'In her outstanding and richly researched book, Lauren Dempster narrates one of the most fascinating stories of transitional justice in Northern Ireland. At the heart of her story are the "disappeared" of the Troubles and the struggle of their families to uncover the truth about the whereabouts of their loved ones. In her masterful analysis, Dempster shows how selective immunity can contribute significantly towards the recovery of the truth for the disappeared, even under the most challenging conditions. Overall, this impeccably documented book is certain to become an important reference text for those interested in transitional justice in Northern Ireland and the politics of victimhood, broadly defined.'

– Iosif Kovras, PhD, Reader (Associate Professor) in Comparative Politics, Department of International Politics, City University of London

'A granular, nuanced look at the efforts to deal with the aftermath of the Troubles, focusing on efforts to recover the bodies of the disappeared. The author writes with authority and compassion, with attention to the shades of grey that accompany civil conflicts, and the importance of trust and time in successful efforts to deal with the past. She shows how the effort to deal with one aspect of the past – finding the bodies of the disappeared – served to shape the larger discussion on transitional justice, for good and ill. A very useful book.'

– Professor Naomi Roht-Arriaza, Albert Abramson '54 Distinguished Professor of Law, University of California, Hastings College of the Law

'Dempster presents, in a meticulously researched book, the most extensive study of its kind on disappearances in Northern Ireland. Through the prism of "the disappeared," wider lessons for the dealing with the past are cogently explored. More broadly, the book takes on many transitional justice tropes, for example, issues such as "innocence" and "guilt", "complicity" and "perpetration". New ideas are introduced such as "quiet" transitional justice, opening novel avenues for reflection and scholarship. All this challenges the reader morally and intellectually, while reshaping the theory and practice of transitional justice more broadly.'

– Professor Brandon Hamber, John Hume and Thomas P. O'Neill Chair in Peace, Ulster University

Transitional Justice and the 'Disappeared' of Northern Ireland

This book employs a transitional justice lens to address the 'disappearances' that occurred during the Northern Ireland conflict – or 'Troubles' – and the post-conflict response to these 'disappearances.' Despite an extensive literature around 'dealing with the past' in Northern Ireland, as well as a substantial body of scholarship on 'disappearances' in other national contexts, there has been little scholarly scrutiny of 'disappearances' in post-conflict Northern Ireland. Although the Good Friday Agreement brought relative peace to Northern Ireland, no provision was made for the establishment of some form of overarching truth and reconciliation commission aimed at comprehensively addressing the legacy of violence. Nevertheless, a mechanism to recover the remains of the 'disappeared' – the Independent Commission for the Location of Victims' Remains (ICLVR) – was established, and has in fact proven to be quite effective. As a result, the reactions of key constituencies to the 'disappearances' can be used as a prism through which to comprehensively explore issues of relevance to transitional justice scholars and practitioners.

Pursuing an interdisciplinary approach, and based on extensive empirical research, this book provides a multifaceted exploration of the responses of these constituencies to the practice of 'disappearing.' It engages with transitional justice themes including silence, memory, truth, acknowledgement, and apology. Key issues examined include the mobilisation efforts of families of the 'disappeared,' efforts by a (former) non-state armed group to address its legacy of violence, the utility of a limited immunity mechanism to incentivise information provision, and the interplay between silence and memory in the shaping of a collective, societal understanding of the 'disappeared.'

Dr Lauren Dempster is a Lecturer in the School of Law, Queen's University Belfast.

Part of the Transitional Justice series

Series editor
Kieran McEvoy, Queen's University Belfast, UK

For information about the series and details of previous and forthcoming titles, see
www.routledge.com/Transitional-Justice/book-series/TRANJ

A GlassHouse book

Transitional Justice and the 'Disappeared' of Northern Ireland

Silence, Memory, and the Construction of the Past

Lauren Dempster

Routledge
Taylor & Francis Group
a GlassHouse book

First published 2019
by Routledge
2 Park Square, Milton Park, Abingdon, Oxon OX14 4RN

and by Routledge
605 Third Avenue, New York, NY 10017

First issued in paperback 2020

a GlassHouse book

Routledge is an imprint of the Taylor & Francis Group, an informa business

British Library Cataloguing in Publication Data
A catalogue record for this book is available from the British Library

Library of Congress Cataloging-in-Publication Data
A catalog record has been requested for this book

ISBN 13: 978-0-367-72795-6 (pbk)
ISBN 13: 978-0-8153-7564-7 (hbk)

Typeset in Galliard
by Taylor & Francis Books

Contents

Preface

This book explores the response to the 'disappearances' that were perpetrated during the Northern Ireland conflict through a transitional justice lens. The evolution of the response to this phenomenon in the Irish context is explored from the perspectives of a number of key constituencies to the 'disappearances': (i) victims' families, (ii) the Republican Movement (who perpetrated many of these acts), (iii) the communities in which these 'disappearances' took place, and (iv), the state. This book uses an interdisciplinary approach, drawing on a broad disciplinary framework including transitional justice, law, criminology, political science, and anthropology. By drawing on this interdisciplinary framework, the responses to the 'disappeared' are used as a prism through which to comprehensively explore a number of key transitional justice themes. These include silence, memory, truth, acknowledgement, and apology. Key issues examined include the utility of a limited immunity mechanism to incentivise information provision, efforts by a (former) non-state armed group to address its legacy of violence, the mobilisation efforts of families of the 'disappeared,' and the interplay between silence and memory in the shaping of the collective memory of the 'disappeared.'

Acknowledgements

To Professor Kieran McEvoy, my mentor, current PI, and former PhD supervisor, thank you so much for your advice, support, and generosity with your time, expertise, and knowledge. Your belief in me means a lot.

This book started out as a PhD thesis, completed at Queen's University Belfast (QUB) in 2016. I am grateful to Kieran and Dr Alastair Ruffell for their supervision, guidance, and encouragement, and to Prof. Brandon Hamber and Dr Cheryl Lawther for examining the thesis and giving such insightful feedback. Thank you also to the Department of Employment and Learning for funding that project.

Further thanks go to Cheryl as my PI between 2016 and 2017, for her always sound advice, enthusiasm for this book, and for being so supportive in ensuring I had time to work on it.

Huge thanks go to all of my interviewees for taking the time to speak with me and for sharing their views and experiences. I am additionally grateful to those of you who helped me to make contact with other potential interviewees – this was vital in helping me represent a range of perspectives. Although I cannot name all of my interviewees here, I must make special mention of Eugene McVeigh and Kieran Megraw: your warmth and patience in discussing your very personal tragedies with me is greatly appreciated.

Special thanks go to Geoff Knupfer of the Independent Commission for the Location of Victims' Remains for always making the time to respond to my queries despite being extremely busy, and for giving me valuable and much-appreciated feedback on the thesis on which this book is based.

I feel very grateful to have so many supportive colleagues at QUB and elsewhere. Thanks to all who have made comments on this manuscript or previous versions of it. I am also grateful for the many valuable conversations about 'disappearances,' transitional justice, publishing, or navigating the world of academia. I make particular mention of Rachel Killean, Kevin Hearty, Anna Bryson, Anne-Marie McAlinden, Luke Moffett, Iosif Kovras, Ron Dudai, and Cath Collins.

To my friends at QUB throughout the PhD process and since – Rachel, Amanda, Andrew, Brendan, Catherine, Sluisie, Connie, Heather, Sarah, Kate, and R-Pats – thank you for all the chats, lunch breaks, and for being such a supportive crew.

I am grateful to the staff at QUB Library, Belfast's Linenhall Library, and the Newspaper library in Belfast Central Library for all of their help in accessing the many resources I needed for completion of this book.

Thanks to all at Routledge, specifically Colin Perrin, Hannah Lovelock, and Nicola Sharpe for their guidance, and of course their patience. I am grateful also to the useful comments and feedback provided by the two anonymous reviewers of my book proposal. Any errors or omissions of course remain my own.

Last but certainly not least, thanks go to my family and my partner, Sam, for their love and support.

Abbreviations

CAIN	Conflict Archive on the Internet
CAJ	Committee on the Administration of Justice
CGP	Consultative Group on the Past
CONADEP	*Comisión Nacional sobre la Desaparición de Personas* (National Commission on the Disappearance of Persons)
CVS	Commission for Victims and Survivors
DE	Dáil Éireann
DUP	Democratic Unionist Party
ESMA	*Escuela Superior de Mecánica de la Armada* (Navy School of Mechanics)
FARC	*Fuerzas Armadas Revolucionarias de Colombia* (Revolutionary Armed Forces of Colombia)
GFA	Good Friday Agreement
HC	House of Commons
HIU	Historical Investigations Unit
HL	House of Lords
HTR	Healing Through Remembering
ICC	International Criminal Court
ICIR	Independent Commission on Information Retrieval
ICLVR	Independent Commission for the Location of Victims' Remains
ICRC	International Committee of the Red Cross
ICTY	International Criminal Tribunal for the former Yugoslavia
INLA	Irish National Liberation Army
IRA	Provisional Irish Republican Army
IRG	Implementation and Reconciliation Group
JVP	*Janatha Vimukthi Peramuna* (People's Liberation Front)
LVR	Location of Victims' Remains legislation
MPTT	Missing Persons Task Team
MRF	Military Reaction Force
NGA	National Graves Association
NGO	Non-Governmental Organisation
NIA	Northern Ireland Assembly
OHA	Oral History Archive

OPONI	Office of the Police Ombudsman for Northern Ireland
OTR	'On The Runs'
PSNI	Police Service of Northern Ireland
RFJ	Relatives for Justice
RUC	Royal Ulster Constabulary
SDLP	Social Democratic and Labour Party
SE	Seanad Éireann
SHA	Stormont House Agreement
SIO	Senior Investigating Officer
TRC	(South African) Truth and Reconciliation Commission
UN	United Nations
UNWGEID	United Nations Working Group on Enforced or Involuntary Disappearances
UUP	Ulster Unionist Party

Introduction

1. 'Disappearances,' Northern Ireland, and 'dealing with' the past

> "Nothing could be worse, for the work of mourning, than confusion or doubt: one has to know who is buried where..."[1]

> "The irreversibility of time means that past injustices both cannot be directly undone and cannot be made to disappear entirely. The past and our memory of it always threatens to resurface."[2]

Between 1972 and 1985, 16 people from Northern Ireland were killed and 'disappeared,' in most cases by the IRA (see footnote 52). In 1998, the signing of the Good Friday Agreement (GFA) brought relative peace to the jurisdiction. That Agreement, however, made no provision for the establishment of some form of overarching truth and reconciliation commission aimed at comprehensively addressing the legacy of violence.[3] In the years since, diverse efforts at truth seeking have been made,[4] all components of what has been described as a 'piecemeal' approach to the past.[5] In 1999, one of these 'pieces,' the Independent Commission for the Location of Victims' Remains (ICLVR) was established to locate the remains of those who had been 'disappeared.'

1 Jacques Derrida, *Specters of Marx*. Trans. Peggy Kamuf (London: Routledge, 1994), p. 9.

2 James W. Booth, 'The Unforgotten: Memories of Justice,' *American Political Science Review*, 95:4, (2001), 777–791 (p. 785).

3 Colm Campbell and Ita Connolly, 'The Sharp End: Armed Opposition Movements, Transitional Truth Processes and the *Rechtsstaat*,' *International Journal of Transitional Justice*, 6:1, (2012), 11–39; Marie Breen Smyth, *Truth Recovery and Justice After Conflict: Managing Violent Pasts* (London: Routledge, 2007): Kieran McEvoy and Anna Bryson, 'Justice, Truth and Oral History: Legislating the Past "From Below" in Northern Ireland,' *Northern Ireland Legal Quarterly*, 67:1, (2016), 67–90.

4 Cheryl Lawther, *Truth, Denial and Transition: Northern Ireland and the Contested Past* (Abingdon: Routledge, 2014).

5 Kieran McEvoy and Graham Ellison, 'Criminological Discourses in Northern Ireland: Conflict and Conflict Resolution,' in Kieran McEvoy and Tim Newburn (eds) *Criminology, Conflict Resolution and Restorative Justice* (Basingstoke: Palgrave Macmillan, 2003), pp. 45–82 (p. 67).

Perpetrated across the globe[6] – 'disappearances' are often carried out by state forces, such as has been the case in Argentina,[7] Iraq,[8] Syria,[9] and Nepal,[10] to name but a few. In a number of contexts, non-state armed groups are responsible for such acts. This has been the case in, for example, Colombia,[11] Mexico,[12] Sri Lanka,[13] and – as this book examines – Northern Ireland. In 2017, the United Nations Working Group on Enforced or Involuntary Disappearances (UNWGEID) reported 45,120 cases of 'disappearance' across 91 states under 'active consideration.'[14] Despite the ubiquity of this practice, much of the existing body of scholarship on the phenomenon of 'disappearances' remains limited to that which addresses the issue from a doctrinal human rights perspective. There is some scholarship which draws on empirical fieldwork,[15] and some which addresses the issue from the perspective of a particular discipline, such as political science[16] or forensic science.[17]

6 Amnesty International, *'Disappearances' and Political Killings: Human Rights Crisis of the 1990s – A Manual for Action* (Amsterdam: Amnesty International, 1994); Francisco Ferrándiz and Antonius C. G. M. Robben (eds), *Necropolitics: Mass Graves and Exhumations in the Age of Human Rights* (Philadelphia: University of Pennsylvania Press, 2015); Iosif Kovras, *Grassroots Activism and the Evolution of Transitional Justice: The Families of the Disappeared* (Cambridge: Cambridge University Press, 2017); Adam Rosenblatt, *Digging for the Disappeared: Forensic Science after Atrocity* (Stanford: Stanford University Press, 2015).

7 Rita Arditti, *Searching for Life: The Grandmothers of the Plaza de Mayo and the Disappeared Children of Argentina* (California: University of California Press, 1999); Antonius C. G. M. Robben, *Political Violence and Trauma in Argentina* (Philadelphia: University of Pennsylvania Press, 2005); Horacio Verbitsky, *Confessions of an Argentine Dirty Warrior* (New York; London: The New Press, 2005).

8 Eric Stover, William D. Haglund and Margaret Samuels, 'Exhumation of Mass Graves in Iraq,' *Journal of the American Medical Association*, 290:5, (2003), 663–666.

9 Kristen Gillespie, 'Enforced Disappearance a "Continuous Practice of the Assads",' *Syria Direct*, 16 September 2014, http://syriadirect.org/main/36-interviews/1566-enforced-disappearance-a-continuous-practice-of-the-assads [accessed 2 August 2018].

10 Simon Robins, 'Towards Victim-Centred Transitional Justice: Understanding the Needs of Families of the Disappeared in Postconflict Nepal,' *International Journal of Transitional Justice*, 5:1, (2011), 75–98.

11 Human Rights Watch, 'Colombia's Zone of Fear,' 26 August 2001, www.hrw.org/news/2001/08/26/colombias-zone-fear-0 [accessed 2 August 2018].

12 Human Rights Watch, 'Mexico's Disappeared,' 20 February 2013, www.hrw.org/reports/2013/02/20/mexicos-disappeared-0 [accessed 2 August 2018]; Human Rights Watch, 'Vanished: The Disappeared of Mexico's Drug War,' 8 January 2014, www.hrw.org/news/2014/01/08/vanished-disappeared-mexicos-drug-war [accessed 2 August 2018].

13 Malathi De Alwis, '"Disappearance" and "Displacement" in Sri Lanka,' *Journal of Refugee Studies*, 22:3, (2009), 378–391.

14 United Nations Working Group on Enforced or Involuntary Disappearances. *Report of the Working Group on Enforced or Involuntary Disappearances*, A/HRC/36/39, 31 July 2017, https://documents-dds-ny.un.org/doc/UNDOC/GEN/G17/229/15/PDF/G1722915.pdf?OpenElement [accessed 2 August 2018].

15 E.g. Robins, n 10.

16 E.g. Kovras, n 6.

17 E.g. Rosenblatt, n 6.

This book uses the case of 'disappearances' in Northern Ireland to address a range of broader theoretical concerns. It draws upon the literature of transitional justice, socio-legal studies, anthropology, criminology, memory studies, and human geography to explore the evolution of the response to this phenomenon in the Irish context. Key issues examined include the utility of a limited immunity mechanism to incentivise information provision, efforts by a (former) non-state armed group to address its legacy of violence, the mobilisation efforts of families of the 'disappeared,' and the interplay between silence and memory in the shaping of a collective, societal understanding of the 'disappeared.' A transitional justice lens is used to analyse the reactions of a number of key constituencies to the 'disappearances': (i) victims' families, (ii) the Republican Movement (who perpetrated many of these acts), (iii) the communities in which these 'disappearances' took place, and (iv), the state. The structure of the book is as follows.

In Chapter 1, 'disappearances' related to the Northern Ireland conflict are situated within the broader international and historical context of 'disappearing.' I chart the central role of 'disappearances' in the evolution of the field of transitional justice, drawing upon the experiences of Argentina, Colombia, Lebanon, Sri-Lanka, and elsewhere to illustrate how 'disappearances' often become iconic legacy issues to be addressed in the transition from authoritarianism or conflict. I will argue that much of the international literature on 'disappearances' retains a state-centric focus, despite the fact that (as in the case of Northern Ireland) non-state actors also routinely engage in the practice.[18] In addition, I explore the impact of 'disappearing' on those left behind, including the notion of 'ambiguous loss,' 'mummification,' and the diminution of trust in social and political relations.[19] I also examine the intersection between 'disappearances' and different forms of amnesties as an illustration of the classic peace versus justice tension in transitional contexts.[20]

18 E.g. Amnesty International, n 6; International Commission of Jurists, *Enforced Disappearance and Extrajudicial Execution: Investigation and Sanction* (Practitioners Guide 9, 2015); Irena Giorgou, 'State Involvement in the Perpetration of Enforced Disappearance and the Rome Statute,' *Journal of International Criminal Justice*, 11, (2013), 1001–1021; Tullio Scovazzi and Gabriella Citroni, *The Struggle Against Enforced Disappearance and the 2007 United Nations Convention* (Leiden; Boston: Martinus Nijhoff Publishers, 2007). For notable exceptions to this trend see e.g. De Alwis, n 13 and Kovras, n 6.

19 Pauline Boss, *Ambiguous Loss: Learning to Live with Unresolved Grief* (Massachusetts: Harvard University Press, 1999); Brandon Hamber and Richard A. Wilson, 'Symbolic Closure Through Memory, Reparation and Revenge in Post-Conflict Societies,' *Journal of Human Rights*, 1:1, (2002), 35–53; Janine Natalya Clark, 'Missing Persons, Reconciliation and the View from Below: a Case Study of Bosnia-Hercegovina,' *Southeast European and Black Sea Studies*, 10:4, (2010), 425–442; Barbara. A. Misztal, *Trust in Modern Societies* (Cambridge: Polity Press, 1996).

20 See e.g. Payam Akhavan, 'Are International Criminal Tribunals a Disincentive to Peace? Reconciling Judicial Romanticism and Political Realism,' *Human Rights Quarterly*, 31:3, (2009), 624–654; Johanna Herman, Olga Martin-Ortega and Chandra L. Sriram, 'Beyond Justice Versus Peace: Transitional Justice and

Finally I explore the complex relationship between 'disappearances,' silence, and memory.[21]

In Chapter 2, I examine the campaigning and mobilisation work of the families of the 'disappeared' of Northern Ireland as an example of victims 'doing' transitional justice.[22] For many families, their responses to the 'disappearance' of their loved ones during the conflict was characterised by silence. Such silence was shaped by uncertainty and misinformation about the fate of their 'disappeared' relatives, fear of paramilitaries, and for some concerns associated with the stigma connected to the 'disappeared' being labelled as informers.[23] However, after the ceasefires in 1994 the families gradually morphed into a small but effective social movement. Drawing in particular from the social movement literature,[24] I explore the ways in which the families managed to frame their campaign as a humanitarian issue and the ways in which the 'disappeared' illuminate key contests concerning legitimate victimhood, victim hierarchy, and the complexity and multiplicity of victim identities.[25]

Chapter 3 focuses on the Republican Movement, which perpetrated the majority of 'disappearances.' This chapter's examination of the Republican Movement's role in, and response to, 'disappearing' provides a case study of how a (formerly) armed opposition movement attempts to engage with one manifestation of the violence it perpetrated in the past. Drawing in particular on the notion

Peacebuilding Strategies,' in Karin Aggestam and Annika Bjorkdahl (eds) *Rethinking Peacebuilding: The Quest for Justice Peace in the Middle East and the Western Balkans* (Abingdon: Routledge, 2013), pp. 1–46.

21 Kathleen Ireton and Iosif Kovras, 'Non-Apologies and Prolonged Silences in Post-Conflict Settings: The Case of Post-Colonial Cyprus,' *Time and Society*, 21:1, (2012), 71–88; Sylvia Karl, 'Rehumanizing the Disappeared: Spaces of Memory in Mexico and the Liminality of Transitional Justice,' *American Quarterly*, 66:3, (2014), 727–748; Michel-Rolph Trouillot, *Silencing the Past: Power and the Production of History* (Boston: Beacon Press, 1995); Eviatar Zerubavel, 'The Social Sound of Silence: Toward a Sociology of Denial,' in Efrat Ben-Ze'ev, Ruth Ginio and Jay (eds) *Shadows of War: A Social History of Silence in the Twentieth Century* (Cambridge: Cambridge University Press, 2010), pp. 32–46.

22 Following Kieran McEvoy and Kirsten McConnachie, 'Victims and Transitional Justice: Voice, Agency and Blame,' *Social and Legal Studies*, (2013), 1–25.

23 Ron Dudai, *The IRA and the Shadow of the Informer: Punishment, Governance, and Dealing with the Past* (Unpublished PhD Thesis, Queen's University Belfast, 2012); Ron Dudai, 'Informers and the Transition in Northern Ireland,' *British Journal of Criminology*, 52, (2012), 32–54; WAVE, *The Disappeared of Northern Ireland's 'Troubles'* (Belfast: WAVE Trauma Centre Publications, 2012).

24 Donnatella Della Porta and Mario Diani, *Social Movements: An Introduction* (Oxford: Blackwell, 2006); Francesca Polletta and James M. Jasper, 'Collective Identity and Social Movements,' *Annual Review of Sociology*, 27, (2001), 283–305.

25 Erica Bouris, *Complex Political Victims* (Connecticut: Kumarian, 2007); Nils Christie, 'The Ideal Victim' in Ezzata A. Fattah (ed.) *From Crime Policy to Victim Policy* (London: Macmillan, 1986), pp. 17–30; Erving Goffman, *Frame Analysis: An Analysis on the Organization of Experience* (Harmondsworth: Penguin, 1975); Kieran McEvoy and Kirsten McConnachie, 'Victimology in Transitional Justice: Victimhood, Innocence and Hierarchy,' *European Journal of Criminology*, 9:5, (2012), 527–538; David A. Snow and Robert D. Benford, 'Ideology, Frame Resonance, and Participant Mobilization,' *International Social Movement Research*, 1, (1988), 197–217.

of embarrassment,[26] this chapter examines how the Republican Movement sought to rationalise the practice of 'disappearing,' the timing of the Republican Movement's engagement in the 'disappeared' issue, and the dialectical relationship between military and political leadership in the 'Movement's' response to the 'disappeared.'[27]

In Chapter 4, Cohen's 'atrocity triangle' of victims, perpetrators, and observers or bystanders[28] is drawn upon to explore the complicity of those who 'stood by' while paramilitaries engaged in the practice of 'disappearance.' Focussing on the aftermath of the 'disappearances,' I explore the reaction of both the local communities in which these 'disappearances' took place and the police who were tasked with investigating these crimes. This chapter draws on the seminal work of Knapp[29] and Das,[30] concerning the role and impact of rumour to examine the ways in which disinformation and untruths compounded paramilitary denial and communal silence. These 'disappearances' took place in a vicious political conflict during which violence became euphemised, normalised, and routinised – nourished by what Taussig describes as '… the intermingling of silence and myth.'[31] However, as I make clear, despite the exigencies of conflict and the undoubted power and influence of the Republican Movement, variants of the truth circulated within Republican communities as a result of what Foucault has described as truth being 'a thing of this world.'[32]

Chapter 5 examines the state's response to the issue of the 'disappeared.' The Location of Victims' Remains legislation is based on a limited immunity from prosecution for the provision of information relating to burial site locations. In this chapter the role of amnesty or amnesty-like mechanisms in incentivising truth provision is analysed,[33] and the development of the ICLVR is examined as an

26 Erving Goffman, 'Embarrassment and Social Organisation,' *American Journal of Sociology*, 62:3, (1956), 264–271; Dacher Keltner and Brenda N. Buswell, 'Embarrassment: Its Distinct Form and Appeasement Functions,' *Psychological Bulletin*, 122:3, (1997), 250–270; June Price Tangney, 'The Self-Conscious Emotions: Shame, Guilt, Embarrassment and Pride,' in Tim Dalgleish and Mick J. Power (eds) *Handbook of Cognition and Emotion* (Chicester: Wiley & Sons Ltd., 1999), pp. 541–568.

27 James MacGregor Burns, *Leadership* (New York: Harper & Row, 1978); Robert Elgie, *Political Leadership in Liberal Democracies* (Basingstoke; London: Macmillan Press Ltd., 1995); Cynthia L. Irvin, *Militant Nationalism: Between Movement and Party in Ireland and the Basque Country* (Minneapolis: University of Minnesota Press, 1999).

28 Stanley Cohen, *States of Denial: Knowing about Atrocities and Suffering* (Cambridge: Polity Press, 2001).

29 Robert H. Knapp, 'A Psychology of Rumour,' *Public Opinion Quarterly*, 8:1, (1944), 22–37.

30 Veena Das, 'Specificities: Official Narratives, Rumour, and the Social Production of Hate,' *Social Identities*, 4:1, (1998), 109–130.

31 Michael T. Taussig, *Shamanism, Colonialism, and the Wild Man: A Study in Terror and Healing* (Chicago; London: Chicago University Press, 1986), p. 8.

32 Michel Foucault, 'Truth and Power,' in James D. Faubion (ed.) *Power: Essential Works of Foucault 1954–1984 (vol. 3)* (London: Penguin Books, 1994), p. 131.

33 Mark Freeman, *Necessary Evils: Amnesties and the Search for Justice* (Cambridge: Cambridge University Press, 2009); Louise Mallinder, *Amnesty, Human Rights and Political Transitions: Bridging the Peace and Justice Divide* (Oxford: Hart Publishing, 2008).

example of what I term 'quiet' transitional justice. I explore the extent to which an amnesty-like measure can in fact be considered as 'victim-centred,' rather than the traditional understanding of amnesties as an instrument of impunity.[34] Drawing upon the political science literature on diplomacy,[35] I use the ICLVR to explore the utility of working 'quietly' on complex and sensitive transitional justice problems. In particular, this chapter is informed by the theoretical literature on trust[36] to explore the quite remarkable relationships which developed between the ICLVR (the public face of which is a retired British police officer) and former IRA members involved in efforts to locate the remains of people killed by that organisation.

In Chapter 6 I explore the broader collective memory of the disappeared in the public consciousness in Ireland and the ways in which this understanding intersects with the politics of the past. Framed within the memory studies literature, the 'threads of narrative'[37] related to the 'disappeared' resonate with key themes in transitional justice including apology, acknowledgement, and truth recovery. The work of Andrieu,[38] Celermajer,[39] Meier,[40] and others[41] is drawn on to analyse the effectiveness of, and reactions to, the apology statements issued by the Republican Movement in relation to 'disappearances.' The value of the 'Movement's' major acknowledgement of involvement in 'disappearing' is explored as an

34 Kris Brown and Fionnuala Ní Aoláin, 'Through the Looking Glass: Transitional Justice Futures Through the Lens of Nationalism, Feminism and Transformative Change,' *International Journal of Transitional Justice*, 9, (2014), 127–149; Vasuki Nesiah, 'Overcoming Tensions Between Family and Judicial Procedures,' *International Review of the Red Cross*, 84:848, (2002), 823–844; Robins, n 10.

35 Michael Johns, 'Quiet Diplomacy, the European Union and Conflict Prevention: Learning from the HCNM on Issues of Social Cohesion,' *International Journal on Minority and Group Rights*, 19, (2012), 243–265; Niall Ó Dochartaigh, 'Together in the Middle: Back-Channel Negotiation in the Irish Peace Process,' *Journal of Peace Research*, 48:6, (2011), 767–780; Anthony Wanis-St. John, 'Back-Channel Negotiation: International Bargaining in the Shadows,' *Negotiation Journal*, 22:2, (2006), 119–144.

36 Morton Deutsch, 'Trust and Suspicion,' *Journal of Conflict Resolution*, 2:4, (1958), 265–279; Geoffrey Hosking, *Trust: A History* (Oxford: Oxford University Press, 2014); Misztal, n 19.

37 Michael Lambek and Paul Antze, 'Introduction: Forecasting Memory,' in Paul Antze and Michael Lambek (eds) *Tense Past* (New York: Routledge, 1996), pp. xi–xxxviii, (xvii).

38 Kora Andrieu, '"Sorry for the Genocide": How Public Apologies Can Help Promote National Reconciliation,' *Millennium: Journal of International Studies*, 38:1, (2009), 3–23.

39 Danielle Celermajer, 'Mere Ritual? Displacing the Myth of Sincerity in Transitional Rituals,' *International Journal of Transitional Justice*, 7, (2013), 286–305.

40 A. J. Meier, 'Conflict and the Power of Apologies,' *Philologie im Netz*, 30, (2004), 1–17.

41 Zohar Kampf and Nava Löwenheim, 'Rituals of Apology in the Global Arena,' *Security Dialogue*, 43:1, (2012), 43–60; Walter Shapiro and Kathleen Adams, 'Mama Mia, That's a Mea Culpa,' *Time*, 146: 26, (1997), 18; Sandra Harris, Karen Grainger and Louise Mullany, 'The Pragmatics of Political Apologies,' *Discourse and Society*, 17:6, (2006), 715–737.

act that speaks to a commitment to a 'new era' of relations,[42] while simultaneously continuing to justify the original killings (but not the 'disappearances') as a legitimate response to informing. I also examine how the collective memory of the disappeared is informed by different types of truth including 'narrow' truth related to the location of the remains,[43] 'geographical' truth relating to past wrongs literally buried in the Irish countryside,[44] and communal truths about shared complicity and silence.[45]

The final chapter locates the issue of the disappeared within the ongoing debates on dealing with the past more broadly in Northern Ireland and elsewhere. In particular I argue that forms of limited immunity are a crucial component of transitional justice and can, in some circumstances, be viewed as a victim-centred approach to dealing with the past. I contend that the importance of building trust manifests itself in several ways: the need to manage expectations, the value of robust guarantees of limited immunity, and the need to allow time for trust to develop between parties. I propose that effective leadership is a central element of the successful functioning of transitional mechanisms, and consideration should be given to the qualities required of those invited to lead legacy institutions. Important also is the role of context and timing in efforts to address past harms – in particular the presence of a sense of momentum or willingness to make change. I argue for the benefits of 'doing' transitional justice quietly, and suggest that there can be a pragmatic value to designing transitional mechanisms 'behind the scenes.' Finally, I emphasise the importance of the spirit in which legacy issues are addressed. The experience of the ICLVR has shown that pragmatism and generosity are essential to progress.

Before exploring efforts to 'deal with' the past in Northern Ireland more closely, in the following section I offer some background detail on 'disappearances' in Northern Ireland. In the final section of this Introduction I outline the methods used in this research.

2. 'Disappearance' in Northern Ireland

> We – my parents missed him from the house … they were concerned about him and … after a given period, I raised concerns with the Gardaí.[46] I mean I actually

42 Michel-Rolph Trouillot, 'Abortive Rituals: Historical Apologies in the Global Era,' *Interventions: International Journal of Postcolonial Studies*, 2:2, (2000), 171–186, (p. 174).

43 Iosif Kovras, 'Explaining Prolonged Silences in Transitional Justice: The Disappeared in Cyprus and Spain,' *Comparative Political Studies*, 20:10, (2012), 1–27; Iosif Kovras, *Truth Recovery and Transitional Justice: Deferring Human Rights Abuses* (London: Routledge, 2014).

44 Derek Gregory, *Geographical Imaginations* (Oxford: Blackwell, 1994); Mark Phelan, 'Not So Innocent Landscapes: Remembrance, Representation and the Disappeared,' in Patrick Anderson and Jisha Menon (eds) *Violence Performed: Local Roots and Global Routes of Conflict* (Palgrave, 2009), pp. 285–316.

45 Stanley Cohen, 'State Crimes of Previous Regimes: Knowledge, Accountability, and the Policing of the Past,' *Law and Social Inquiry*, 20:1, (1995), 7–50; Richard A. Wilson, *The Politics of Truth and Reconciliation in South Africa: Legitimizing the Post-Apartheid State* (Cambridge: Cambridge University Press, 2001).

46 *An Garda Síochána* – the Republic of Ireland's police force.

> thought he had … maybe, just gone off somewhere … just, you know, when I say 'disappeared' I mean 'disappeared' in a different way … like young people do. And there wasn't the same social media outlets, there was no Twitter, no Facebook … phones were phone boxes … So you couldn't even think that everybody would have … a means of communication … I went to the Gardaí in Dublin about it at the behest of my parents, to reassure them or to bring them back some information. But they had no information at that time obviously.[47]
>
> Eugene McVeigh, brother of Columba McVeigh

> On the Saturday … he'd been in the town in the morning with my Mum and … then was going on up to Twinbrook where he lived with his wife … when he got in … there was 8 or 9 people waiting for him … he was taken away and they said to his wife, 'don't be telling the police, he's going to be back.' And, obviously as we know … he didn't come back. So eventually it was reported to the police and there was a media moment on TV, we made an appeal … But, back to the late '70s … communication was a lot slower and, at the time we always thought that he would be coming back. And, it might have been a couple of days, you thought, or at the week, a couple of months, then … his daughter getting born in October – and then Christmas time we thought definitely he'd come back but it never happened.[48]
>
> Kieran Megraw, brother of Brendan Megraw

Columba McVeigh and Brendan Megraw were both 'disappeared' during the conflict or 'Troubles' in Northern Ireland. Columba McVeigh was from Donaghmore in County Tyrone, Northern Ireland. In November 1975 he was living in Dublin, from where he was 'disappeared.' In April 1978, Brendan Megraw was abducted as he returned to his home in Belfast from a shopping trip. In 1999, the Provisional Irish Republican Army (the IRA) admitted to 'disappearing' McVeigh, Megraw, and seven other individuals. In October 2014, Brendan Megraw's remains were recovered from bogland in Oristown, County Meath, by the Independent Commission for the Location of Victims' Remains (ICLVR/the Commission). The following month, his funeral was held in Belfast, 36 years after his 'disappearance.'[49] A number of searches have taken place for Columba McVeigh's remains in bogland at Bragan, County Monaghan, Republic of Ireland. At the time of writing, his remains are yet to be found.[50]

Sixteen individuals were 'disappeared' between 1972 and 1985.[51] Joe Lynskey, Kevin McKee, and Seamus Wright were 'disappeared' in 1972; Peter Wilson was

47 Interview, Eugene McVeigh, August 2015.

48 Interview, Kieran Megraw, October 2015.

49 'IRA Investigation Locates Grave Sites,' *An Phoblacht*, 1 April 1999; WAVE, n 23; Gerry Moriarty, 'Funeral Held for IRA Murder Victim Brendan Megraw,' *The Irish Times*, 14 November 2014.

50 Tom Brady, 'Hunt for Bodies of Northern Ireland's Remaining Disappeared Intensifies,' *Belfast Telegraph*, 25 June 2018; WAVE, n 23.

51 It should be noted that there are two individuals, Gareth O'Connor and Lisa Dorrian, who are not included in this list and who have 'disappeared' in suspicious circumstances in which paramilitary involvement is suspected. These cases occurred after the

'disappeared' in 1973; and Eamonn Molloy in 1975. Robert Nairac was 'disappeared' in 1977. In 1978, John McClory and Brian McKinney were 'disappeared.' Gerry Evans was 'disappeared' in 1979; and Charlie Armstrong, Danny McIlhone, and Eugene Simons were 'disappeared' in 1981. The only woman to be 'disappeared' – Jean McConville – was abducted from her home in west Belfast in 1972. In most of these cases, the IRA has admitted responsibility.[52] In the majority of cases, the 'disappeared' were abducted from Northern Ireland, and buried in the Republic of Ireland. Seamus Ruddy was 'disappeared' in France by the Irish National Liberation Army (INLA – a smaller Republican armed group) in 1985.[53] To date, the remains of 13 of the 'disappeared'

April 1998 cut-off date, and thus do not fall under the Commission's remit (see e.g. *BBC News* [online], 'Timeline: The Disappearance of Lisa Dorrian,' 28 February 2017, www.bbc.co.uk/news/uk-northern-ireland-39116502 [accessed 11 September 2018]; WAVE, n 23). This book focuses on those cases which come under the remit of the ICLVR.

52 The IRA has released statements acknowledging responsibility for the 'disappearances' of Joe Lynskey, Kevin McKee, Seamus Wright, Jean McConville, Eamonn Molloy, Columba McVeigh, Robert Nairac, Brendan Megraw, John McClory, Brian McKinney, and Danny McIlhone ('Investigation Confirms 1972 Disappearance,' *An Phoblacht*, 11 February 2010; 'IRA Investigation Locates Grave Sites' supra n 49; 'SAS Captain Executed,' *Republican News*, 21 May 1977). Although media speculation linked the IRA to Peter Wilson's 'disappearance' (e.g. Allison Morris, 'Exclusive – "Secret" IRA Victim on Disappeared List,' *The Irish News*, 30 October 2009) and Gerry Adams confirmed his death to the family (account of Patricia Wilson in WAVE, n 23), an IRA spokesperson denied IRA involvement in a statement issued to journalist Brian Rowan (Brian Rowan, 'Move to Distance IRA from Missing West Belfast Man,' *Belfast Telegraph*, 2 November 2009). With regards to Eugene Simons, although news reports linked the IRA to his 'disappearance' (e.g. 'Body Found in Bog Identified,' *The Irish Times*, 23 May 1984), I have found no statements of responsibility from any organisation. I have also found no statements of responsibility for the 'disappearances' of Gerry Evans or Charlie Armstrong. An IRA source told reporter Suzanne Breen that the IRA was responsible in these cases, however Gerry Adams has stated that the IRA has said it is not responsible for either of these two cases (Suzanne Breen, 'Put That Family Out of its Misery,' *Sunday Tribune*, 18 January 2009; Noel McAdam, 'Pressure Steps Up On Disappeared,' *Belfast Telegraph*, 4 August 2006). In 2013, Gerry Adams referred to 13 cases for which the IRA had acknowledged involvement; however I have found statements of acknowledgement for only the 11 cases listed earlier ('Gerry Adams Appeals for Information on Victims Secretly Buried by the IRA,' *An Phoblacht*, 21 June 2013).

53 As noted, Columba McVeigh was abducted from Dublin. The remains of Peter Wilson were found on a beach in County Antrim, Northern Ireland. In all other cases (with the exception of Seamus Ruddy), remains have been found, or are believed to be buried, in the Republic of Ireland. In 1995, a spokesperson for the Irish Republican Socialist Party, the political wing of the INLA (Irish National Liberation Army), stated that they 'accepted' that Ruddy was dead and would assist in efforts to locate his remains (Suzanne Breen, 'IRSP "accepts" that Former Member Dead,' *The Irish Times*, 19 December 1995. See also BBC Radio Foyle, Willie Gallagher in Interview, BBC Radio Foyle, 8 May 1999. Available at http://rfe123.org/willie-gallagher-bbc-radio-foyle-interview-transcript-8-may-2017 [accessed 30 June 2018] and WAVE, n 23).

have been recovered.[54] The remains of Joe Lynskey, Columba McVeigh, and Robert Nairac are yet to be found.

3. Dealing with the past in Northern Ireland

As mentioned earlier, the GFA made only limited mention of addressing the needs of victims and did not include any overarching mechanism aimed at comprehensively 'dealing with' the past – such as a truth and reconciliation commission.[55] Where such processes have occurred it has been on an *ad hoc* [56] or 'piecemeal' basis,[57] via, for example, public inquiries, the coronial inquest system, the Office of the Police Ombudsman, the Historical Enquiries Team, the Criminal Cases Review Commission, civil actions, and various 'bottom up' initiatives.[58]

There have been four major attempts to develop an overarching mechanism or series of mechanisms to respond to the legacy of the 'Troubles.'[59] In 2006 the NGO, *Healing Through Remembering*, produced a report detailing a range of options aimed at practically responding to the effects of the conflict.[60] This report is said to have 'directly informed' the subsequent attempt at 'dealing with' the past: that made by the Consultative Group on the Past (CGP), which published its report in 2009.[61] Chaired by former Church of Ireland primate, Lord Eames, and former vice-chairman of the Policing Board, Denis Bradley, the CGP was established by the British government in 2007.[62] Central to the proposals made by the CGP was the creation of a Legacy Commission, chaired by an International Commissioner and mandated with assisting societal reconciliation, reviewing and investigating historical cases, conducting an information recovery process and examining linked cases or themes emerging from the conflict. These proposals were overshadowed by one recommendation – that a £12,000 'recognition payment' be made to the nearest relative of a person killed as a result of the conflict. Tied into more widespread controversy over who could be termed a 'victim' (see Chapter 2), this recommendation resulted in angry protests at the Report's

54 See 'The Disappeared' at www.iclvr.ie/en/iclvr/pages/thedisappeared [accessed 2 August 2018]. The remains of Eugene Simons were found in 1984, prior to the establishment of the ICLVR.

55 Campbell and Connolly, n 3; Smyth, n 3; McEvoy and Bryson, n 3.

56 Aoife Duffy, 'A Truth Commission for Northern Ireland?' *International Journal of Transitional Justice*, 4:1, (2010), 26–46.

57 McEvoy and Ellison, n 5.

58 See e.g. Campbell and Connolly, n 3; Healing Through Remembering, *Dealing with the Past? An Overview of Legal and Political Approaches Relating to the Conflict in and about Northern Ireland* (Belfast: Healing Through Remembering, 2013); Kieran McEvoy, *Making Peace with the Past: Options for Truth Recovery Regarding the Conflict in and about Northern Ireland* (Belfast: Healing Through Remembering, 2006); McEvoy and Bryson, n 3.

59 McEvoy and Bryson, n 3.

60 McEvoy, n 58; Healing Through Remembering, n 58.

61 Healing Through Remembering, n 58 at 3.

62 Patricia Lundy, 'Can the Past be Policed? Lessons from the Historical Enquiries Team Northern Ireland,' *Journal of Law and Social Challenges*, 11, (2009), 109–156.

launch, negatively impacted upon public attitudes to the Report as a whole, and resulted in the Report's rejection by the Conservative-led Coalition government which took power in 2010.[63] In 2013, Northern Ireland's political parties failed to reach agreement on proposals developed during a series of talks chaired by US diplomat Richard Haass and academic Meghan O'Sullivan, aimed at addressing the issues of flags, parades, and the past.[64] Haass and O'Sullivan's draft proposals for 'contending with the past' comprised three structures: an Historical Investigations Unit (HIU), an Independent Commission on Information Retrieval (ICIR), and an archive for oral histories, documents, and other conflict-related materials.[65] More recently, all-party talks held at Stormont House in 2014 resulted in the Stormont House Agreement (SHA). This document also proposes an HIU and an ICIR, together with an Oral History Archive (OHA) and an Implementation and Reconciliation Group.[66] At the time of writing, a period of public consultation on these proposals, launched by the Secretary of State for Northern Ireland, is ongoing.[67]

Against this backdrop of a lack of consensus on how to deal with the past, and the continued absence of an overarching series of transitional mechanisms,[68] a process was put in place to locate the remains of the 'disappeared.' In 1999 the ICLVR was established via an intergovernmental treaty between the British and Irish governments and legislation passed in each of these jurisdictions.[69] As the Northern Ireland (Location of Victims' Remains) Act 1999 states, the ICLVR was tasked with 'locating the remains of persons killed before 10th April 1998 as a result of unlawful acts of violence committed on behalf of, or in connection with, proscribed organisations; and for connected purposes.'[70]

63 Healing Through Remembering, n 58; McEvoy and Bryson, n 3.

64 Mark Devenport, 'Richard Haass Talks: Back at a Crossroads,' *BBC News* [online], 31 December 2013, www.bbc.co.uk/news/uk-northern-ireland-25563061 [accessed 14 August 2018]; McEvoy and Bryson, n 3.

65 Richard Haass, 'An Agreement Among the Parties of the Northern Ireland Executive on Parades, Select Commemorations, and Related Protests; Flags and Emblems; and Contending with the Past,' Proposed Agreement 31 December 2013, http://cain.ulst.ac.uk/events/peace/haass-talks/haass_2013-12-31.pdf> [accessed 2 August 2018].

66 Stormont House Agreement, www.gov.uk/government/publications/the-stormont-house-agreement [accessed 16 August 2018].

67 Northern Ireland Office and The Rt Hon Karen Bradley MP, 'Press Release,' 11 May 2018, www.gov.uk/government/news/secretary-of-state-launches-public-consultation-on-proposals-to-address-the-legacy-of-northern-irelands-past [accessed 16 June 2018]. See McEvoy and Bryson, n 3, for further details of events following the agreement of the SHA in 2014.

68 Healing Through Remembering, n. 58; Cheryl Lawther, 'Unionism, Truth Recovery and the Fearful Past,' *Irish Political Studies*, 26:3, (2011), 361–382; McEvoy and Bryson, n 3; Bill Rolston, 'Dealing with the Past: Pro-State Paramilitaries, Truth and Transition in Northern Ireland,' *Human Rights Quarterly*, 28:3, (2006), 652–675.

69 Criminal Justice (Location of Victims' Remains) Act 1999; Northern Ireland (Location of Victims' Remains) Act 1999.

70 Northern Ireland (Location of Victims' Remains) Act 1999. 10 April 1998 is the date the GFA was agreed.

The ICLVR has two commissioners, one appointed by each of the two governments. As will be examined in greater detail in Chapter 5, information given to the ICLVR cannot be used in criminal proceedings and forensic testing on human remains found is restricted to that required for confirming the identity of the deceased, establishing – for the purposes of an inquest – how, when, and where that person died, and to ensure that remains can be moved safely.[71] The Commission can therefore serve as a confidential conduit for information relating to the burial locations of the 'disappeared.' Those with information can provide it to the Commission without fear that this engagement would result in their prosecution, and the Commission can use that information to search for the burial sites of the 'disappeared.' As I will argue in this book, the process facilitated by the ICLVR has been relatively effective and lessons can be learned from this approach that are relevant for both dealing with the past in Northern Ireland and for transitional justice more broadly.

4. Methods

This book uses archival (mainly news media archives) and qualitative interview-based research. Interviews were conducted between 2012 and 2015. In selecting interviewees, I sought to represent a range of perspectives on the 'disappeared' issue, including those of three of the key actors examined in this book: the families of the 'disappeared,' the Republican Movement, and the state. Twenty semi-structured interviews were conducted with relatives of the 'disappeared,' victim advocates and representatives of victim support organisations, Republican ex-combatants, staff of the ICLVR, academics, journalists, politicians, and others with experience of conflict legacy issues in the context of Northern Ireland.

Although this is a relatively small sample size, it includes key actors and has, in my view, facilitated the provision of in-depth, informed viewpoints. Purposive, or targeted sampling[72] was used to select interviewees who represent a variety of perspectives in relation to the 'disappeared.' In qualitative research, small samples can be effective as even a single interview can produce useful information.[73] 'Improved understanding of complex human issues'[74] and diversity in participants[75] are argued to be more important than generalisability of results. Thus, small-scale interviews, rather than an extensive sample size, can produce conceptual depth in research.[76] For Patton, 'The validity, meaningfulness, and insights

71 Ibid.
72 Ibid.
73 Johnny Blair, Frederick Conrad, Allison Castellano Ackermann and Greg Claxton, 'The Effect of Sample Size on Cognitive Interview Findings,' *Proceedings of the American Statistical Association, Section on Survey Research Methods*, (2006), 4041–4046.
74 Martin N. Marshall, 'Sampling for Qualitative Research,' *Family Practice*, 13:6, (1996), 522–525, (p. 524).
75 Nigel King and Christine Horrocks, *Interviews in Qualitative Research* (London: SAGE Publications Ltd., 2010).
76 Mira Crouch and Heather McKenzie, 'The Logic of Small Samples in Interview-Based Qualitative Research,' *Social Science Information*, 45:4, (2006), 483–499

generated from qualitative inquiry have more to do with the information richness of the cases selected and the observational/analytical capabilities of the researcher than with sample size.'[77]

In using a small sample of interviewees, 'all the emerging material can be kept in the researcher's mind as a totality under investigation.'[78] In this regard, Crouch and McKenzie argue, small-scale interviews can be 'conceptually generative.'[79] This has been evidenced in the writing of this book. Being able to keep in mind much of the material collected in interviews as I developed my arguments has been valuable, and the interviews conducted have significantly shaped the arguments made.

Ethical approval was obtained from my institution prior to beginning fieldwork. Of course, the consideration of ethical issues is not limited to the passing of an application by an institution but is something that should be taken into account at all stages of research.[80] Thought had to be given throughout fieldwork to the sensitive nature of the topic under discussion.

When researching sensitive topics, areas of potential concern include issues of harm, consent, deception, privacy, and confidentiality. One of the most efficient and direct ways to allay any concerns of this nature is to be open with interviewees and to elucidate all aspects of the interview process with them, explaining clearly your role as researcher and the purposes of your research.[81] For this research, interviewees were provided with an overview of the purposes of the research, reasons for wanting to speak with them, what an interview would entail, and what would happen to the information they provided in my first communication (either email or letter). At the time of the interview, this information was clarified again in a Research Information Document which included information about me and my research, why the interviewee had been chosen, who else would be taking part (in terms of the broad categories into which interviewees fit, rather than named persons), and what the interviewee's involvement would consist of. Informed consent was obtained from all participants. All interviewees were offered anonymity. Where interviewees wished to remain anonymous, their views have of course been respected. The majority of interviewees were happy to be named and have been so. A brief description of each interviewee is included the first time they are referred to in each chapter, and listed in Appendix 1.

Aware of the potentially particular sensitivity of interviewing relatives of victims, these interviewees were not 'cold called,' rather contact was made first via other

77 Michael Quinn Patton, *Qualitative Research and Evaluation Methods* (3rd ed.) (London: SAGE, 2002), p. 245.

78 Crouch and McKenzie, n 76 at 495.

79 Ibid. at 492.

80 Joan E. Sieber and Barbara Stanley, 'Ethical and Professional Dimensions of Socially Sensitive Research,' *American Psychologist*, 43:1, (1988), 49–55; Rose Wiles, *What are Qualitative Research Ethics?* (Bloomsbury Publishing, 2012).

81 Uwe Flick, *An Introduction to Qualitative Research* (4th ed.) (London: SAGE Publications Ltd., 2009). See also Anna Bryson and Sean McConville, *The Routledge Guide to Interviewing* (Abingdon: Routledge, 2014).

interviewees who had existing relationships with them. As Bryson and McConville advise, interviewees were provided with an overview of the research and the interview process, and given some time to consider the invitation.[82] The questions in the Research Instrument were designed in such a way so as not to focus on the details of specific cases of 'disappearance' (although, as evidenced by the quotes earlier, some of this information was shared during the interviews). Rather the questions were thematised according to the responses to the issue of 'disappearing' by Republicans, by families, by the state, and the local community. Questions were also asked on the intersection between the issue of the 'disappeared' and key transitional justice themes of apology, acknowledgement, truth recovery, the role of amnesty, and memory. As Wiles advises,[83] it was made clear to participants that their participation was voluntary, and they could decline to answer any questions they wished. Questions asked were open-ended, so that participants could give as much, or as little information as they liked.

This is a topic of extreme sensitivity for the Republican Movement. While of course not unaware of the horror of the practice of 'disappearing,' I was nevertheless cognisant that an academic work is not the place to mete out condemnation. Rather I was keen to engage with Republicans in a version of what Matza has described as an appreciative stance. This is one which seeks to engage with and comprehend the subjectivity, diversity, and complexity of human behaviour, rather than a critical or 'correctional' stance which focuses solely on problems.[84] Following Liebling et al.'s use of the appreciative inquiry method as part of a 'search for understanding and explanation,' I approached interviewees from a place of interest, rather than condemnation or judgment.[85] Questions asked of interviewees covered the responses of all the groups analysed in this book, in order to allow me to engage in informed, measured, and critical scholarly reflection on the actions and reactions of all parties. The first of these groups analysed will be the families of the 'disappeared' (Chapter 2). Prior to examining the families' response to the 'disappearances,' Chapter 1 explores the international context of 'disappearing.'

82 Bryson and McConville, ibid.

83 Wiles, n 80.

84 Alison Liebling, David Price and Charles Elliott, 'Appreciative Inquiry and Relationships in Prison,' *Punishment and Society*, 1:1, (1999), 71–98; David Matza, *Becoming Deviant* (New Jersey: Prentice Hall, 1969).

85 Liebling et al., n 75.

1 'Disappearing' in international context

Memory, silence, and the law

1. Introduction

This chapter will introduce the concept of 'disappearing' by giving a brief historical overview of the use of the practice, examining how the act is defined in legal terms and analysing the impact on those left behind. The 'rationales' presented for 'disappearing' in various international contexts will then be examined. Subsequently, some of the literature on silence and memory will be introduced, as these are two themes that underlie all stages of a 'disappearance,' from the perpetration of the abduction through to campaigns by victims' families to uncover the truth. Finally, international efforts to recover the 'disappeared' will be briefly outlined, and the case of Northern Ireland situated against this backdrop.

2. 'Disappearing': origins and international context

To analyse the 'disappearances' that occurred during the conflict in Northern Ireland, it is useful to begin by situating 'disappearing' in its historical and international context. One of the earliest twentieth century manifestations of the practice discussed in the literature is the Nazi *Nacht und Nebel Erlass* (Night and Fog Decree) of December 1941. This policy ordered the secret removal of those people in occupied territories who were believed to be a security threat and their return to Germany. No information was to be provided to the individual's family or loved ones.[1] These people were effectively, "made to disappear."[2] The term *desaparecido* or 'disappeared' subsequently came into regular parlance in the 1960s

1 Reed Brody and Felipe González, 'Nunca Más: An Analysis of International Instruments on "Disappearances,"' *Human Rights Quarterly*, 19:2, (1997), 365–405; United Nations Commission on Human Rights (UNCHR), *Civil and Political Rights, Including Questions of: Disappearances and Summary Executions, Report Submitted by Mr Manfred Nowak, Independent Expert Charged with Examining the Existing International Criminal and Human Rights Framework for the Protection of Persons from Enforced or Involuntary Disappearances*, E/CN.4/2002/71 (8 January 2002), www.icaed.org/fileadmin/user_upload/G0210026.pdf [accessed 2 August 2018].

2 Testimony of Wilhelm Keitel, Nuremberg Trial Proceedings Volume 10, 4 April 1946 (Morning Session), http://avalon.law.yale.edu/imt/04-04-46.asp#keitel2 [accessed 20 June 2018].

to refer to the abduction and assassination of anti-government forces in Guatemala by so-called 'death squads.'[3] Such practices became widespread across Latin America in the 1970s and 1980s,[4] though it is perhaps with the thousands of alleged 'subversives' who were 'disappeared' during Argentina's 'dirty war' that the term became most commonly associated.[5]

Between 10,000 and 30,000 individuals were 'disappeared' in Argentina between 1976 and 1983.[6] Abducted by state forces and held in secret detention centres, these people were often tortured before being executed and their bodies cremated or buried in mass graves. In some cases, they were taken on what was known as a 'death flight,' where individuals were sedated and thrown from planes into the sea. During this time and for years afterwards, state agents not only denied victims' families information on their whereabouts, but in most cases denied having had these individuals in their custody.[7] Following the 1983 election of Raúl Alfonsín, the National Commission on the Disappearance of Persons (*Comisión Nacional sobre la Desaparición de Personas* – CONADEP) was set up to investigate these 'disappearances.' Although the term 'truth commission' was not adopted until a decade later, this Commission was one of the first of many such institutions established to catalogue and investigate human rights abuses in post-conflict contexts.[8]

Political 'disappearances' have become a much-discussed human rights issue and a significant literature now exists on 'disappearances' across the globe.[9] The campaign of the *Madres* of the Plaza de Mayo – the mothers of those 'disappeared' by the Argentinian junta – is perhaps one of the best known of such mobilisation

3 Maureen R. Berman and Roger S. Clark, 'State Terrorism: Disappearances,' *Rutgers Law Journal*, 13, (1981), 531–558 (p. 531).

4 Tullio Scovazzi and Gabriella Citroni, *The Struggle Against Enforced Disappearance and the 2007 United Nations Convention* (Leiden; Boston: Martinus Nijhoff Publishers, 2007).

5 Rita Arditti, *Searching for Life: The Grandmothers of the Plaza de Mayo* (California: University of California Press, 1999), p. 7.

6 Priscilla B. Hayner, *Unspeakable Truths: Transitional Justice and the Challenge of Truth Commissions* (2nd ed.) (New York; Oxon: Routledge, 2011).

7 Uki Goñi, 'Argentina "Death Flight" Pilots Sentenced for Deaths Including Pope's Friend,' *The Guardian*, 29 November 2017; Antonius C. G. M. Robben, *Political Violence and Trauma in Argentina* (Philadelphia: University of Pennsylvania Press, 2005); Horacio Verbitsky, *Confessions of an Argentine Dirty Warrior* (New York; London: The New Press, 2005).

8 Hayner, n 6.

9 For accounts of 'disappearances' in a range of contexts see e.g. Amnesty International, *'Disappearances' and Political Killings: Human Rights Crisis of the 1990s – A Manual for Action* (Amsterdam: Amnesty International, 1994); Francisco Ferrándiz and Antonius C. G. M. Robben (eds) *Necropolitics: Mass Graves and Exhumations in the Age of Human Rights* (Philadelphia: University of Pennsylvania Press, 2015); Iosif Kovras, *Grassroots Activism and the Evolution of Transitional Justice: The Families of the Disappeared* (Cambridge: Cambridge University Press, 2017); Adam Rosenblatt, *Digging for the Disappeared: Forensic Science after Atrocity* (Stanford: Stanford University Press, 2015).

efforts.[10] 'Disappearances' have occurred elsewhere in Latin America,[11] as well as in Africa,[12] Asia,[13] and Europe.[14] In 2017, 45,120 cases across 91 states were reported to be under 'active consideration' by the United Nations Working Group on Enforced or Involuntary Disappearances (UNWGEID).[15] As the next section will examine, despite the prevalence and diversity of the practice, the definition of a 'disappearance' retains a state-centric focus that does not fit comfortably with the notion of 'disappearing' as experienced in Northern Ireland.

3. Defining 'disappearances'

Although there are some exceptions (see below), one of the features of the international literature on 'disappearances' is that, historically at least, much of the discussion has been based on the premise that it was primarily states which were responsible for such activities. This state-centricity is illustrated by some of the historical commentary on the phenomenon by influential human rights

10 Arditti, n 5; Emilio Crenzel, *Memory of the Argentina Disappearances: The Political History of Nunca Más* (New York: Routledge, 2011); Emilio Crenzel, 'Argentina's National Commission on the Disappearance of Persons: Contributions to Transitional Justice,' *International Journal of Transitional Justice*, 2:2, (2008), 173–191; Antonius C.G.M. Robben, 'Disappearance and Reburial in Argentina,' in Jeffrey A. Sluka (ed.) *Death Squad: The Anthropology of State Terror*, (Philadelphia: University of Pennsylvania Press, 2000), pp. 93–113; Robben, n 7; Jennifer G. Schirmer, '"Those Who Die for Life Cannot be Called Dead": Women and Human Rights Protest in Latin America,' *Feminist Review*, 32, (1989), 3–29 (p. 5).

11 See e.g. Jo-Marie Burt, 'Guilty as Charged: The Trial of Former Peruvian President Alberto Fujimori for Human Rights Violations,' *International Journal of Transitional Justice*, 3:3, (2009), 384–405; Crenzel (2011), n 10.; Hayner, n 6; Ralph Rozema, 'Forced Disappearance in an Era of Globalization: Biopolitics, Shadow Networks, and Imagined Worlds,' *American Anthropologist*, 113:4, (2011), 582–593.

12 Amnesty International, n 9; Joost Fontein, 'Between Tortured Bodies and Resurfacing Bones: The Politics of the Dead in Zimbabwe,' *Journal of Material Culture*, 15:3, (2010), 423–448; Human Rights Watch, 'Time for Reckoning: Enforced Disappearances and Abductions in Algeria' (February 2003), www.hrw.org/reports/2003/algeria0203/algeria0203.pdf [accessed 2 August 2018].

13 Malathi De Alwis, '"Disappearance" and "Displacement" in Sri Lanka,' *Journal of Refugee Studies*, 22:3, (2009), 378–391; Simon Robins, 'Towards Victim-Centred Transitional Justice: Understanding the Needs of Families of the Disappeared in Postconflict Nepal,' *International Journal of Transitional Justice*, 5:1, (2011), 75–98; Eric Stover, William D. Haglund and Margaret Samuels, 'Exhumation of Mass Graves in Iraq,' *JAMA: the Journal of the American Medical Association*, 290:5, (2003), 663–666; Michael Young, 'The Sneer of Memory: Lebanon's Disappeared and Postwar Culture,' *Middle East Report*, 217, (2000), 42–45.

14 Kovras n 9; Layla Renshaw, *Exhuming Loss: Memory, Materiality and Mass Graves of the Spanish Civil War* (California: Left Coast Press, 2011).

15 United Nations Working Group on Enforced or Involuntary Disappearances. *Report of the Working Group on Enforced or Involuntary Disappearances*, A/HRC/36/39 (31 July 2017), https://documents-dds-ny.un.org/doc/UNDOC/GEN/G17/229/15/PDF/G1722915.pdf?OpenElement [accessed 2 August 2018].

organisations and institutions. The UN 1992 Declaration on the Protection of all Persons from Enforced Disappearance describes the phenomenon as follows:

> persons are arrested, detained or abducted against their will or otherwise deprived of their liberty by officials of different branches or levels of Government, or by organised groups or private individuals acting on behalf of, or with the support, direct or indirect, consent or acquiescence of the Government, followed by a refusal to disclose the fate or whereabouts of the persons concerned or a refusal to acknowledge the deprivation of their liberty, which places such persons outside the protection of the law.[16]

The International Convention for the Protection of All Persons from Enforced Disappearance defines an 'enforced disappearance' as one committed 'by agents of the State or by persons or groups … acting with the authorisation, support or acquiescence of the State.'[17] The mandate of the UNWGEID thus remains limited to those cases where there is some form of state involvement or collusion, however the Group recognises that opposition forces may perpetrate 'disappearances' in contexts of internal armed conflict and condemns the use of the practice by any perpetrator.[18]

As in the Irish context, however, there are of course examples where 'disappearances' are perpetrated by non-state armed groups or criminal gangs. To name a few examples, of the tens of thousands of 'disappearances' that have been committed in Sri Lanka, some, albeit a minority, were carried out by the JVP (*Janatha Vimukthi Peramuna* or People's Liberation Front) during their uprising against the ruling government of 1987–1990.[19] In Colombia, although the majority of the country's 'disappearances' can be attributed to right-wing paramilitary groups acting with the acquiescence or support of the military, FARC (*Fuerzas Armadas Revolucionarias de Colombia* or Revolutionary Armed Forces of Colombia) insurgents are also known to have been involved in abductions.[20] Similarly, in Syria 'disappearances' are carried out by both pro-state militia with different levels of collusive relations with the state and by traditional 'rebel' groups

16 United Nations, *Declaration on the Protection of all Persons from Enforced Disappearance*, A/RES/47/133 (18 December 1992), www.un.org/documents/ga/res/47/a47r133.htm [accessed 2 August 2018].

17 United Nations General Assembly (UNGA), *International Convention for the Protection of All Persons from Enforced Disappearance*, A/RES/61/177 (20 December 2006), www.ohchr.org/en/hrbodies/ced/pages/conventionced.aspx [accessed 2 August 2018].

18 United Nations Economic and Social Council, *Civil and Political Rights, Including the Questions of: Disappearances and Summary Executions – Report of the Working Group on Enforced or Involuntary Disappearances*, E/CN.4/2006/56 (27 December 2005), www.ijdh.org/wp-content/uploads/2005/12/Disappearances-working-group-report_UN2005.pdf [accessed 2 August 2018].

19 De Alwis, n 13.

20 Human Rights Watch, 'Colombia's Zone of Fear' (26 August 2001), www.hrw.org/news/2001/08/26/colombias-zone-fear-0 [accessed 2 August 2018].

who are fighting against the state.[21] A number of 'disappearances' from Mexico's drug war are linked to criminal gangs, and the settling of scores between rival drug cartels.[22]

Perhaps in recognition of the growing significance of non-state actors, the Rome Statute of the International Criminal Court defines the process more broadly, as a crime carried out 'by, or with the authorisation, support or acquiescence of, a State or political organisation.'[23] In his report submitted to the UN Commission on Human Rights, Nowak suggests that the inclusion of 'political organisation' opens up the definition to include non-state organisations.[24] It has been suggested that this serves to 'delink[ing] these offences from official action'[25] and render the definition more applicable to 'the peculiarities of modern non-international conflicts.'[26] As Nowak's report summarises, the definition of enforced disappearance is not consistent across international law. Although international criminal law allows for the inclusion of non-state actors if operating as a political organisation, direct or indirect state involvement remains a defining feature of the violation in international human rights law.[27]

One of the reasons why the creation of a satisfactory, all-encompassing definition for 'disappearing' is difficult is that it is a method of violence that can take multiple forms.[28] Although the example of Argentina, as noted earlier, perhaps for many shapes their expectations of how 'disappearing' manifests itself, globally 'disappearance' can differ between, and within, contexts. In Morocco, many of the 'disappeared' were not executed, but held in secret detention centres for decades.[29] The bodies of Sri Lanka's 'disappeared' were often not hidden but left in a

21 UNGA, *Report of the Independent International Commission of Inquiry on the Syrian Arab Republic*, A/HRC/27/60 (13 August 2014), www.ohchr.org/Documents/HRBodies/HRCouncil/CoISyria/A.HRC.27.60_Eng.pdf [accessed 2 August 2018]; Independent International Commission of Inquiry on the Syrian Arab Republic, *Conference Room Paper: Without a Trace: Enforced Disappearances in Syria* (19 December 2013), www.ohchr.org/Documents/HRBodies/HRCouncil/CoISyria/ThematicPaperEDInSyria.pdf [accessed 2 August 2018].

22 Human Rights Watch, 'Mexico's Disappeared,' (20 February 2013), www.hrw.org/reports/2013/02/20/mexicos-disappeared-0 [accessed 2 August 2018]; Human Rights Watch, 'Vanished: The Disappeared of Mexico's Drug War,' (8 January 2014), www.hrw.org/news/2014/01/08/vanished-disappeared-mexicos-drug-war [accessed 2 August 2018].

23 Rome Statute of the International Criminal Court (17 July 1998), www.icc-cpi.int/NR/rdonlyres/ADD16852-AEE9-4757-ABE7-9CDC7CF02886/283503/RomeStatutEng1.pdf [accessed 2 August 2018].

24 UNCHR, n 1.

25 George A. Andreopolis and Peter Zehra Juviler, *Non-State Actors in the Human Rights Universe* (USA: Kumarian Press, 2006), p.149.

26 Irena Giorgou, 'State Involvement in the Perpetration of Enforced Disappearance and the Rome Statute,' *Journal of International Criminal Justice*, 11, (2013), 1001–1021 (p. 1021). See also Lisa Ott, *Enforced Disappearance in International Law* (Cambridge: Intersentia Ltd., 2011).

27 UNCHR, n 1.

28 Brody and González, n 1.

29 Hayner, n 6.

public place, the bodies having been burned or so badly mutilated as to be unidentifiable.[30] Similar strategies have been seen in Colombia.[31] The 'disappeared' of Spain's civil war were those buried in unmarked graves, and yet in some cases the locations of these graves, and whose remains they contain, were known by local people who had witnessed the killings.[32]

Given the apparent absence of the element of state involvement, the 'disappearances' perpetrated in Northern Ireland do not fit neatly with the legal definitions provided.[33] As such, the cases could arguably be described using the term 'the missing,' which has a much broader meaning, encompassing any person unaccounted for as a result of armed conflict or internal violence, or indeed outside of conflict settings.[34] However, as suggested earlier, 'disappeared' has become a 'generic term,'[35] applied to a range of forms of 'disappearance' carried out by a variety of perpetrators, both connected to the state, and not. In his book published in 2000, Seamus McKendry (son-in-law of Jean McConville) explains his decision to use the term 'disappeared' as designed to reflect the atrocities committed by the Argentinian Junta.[36] Although McKendry's use of the term in the Irish context was not new, as it has been used as far back as a 1983 newspaper article,[37] the connections between those 'disappearances' that occurred in Latin America and those that happened in Ireland have been drawn on elsewhere. For example, one critic of Sinn Féin (and Gerry Adams in particular), Ed Moloney, argued that 'by the standards of Chile, Argentina or Peru, the IRA's use of this practice was mild, but arguably it is not the scale of the practice that matters as much as the fact it happened at all.'[38] The use of

30 De Alwis, n 13; Amnesty International, n 9.

31 Amnesty International, n 9.

32 Renshaw, n 14; Luis Ríos, José Ignacio Casado Ovejero and Jorge Puente Prieto, 'Identification Process in Mass Graves from The Spanish Civil War I,' *Forensic Science International*, 199, (2010), e27–e36.

33 It should of course be noted here that, as Nowak states, it can be difficult to establish with any certainty the presence, or extent, of state involvement in a 'disappearance,' as by the nature of the act, facts are concealed (UNCHR, n 1). With regards to the Irish cases, we cannot be certain whether or not state agents within the IRA were involved in carrying out these acts. For example, Margaret Perry (not on the ICLVR's list of 'disappeared' as her remains were found a year after her murder) was killed and secretly buried by IRA members who were at that time allegedly working as informers for the Royal Ulster Constabulary (RUC). Perry was last seen in Portadown on 21 June 1991. Her body was found in County Sligo, 30 June 1992 (see David McKittrick, Seamus Kelters, Brian Feeney, Chris Thornton and David McVea, *Lost Lives: The Stories of the Men, Women and Children Who Died as a Result of the Northern Ireland Troubles* (Edinburgh; London: Mainstream Publishing, 2007); Peter Taylor, *States of Terror: Democracy and Political Violence* (Harmondsworth: Penguin, 1994)).

34 Kovras, n 9

35 Ibid., at 14.

36 Seamus McKendry, *Disappeared: The Search for Jean McConville* (Dublin: Blackwater, 2000).

37 Fionnuala O'Connor, 'Suspicion and Fear Over the "Disappeared",' *The Irish Times*, 20 July 1983.

38 Ed Moloney, *Voices from the Grave: Two Men's War in Ireland* (London: Faber and Faber, 2011), p. 111.

the term in the Irish context is arguably demonstrative of the use of an emotive and instantly recognisable label for the purposes of activism and mobilisation, rather than particularly legalistic reasons.

4. The impact of 'disappearing'

Despite the variation present in the range of victims, perpetrators, and methods of 'disappearance,' elements of its social, political, and personal impact are comparable, and widely discussed. De Alwis describes forced 'disappearance' as 'one of the most insidious forms of violence as it seeks to obliterate the body and indefinitely extends and exacerbates the grief of those left behind.'[39] From such a vantage point, 'disappearance' is a dual punishment or 'double harm'[40] – first by killing the victim, and second, in withholding information from families. The suffering on the part of the families has led to calls for them to also be considered 'victims.' In his 2002 Report, Nowak states:

> Often the disappeared persons are killed immediately, but their children, parents or spouses continue to live for many years in a situation of extreme insecurity, anguish and stress, torn between hope and despair. They must, therefore, also be considered as victims of enforced disappearance.[41]

Boss's theory of 'ambiguous loss'[42] is drawn on in the literature to illustrate this impact.[43] 'Ambiguous loss' manifests itself in two forms. The first is physical absence: a loved one is perceived as present, though may be physically gone, such as a soldier missing in action, or, as we are dealing with here, a person has been 'disappeared.' The second form of ambiguous loss is where a person is physically present but psychologically absent, for example as a result of Alzheimer's disease or addiction.[44] For Boss, both of these types of loss share similar effects.

First, ambiguous loss can be immobilising, people may struggle to problem-solve as they do not know the nature of the problem, specifically whether the situation is temporary or permanent.[45] Internationally this can have practical and

39 De Alwis, n 13 at 378.
40 Robben, n 7 at 269.
41 UNCHR, n 1.
42 Pauline Boss, *Ambiguous Loss: Learning to Live with Unresolved Grief* (Massachusetts: Harvard University Press, 1999).
43 See e.g. Jay D. Aronson, 'The Strengths and Limitations of South Africa's Search for Apartheid-Era Missing Persons,' *International Journal of Transitional Justice*, 5:2, (2011), 262–281; Janine Natalya Clark, 'Missing Persons, Reconciliation and the View from Below: a Case Study of Bosnia-Hercegovina,' *Southeast European and Black Sea Studies*, 10:4, (2010), 425–442; Simon Robins, 'Ambiguous Loss in a Non-Western Context: Families of the Disappeared in Postconflict Nepal,' *Family Relations*, 59:3, (2010), 253–268; Robins, n 13; Eric Stover and Rachel Shigekane, 'The Missing in the Aftermath of War: When do the Needs of Victims' Families and International War Crimes Tribunals Clash?' *International Review of the Red Cross*, 84:848, (2002), 845–866; Stover et al., n 13.
44 Boss, n 42.
45 Boss, ibid.

legal implications as families may often be unable to claim reparations or other support if the fate of their relative is unknown.[46] This immobility is captured by Hamber and Wilson's notion of 'uncanny space': the 'symbolically liminal social space' occupied by families of the 'disappeared.' In this 'uncanny space' families are unable to move forward, and bedrooms and homes become 'mummified' as they are kept in an unchanged state, waiting for a loved one's return.[47] As Radislav Krstic was convicted of, and sentenced for, genocide at the International Criminal Tribunal for the former Yugoslavia (ICTY), the presiding judge described the 'amputated lives' of victims' families.[48] Such terminology is equally relevant in the Irish context, where families were 'left in limbo for decades.'[49]

Second, ambiguity of circumstance may prevent family members from re-organising their roles and relationships, as they hold on to the hope that their relative may return.[50] Those researching 'disappearances' internationally have encountered such issues. For example, Clark describes how the mothers of victims of the Srebrenica massacre struggle to move on with their lives, as, without the bodies of their children being found, they struggle to achieve a sense of closure.[51] Ambiguity of circumstances can have practical implications. In Nepal, Robins found that as women traditionally join their husband's household, if their husband is 'disappeared' they become alienated. Though an economic burden to their husband's family, they are unable to leave because of the social stigma attached.[52]

Third, the act of 'disappearing' denies loved ones the symbolic rituals that socially, psychologically, and culturally designate a clear loss.[53] McEvoy and Conway draw on the work of Cohen to suggest that although in a number of contexts (including Northern Ireland), people more or less *know* what happened, it is only through dealing with the dead that genuine *acknowledgement* can take place.[54] As the treatment of the body is central to the grieving process, and consequently any attempts to achieve 'closure,' the grieving process is impeded when the fate of the dead, and the location of their remains, is unknown. Across cultures, groups have their own ideas and practices about what makes a 'good death,' in particular with regards to how the dead should be treated, and what the

46 Hayner, n 6.

47 Brandon Hamber and Richard A. Wilson, 'Symbolic Closure Through Memory, Reparation and Revenge in Post-Conflict Societies,' *Journal of Human Rights*, 1:1, (2002), 35–53 (pp. 39–40).

48 International Criminal Tribunal for the Former Yugoslavia, 'Radislav Krstic Becomes the First Person to be Convicted of Genocide at the ICTY and is Sentenced to 46 Years Imprisonment,' [Press Release], OF/P.I.S/609e (2 August 2001), www.icty.org/sid/7964 [accessed 2 August 2018].

49 Allison Morris, 'The Disappeared – Secretly Buried Remains May Have Been Moved Before,' *The Irish News*, 10 December 2010.

50 Boss, n 42.

51 Clark, n 43.

52 Robins, n 13.

53 Boss, n 42.

54 Kieran McEvoy and Heather Conway, 'The Dead, the Law, and the Politics of the Past,' *Journal of Law and Society*, 31:4, (2004), 539–562.

repercussions will be if they are not dealt with properly.[55] Internationally this is seen as a particular point of suffering with regards the 'disappeared.'[56] For instance, in Argentina, it is said that 'disappearances' created 'a rupture with respect to the conception of death traditionally held.'[57]

A fourth effect suggested by Boss is that, due to the absurdity and irrationality of the situation, those who would provide support in the case of an unambiguous loss, will instead withdraw.[58] Crenzel and Robben have described such behaviour in Argentina, where families of the 'disappeared' experienced isolation from others in the community.[59] Tully found that, in Nicaragua, the 'lack of discourse' at a national, community, and family level further enhanced the suffering of the mothers of the 'disappeared' and made it more difficult for them to reintegrate and resume their lives.[60]

Finally, Boss argues that continuing uncertainty physically and emotionally exhausts those affected.[61] The lasting impact is elucidated by Robben in his account of the suffering of Argentinian families: 'The abduction and disappearance of loved ones, the interminable search, the attempt to provide a proper burial, the years of silence in fear … and a never-ending anguish.'[62]

In the Northern Ireland context, research has found that healing or resolution is seldom possible without more knowledge of the circumstances of a loved one's death.[63] Brian McKinney's father articulated this, describing the pain, "like a toothache, it never goes away … the pain is always there."[64]

There is also a range of lasting socio-psychological consequences discussed in the literature associated with 'disappearances.' For example, Clark observed during her research in Bosnia-Hercegovina that the issue of 'disappearances' can impact negatively on chances of reconciliation. She contends that the prolonged trauma experienced by relatives renders them less open to the restoration of relationships, consumed with their own feelings of guilt, unable to come to terms with their own 'ambiguous loss' and therefore less accepting of the suffering experienced by

55 Katherine Verdery, *The Political Lives of Dead Bodies: Reburial and Postsocialist Change* (New York: Columbia University Press, 1999).
56 Crenzel (2011), n 10; Zoe Crossland, 'Buried Lives,' *Archaeological Dialogues*, 7:2, (2000), 146–159; Iosif Kovras, 'Explaining Prolonged Silences in Transitional Justice: The Disappeared in Cyprus and Spain,' *Comparative Political Studies*, 20:10, (2012), 1–27; Robben n 7; Gabriel Ruiz Romero, 'Voices Around Us: Memory and Community Empowerment in Reconstruction Efforts in Colombia,' *International Journal of Transitional Justice*, 6:3, (2012), 1–11.
57 Crenzel (2011), n 10 at 16.
58 Boss, n 42.
59 Crenzel (2011), n 10; Robben n 7.
60 Sheila R. Tully, 'A Painful Purgatory: Grief and the Nicaraguan Mothers of the Disappeared,' *Social Science and Medicine*, 40:12, (1995), 1597–1610 (p. 1597).
61 Boss, n 42.
62 Robben, n 7 at 263.
63 Marie Smyth, *Residual Matters Relating to Victims of the Troubles in Light of the Agreement Document*, Submission to the Northern Ireland Commission on Victims, 22 April 1998 (INCORE).
64 Gerry Moriarty, 'IRA Victims Campaign Stepped Up,' *The Irish Times*, 27 June 1995.

the 'other side.' When families believe that members of other ethnic groups are withholding information that could help locate remains, this can fuel inter-ethnic mistrust.[65] In addition, there may be economic consequences for those left behind.[66] For example in Nepal, where the majority of the 'disappeared' are men – the traditional breadwinners in Nepalese society – economic support was one of the main needs of victims' families.[67] The gendered impact of 'disappearing' is evidenced elsewhere internationally, as men constitute a significant proportion of the 'disappeared.' As a result the effects of 'disappearance' can particularly affect women, and, as illustrated by the *Madres* of the Plaza de Mayo and similar campaigns, women often take the lead in campaigns for truth and justice.[68]

In Tully's account of the struggles faced by mothers of the 'disappeared' in Nicaragua, she describes the lasting effects of 'disappearing':

> Each story told by a wife, sister or mother begins with the routine of the every day. Quickly, that is smashed. The rupture – the disappearance – occurs and nothing is ever the same. The story descends into a harrowing description of uncertainty, fear and surreality.[69]

This lasting impact has resulted in 'disappearing' being described as a 'continuous violation,'[70] with the UN Declaration on the Protection of All Persons from Enforced Disappearance stating that 'acts constituting enforced disappearance shall be considered a continuing offence as long as the perpetrators continue to conceal the fate or whereabouts of persons.'[71] The continuous nature of the violation renders the state responsible for investigating to bring the offence to an end by establishing the fate of a 'disappeared' person.[72]

In the 2006 Castillo Páez case in Peru, the Permanent Criminal Chamber of Peru's Supreme Court of Justice stated in relation to a 'disappearance' being a 'continuous offence' that 'in this sense the offence is not part of the past.'[73] Tully picked up on this theme in her work on the Nicaraguan Mothers of the Disappeared, for whom 'the war has not ended.'[74] The sense of a 'disappearance' not being 'part of the past' is fundamental in understanding the place for 'dealing with' 'disappearance' through a transitional justice mechanism. Although, as

65 Clark, n 43.
66 Stover et al., n 13.
67 Robins, n 13.
68 David Tolbert, 'Enforced Disappearances: Justice for the Disappeared has a Woman's Face,' *The International Centre for Transitional Justice* (30 August 2013), https://ictj.org/news/justice-disappeared-has-woman's-face [accessed 2 August 2018].
69 Tully, n 60 at 1598.
70 See Scovazzi and Citroni, n 4, specifically at 309–314, and the International Committee of the Red Cross (ICRC), 'Practice Relating to Rule 98. Enforced Disappearance,' www.icrc.org/customary-ihl/eng/docs/v2_rul_rule98 [accessed 2 August 2018].
71 UNGA, n 17.
72 Scovazzi and Citroni, n 4.
73 ICRC, n 70.
74 Tully, n 60 at 1599.

previously argued, those 'disappearances' that were carried out in Northern Ireland do not fit comfortably with the legal definition of 'enforced disappearance' as they were conducted by a non-state group, these acts share many of the same characteristics as 'ongoing violations.' As Gerry Evans' mother, Mary, described: "Everything stopped for our family 30 years ago. We haven't been able to move on."[75] It is important to recognise here that relatives of a 'disappeared' person face a different set of challenges to others affected by conflict. Until the fate of their loved one is known they are effectively a stage behind other victims. If a 'disappeared' person has been killed, this must be established before plans are made to locate and exhume remains; if families are calling for prosecution then it is necessary to know what crimes are being prosecuted. These families therefore have a longer road to travel before they can enter into the debate at the same stage as other victims, vis-à-vis calls for reparations, prosecutions, or truth recovery.

5. 'Rationalising' 'disappearance': history, power, and silencing

In the transitional justice literature there is attention paid to victim mobilisation, exhumations, reparations, and trials of perpetrators. However, in the flurry of scholarship on post-'disappearance' behaviours and responsive action, there is comparatively little exploration of the motivating factors that instigated use of the practice in the first place by the 'disappearer' state or organisation. In reviewing the relevant academic and policy literature as well as the relevant case-law, I have identified four, at times overlapping, rationales for 'disappearing' internationally: 'disappearing' as continuity with the past, 'disappearing' to remove 'unwanted categories,'[76] 'disappearing' as a 'technique of terror,'[77] and 'disappearing' as 'the perfect crime.'[78] As will be argued in this section, these rationales demonstrate that a key motivating factor in the perpetration of 'disappearances' is the desire and power to silence: silencing perceived opposition or dissent by 'disappearing' those considered to be a threat to the status quo, silencing their supporters and the wider populous though instilling fear, and silencing knowledge of the killing itself by attempting to hide all traces of crimes committed.

In several contexts, historical use of 'disappearing' as a method of silencing perceived political opponents has been argued to be one element of the practice's repeated use. For instance, the 'disappearance' in Guatemala in 1967 of 28 Communist party and union leaders is suggested to have established a precedent for the method and use of 'disappearing' elsewhere in Latin America.[79] In Argentina, Robben contends that perpetration of 'disappearances' by state forces

75 Suzanne Breen, 'Put That Family Out of its Misery,' *Sunday Tribune*, 18 January 2009.

76 Rozema, n 11 at 583.

77 Olivier de Frouville, Chair and Rapporteur of the WGEID in interview, *Oxford University Press Blog*, 'How Can a Human Being "Disappear"?' (2013), http://blog.oup.com/2013/08/enforced-disappearance-international-law-pil [accessed 2 August 2018].

78 Schirmer, n 10 at 5.

79 Schirmer, n 10. See also Rosenblatt, n 9.

was rooted in a political fixation on the dead body and the spirit, and historical practices of desecration of the corpse of political opponents.[80] The head of the Syrian Commission for Transitional Justice describes the practice of 'disappearing' there as a "continuous practice of the Assads" that had been used since the 1970s, and constituted a "historical phenomenon" that would only stop with the end of the Assad regime.[81] These examples suggest that cultural, political, and military history can be a source of rationalising 'disappearing.' However, while history may provide a source for the strategic choice to 'disappear,' the ability to 'disappear' requires power – power to 'disappear' and the power to cover one's tracks and avoid accountability.[82]

The expression of power over life and death has been described as the ultimate evidence of sovereignty:[83] 'where power speaks through blood.'[84] Foucault elaborates, particularly through his account of the sentencing of Damiens the regicide to the *amende honorable*, how, prior to the emergence of the prison as the primary form of punishment in the late eighteenth century, 'the body was the major target of penal repression.' Punishment was a 'spectacle,' a public display symbolising the power of the punisher over the punished, the severity of the crime matched by the severity of the tortures inflicted.[85] As McEvoy and Conway articulate, drawing on Foucault:

> the body of an accused person was itself the primary canvas upon which the lawful power of the state or sovereign was inscribed. Historically, the physical and symbolic destruction of the body *after* death was an important aspect of the sentence of the court.[86]

Such control marked a 'hold on the body,'[87] feeding into ideas of power and ownership of the dead. Bodies – and the manipulation of them – can serve as 'symbols of political order.'[88] Punishment, Foucault argues, as an expression of sovereign power, demands elements of both redress and revenge.[89] The treatment

80 Robben, n 10.
81 Kristen Gillespie, 'Enforced Disappearance a "Continuous Practice of the Assads",' *Syria Direct*, 16 September 2014, http://syriadirect.org/main/36-interviews/1566-enforced-disappearance-a-continuous-practice-of-the-assads [accessed 2 August 2018].
82 See e.g. as Kovras (n 9 at 186) remarks with regards the clandestine burial of activists who died in secret detention or in extrajudicial operations in South Africa, 'there must be a high level of coordination among different sectors of the repressive state, infrastructural support and other material resources to hide bodies.'
83 Achille Mbembe (trans.), 'Necropolitics,' *Public Culture*, 15:1, (2003), 11–40.
84 Suvendrini Perera, '"They Give Evidence": Bodies, Borders and the Disappeared,' *Social Identities*, 12:6, (2006), 637–656 (p. 647).
85 Michel Foucault, *Discipline and Punish: The Birth of the Prison* (London: Penguin Books, 1977), p. 8.
86 McEvoy and Conway, n 54 at 552.
87 Foucault, n 85 at 10.
88 Verdery, n 55 at 28.
89 Foucault, n 85.

of the body can be used to express 'outrage and vengeance' for the actions of the deceased in life.[90] In the Irish context, Ron Dudai draws on the work of Garland to argue that 'disappearing' is an example of 'penal excess,' a form of retribution that is "self-consciously excessive."[91] He suggests that the 'disappearing' of those believed to be informers (see Chapter 3) by the IRA is indicative of an emotional response to their alleged actions which 'goes beyond the rational calculation of operational loss.'[92]

The removal of those perceived as a threat is one rationale for 'disappearing' that (as I argue elsewhere) has been presented in Ireland[93] and internationally. The term *desaparecido* was first used to refer to the Latin American practice of eliminating 'real or imagined government opponents.'[94] In such contexts, the practice of enforced disappearance has been described as a 'counter-subversive strategy'[95] used to 'control political space.'[96] A survey of cases of 'disappearance' internationally indicates that it can be a response to a real or perceived threat (especially of a political nature), in which those regarded as posing a risk to the status quo are controlled or removed through 'disappearing.' In Argentina, El Salvador, Mexico, Chile, Syria, and Uruguay, 'disappearing' was (and is in some cases) used to remove those believed to be involved in political activism or who represent the political opposition.[97] In Nepal and Indonesia 'disappearances' were perpetrated by state forces against those considered to be involved in the insurgency.[98] Individuals may be 'disappeared' because of their ethnicity, their religion,

90 McEvoy and Conway, n 54 at 553.

91 Ron Dudai, *The IRA and the Shadow of the Informer: Punishment, Governance, and Dealing with the Past* (Unpublished PhD Thesis, Queen's University Belfast, 2012), p. 85. And see David Garland, 'Penal Excess and Surplus Meaning: Public Torture Lynchings in Twentieth-Century America,' *Law and Society Review*, 39:4, (2005), 793–833.

92 Dudai, ibid. at 69. See also Chapter 3.

93 Lauren Dempster, 'The Republican Movement, "Disappearing" and Framing the Past in Northern Ireland,' *International Journal of Transitional Justice*, 10:2, (2016), 250–271.

94 Stover and Shigekane, n 43 at 849. See also Paloma Aguilar and Iosif Kovras, 'Explaining Disappearances as a Tool of Political Terror,' *International Political Science Review*, (2018).

95 De Frouville, n 77

96 Kevin M. DeJesus, Fernando Bosco and Iman Humaydan, 'Enforced Disappearance: Spaces, Selves, Societies, Suffering,' *ACME*, 13:1, (2014), 73–78 (p. 73).

97 Crenzel (2008), n 10; Soledad Galiana, 'Searching for the Disappeared,' *An Phoblacht*, 28 January 1999; Onur Bakiner, 'From Denial to Reluctant Dialogue: The Chilean Military's Confrontation with Human Rights (1990–2006),' *International Journal of Transitional Justice*, 4:1, (2010), 47–66; Human Rights Watch, 'Where are Syria's Disappeared, Detained, and Kidnapped?' 28 October 2017, www.hrw.org/news/2017/10/28/where-are-syrias-disappeared-detained-and-kidnapped [accessed 2 August 2018]; Independent International Commission of Inquiry on the Syrian Arab Republic, n 21; Wolfgang S. Heinz, 'Motives for "Disappearances" in Argentina, Chile and Uruguay,' *Netherlands Quarterly Human Rights*, 13, (1995), 50–64; Ernesto Schwarz-Marin and Arely Cruz-Santiago, 'Pure Corpses, Dangerous Citizens,' *Social Research*, 83:2, (2016), 483–510; Lynn Stephen, 'Women's Rights are Human Rights,' *American Ethnologist*, 22:4, (1995), 807–827.

98 Renée Jeffery, 'Amnesty and Accountability: The Price of Peace in Aceh, Indonesia,' *International Journal of Transitional Justice*, 6:1, (2012), 60–82; Robins, n 13.

or because they are members of an indigenous community, such as has happened in Colombia,[99] in Guatemala,[100] and in Lebanon.[101]

In these cases, 'disappearing' served, as described by Rozema, as a way of 'removing unwanted categories.'[102] Internationally, the 'removal' of the 'disappeared' as the removal of a threat is a feature of those 'disappearances' perpetrated by, or on the part of, state forces. For Argentina's General Videla, the 'disappeared' were evidence of state attempts to destroy the "forces of evil."[103] During his account of his involvement in the *Nacht und Nebel* decree, Wilhelm Keitel stated that from a "military point of view", an "enormous increase" in "resistance movements, sabotage and everything connected with it" *necessitated* "an elimination of ordinary legal procedures."[104]

To return to Foucault, what he has suggested is worse than 'excessive' physical punishment of the body is 'a penalty that seems to be without bounds.'[105] In his analysis of Foucault, Robben points out that public torture and destruction of the body, while displaying the power of the sovereign, 'also showed spectators the limits of that power.' In maintaining secrecy, 'violent death was taken away from the eye and control of the people.'[106] Foucault's accounts of the violent executions of Damiens the regicide and others exist because they were recorded in the newspapers of the day. Individuals bore witness to these acts, and immortalised their brutality in writings that we can access today. Once we remove these witnesses the possibilities of punishment become boundless.

This notion of the boundlessness of punishment relates particularly to another of the rationales for 'disappearing,' that it is a 'technique of terror' – a way of silencing potential opposition or dissent through instilling fear.[107] For example in Nepal, it has been suggested that 'disappearing' reinforced power dynamics between landlords and indigenous communities, and created an 'atmosphere of terror.'[108] In Mexico, the practice has been described as a form of 'state terrorism.'[109] The instilling of fear has been proposed as a rationale for 'disappearing' by state forces in Argentina,[110] and by state and non-state groups in Colombia[111] and Syria.[112] In Argentina, Robben contends, terror was 'intended to debilitate people

99 Council on Hemispheric Affairs, 'Forced Disappearance in Colombia' (2011), www.coha.org/forced-disappearances-in-colombia/#_ftn2 [accessed 2 August 2018].
100 Schirmer, n 10.
101 Young, n 13.
102 Rozema, n 11 at 583.
103 Cited in Schirmer, n 10 at 9; 10.
104 Nuremberg Trial Proceedings, n 2.
105 Foucault, n 85 at 90.
106 Robben, n 10 at 96.
107 De Frouville, n 77. See also Aguilar and Kovras, n 94.
108 Robins, n 13 at 82.
109 Galiana, n 97.
110 Robben, n 10.
111 Council on Hemispheric Affairs, n 99.
112 Independent International Commission of Inquiry on the Syrian Arab Republic, n 21.

politically and emotionally.'[113] During the Spanish Civil War, General Emilio Mola stated: 'the action has to be violent in the extreme to reduce the enemy … We must sow terror … We must create the sense of absolute power.'[114]

This 'terror' may be a powerful tool for those seeking to diminish potential resistance. In Syria, the 'disappeared' include relatives of those wanted by Syrian security forces and who are involved in activism as a means of instilling fear in remaining family members and deterring them from involvement.[115] In Argentina, 'disappearing' sowed uncertainty, disrupting the activities of the various revolutionary organisations.[116] In Argentina and Chile, 'disappearing' is argued to have 'spread a culture of fear intended to terrorize people into political paralysis.'[117] Retired Argentine naval officer Adolfo Scilingo, recounting to Horacio Verbitsky why the fate of the junta's victims was kept secret from their comrades, explained that it was believed that withholding information would "create uncertainty" and "undermine their morale."[118] Research into the treatment of drowned asylum seekers by the Australian government found that the 'value' of unidentified bodies 'as "deterrents" resides in their very anonymity.'[119] Here, the fear of being 'unknown' in death, arguably adds an extra element of threat for those considering attempting such a crossing. Referring to Argentina, Robben has written of: 'the fear of an unknown threat, impossible to describe.'[120]

In some contexts, this object of terrorising reaches those who might, or have, become involved in campaigning for the return of the 'disappeared' or for the establishment of truth. In Lebanon, one woman whose husband was 'disappeared' commented on her surprise at the turnout of hundreds to a gathering she called for those who had a loved one abducted during the Lebanese civil war as at that time: 'most people were paralyzed by a deep-seated fear that reporting the problem to the police might have an adverse effect on their loved ones, if they were still in custody.'[121] Campaigners for the 'disappeared' have been harassed – for example in Algeria,[122] threatened and abducted in Sri Lanka,[123] and 'disappeared'

113 Robben, n 10 at 94.
114 Ermengol Gassiot Ballbé and Dawnie Wolfe Steadman, 'The Political, Social and Scientific Contexts of Archaeological Investigations of Mass Graves in Spain,' *Archaeologies: Journal of the World Archaeological Congress*, 4:3, (2008), 429–444, (p. 431).
115 Independent International Commission of Inquiry on the Syrian Arab Republic, n 21.
116 Robben, n 10. See also Antonius C. G. M. Robben, 'Exhumations, Territoriality, and Necropolitics in Chile and Argentina,' in Francisco Ferrándiz and Antonius C. G. M. Robben (eds) *Necropolitics* (Philadelphia: University of Pennsylvania Press, 2015), pp. 53–75.
117 Robben (2015), ibid.
118 Adolfo Scilingo, retired officer of the Argentinian navy, cited in Verbitsky, n 7 at 20.
119 Perera, n 84 at 648.
120 Robben, n 7 at 274.
121 Kovras, n 9 at 129.
122 Human Rights Watch, *World Report 2014*, www.hrw.org/sites/default/files/wr2014_web_0.pdf [accessed 2 August 2018].
123 Asian Human Rights Commission, 'Sri Lanka: Mayuri Inoka, Wife Campaigning for Disappeared Husband, Abducted' (2014), www.humanrights.asia/news/press-releases/AHRC-PRL-023-2014 [accessed 2 August 2018].

in Argentina.[124] Following the 'disappearance' of a number of their members, the *Madres* of the Plaza de Mayo declared: "They kidnapped these women to muzzle us."[125] As these cases demonstrate, the terror created by 'disappearance' can silence others in such a way as to render the effects of the 'disappearance' almost self-perpetuating.

The fear and silence created forge further barriers between the 'disappeared' person and any hope of their being recovered or the truth being made known. As Taussig describes, 'The point about silencing and the fear behind silencing is not to erase memory. Far from it. The point is to drive the memory deep within the fastness of the individual so as to create more fear and uncertainty.'[126]

Such fear has been witnessed in the context of Irish 'disappearances.' In 2014, with arrests being made over the abduction of his mother, Michael McConville, son of Jean, told media that despite having witnessed his mother's abduction 42 years previously, he would continue to refuse to name those involved, out of fear.[127]

Finally, a perpetrator may 'disappear' in an attempt to silence knowledge of the crime being made known. For Schirmer,[128] 'disappearing' is 'the perfect crime' as the crime is 'invisible' except to the family and friends of the victim. This 'invisibility' allows perpetrators to avoid accountability and the accompanying damage to their reputation. Keitel, during his testimony at the Nuremberg Trials, suggested that this was part of Hitler's rationale behind the *Nacht und Neber* decree (emphasis author's own):

> he said to me that ... death sentences by court-martial against saboteurs and their accomplices were increasing ... he did not wish this to occur, since ... *it made appeasement and relations with the population only more difficult* ... instead ... the suspect ... should be deported to Germany without the knowledge of their families and be interned or imprisoned *instead of lengthy court-martial proceedings with many witnesses.* [129]

In Argentina, Crenzel suggests, 'the disappearances encapsulated the perpetrators' determination to go unpunished.'[130] One Argentinian brigadier general of the Supreme Court of the Armed Forces told Robben that 'guerillas' were 'disappeared' so as to avoid the risk of revenge being perpetrated against their executioner or those involved in their trials, that may occur after a public

124 Schirmer, n 10.
125 Schirmer, ibid at 8.
126 Michael T. Taussig, *The Nervous System* (New York: Routledge, 1992), p. 27.
127 Michael McHugh and David Young, 'Gerry Adams Latest: Jean McConville's Son Fears for His Life, Sinn Féin Hits Out at Unionist "Old Guard",' *Belfast Telegraph*, 1 May 2014; Fionola Meredith, 'We Live Distorted Normality Where Fear Still Reigns,' *Belfast Telegraph*, 9 May 2014.
128 Schirmer, n 10 at 5. See also Aguilar and Kovras, n 94.
129 Nuremberg Trial Proceedings, n 2.
130 Crenzel (2011), n 10 at 175.

execution.[131] Two further facets to the avoidance of accountability in Argentina were the desire to avoid both historical judgment by future governments and the condemnation of the international community.[132] 'Disappearing' to hide the perpetration of extra-judicial killings from the global gaze is also suggested to be a motivating factor in Mexico.[133] The mother of one 'disappeared' accused the government of being "two-faced ... The nice face is for the international audience. The horrible face is presented to the Mexicans themselves."[134]

In a 'disappearance,' efforts are made to conceal the remains either through secret burial or through treating the body in such a way as to make identification difficult (or almost impossible), or a combination of these actions. For example, following the genocide at Srebrenica, efforts were made to hide what had been done. Personal items that may have helped identify remains were removed, and remains were exhumed and redeposited in secondary graves.[135] In Argentina, bodies were cremated, interred as unidentified at cemeteries, or abandoned. Documentation relating to detainees was destroyed.[136] Bodies can be so mutilated as to make identification impossible.[137] In Sri Lanka, bodies were cremated on pyres of rubber tyres, or dumped in rivers.[138] As one interviewee suggested, those involved in 'disappearing' in Northern Ireland perhaps thought it "was the easiest thing to do. You know to not be traced, to cover their tracks, to get away with it."[139] Though it should be noted that in the Irish context:

> the bodies weren't stripped, as in left naked, without any identifiable [items] ... some of them had medals, medallions and things in the event that they were found. So it wasn't a concealment of their identity, in other words that if they are found, that they will be able to be given to the relatives.[140]

As outlined earlier, these rationales are rooted in the notion of silencing and indicate that the perpetrator has the power, means, and – from their perspective – motive to silence. 'Disappearing' is to a significant extent *about* silencing: silencing those 'disappeared,' their loved ones, perceived political opposition or specific groups, silencing knowledge of the crimes committed and, by extension, efforts to apportion blame or hold perpetrators accountable. Silence has been described as an 'ally of fear,'[141] and is, arguably, the defining aspect of a 'disappearance': a

131 Robben, n 10.
132 Crenzel (2008), n 10 and Robben, n 10.
133 Galiana, n 97; Sylvia Karl, 'Rehumanizing the Disappeared: Spaces of Memory in Mexico and the Liminality of Transitional Justice,' *American Quarterly*, 66:3, (2014), 727–748.
134 Galiana, n 97.
135 Stover and Shigekane, n 43.
136 Robben, n 10.
137 De Alwis, n 13; Schirmer n 10.
138 Amnesty International, n 9.
139 Interview, journalist and writer Susan McKay, July 2014.
140 Interview, retired *An Garda Síochána* Detective Inspector, Brendan McArdle, January 2015.
141 Romero, n 56 at 6.

person may be abducted or arbitrarily detained, but it is the silencing of information regarding their whereabouts or fate that renders them 'disappeared.' One way in which this silencing is combatted by those campaigning on issues related to 'disappearing' is through mobilising to bring the memories of the 'disappeared' and what happened to them into the public domain.

6. 'Disappearances,' silence, and memory

It is argued in some of the transitional justice literature that 'erasure' is the ultimate goal of 'disappearing':[142] 'to be disappeared is to become anonymous.'[143] Internationally, various strategies have been used in order to bring the memory of the 'disappeared' into public view – both to honour their memory, and to draw attention to the suffering of families. For example, internationally, every year on 30 August, the International Day of the Disappeared is marked by photograph exhibits, publications, and speeches.[144] In the Northern Ireland context, WAVE – a cross-community organisation supporting those impacted by the conflict – has, among other activities and campaigns, published a book of the families' stories, in part as a 'reminder' that there are remains yet to be found.[145] This section will introduce the body of research that exists on silence and memory, as concepts that recur in accounts of 'disappearances' and their aftermath.

I would like to enter one caveat at this juncture. While it is tempting to frame this discussion as one of binary opposition with silence and forgetting on the one hand, and voice and memory on the other,[146] it must be emphasised that silence is not simply a void and memory is not the filling of this void. Instead, as I will argue, there is interplay between the two. The conclusion of this interplay is the production of a narrative about the past that includes that which has been selectively remembered and excludes that which has been silenced. The producers of these narratives, who decide what is silenced and what is remembered, have the power to create a version of history that meets their needs. The 'erasure' of the 'disappeared,' which begins with their abduction, will continue with their exclusion from history, unless those who were close to them succeed in bringing their own accounts of the past to the fore.

142 De Alwis, n 13.
143 Tully, n 60 at 1598.
144 International Committee of the Red Cross, 'Living with Absence: Helping the Families of the Missing' (ICRC, 2014), www.icrc.org/eng/resources/documents/publication/p4152.htm [accessed 9 August 2018].
145 WAVE, *The Disappeared of Northern Ireland's 'Troubles'* (Belfast: WAVE Trauma Centre Publications, 2012), p. vii.
146 Jay Winter, 'Thinking About Silence,' in Efrat Ben-Ze'ev, Ruth Ginio and Jay (eds) *Shadows of War: A Social History of Silence in the Twentieth Century* (Cambridge: Cambridge University Press, 2010), pp. 3–31.

6.1. 'Disappearances,' silence, and power

A starting point for a discussion on silence is to state clearly that silence is not just the absence of sound. It is socially constructed.[147] For Zerubavel, this construction begins with the active avoidance of certain topics.[148] As in a normal conversation, noise on a particular topic may serve to silence another.[149] Winter argues that the sense of a binary opposition between silence and memory is rooted in the body of literature dedicated to the Holocaust, where initial oblivion is succeeded by public memory.[150] He describes a more complex role for silence, as a 'socially constructed space,' in which silence can be chosen as a response when other possibilities exist.[151] It should not necessarily be equated with forgetting or being mute as it can be a deliberate strategy initiated because of, or motivated by, a number of factors.[152]

Silence is a complex phenomenon.[153] It can be a response to fear, pain, shame, embarrassment, the desire to avoid further violence, a way of protecting oneself and others, and it can be motivated or shaped by social convention.[154] Silence, and the forms in which it is presented, relates to the wider social and political context.[155] For example, Eastmond and Selimovic, writing about Bosnia and Herzegovina, argue that silence can convey a range of social meanings, and must be understood within its proper social context, rather than considered from a western perspective where the tendency is to prioritise speech over silence.[156] They argue that there is a time to be silent, just as there is a 'time to speak.'[157] Within this framework, this 'temporal dimension'[158] is perhaps especially significant during a transition from conflict, when silence can be 'more emotionally charged and contentious.'[159] A lasting silence following a period of transition from conflict can indicate that political and social conditions are not yet conducive to the narration of particular past events or acts of violence.[160] In terms of dealing

147 Ibid.

148 Eviatar Zerubavel, 'The Social Sound of Silence: Toward a Sociology of Denial,' in Efrat Ben-Ze'ev, Ruth Ginio and Jay (eds) *Shadows of War: A Social History of Silence in the Twentieth Century* (Cambridge: Cambridge University Press, 2010), pp. 32–46.

149 Ibid.

150 Winter, n 146.

151 Ibid., at 4.

152 Marita Eastmond and Johanna Mannergren Selimovic, 'Silence as Possibility in Postwar Everyday Life,' *International Journal of Transitional Justice*, 6:3, (2012), 502–524.

153 Fiona C. Ross, 'An Acknowledged Failure: Women, Voice, Violence, and the South African Truth and Reconciliation Commission,' in Rosalind Shaw and Lars Waldorf (eds) *Localizing Transitional Justice* (California: Stanford University Press, 2010), pp. 69–91.

154 Ibid.; Zerubavel, n 148.

155 Eastmond and Selimovic, n 152.

156 Ibid.

157 Ibid. at 524.

158 Ross, n 153.

159 Eastmond and Selimovic, n 152 at 506.

160 Victor Igreja, 'Memories as Weapons: The Politics of Peace and Silence in Post-Civil War Mozambique,' *Journal of Southern African Studies*, 34:3, (2008), 539–556.

with a contentious past, political contestation over such an endeavour is often focused on 'who or what is entitled to speak for that past in the present.'[161] This suggests that in a way, control over the past lies with whoever has the power to speak of it, rather than with what actually took place. From this perspective, silence, and its breakage, must be considered in light of its social and cultural context, historical temporality, and existing power relations. Of relevance to an analysis of the response to 'disappearances' are therefore questions of who is silent and who speaks, and when and why individuals or groups may choose to speak out, or remain silent.

With the power to speak comes the power to render others 'silencable.'[162] In a context of violence, speaking out can be dangerous if it is seen as a challenge to the dominant power.[163] Silence, in these cases, can be considered evidence of the exertion of power, where fear stops the oppressed and the violated from speaking out. Some suggest that to speak out is a way of expressing power over one's own situation, in order to counteract rival narratives. For Winter, in speaking out, one becomes the author of one's life.[164] Where dominant discourses can silence civil society,[165] voicing dissent and spreading stories can be a way of resisting this silencing.[166] Of course, voices can also be instrumentalised or co-opted for political ends.[167] A site of conflict exists between those with the power to speak and those without it. The relationship between silence and power can be multifaceted, subtle, and pervasive.[168]

Trouillot's *Silencing the Past* is instructive here.[169] In his consideration of the relationship between silence and power in the production of history, he considers

161 Katharine Hodgkin and Susannah Radstone, 'Introduction: Contested Pasts,' in Katherine Hodgkin and Susannah Radstone (eds) *Contested Pasts: The Politics of Memory* (London; New York: Routledge, 2003), 1–22.

162 Jelena Obradovic-Wodnik, 'The "Silent Dilemma" of Transitional Justice: Silencing and Coming to Terms with the Past in Serbia,' *International Journal of Transitional Justice*, 7:2, (2013), 328–347 (p. 336).

163 Fiona C. Ross, 'On Having Voice and Being Heard: Some After-Effects of Testifying Before the South African Truth and Reconciliation Commission,' *Anthropological Theory*, 3:3, (2003), 325–341.

164 Winter, n 146.

165 Kathleen Ireton and Iosif Kovras, 'Non-Apologies and Prolonged Silences in Post-Conflict Settings: The Case of Post-Colonial Cyprus,' *Time and Society*, 21:1, (2012), 71–88.

166 Obradovic-Wodnik, n 162.

167 Cheryl Lawther, 'The Construction and Politicisation of Victimhood,' in Orla Lynch and Javier Argomaniz (eds) *Victims of Terrorism: A Comparative and Interdisciplinary Study* (Abingdon: Routledge, 2016), pp. 10–30; Tshepo Madlingozi, 'On Transitional Justice Entrepreneurs and the Production of Victims,' *Journal of Human Rights Practice*, 13:2 (2010), 208–228; Kieran McEvoy and Kirsten McConnachie, 'Victims and Transitional Justice: Voice, Agency and Blame,' *Social and Legal Studies*, (2013), 1–25.

168 Maria-Luisa Achino-Loeb, 'Introduction: Silence as the Currency of Power,' in Maria-Luisa Achino-Loeb (ed.) *Silence: The Currency of Power* (Oxford: Berghahn Books, 2006), pp. 1–22; Michel-Rolph Trouillot, *Silencing the Past: Power and the Production of History*, (Boston: Beacon Press, 1995).

169 Trouillot, ibid.

the extent to which we can separate what happened from what is said to have happened. While mindful of Appadurai's contention that history is never 'infinitely susceptible to invention,'[170] Trouillot demonstrates the role played by power in silencing certain aspects of the past. For him, historical production involves both social process and narratives about that process, and many opportunities exist for power to impact upon the story created. Silences are inescapable in history, as to produce a trace is to create a silence – to focus on one thing silences something else.[171] Whoever then has the power to choose what is silenced and what is mentioned is in a strategic position to determine what is included in narratives of the past. Given this role for power in the production of history, if nobody speaks out to counteract the dominant narrative, the 'disappeared' could be forever silenced.

Debate exists over the societal and political effects of silence. It can protect, and help the establishment of peace and democracy, but it can also be politically damaging, particularly when past events are drawn on to be used as weapons.[172] A break in silence can allow the expression of previously repressed memories, and the silence can in some cases have nourished the story by allowing for a period of reflection. Conversely, a silence can be so long-lasting as to efface memory.[173] Silence can legitimise violence, as by not speaking out, violence can go unacknowledged, and unpunished.[174] For some, a key role of transitional justice is 'combating silence,' implicitly suggesting of course that the act of speech is healing.[175]

Others point to examples where silence has value. Speech can be damaging.[176] The giving of testimony does not always have a satisfactory outcome for the witness.[177] Silence can be a pragmatic strategy in achieving successful coexistence in post-conflict scenarios.[178] During their research in Bosnia and Herzegovina, Eastmond and Selimovic's interviewees suggested a number of benefits to remaining silent about the war. These included the protection of the younger generation from inheriting old hatreds, and thus breaking the pattern of violent conflict, silence as a way of demonstrating an understanding of shared suffering

170 Arjun Appadurai, 'The Past as a Scarce Resource,' *Man*, 16:2, (1981), 201–219; Trouillot, n 168 at 8.
171 Trouillot n 168.
172 Igreja, n 160; Luisa Passerini, 'Memories Between Silence and Oblivion,' in Katherine Hodgkin and Susannah Radstone (eds) *Contested Pasts: The Politics of Memory* (London; New York: Routledge, 2003), pp. 238–254.
173 Passerini, ibid.
174 Ross, n 153.
175 Ibid.
176 Ibid.
177 Harvey M. Weinstein, 'Editorial Note: The Myth of Closure, the Illusion of Reconciliation: Final Thoughts on Five Years as Co-Editor-in-Chief,' *International Journal of Transitional Justice*, 5:1, (2011), 1–10.
178 Eastmond and Selimovic, n 152; Ann Nee and Peter Uvin, 'Silence and Dialogue: Burundians' Alternatives to Transitional Justice,' in Rosalind Shaw and Lars Waldorf (eds) *Localizing Transitional Justice* (California: Stanford University Press, 2010), pp. 157–182.

and showing respect for those who had lost loved ones, and silence as a demonstration of agency. This latter category included Bosniaks for whom merely being present in a place from which they were once expelled was sufficient to demonstrate their opposition to attempts at ethnic cleansing, without the need to verbalise their experiences.[179] Demonstrating agency through silence is a theme explored by Veena Das, who found that, during the Partition of India, women brought back to their families after being abducted often remained silent to protect themselves from it becoming known that they had been violated. Rather than being empowered through speech, women were empowered through silence to protect their reputations and continue with everyday life.[180] In her analysis of Holocaust survivors, Kidron found that their silence was actually a means of preserving memory. Finding that survivors silently incorporated the memory of the Holocaust into daily life, Kidron asserts that this is a way of maintaining 'the imminent presence of the past in the present.'[181] In these cases, silence is not 'negatively marked absence.' Rather it is 'a medium of expression, communication, and transmission of knowledge in its own right.'[182] Such silent memorialisation has been witnessed in the context of Northern Ireland's 'disappeared.' The families hold an annual 'Silent Walk for the Disappeared' during which they lay a wreath at Stormont – Northern Ireland's Parliament Buildings. On the wreath are white lilies which represent those still missing.[183]

By its very nature a form of absence, silence can be difficult to identify.[184] At times it is only in retrospect that one can hear those voices that may have previously been silenced.[185] In cases of 'disappearance' in Northern Ireland (see Chapter 4), and internationally, there are suggestions, and in some cases, it is widely known, that there are those, beyond the individuals directly involved, who know what has taken place. To use Zerubavel's term, a 'conspiracy of silence' exists, in which people collectively ignore something of which they are each personally aware.[186] For Zerubavel the existence of such a 'conspiracy' underscores the difference between knowledge and acknowledgement, between personal cognisance and public discourse. One of the motivations for this can be 'the chillingly symmetrical dynamics of silence between the fearsome perpetrators and fearful witnesses of atrocities.'[187] As detailed earlier, such fear-induced silence is evidenced internationally in cases of 'disappearance,' where the perpetration of such acts instils terror and creates a culture of fear.[188] Passerini argues that 'certain

179 Eastmond and Selimovic, ibid.

180 Veena Das, *Life and Words: Exploring Violence and the Descent into the Ordinary* (California: University of California Press, 2006).

181 Carol A. Kidron, 'Toward an Ethnography of Silence,' *Current Anthropology*, 50:1, (2009), 5–27 (p. 15).

182 Ibid. at 6; 7.

183 'Families "Will Stand Together Until All the Disappeared are Brought Home",' *Belfast Telegraph*, 2 November 2017.

184 Passerini, n 172.

185 Trouillot, n 168.

186 Zerubavel, n 148 at 32.

187 Ibid. at 37.

188 Robben n 7; Rozema, n 11.

silences are observable only when they are broken or interrupted'[189] and breaking the fear-induced silence through memorialisation of the 'disappeared' has emerged as one strategy used by those seeking to establish the fate of the 'disappeared.' In Colombia, for example, relatives of the 'disappeared' in Granada initiated a project, the *Salón de Nunca Más* or Hall of Never Again, where photographs and stories about the 'disappeared' could be publicly displayed.[190] In Argentina, human-sized silhouettes representing the 'disappeared' were placed on the railings at the entrance to ESMA (the *Escuela Superior de Mecánica de la Armada* – one of the most infamous detention centres of the military dictatorship) as a way of acknowledging the absence of the 'disappeared.'[191] The value of memory for those seeking knowledge of the 'disappeared' will be examined in the next section.

6.2. 'Disappearances,' memory, and politics

In his discussion of memory as duty, Booth draws on Czeslaw Milosz's Nobel Lecture: "Those who are alive receive a mandate from those who are dead and silent forever: to preserve the truth about the past."[192] If Booth had included Milosz's next line, he would have presented us with one of the key impediments to such an endeavour: "They can fulfil their duties only by trying to reconstruct precisely things as they were, and by wresting the past from fictions and legends."[193] That memory is often looked to for establishing the truth about the past assumes a direct correlation between what took place and how it is remembered[194] that in reality, arguably does not exist.

One important work for current purposes is Halbwach's *On Collective Memory*,[195] in which he argues for the social construction of memory. As memory is acquired, recalled, recognised, and localised in society, it is framed within its boundaries, and consequently, 'the past is not preserved but is reconstructed on the basis of the present.'[196] As with silence, memory is something intangible, and defined and described in various ways by scholars. It is a 'duty' the living owe to the dead.[197] It is also a 'screen' that both reveals and hides traces of what has taken place.[198] And it can be a 'weapon' that is drawn on when needed to be wielded

189 Passerini, n 172 at 239.
190 Romero, n 56.
191 Vincent Druliolle, 'Silhouettes of the Disappeared: Memory, Justice and Human Rights in Post-Authoritarian Argentina,' *Human Rights and Human Welfare*, 9, (2009), 77–89.
192 W. James Booth, 'The Unforgotten: Memories of Justice,' *American Political Science Review*, 95:4, (2001), 777–791 (p. 782).
193 Czeslaw Milosz, Nobel Lecture (1980), www.nobelprize.org/nobel_prizes/literature/laureates/1980/milosz-lecture.html [accessed 2 August 2018].
194 Hodgkin and Radstone, n 161.
195 Maurice Halbwachs, *On Collective Memory* (ed. trans. Lewis A. Coser) (Chicago: University of Chicago Press, 1992).
196 Ibid. at 40.
197 Booth, n 192.
198 Passerini, n 172.

against political opponents.[199] Like silence, memory is also a construct. Memory as representation is a recurring theme, where memory is a construction of the past influenced by the present, that can be both consciously manipulated and unconsciously absorbed.[200] Memory is then not a passive reflection of past events, but a complex and dynamic medium. To consider memory is to consider a version, or collection of versions, of the past.

The role of memory is in some accounts promoted as enabling the countering of official 'lies' with grassroots 'truth.'[201] This binary opposition of grassroots 'truth' versus top down 'lies,' which one sees in some of the more eulogising accounts of truth recovery, is something of a simplification. Critical variants of memory theory have developed further to consider memory as process, examining the complexities of how different versions of the past can be promoted, reformulated, or even silenced.[202] As discussed, memory is socially constructed,[203] and the way in which it is formed and communicated relates to the present day context, as much as to the period being remembered. For the sake of brevity, I am going to summarise some of the key aspects of this politics of memory literature across four themes – the formation of collective memory, the relationship between memory and dealing with the past, its impact on everyday politics, and the role of memory in responding to 'disappearances.'

The formation and preservation of collective memory is closely linked to a group's identity and sense of continuity with its past. Thus, it is considered to play a role in group cohesion through the creation of a collective image of a shared past.[204] Olick and Levy propose that collective memory is an ongoing negotiation between past and present that impacts upon political claims-making both mythically and rationally – mythically, through the power of the past over the present, and rationally, through the power of the present over the past.[205] This function of memory as structuring and strengthening a group's identity then necessitates the formation of a collective identity that is consistent with the group's ideology yet at the same time promotes their current goals. For Kansteiner, 'historical representations are negotiated, selective, present-oriented, and relative.'[206] Wood

199 Igreja, n 160.

200 Hodgkin and Radstone, n 161; Wulf Kansteiner, 'Finding Meaning in Memory: A Methodological Critique of Collective Memory Studies,' *History and Theory*, 41, (2002), 179–197 (p.180); Passerini, n 172; Elizabeth Tonkin, *Narrating Our Pasts: The Social Construction of Oral History* (Cambridge: Cambridge University Press, 1992).

201 Hodgkin and Radstone, n 161.

202 Ibid.

203 Halbwachs, n 195.

204 Benedict Anderson, *Imagined Communities: Reflections on the Origin and Spread of Nationalism* (London; New York: Verso, 2006); Barbara A. Misztal, *Theories of Social Remembering* (Maidenhead: Open University Publishing, 2003).

205 Jeffrey K. Olick and Daniel Levy, 'Collective Memory and Cultural Constraint: Holocaust Myth and Rationality in German Politics,' *American Sociological Review*, 62:6, (1997), 921–936.

206 Kansteiner, n 200 at 195.

expresses a similar view, arguing that 'public memory' is usually in practice selected, organised, and shaped by some social group or other manifestation of power. For Wood, the relationship between memory and power is inherent in the production of collective memory, as those representations of the past that enter the public domain 'embody an intentionality … that promotes or authorises their entry.'[207] From such a perspective, any collective memory presented in the public domain will be a representation of the intention of the group, party, or institution from which it originates, designed to meet their needs at that particular time.

The wisdom of drawing out memories of past violence during a period of transition has been fiercely debated. For some, the imposition of a silence or amnesia regarding the past is at times more conducive to the development of a peaceful future than remembering the violence that took place.[208] The political inclinations of the groups involved impact upon the timing of engagement with the memory of the past, especially a negative one, and so this is something that will only take place in an atmosphere that is conducive to dealing with the issues raised.[209] It has also been suggested that a period of collective amnesia readies the ground for recovering collective memory at a later stage.[210] In considering the timing of engaging with memory, it is not only a case of considering its production, but also that the audience is ready to embrace it.[211]

A further consideration with respect to timing is that as memories can be powerful tools to injure an opponent, they can be 'kept in reserve' to be used at a time when they will have maximum impact.[212] Igreja found that in post-civil war Mozambique, 'unsettled histories' provided opportunities in everyday politics for political figures to exploit differing versions of past violence for their own political ends and, in this way, memories were used to injure political opponents.[213] These conflicts suggest that, just as a conducive atmosphere is required for memory to be produced and embraced, the absence of a process or means of facilitating this engagement with the past creates an atmosphere conducive to political point-scoring using competing versions of past actions. There exists an interplay between memory and power that manifests itself in political life, particularly at a time of transition. At this point it is useful to consider how one decides when the time is right to engage with the memory of past violence, and who is involved in making this decision. Orwell's frequently repeated quote, 'Whoever controls the past,

207 Nancy Wood, *Vectors of Memory: Legacies of Trauma in Postwar Europe* (Oxford: Berg, 1999), p. 2.

208 Booth, n 192; Paul Connerton, 'Seven Types of Forgetting,' *Memory Studies*, 1:1, (2008), 59–71; Igreja, n 160; Reinhart Kössler, 'Facing a Fragmented Past: Memory, Culture and Politics in Namibia,' *Journal of Southern African Studies*, 33:2, (2007), 361–382; Misztal, n 204; Passerini, n 172.

209 Igreja, n 160; Kansteiner, n 200.

210 Susanne Karstedt, 'From Absence to Presence, From Silence to Voice: Victims in International and Transitional Justice Since the Nuremberg Trials,' *International Review of Victimology*, 17:9, (2010), 9–30.

211 Kansteiner, n 200.

212 Igreja, n 160.

213 Ibid.

controls the future. Whoever controls the present controls the past'[214] points to the powerful as those who decide if, when, and how to explore the memory of the past. Indeed, in some contexts, it is only the political elites or state authorities that have a voice in determining if and when the memory of the past is dealt with.[215] However, there are some who argue for an increasingly dominant role for the voices of victims in combatting impunity over past violence by engaging with their memories of what took place, and mobilising to pressurise the state into doing the same.[216] Misztal summarises that ultimately, accessing the closest approximation of what really took place in the past comes from considering a plurality of diverse narratives.[217] Of course, it should be noted that the incorporation of victims' voices is not a 'quick fix' to power imbalances. As will be discussed further in Chapter 2, victims are not a monolith, and any decision to include victims' voices is likely to be followed by decisions as to which voices are selected, listened to, and have impact.[218] The link between 'having voice' and 'being heard' is not unproblematic.[219]

Hodgkin and Radstone describe how memory involves the clashing of the personal, social, public, and political.[220] This clashing is exemplified keenly in the case of 'disappearances,' in which something that is in many ways immensely personal is, at the same time, bound up in the political and social context in which the 'disappearance' takes place, and in which public efforts are made to respond to the issue. It can be the case that through bringing personal memories into the public sphere, action is taken in dealing with these atrocities. Remembering allows those who are absent to live on, bringing those who have passed away into the present, through memory,[221] and highlighting the 'vacuum created' by their disappearance.[222] In cases of 'disappearance,' memory is at once an expression of remembrance of the victim, and a form of activism in making visible the wrong that was committed, through voicing memories in order to silence denial. Relatives of the 'disappeared' in Colombia assert that 'making their voices heard was the best way of confronting perpetrators' stories.'[223] In Argentina it is argued that it was the presentation of thousands of *habeas corpus* petitions to the courts by relatives that left the first traces of memory of the 'disappeared.'[224] Burchianti

214 Cited in Misztal, n 204 at 120.
215 Margaret E. Burchianti, 'Building Bridges of Memory: The Mothers of the Plaza de Mayo and the Cultural Politics of Maternal Memories,' *History and Anthropology*, 15:2, (2004), 133–150; Iolanda Jaquemet, 'Fighting Amnesia: Ways to Uncover the Truth about Lebanon's Missing,' *International Journal of Transitional Justice*, 3:1, (2008), 69–90.
216 Burchianti, ibid.; Karstedt, n 210; Romero, n 56.
217 Misztal, n 204.
218 McEvoy and McConnachie, n 167.
219 Ross, n 153.
220 Hodgkin and Radstone, n 161.
221 Booth, n 192; Romero, n 56.
222 Romero, ibid.
223 Ibid. at 6.
224 Crenzel (2011), n 10.

quotes one of the *Madres* of the Plaza de Mayo as describing memory as "the basis on which claims for justice and truth are made."[225] Furthermore, it has been suggested that in Spain, the search for, and excavation of, remains of the 'disappeared' has helped to generate interest in understanding what happened, and to motivate the production of a narrative of the events that took place.[226] These examples show that memory can be a powerful device for families of the 'disappeared.' Yet, the politics of memory impact upon its effectiveness. Kössler, for example, argues that different groups have differing levels of opportunity to voice their version of the past; for him, public memory is bound up with political actions, political strategies, and inequality.[227]

At a time of transition from conflict, Booth contends, 'the weight of the claims of the past, and their clash with those of the present and future, are most visible.'[228] During transition, remembering the past and attempting to silence it have been presented as polar opposite strategies.[229] However, as has been argued, the construction of both silence and memory belies any such polarisation. The timing and motivations for engaging with the memory of past events can be complex, and the memory that is then produced is itself a representation of the past, rather than a reproduction of it. Within this representation there may be aspects of the past that are silenced or missing through not having been selected for inclusion. Silence and memory are both constructs that can be appropriated and manipulated for political ends, and although there is an inevitable link between dominant accounts of the past and power relations,[230] the memories of past violence and violations, or the decision to silence those memories, represent powerful tools that can be used by various different groups, both within the political elite and civil society. As discussed previously, just as 'disappearances' are about power and about silencing, when families and others speak out against 'disappearing,' they exert their own collective power to combat the efforts of state forces or non-state armed groups to 'silence' those they 'disappeared.' As Tully articulates, to mobilise against 'disappearing' is to 'challenge … collective silences and … confront … public forgetting.'[231]

225 Burchianti, n 215 at 133.
226 Romero, n 56; Renshaw n 14; Mary Vincent, 'Breaking the Silence? Memory and Oblivion Since the Spanish Civil War,' in Efrat Ben-Ze'ev, Ruth Ginio and Jay Winter (eds) *Shadows of War: A Social History of Silence in the Twentieth Century* (Cambridge: Cambridge University Press, 2010), pp. 47–67. Of course, it should be noted that many silences remain (see e.g. Francisco Ferrándiz, 'Mass Graves, Landscapes of Terror,' in Francisco Ferrándiz and Antonius C. G. M. Robben (eds) *Necropolitics* (Philadelphia: University of Pennsylvania Press, 2015), pp. 92–118.
227 Kössler, n 208.
228 Booth, n 192.
229 Passerini, n 172; Kössler, n 208.
230 Hodgkin and Radstone, n 161.
231 Tully, n 60 at 1597.

7. Recovering the 'disappeared': the international experience

Where this mobilisation has led to the location of the remains of those who have been 'disappeared,' this is rarely as a result of the activism of relatives of the 'disappeared' and their supporters alone.[232] As this book examines in the context of Northern Ireland, the recovery of the 'disappeared' often requires action from families and NGOs or support groups, from the state, and from the perpetrators themselves. This need for information from perpetrators, and the use of limited immunity or amnesty-like measures in exchange for this information, offers an illustration of the classic peace versus justice tension which is often encountered in transitional contexts.[233]

Perpetrators often 'have a monopoly on information about gravesites.'[234] For example, Stover and Shigekane report in relation to Rwanda and the former Yugoslavia that the recovery of remains can be 'difficult, if not impossible, without the cooperation of the actual perpetrators who for obvious reasons would rather remain anonymous.'[235] The exhumation and identification of the remains of the 'disappeared' often necessitates the provision of 'incentives to convince perpetrators to come forward with valid information on burial sites. These … may include immunity from prosecution, anonymity and confidentiality.'[236] To this end, in a number of contexts, states have introduced limited immunity mechanisms to incentivise and facilitate the provision of information on burial site locations by perpetrators.

In Cyprus, information circulated within the Committee on Missing Persons was to be confidential; those who provided 'critical information' would not be politically or legally liable; and the information provided would not be used against them. This – combined with agreement between the leaders of the two Cypriot communities that all information available on burial sites should be circulated and investigated – resulted in the location of the remains of over a thousand disappeared persons within ten years.[237] In Colombia, although described as 'controversial' due in part to the provision of a 'de facto amnesty to paramilitary groups' offered in the first version of the legislation,[238] the

232 Exceptions to this include exhumation of mass graves in Iraq by communities of mourners (Rosenblatt, n 9) and 'citizen forensics' in Mexico (see Ernesto Schwarz-Marin and Arely Cruz-Santiago, 'Forensic Civism: Articulating Science, DNA and Kinship in Contemporary Mexico and Colombia,' *Human Remains and Violence: An Interdisciplinary Journal*, 2:1, (2016), 58–74).

233 See e.g. Payam Akhavan, 'Are International Criminal Tribunals a Disincentive to Peace? Reconciling Judicial Romanticism and Political Realism,' *Human Rights Quarterly*, 31:3, (2009), 624–654; Johanna Herman, Olga Martin-Ortega and Chandra L. Sriram, 'Beyond Justice Versus Peace: Transitional Justice and Peacebuilding Strategies,' in Karin Aggestam and Annika Bjorkdahl (eds) *Rethinking Peacebuilding: The Quest for Justice Peace in the Middle East and the Western Balkans* (Abingdon: Routledge, 2013), pp. 1–46.

234 Kovras, n 9 at 177.

235 Stover and Shigekane, n 43.

236 Kovras, n 9 at 239.

237 Ibid.

238 Louise Mallinder and Kieran McEvoy, 'Rethinking Amnesties: Atrocity, Accountability and Impunity in Post-Conflict Societies,' *Contemporary Social Science*, 6:1, (2011), 107–128 (p. 124). See also Catalina Diaz, 'Challenging Impunity from

'Justice and Peace Law' has facilitated the recovery of some 3000 'disappeared' persons.[239] In Uruguay, the *Comisión para la Paz* was tasked with gathering information in relation to the detained and 'disappeared' and determining their fate, but not to identify perpetrators. The Commission met regularly with victims' families and victims' organisations, and held confidential meetings with members of the armed forces in order to gather information.[240] In South Africa, where many of those missing are buried in individual graves, Madeline Fullard of the Missing Persons Task Team (MPTT) has reported that, they "can essentially do nothing in certain cases without some assistance from the perpetrators."[241] Kovras has reported that approximately one third of the bodies recovered by the MPTT have been so as a result of information provided via the South African Truth and Reconciliation Commission's amnesty hearings. It should be noted, however, that he described the design of these hearings as 'flawed' in this regard, as amnesty could be granted on the basis of the provision of information which was not of sufficient detail to facilitate the location of remains.[242] As this book will examine, Northern Ireland is another case where information from the perpetrators has been required to locate burial sites and this has been facilitated by the use of a limited immunity mechanism (see Chapter 5).

8. Conclusion

As this chapter has analysed, 'disappearances' are a 'universal phenomenon.'[243] They are often perpetrated by those with the power and desire to silence – to silence those they 'disappear,' their loved ones and supporters, and to silence the prospect of accountability. Often, it is the families who become the 'silence breakers,' the first to speak out against what has happened.[244] As examined in the preceding section, however, action is also often required on the part of the state, and on the part of the perpetrator, in order to facilitate the locating of remains. The response to Northern Ireland's 'disappeared' will be examined from each of these perspectives in this book, beginning with the families in Chapter 2.

Below: The Contested Ownership of Transitional Justice in Colombia,' in Kieran McEvoy and Lorna McGregor (eds) *Transitional Justice from Below* (Oxford: Hart Publishing, 2008), 189–216.

239 Kovras, n 9.

240 Louise Mallinder, 'Uruguay's Evolving Experience of Amnesty and Civil Society's Response.' Working paper (2009) Transitional Justice Institute Research. Available at SSRN: https://ssrn.com/abstract=1387362.

241 Cited in Kovras, n 9 at 195.

242 Kovras, n 9 at 193. The MPTT was also provided with information on burial site locations by Eugene de Kock, during his imprisonment (see Justine van der Leun, 'The Odd Couple: Why an Apartheid Activist Joined Forces with a Murderer,' *The Guardian*, 6 June 2015).

243 UNCHR, n 1.

244 See e.g. Burchianti, n 215; Jaquemet, n 215; Kovras, n 9; Renshaw, n 14; Robben, n 7; Schirmer, n 10.

2 The victims

Mobilisation, the politics of victimhood, and constructing the 'disappeared'

1. Introduction

In a number of contexts, 'disappearances' have created the impetus for mobilisation by victims' families.[1] For Robins, out of all violations, 'disappearance' has played the most significant role in developing transitional justice processes beyond prosecution, because of the need for information and establishing truth.[2] Indeed, it can be argued that mobilisation by families of the 'disappeared' of Argentina, prompted the establishment of the National Commission on the Disappearance of Persons (CONADEP), one of the first truth commissions.[3] More broadly, protests against the Latin American 'disappearances' by families and the Latin American NGO sector 'were eventually to have repercussions far beyond Latin America,'[4] influencing the development of elaborate international protections against 'disappearing.'[5] Lobbying by various national and international human rights organisations influenced the introduction of the UN Declaration for the Protection of All Persons from Enforced Disappearance in 1992, the Inter-American Convention on Forced Disappearance of Persons in 1994, and the International Convention for the Protection of All Persons from Enforced Disappearance in 2006.[6]

1 See e.g. Iolanda Jaquemet, 'Fighting Amnesia: Ways to Uncover the Truth about Lebanon's Missing,' *International Journal of Transitional Justice*, 3:1, (2008), 69–90; Iosif Kovras, *Grassroots Activism and the Evolution of Transitional Justice: The Families of the Disappeared* (Cambridge: Cambridge University Press, 2017); Michael Young, 'The Sneer of Memory: Lebanon's Disappeared and Postwar Culture,' *Middle East Report*, 217, (2000), 42–45. Layla Renshaw, *Exhuming Loss: Memory, Materiality and Mass Graves of the Spanish Civil War* (California: Left Coast Publishing, 2011).

2 Simon Robins, 'Towards Victim-Centred Transitional Justice: Understanding the Needs of Families of the Disappeared in Postconflict Nepal,' *International Journal of Transitional Justice*, 5:1, (2011), 75–98.

3 Priscilla B. Hayner, *Unspeakable Truths: Transitional Justice and the Challenge of Truth Commissions* (2nd ed.) (New York; Oxon: Routledge, 2011).

4 Wilder Tayler, 'Background to the Elaboration of the Draft International Convention for the Protection of All Persons from Enforced Disappearance,' *The Review/International Commission of Jurists*, 62–63, (2001), 63–72 (p. 63).

5 Ibid.; Kovras, n 1.

6 Lisa Ott, *Enforced Disappearance in International Law* (Cambridge: Intersentia Ltd., 2011); Tayler, n 4.

The campaign by families of the 'disappeared' in Northern Ireland is argued to be 'illustrative of the political and moral power of victim-focussed initiatives.'[7] It can be situated in this international landscape of campaigns by families of the 'disappeared' which exemplify the ability of victims to '"do" transitional justice,'[8] while also responding to specific characteristics of the Northern Ireland context, including the contemporary political context, and subjectivities of the victim hierarchy.

The next section will examine the relevance of this example of victim agency in relation to continuing debate on the extent to which transitional justice processes internationally are (or are not) 'victim-centred.' Then the focus will shift to Northern Ireland, and the contours of the 'silence' experienced by families in the aftermath of the 'disappearance.' Subsequently, drawing on the social movement literature, the families' mobilisation efforts will be examined, with a particular focus on how the 'disappeared' have been 'framed' by families, and the political opportunities available to them. Finally, some of the potential challenges facing the families will be highlighted.

2. Victims in transitional justice

As set out in Chapter 1, the families of those who have been 'disappeared' can also be considered to be victims. They can, therefore, have a dual role, as both victim and victims' campaigner. Despite claims that victims constitute the 'moral centre' of transitional justice,[9] some point to a disjuncture between the prominence of the category and the level of scholarly commitment to understanding the political and social subjectivities inherent in the construction of victimhood and attribution of the victim 'label.'[10] These varying points of view are manifest in discussions around the identification of who victims are, and the centrality of victims within transitional justice processes. In this section, the place of the families of the 'disappeared' as both victim and advocate will be considered in light of these debates.

Defined as 'the identity, meaning and status of victims in society,' for Druliolle, victimhood is a historical and social construction, which does not necessarily correlate to harm suffered.[11] As Smyth suggests, 'legitimate victimhood is a contested category.'[12]

7 Kieran McEvoy, *Making Peace with the Past: Options for Truth Recovery Regarding the Conflict in and about Northern Ireland* (Belfast: Healing Through Remembering, 2006), p. 62.

8 Following Kieran McEvoy and Kirsten McConnachie, 'Victims and Transitional Justice: Voice, Agency and Blame,' *Social and Legal Studies*, (2013), 1–25.

9 Kris Brown and Fionnuala Ní Aoláin, 'Through the Looking Glass: Transitional Justice Futures Through the Lens of Nationalism, Feminism and Transformative Change,' *International Journal of Transitional Justice*, 9, (2014), 127–149 (p. 140).

10 Vincent Druliolle, 'Recovering Historical Memory: A Struggle against Silence and Forgetting? The Politics of Victimhood in Spain,' *International Journal of Transitional Justice*, 9:2, (2015), 316–335; Kieran McEvoy and Kirsten McConnachie, 'Victimology in Transitional Justice: Victimhood, Innocence and Hierarchy,' *European Journal of Criminology*, 9:5, (2012), 527–538.

11 Druliolle, ibid. at 320.

12 Marie Breen Smyth, *Truth Recovery and Justice After Conflict: Managing Violent Pasts* (London: Routledge, 2007), p. 77. See also Marie Breen Smyth, 'The Uses of

The label of 'victim' is often intrinsically linked to the concept of 'innocence' which, as McEvoy and McConnachie explore, is a problematic notion in post-conflict or post-dictatorship contexts as 'such a malleable term is often used to describe victims from 'our' community rather than 'theirs.'[13] Victimhood is subjective and the 'victim' label may be attributed on the basis of the political, social, and cultural perspectives of the labeller, rather than the harm experienced by the labelled. Transitional justice measures can therefore be politicised by attempts to identify who the victims are.[14]

Just as the task of attributing victim status is a site of dispute, so too are discussions surrounding the role and position of victims in transitional justice processes. For some, there is an important place for civil society actors and grassroots initiatives during transitions from conflict, with victims' rights and needs a central consideration in post-peace settlement contexts.[15] Karstedt charts the emergence of victims' voices in international and transitional justice from the Nuremberg trials of the 1940s to more recent processes such as the South African Truth and Reconciliation Commission (TRC) and the International Criminal Tribunal for the former Yugoslavia (ICTY), arguing that victims' voices have become more prominent over time.[16] In their assessment of the International Criminal Court (ICC), Pena and Carayon found that, although not yet achieving its full potential in terms of victim participation, victims left in a state of disempowerment by violence can empower themselves through making decisions.[17] In Colombia, the introduction of a broadly defined legal category of 'victim' is said to have opened up a 'legal and legitimate avenue to raise claims with the state,' the effects of which were felt by victims and wider Colombian society.[18]

Suffering: Victims as Moral Beacons or Icons of Grievance,' in Vincent Druliolle and Roddy Brett (eds) *The Politics of Victimhood in Post-Conflict Societies* (Cham, Switzerland: Palgrave Macmillan, 2018), pp. 211–236.

13 McEvoy and McConnachie, n 10 at 533.

14 Druliolle, n 10; Vincent Druliolle and Roddy Brett, 'Introduction,' in Vincent Druliolle and Roddy Brett (eds) *The Politics of Victimhood in Post-Conflict Societies* (Cham, Switzerland: Palgrave Macmillan, 2018), pp. 1–22.

15 Laura Arriaza and Naomi Roht-Arriaza, 'Social Reconstruction as a Local Process,' *International Journal of Transitional Justice*, 2:2, (2008), 152–172; Ron Dudai and Hillel Cohen, 'Dealing with the Past when the Conflict is Still Present,' in Rosalind Shaw and Lars Waldorf (eds) *Localizing Transitional Justice* (California: Stanford University Press, 2010), pp. 228–252; Wendy Lambourne, 'Transitional Justice and Peacebuilding after Mass Violence,' *International Journal of Transitional Justice*, 3:1, (2008), 28–48; John Brewer and Bernadette Hayes, 'Victimhood Status and Public Attitudes Towards Post-Conflict Agreements: Northern Ireland as a Case Study,' *Political Studies*, 61:2, (2013), 442–461.

16 Susanne Karstedt, 'From Absence to Presence, From Silence to Voice: Victims in International and Transitional Justice Since the Nuremberg Trials,' *International Review of Victimology*, 17:1, (2010), 9–30.

17 Mariana Pena and Gaelle Carayon, 'Is the ICC Making the Most of Victim Participation?' *International Journal of Transitional Justice*, 7:3, (2013), 518–535.

18 Jemima García-Godos and Knut Andreas O. Lid, 'Transitional Justice and Victims' Rights before the End of a Conflict,' *Journal of Latin American Studies*, 42:3, (2010), 487–516 (pp. 514–515).

Despite the supposed centrality of victims to transitional justice processes, some critical commentators question whether the rhetoric matches the delivery.[19] This is in terms of both the extent to which victims' needs and voices are prioritised in transitional mechanisms, as well as the apparent gulf that exists between theory and practice.[20] Robins argues that transitional justice processes in general continue to operate in a top-down fashion. Although the term 'victim-centred' is commonly used to describe transitional mechanisms, victims are often not at the centre of these processes.[21] They can be neglected.[22] McEvoy and McConnachie highlight a 'mismatch' between the 'rhetoric' surrounding the victim-centred nature of transitional justice processes, and the 'reality' of the victim experience, where victims' needs can be side-lined or 'instrumentalised' in favour of broader political and social aims.[23] For example in Peru, the use of victimhood as a tool by politicians is argued to have resulted in inconsistency in the granting of victim status and provision of reparations.[24] As Dixon and Tenove summarise with regards to international criminal justice specifically, although there have been changes in the representation of, and approach to, victims, they continue to lack agency.[25] In a similar vein, in truth commissions as well as international trials, Doak suggests, the victim's role is 'purely instrumental.' In the former, victims are information-providers contributing to a process aimed at achieving societal reconciliation. In the latter, victims are evidence-providers, contributing to the building of a case to prosecute perpetrators.[26] Humphrey suggests that in participating in such processes, 'victimhood becomes quite detached from the reality of the experiences that produced it.'[27]

19 E.g. Marie-Bénédicte Dembour and Emily Haslam, 'Silencing Hearings? Victim-Witnesses at War Crimes Trials,' *European Journal of International Law*, 15:1, (2004), 151–177; Peter Dixon and Chris Tenove, 'International Criminal Justice as a Transnational Field: Rules, Authority and Victims,' *International Journal of Transitional Justice*, 7:3, (2013), 393–412; Drulliole and Brett, n 14; McEvoy and McConnachie, n 8.

20 Rosalind Shaw and Lars Waldorf, 'Introduction: Localizing Transitional Justice,' in Rosalind Shaw and Lars Waldorf (eds) *Localizing Transitional Justice* (California: Stanford University Press, 2010), pp. 3–26.

21 Robins, n 2.

22 Jonathan Doak, 'The Therapeutic Dimension of Transitional Justice: Emotional Repair and Victim Satisfaction in International Trials and Truth Commissions,' *International Criminal Law Review*, 11:2, (2011), 263–298.

23 McEvoy and McConnachie, n 10 at 528. See McEvoy and McConnachie, n 8.

24 Mijke de Waardt, 'Are Peruvian Victims Being Mocked? Politicization of Victimhood and Victims' Motivations for Reparations,' *Human Rights Quarterly*, 35:4, (2013), 830–849.

25 Dixon and Tenove, n 19. See also Emily Haslam, 'Subjects and Objects: International Criminal Law and the Institutionalization of Civil Society,' *International Journal Transitional Justice*, 5:2, (2011), 221–240 and Rachel Killean, *Victims, Atrocity and International Criminal Justice: Lessons from Cambodia* (London: Routledge, 2018).

26 Doak, n 22 at 264.

27 Michael Humphrey, 'From Victim to Victimhood: Truth Commissions and Trials as Rituals of Political Transition and Individual Healing,' *The Australian Journal of Anthropology*, 14:2, (2003), 171–187, (p. 173).

In Northern Ireland, the 'rhetorical and political force' of the victim 'issue' has resulted in accusations of the instrumentalisation of victimhood,[28] which 'remains highly politicised … with victims having been historically squeezed "like a grape in a vice" between the competing narratives of nationalist and unionist politicians seeking to blame the Other for the violence of the past.'[29]

With regards the 'disappeared,' the need for communication with those responsible for perpetrating these acts, and the subsequent requirement for a limited immunity to facilitate the recovery of remains, made the victims' families' campaign ripe for exploitation by politicians (see Chapter 5). As will be examined later in this book (Chapters 3 and 6), where Republicans would seek to emphasise the efforts of 'their side' in the search process, their opponents are equally ready to use the issue as a 'weapon' in their efforts to politically damage Sinn Féin.

As introduced earlier, campaigns to establish information about, or recover remains of, the 'disappeared' can be prime examples of grassroots initiatives in transitional contexts, as it is often the families of victims who drive forward recovery efforts by putting pressure on the state to act. Defined by Lederach, the grassroots level consists of those individuals from local communities with direct experience of the reality of suffering. Via 'bottom-up' efforts, the grassroots exert pressure on those higher up in order to effect change.[30] Advocates of bottom-up approaches argue that they have value in promoting agency in those affected by conflict and by reflecting the diversity of conflict experience.[31] Drawing on this body of work, McEvoy and McConnachie suggest that 'a common theme that runs through this work is that there is a real potential for forms of mobilisation amongst victims … that … challeng[e] the assumption that only '"state-like" legal institutions can "do" transitional justice.'[32]

Families of the 'disappeared' can successfully exercise their agency in speaking out about the fate of their loved ones. They can break the silence that follows a 'disappearance,' mobilise support for their cause, research and promote recovery and identification measures, and ensure the memory of the 'disappeared' remains part of the public consciousness.[33] Despite the apparent gulf between the rhetoric and reality of 'victim-centeredness,' campaigns by families of the 'disappeared' offer examples of those at the grassroots level providing the impetus for state action. Grassroots initiatives have value in 'sending an important message' that those on the ground can 'confront past abuses and suffering.'[34] Both internationally and in

28 Ruth Jamieson, 'Framing Blame and Punishment: Former Politically-Motivated Prisoners in Post-Conflict Northern Ireland,' *Criminal Justice Matters*, 89:1, (2012), 30–31, (p. 30).

29 Nevin T. Aiken, 'Learning to Live Together: Transitional Justice and Intergroup Reconciliation in Northern Ireland,' *International Journal of Transitional Justice*, 4:2, (2010), 166–188 (p. 176).

30 John Paul Lederach, *Building Peace: Sustainable Reconciliation in Divided Societies* (Washington: United States Institute of Peace Press, 1997).

31 Arriaza and Roht-Arriaza, n 15.

32 McEvoy and McConnachie, n 8 at 11.

33 E.g. Kovras, n 1; Jaquemet n 1; Renshaw, n 1; Adam Rosenblatt, *Digging for the Disappeared: Forensic Science After Atrocity* (Stanford: Stanford University Press, 2015).

34 Dudai and Cohen, n 15 at 251.

Northern Ireland, families of the disappeared have done just that. As this book explores, factors external to the families' campaign have impacted upon the campaign's relative success, however the efforts by families have been crucial. In a context where political stalemate has repeatedly stalled progress in responding to the legacy of the conflict, the actions of the families of the 'disappeared' exemplify one way in which victims can 'do' transitional justice.

3. From silence to voice: collective identity, innocence, and constructing victimhood

As explored in Chapter 1, silence permeates multiple stages of a 'disappearance,' from the act itself through to efforts to seek the truth and locate remains. In Northern Ireland, similar silences have been encountered. The silence on the part of the Republican Movement will be examined in Chapter 3, and in Chapter 4 the silences that existed at various levels within the community will be explored. This section will introduce the silence as experienced by the families, and examine how they captured their voice.

During the conflict in Northern Ireland, it has been said that many people would, as a rule, 'keep their heads down,' out of fear.[35] The place of silence as an 'ally of fear'[36] emerges through the families' accounts, as they describe a context where fear of non-state armed groups proved a barrier to both the enquiries families made directly to those groups, and arguably also to the emergence of the truth from others (see Chapter 4). A further potential element of this silencing, as examined later in this chapter, and also later in this book, may have resulted from the stigma connected to the 'disappeared' being labelled as informers. Fear features both subtly, and more explicitly, in a number of the accounts of families. Brian McKinney's father, Billy, suggested that "All roads point to the IRA,"[37], yet, Brian's mother Margaret's enquiries were met with 'a wall of silence.'[38] Charlie Armstrong's daughter, Anna McShane, has described how "a blanket of silence came down in an area where everybody knows everything."[39] Speaking out against the IRA was, Margaret McKinney has said, "taboo."[40]

In some cases, fear is more explicit. One family was warned not to ask 'too many questions'; another was threatened against going public with their story.[41]

35 Susan McKay, *Bear in Mind These Dead* (London: Faber and Faber, 2008), p. 4.
36 Gabriel Ruiz Romero, 'Voices Around Us: Memory and Community Empowerment in Reconstruction Efforts in Colombia,' *International Journal of Transitional Justice*, 6:3, (2012), 1–11.
37 Suzanne Breen, 'Missing Presumed Dead,' *The Irish Times*, 13 August 1994.
38 WAVE, *The Disappeared of Northern Ireland's 'Troubles'* (Belfast: WAVE Trauma Centre Publications, 2012), p. 53.
39 Toby Harnden, *'Bandit Country': The IRA and South Armagh* (London: Hodder and Stoughton, 1999), p. 209.
40 WAVE, n 38 at 53.
41 WAVE, n 38: see accounts relating to Brian McKinney and Seamus Ruddy.

Peter Wilson's sister has described how their mother was afraid to speak about what had happened, for fear something would happen to the family.[42] One of the first to speak out publicly about the fate of the 'disappeared' was Helen McKendry, daughter of Jean McConville. Of this experience – a 1994 BBC Radio *Talkback* interview – she has said "I was very frightened … People had known there were people who had disappeared, but they were too afraid to speak."[43]

Telling stories is one way of resisting silencing by a dominant discourse,[44] and the Republican Movement's discourse – or lack thereof – had until that time been dominant. In telling their stories, the families began the process of resisting this silencing. As will be examined, speaking out was only the beginning of a process, the outcome of which was uncertain.

In the mid-1990s, families began to become aware that there existed others who had shared similar experiences of 'disappearance.' In some accounts, the efforts of Seamus McKendry, son-in-law of Jean McConville, in bringing families together, are highlighted.[45] Others point to the work of WAVE, a cross-community organisation supporting those injured, traumatised, or bereaved during the conflict in Northern Ireland.[46] The development of bonds between the families supports Simic and Daly's assertion that when those with shared experiences are brought together, social bonds can form.[47] One interviewee spoke of the "collaborative network of support" that formed between the families.[48] For example, Eileen McClory described how 'hearing about other families made us feel not so alone.'[49] In interview, the brother of one of the 'disappeared' highlighted the particular bond of the mothers:

> I think … from my Mum's point of view … at times where if they were sitting having a meeting and all the mothers … were able to obviously understand how each one of them felt. This is my brother that went missing but still for

42 WAVE, n 38.

43 'David Never got Over the Passing of his Beloved Wife,' *Belfast Telegraph*, 2 July 2011.

44 Kathleen Ireton and Iosif Kovras, 'Non-Apologies and Prolonged Silences in Post-Conflict Settings: The Case of Post-Colonial Cyprus,' *Time and Society*, 21:1, (2012), 71–88; Jelena Obradovic-Wodnik, 'The "Silent Dilemma" of Transitional Justice: Silencing and Coming to Terms with the Past in Serbia,' *The International Journal of Transitional Justice*, 7:2, (2013), 328–347.

45 Seamus McKendry, *Disappeared: The Search for Jean McConville* (Dublin: Blackwater Press, 2000); WAVE, n 38.

46 E.g. Margaret McKinney in WAVE, ibid. Interviews with Monica McWilliams, a senior academic who has been involved with WAVE and the families' campaign, September 2014; Eugene McVeigh, brother of Columba McVeigh, August 2015. See also www.wavetraumacentre.org.uk/about-us [accessed 7 June 2018].

47 Olivera Simic and Kathleen Daly, '"One Pair of Shoes, One Life": Steps Towards Accountability for Genocide in Srebenica,' *International Journal of Transitional Justice*, 5:3, (2011), 477–491.

48 Interview, Monica McWilliams.

49 WAVE, n 38 at 61.

> her it was her son and I think it was the same for all the mothers; it's a more powerful loss for them.[50]

In addition to their shared experience, the families acted together to progress their campaign. Collective action can produce new identities,[51] and the joint action on the part of families helped create a new collective identity. Polletta and Jasper define collective identity as 'an individual's cognitive, moral and emotional connection with a broader community, category, practice or institution,' and this can include 'the perception of shared status.'[52] The families' 'shared status' came from having loved ones who had shared the same fate. Through their campaign, the families restored identity to their loved ones through sharing their stories, and produced a new identity for themselves as advocates for change, representing an unresolved issue from the conflict. This identity was formalised through the formation and official launch of Families of the Disappeared in June 1995.[53]

Another facet to the families coming together as a group was that their collective status enabled them to find and amplify their voice. It is argued that 'demanding recognition for a new or changed identity can both secure concessions and permanently change the terrain of political conflict.'[54] The recognition of the Families of the Disappeared was in turn recognition of the 'disappeared' and through their mobilisation, the families created a platform for themselves in the 'political conflict' of the mid-1990s.

Polletta and Jasper propose that those sharing a collective identity may represent themselves to certain audiences as more homogenous than they really are,[55] and that appears to be the case with the families of the 'disappeared.' Although the families have been affected by the same form of violent act, and (at least at that time) have a shared goal, their collectivity arguably obscures a heterogeneity in terms of the characteristics of the 'disappeared' themselves.

As introduced earlier, in transitional contexts across the world, victims' rights and needs have been contested. Northern Ireland is no exception.[56] Although the

50 Interview, Kieran Megraw, October 2015.
51 Donnatella Della Porta and Mario Diani, *Social Movements: An Introduction* (Oxford: Blackwell, 2006).
52 Francesca Polletta and James M. Jasper, 'Collective Identity and Social Movements,' *Annual Review of Sociology*, 27, (2001), 283–305 (p. 285).
53 Tanya Acheson, 'Ribbon to Remember Missing,' *Belfast Telegraph*, 21 June 1995; Martin Hill, 'Clinton and Mandela get Grief Symbol,' *Belfast Telegraph*, 26 June 1995; *Press Association News*, 26 June 1995.
54 Polletta and Jasper, n 52 at 297.
55 Ibid.
56 Brewer and Hayes, n 15; Pablo de Greiff, *Report of the Special Rapporteur on the Promotion of Truth, Justice, Reparation and Guarantees of Non-Recurrence, on his Mission to the United Kingdom of Great Britain and Northern Ireland*, A/HRC/34/62/Add.1 (17 November 2016), https://digitallibrary.un.org/record/861416/files/A_HRC_34_62_Add-1-EN.pdf [accessed 7 August 2018]; McEvoy and McConnachie, n 10; Cheryl Lawther, 'The Construction and Politicisation of Victimhood,' in Orla Lynch and Javier Argomaniz (eds) *Victims of Terrorism: A Comparative and Interdisciplinary Study* (Abingdon: Routledge, 2016), pp. 10–30.

Good Friday Agreement (GFA) made provision for acknowledging and addressing 'the suffering of the victims of violence,' how to do this has been a source of controversy.[57] It is suggested that 'almost every aspect of victimhood is contested and challenged.'[58] One of the central areas of contention is the definition of who constitutes a 'legitimate' victim, and specifically, the attempted differentiation between 'innocents' and those who perpetrated violence.[59] In Northern Ireland, as in other post-conflict contexts,[60] such differentiation between victims has contributed to the development of a 'hierarchy' of victimhood, based on perceived levels of innocence and the extent to which the 'victim' label is considered to be applicable.[61]

The 'disappeared' cannot be placed neatly in any such hierarchy. Ní Aoláin and Turner contend that certain victims are often 'privileged' within a hierarchy and 'left out … are those whose victimhood may be more complex or compromised.'[62] The 'disappeared,' – as will be examined – exemplify 'complex' victimhood and yet as a group have received significant attention in the context of Northern Ireland. They have emerged as a distinct category of victim, with Sir Kenneth Bloomfield, in his report as Victims Commissioner, remarking that their families are in a 'special predicament.'[63]

Bouris describes how images of victims play a powerful role in motivating a response to violations and in attracting international attention.[64] Yet, as noted earlier, the image of the victim is often intertwined with the concept of innocence.[65] As Christie contends, those who are considered vulnerable and innocent, victimised by a 'bad' offender who is unknown to them, are 'most readily … given

57 Brewer and Hayes, n 15.
58 Neil Ferguson, Mark Burgess and Ian Hollywood, 'Who are the Victims? Victimhood Experiences in Postagreement Northern Ireland,' *Political Psychology*, 31:6, (2010), 857–886, (p. 858).
59 Brewer and Hayes, n 15; Kevin Hearty, '"Victims of" Human Rights Abuses in Transitional Justice: Hierarchies, Perpetrators and the Struggle for Peace,' *The International Journal of Human Rights*, 22:7, (2018), 888–909.
60 Fionnuala Ní Aoláin and Catherine Turner, 'Gender, Truth and Transition,' *UCLA Women's Law Journal*, 16, (2007), 229–279; McEvoy and McConnachie, n 10; Mijke de Waardt. 'The Politics of Victimhood at the Grassroots Level: Inclusion and Exclusion Among Peruvian Victim Organisations,' in Vincent Druliolle and Roddy Brett (eds) *The Politics of Victimhood in Post-conflict Societies* (Cham, Switzerland: Palgrave Macmillan, 2018), pp. 133–158.
61 Christine Bell, 'Dealing with the Past in Northern Ireland,' *Fordham International Law Journal*, 26, (2002), 1095–1147; John Brewer and Bernadette Hayes, 'Victims as Moral Beacons: Victims and Perpetrators in Northern Ireland,' *Contemporary Social Science*, 6:1, (2011), 73–88; Ferguson et al., n 58; Hearty, n 59; Lawther, n 56; Smyth (2018), n 12.
62 Ní Aoláin and Turner, n 60 at 265.
63 Sir Kenneth Bloomfield, '*We Will Remember Them': Report of the Northern Ireland Victims Commissioner* (Belfast: HMSO, 1998), p. 38.
64 Erica Bouris, *Complex Political Victims* (Connecticut: Kumarian, 2007).
65 Bouris, ibid.; Sharon Lamb, *The Trouble with Blame: Victims, Perpetrators and Responsibility* (London: Harvard University Press, 1996); McEvoy and McConnachie, n 10.

the complete and legitimate status of being a victim.' They are the 'ideal victims.'[66] Critical scholars question the reliability of conventional dichotomies of victim versus perpetrator, good versus evil, innocent versus guilty, mooting the possibility that such separations are not readily applicable in all contexts, particularly those of ethnic or civil conflict. In these circumstances, the categories of 'victim' and 'perpetrator' can be blurred, subjective, and both applicable to the same individual.[67]

The focus on 'innocent victims' can produce a somewhat blinkered view of the past, as can an emphasis on the 'guilty perpetrator.'[68] Simplistic imagery and limited understanding of who constitutes a 'victim' can impact upon long-term stability, as the images of the victim shape the response policies that are put in place.[69] Furthermore, assigning guilt to particular individuals or groups creates a false sense that good is pervasive in everyone else.[70] To attempt to allow for analysis of this complexity, Bouris calls for 'a discourse of the gray victim,'[71] drawing on the work of Arendt to argue that a true rebuilding of a community is only possible if the complexities of victimisation are considered. Similarly, Borer directs our gaze to the 'shades of gray': 'not all victims are the same, nor are all perpetrators the same, and … some victims are also perpetrators.'[72] While some might argue that 'disappearing' is an issue that is black and white, the often political nature of the act (Chapter 1) means that those who have been 'disappeared' may not sync with the image of a typical innocent victim. A more nuanced understanding of who constitutes a victim is required.

In some contexts, the heinousness of the act of 'disappearing' serves to transcend political, ideological, or cultural divides. Even in deeply divided societies, widespread sympathy can be mobilised for the 'disappeared.'[73] Kovras has detailed the experience of Cyprus, where Greek-Cypriots and Turkish-Cypriots have 'worked together to solve' the 'sensitive issue' of how to begin recovering the 'disappeared.'[74] In Chile, Schirmer describes, ideological differences between

66 Nils Christie, 'The Ideal Victim' in Ezzata A. Fattah (ed.) *From Crime Policy to Victim Policy* (London, Macmillan, 1986), pp. 17–30.

67 Bouris, n 64.; Druliolle, n 10; Karstedt, n 16; Lamb, n 65.; McEvoy and McConnachie, n 10; Nneoma v. Nowgu, 'When and Why It Started: Deconstructing Victim-Centered Truth Commission in the Context of Ethnicity-Based Conflict,' *International Journal of Transitional Justice*, 4:2, (2010), 275–289.

68 Bouris, n 64.

69 Bouris, n 64. See also Jemima García-Godos, 'Victims and Victimhood in Reparation Programs: Lessons from Latin America,' in Vincent Druliolle and Roddy Brett (eds) *The Politics of Victimhood in Post-conflict Societies* (Cham, Switzerland: Palgrave Macmillan, 2018), pp. 25–52.

70 Jamieson, n 28.

71 Bouris, n 64 at 7.

72 Tristan Anne Borer, 'A Taxonomy of Victims and Perpetrators: Human Rights and Reconciliation in South Africa,' *Human Rights Quarterly*, 25:4, (2003), 1088–1116, (p. 1116; p. 1115).

73 Iosif Kovras and Neophytos Loizides, 'Delaying Truth Recovery for Missing Persons,' *Nations and Nationalism*, 17:3, (2011), 520–539.

74 Kovras, n 1 at 174.

members of *Agrupación* (The Group of Relatives of the Detained-Disappeared) did not create division: 'the traumatic experience of having a disappeared relative over-powered any class or political distinctions.'[75] Yet, political, social, or cultural factors can impact upon cohesion between families or the support families of the 'disappeared' receive. In Lebanon, for example, the groups of relatives are fragmented, with different groups established in response to disappearances by particular perpetrator organisations.[76] One leading member of a relatives' organisation remarked that "one murderer at this group can be the hero of another group."[77] In that context, sectarian division and fear of renewing conflict is argued to have fed into a lack of support for relatives of the 'disappeared.'[78] In Nicaragua, mothers of the 'disappeared' received little support from political leaders, the Catholic church, or indeed the wider public, as a result of continuing political instability, the political alignment of human rights groups along pro- and anti-Sandinista lines, and the open alignment of many senior Church figures with the political right.[79] A better known example is the nicknaming of the *Madres* of the Plaza de Mayo as *Las Locas*, because they 'no longer embodied the state's vision of a reconciled nation.'[80] Brendan Megraw's brother Kieran, recounted a similar experience: 'I remember attending a meeting along with other members of Families of the Disappeared with a Minister in the Republic of Ireland. He said that the families need to move on and embrace the peace process.'[81]

Being a victim of a 'disappearance' does not immediately qualify one for sympathy or support. In a civil conflict, such as that in Northern Ireland, communities often see themselves as the victim and the 'other' primarily as perpetrator.[82] Arguably, given the contested victimhood terrain of Northern Ireland,[83] that the families' campaign has garnered such widespread support is perhaps not as inevitable as it may first seem.

3.1. Innocence and the 'greying' of victimhood

While seeking not to undermine the impact of 'disappearing,' create a 'hierarchy of victims,' or in any way justify the actions of those who perpetrate these acts,

75 Jennifer G. Schirmer, '"Those Who Die for Life Cannot be Called Dead": Women and Human Rights Protest in Latin America,' *Feminist Review*, 32, (1989), 3–29 (p. 17).
76 'Disappearances' were perpetrated by the Lebanese and Israeli armies, as well as Christian and Muslim militias, and later by Hezbollah and Lebanese security forces under the control of the Syrian regime (Kovras, n 1).
77 Kovras, n 1 at 137.
78 Jaquemet, n 1.
79 Sheila R. Tully, 'A Painful Purgatory: Grief and the Nicaraguan Mothers of the Disappeared,' *Social Science and Medicine*, 40:12, (1995), 1597–1610.
80 Brandon Hamber and Richard A. Wilson, 'Symbolic Closure Through Memory, Reparation and Revenge in Post-Conflict Societies,' *Journal of Human Rights*, 1:1, (2002), 35–53.
81 WAVE, n 38 at 50.
82 Roman David, 'International Criminal Tribunals and the Perception of Justice: The Effect of the ICTY in Croatia,' *International Journal of Transitional Justice*, 8:3, (2014), 476–495.
83 See e.g. Brewer and Hayes, n 15; de Greiff, n 56; Lawther, n 56; McEvoy and McConnachie, n 10.

looking more closely at Northern Ireland's 'disappeared' provides some insight into the multiplicity of identities during conflict. It also speaks to the fluid nature of labels such as 'perpetrator' and 'victim' – temporary states which individuals can shift into at different times depending on a range of circumstances.[84] A consideration of the 'disappeared' in light of the 'constants' of victim identity as suggested by Bouris[85] – innocence, purity, moral superiority, a lack of responsibility, and the absence of guilt – suggests that many do not neatly fit with such characteristics.

As will be explored in Chapter 3, the majority of the 'disappeared' were, according to IRA statements, 'guilty' of either informing, stealing IRA weapons, or some other internal disciplinary violation. Some were also said to be IRA members.[86] Several accounts beyond the IRA statements support these assertions of IRA membership.[87] Such claims are supported by some families,[88] but not others.[89] Several of the 'disappeared' were alleged to have been involved in petty crime.[90] The families of Brian McKinney and John McClory have spoken of their connection to a robbery at the Clubhouse Bar on the Glen Road in Belfast, which was run at that time by the IRA.[91] The IRA has claimed that Danny McIlhone was a 'civilian' who was 'involved in armed robberies in Belfast and Dublin.'[92] The brother of Seamus Ruddy, reportedly 'disappeared' as a result of links to weapons-running and an INLA (Irish National Liberation Army) feud,[93] has said "you see Seamus was no angel, he was involved with people at the time during the Troubles … [he] had been involved in acquiring arms."[94]

The majority of the 'disappeared'[95] have been accused by the IRA of involvement in informing. The sister of Kevin McKee has said that she believed he might

84 McEvoy and McConnachie, n 10; Nowgu, n 67.
85 Bouris, n 64.
86 'IRA Investigation Locates Grave Sites,' *An Phoblacht*, 1 April 1999; 'Investigation Confirms 1972 Disappearance,' *An Phoblacht*, 11 February 2010.
87 E.g. Harnden, n 39; Martin Dillon, *The Dirty War* (London: Arrow Books, 1991); Ed Moloney, *A Secret History of the IRA* (London: Penguin Books, 2007); Ed Moloney, *Voices from the Grave: Two Men's War in Ireland* (London: Faber and Faber, 2011).
88 See account by Kevin McKee's sister in WAVE, n 38 and statement by Briege Wright, 'My Brother, Seamus Wright,' *An Phoblacht*, 15 November 2013.
89 WAVE, n 38: see accounts from relatives of Eugene Simons, Gerry Evans, and Eamonn Molloy.
90 'IRA Investigation Locates Grave Sites,' n 86.
91 Jilly Beattie and Martin Breen, 'Missing Bodies of IRA Victims Buried Under Family Homes,' *The People*, 29 June 1997; Una Bradley, '"Disappeared" Man's Mother "Shattered by End of Search",' *Belfast Telegraph*, 23 December 1998; Nick Thorpe, 'Mother's Hope She Can Lay Her Son to Rest,' *The Scotsman*, 27 June 1998; Accounts by Margaret McKinney and Eileen McClory in WAVE, n 38; *The Forgiveness Project*, 'Margaret McKinney,' http://theforgivenessproject.com/stories/margaret-mckinney-northern-ireland/ [accessed 7 June 2018].
92 'IRA Statement,' *An Phoblacht*, 15 August 2002.
93 Dillon, n 87. See also Ian Geldard and Keith Craig, *IRA, INLA: Foreign Support and International Connections* (London: Institute for the Study of Terrorism, 1988). The INLA was a smaller Republican armed group.
94 Donal McMahon, 'Family Emotions Run High,' *Newry Reporter*, 10 May 2017.
95 'IRA Investigation Locates Grave Sites,' n 86.

have been recruited by Special Branch.[96] Columba McVeigh's brother Eugene does not believe he was in the IRA but thinks:

> my brother was probably recruited by British Military Intelligence … why he was recruited I don't know, because he wasn't in any way valuable to them. He wasn't in the Organisation but they must have believed that he was ….[97]

Brendan Megraw's family suggested that he may have been taken because he spoke to police following a shooting[98] and Peter Wilson is said to have talked to the British soldiers on patrol in his local area,[99] and to be considering joining the British Army.[100] Although neither were known to be involved with the IRA or in non-political crime, given that 'whatever you say, say nothing' is a common refrain in Republican propaganda, some may have considered these actions worthy of punishment. Another of Columba McVeigh's brothers, Oliver, has said: "My theory on all of the disappeared is: he knew something and he had to be shut up" – that these individuals were killed "to protect informers at a higher level."[101] Several families, such as those of Jean McConville and Eamonn Molloy, have said that they do not believe that their loved ones are guilty of the charges alleged by the IRA.[102]

The case of Jean McConville demonstrates how subjective perceptions of 'innocence' and 'guilt' can be. Arguably the most well-known of the 'disappeared' victims, McConville in many ways fits the image of a typical 'innocent' victim:[103] female, a mother, vulnerable (both practically, through being a widow, and psychologically – her children have spoken of how she suffered from depression), and already marginalised as a result of her mixed marriage.[104] Her family has repeatedly insisted that she was innocent of the informer allegations made against her[105] and in 2006 the Police Ombudsman of Northern Ireland, Nuala O'Loan, found

96 WAVE, n 38.
97 Interview, Eugene McVeigh, August 2015.
98 David McKittrick, Seamus Kelters, Brian Feeney, Chris Thornton and David McVea, *Lost Lives: The Stories of the Men, Women and Children who Died as a Result of the Northern Ireland Troubles* (Edinburgh; London: Mainstream Publishing, 2007).
99 Allison Morris, 'The Disappeared: Peter Wilson,' *The Irish News*, 31 October 2009.
100 Walter Ellis, 'Army Used Retarded Man – Claim,' *The Irish Times*, 19 September 1973; 'Retarded Man Still Missing,' *The Irish Times*, 29 September 1973; WAVE, n 38.
101 Keith Duggan, 'Columba McVeigh: A Lost Life Brought into Sharper Focus,' *The Irish Times*, 19 May 2018.
102 WAVE, n 38.
103 Bouris, n 64. See also Christie, n 66.
104 Jim Cusack, 'McConville Found Herself Isolated as Falls Rejected British Army Role,' *The Irish Times*, 31 May 1999; Susan McKay, 'Northern Ireland's Peace is Haunted by Ghosts Who Will Not be Silenced,' *The Guardian*, 4 May 2014; McKendry, n 45.
105 See e.g. Elizabeth Day, 'Jean McConville's Daughter: "If I Give Up Fighting, They've Won",' *The Observer*, 6 July 2014; Marie Foy, 'Provo Victim Jean's Family Hit Back,' *Belfast Telegraph*, 27 January 2005; Dan Keenan and Liam Reid, 'IRA Derided Over its Defence of McConville Murder,' *The Irish Times*, 10 July 2006;

no evidence to support the IRA's claims that she was an informer.[106] The IRA responded with a statement reiterating McConville's guilt,[107] and some in the Republican Movement, even if they do not agree with the extent of her punishment, maintain that she was involved in informing activity (see Chapter 3). If such allegations were to be true, from a Republican perspective, McConville would not be without guilt.

According to the information currently available from media archives and as suggested by interviewees, with the exception of Charlie Armstrong,[108] there is evidence that arguably 'greys' the victimhood of many of the 'disappeared' – depending on one's perspective of course. Those who were involved in criminal activity and those who were actively involved in the IRA do not fit easily with the notion of the 'innocent' victim. Those who were involved in informing would have been seen as deserving of some form of punishment by most Republicans (see Chapter 3). This group of victims reflects the practical difficulty, especially in the messy reality of conflict, of the perpetrator/victim, innocent/guilty dichotomies, and shows how subjective 'innocence' can be as a concept.[109]

It has been argued that transitional justice mechanisms may struggle when dealing with victims who are not completely without blame.[110] However, as will be explored in the next section, the families of the 'disappeared' have succeeded in framing the 'disappeared' in such a way as to mobilise widespread support for their cause.

4. Victims' families, political opportunity, and framing the 'disappeared'

Monica McWilliams said of the families: "I just pay credit to them as a social movement – a very small social movement – but they are a social movement."[111] Defined as 'individuals sharing resources in pursuit of collective goals,'[112] the families behave – as McWilliams suggested – like a small social movement. Indeed, Della Porta and Diani point out that much of the analysis directed at social

'McConville Son Says Family Endured 31 Years of "Hell",' *The Irish Times*, 5 April 2004; McKendry, n 45.

106 Office of the Police Ombudsman for Northern Ireland, *Report into the Complaint by James and Michael McConville Regarding the Police Investigation Into the Abduction and Murder of Their Mother Mrs Jean McConville* (Belfast: Office of the Police Ombudsman for Northern Ireland, 2006).

107 'IRA Carried Out "Thorough Investigation" Into McConville Death,' *An Phoblacht*, 13 July 2006.

108 Charlie Armstrong was 'disappeared' on his way to collect a neighbour to take her to mass. No organisation has made any allegations against him and his family have been given information by an un-named source that his killing may have been a mistake (see e.g. 'Families get Closure with Verdicts of Unlawful Killing on Disappeared,' *Belfast Telegraph*, 22 September 2011; WAVE, n 38).

109 Bouris, n 64; Druliolle, n 10; Karstedt, n 16; Lamb, n 65; McEvoy and McConnachie, n 10.

110 McEvoy and McConnachie, n 8.

111 Interview, Monica McWilliams, September 2014.

112 Della Porta and Diani n 51 at 19.

movements can equally be applied to political and cultural collective action more generally.[113] This section will draw on the literature on social movements and framing to consider how the families mobilised support, in particular through analysing the political opportunities available to them, and the framing of their cause.[114]

4.1. Political opportunity and the timing of the families' response

The first hurdle for families of those who have been disappeared is to make sure their predicament is *known*.[115] In states where the past is not being dealt with, families of the 'disappeared' can be marginalised,[116] and as examined earlier, the period following the 'disappearances' is for many relatives characterised by silence. Yet, as is evident from media reports in Northern Ireland and elsewhere from the mid-1990s onwards, the "families were becoming louder."[117] The following paragraphs will examine how the families transformed their discontent into the mobilisation that shifted their experiences from the private to the public domain.[118]

The backdrop to the passing of the Location of Victims' Remains legislation should be given some attention, as the extent to which law matters is often dependent on the context in which change is sought.[119] The political opportunity model outlined in the social movement literature – specifically Tarrow's five dimensions of political opportunity – can be used to structure this consideration of context.[120]

113 Della Porta and Diani, ibid.

114 Robert D. Benford and David A. Snow, 'Framing Processes and Social Movements: An Overview and Assessment,' *Annual Review of Sociology*, 26, (2000), 611–639; Della Porta and Diani, n 51; Sidney Tarrow, *Power in Movement: Social Movements and Contentious Politics* (Cambridge: Cambridge University Press, 1998).

115 Robins, n 2.

116 Jaquemet, n 1.

117 Interview, Brian Rowan, journalist, commentator, and former BBC security correspondent, September 2014.

118 Della Porta and Diani, n 51.

119 Sandra R. Levitsky, 'Law and Social Movements: Old Debates and New Directions,' in Austin Sarat and Patricia Ewick (eds) *The Handbook of Law and Society* (Wiley Online: 2015), pp. 382–398; Holly J. McCammon and Allison R. McGrath, 'Litigating Change? Social Movements and the Court System,' *Sociology Compass*, 9:2, (2015), 128–139; Michael McCann, 'Law and Social Movements: Contemporary Perspectives,' *Annual Review of Law and Social Science*, 2, (2005), 17–38; Douglas NeJaime, 'Constitutional Change, Courts, and Social Movements,' *Michigan Law Review*, 111:6, (2013), 877–902.

120 NeJaime, ibid.; Tarrow, n 114. It should be noted that a number of criticisms have been directed at the political opportunity model. These include, for example, that the model places too much emphasis on the agency on external actors, and not enough on the movements themselves; that Tarrow is not clear enough as to which dimensions have most impact on a movement's chances of success; and that the model does not adequately capture the complexities of how social movements operate (see e.g. Jack A. Goldstone, 'More Social Movements or Fewer? Beyond Political Opportunity Structures to Relational Fields,' *Theory and Society*, 33:3–4, (2004), 333–365; Aldon Morris, 'Reflections on Social Movement Theory: Criticisms and Proposals,' *Contemporary Sociology*, 29:3, (2000), 445–454). However,

Although Tarrow's examples draw on state-level democratic crises and larger scale social movements, his five factors can be witnessed in the context being considered here.

The first of Tarrow's 'dimensions of opportunity' is an increase in access to allow new actors to participate.[121] Arguably, following the announcement of the ceasefires[122] and the gradual move towards all-party talks, the shift in the conversation from how to control the conflict towards how to build peace provided the families with an opportunity to participate in the debate. The families, supported by WAVE, were involved in "different kinds of lobbying and advocacy going on at different levels."[123] In 1995 alone this included meetings with then Prime Minister John Major,[124] shadow Northern Ireland spokeswoman Mo Mowlam,[125] and Security Minister Sir John Wheeler.[126] In October 1995, families attended the Labour party conference in Brighton to lobby further support.[127] This was at the invitation of Labour MP Harry Barnes, who tabled a motion in the House of Commons calling on the Republican Movement to respond to the families' pleas.[128]

Second, the shifting of political alignments can create an atmosphere of uncertainty in which others may choose to act.[129] The shift in the Republican Movement away from violence and towards a focus on purely political means provided an opportunity for families to criticise Sinn Féin, and Adams in particular, in a way that might not previously have been possible. A flyer related to the Families' campaign reads: 'In the light of recent developments towards a lasting peace, we, the families of the disappeared believe that pressure must be put on the Republican Movement to inform us of the whereabouts of our loved ones.'[130] This was

this model is used here as the context of the families' campaign was highlighted by a number of interviewees as relevant. Furthermore, the agency of the families is addressed throughout this chapter in terms of both their availing of the opportunities available to them, and the framing of their cause.

121 Tarrow, n 114.

122 On 31 August 1994 the IRA announced a 'complete' cessation of violence. Republicans grew increasingly dissatisfied with the lack of political progress being made and this ceasefire was ended on 9 February 1996 with the IRA's bombing of London's Canary Wharf, which killed two people, injured more than 100, and caused some £85 million worth of damage. The IRA released a statement resuming its ceasefire on 19 July 1997 (Deaglán de Bréadún, *The Far Side of Revenge: Making Peace in Northern Ireland* (Cork: The Collins Press, 2008)).

123 Interview, Monica McWilliams, September 2014.

124 Oliver McGuckin, 'Pledge on "Disappeared",' *Belfast Telegraph*, 3 May 1995.

125 Tanya Acheson, 'End Families' Torment,' *Belfast Telegraph*, 9 August 1995.

126 Marie Foy, 'Wheeler Pledge Over "Disappeared",' *Belfast Telegraph*, 8 September 1995.

127 Tanya Acheson, 'Grieving Families Lobby MPs,' *Belfast Telegraph*, 2 October 1995.

128 McGuckin, n 124.

129 Tarrow, n 114.

130 'Disappeared,' undated flyer linked to campaign located in Linenhall Library's collection of ephemera on victim support organisations.

an opportunity that could be exploited by the media also, as historian Richard English suggested:

> This gained momentum partly because of some of the families, partly because of some journalists, partly … because of some anti-Adams momentum … whatever the motivation about that, it had the benign effect of allowing people who otherwise would have been buried again in terms of their own voice, to become vocal.[131]

The third dimension exists when there are political divisions among the elite.[132] The inevitable political contests between the 'elites' of Sinn Féin and Unionism allowed the families to monopolise the strategic nature of Adams' position as a lynchpin between the IRA's violent past and Sinn Féin's political present. One of the earliest reports on the 'disappeared,' in the *Belfast Telegraph* in April 1995, is explicit about this connection in the headline: 'Give Us Back Our Dead, Mr Adams.'[133] At a time characterised by deal-making and compromises, this linkage was a powerful move by families to not only situate their predicament among the issues to be 'dealt with' as part of the peace negotiations, but also to connect their campaign to one of the key figures of those negotiations. In 1996 Margaret McKinney told the *News Letter* that she believed that 'those high up in the Republican movement should be able to exert pressure further down to get information.'[134]

Fourth, the presence of influential allies can give added support to challengers.[135] In 1995, Helen McKendry wrote to President Clinton requesting him "to force Sinn Féin … to atone for their heinous deeds."[136] Two weeks later, Clinton referred to the plight of the families in his speech at the Washington Investment conference, saying: "It is time to allow families to be whole again."[137] The USA's support for the families was significant, and Clinton's comments are said to have been a 'huge boost' for the campaign.[138] In 1998, Margaret McKinney met with Clinton at the White House and she has said that after this meeting, 'things really began to happen … ten months after the White House meeting Gerry Adams came to the house to tell me I was going to get Brian's body.'[139] For Kieran Megraw, Clinton's involvement was:

131 Interview, Richard English, August 2014.
132 Tarrow, n 114.
133 Tanya Acheson, 'Give Us Back Our Dead, Mr Adams,' *Belfast Telegraph*, 28 April 1995.
134 Donna Carton, 'Where are the Bodies?' *News Letter*, 19 April 1996.
135 Tarrow, n 114.
136 Tanya Acheson, 'Family Asks Clinton to Help Find Bodies,' *Belfast Telegraph*, 12 May 1995.
137 Vincent Kearney and Martina Purdy, 'Clinton to Visit in Autumn,' *Belfast Telegraph*, 26 May 1995.
138 McKittrick et al., n 98 at 302.
139 WAVE, n 38 at 54.

> massive … it was a big breakthrough that he was going to be pushing it and then … it was being mentioned in the Good Friday Agreement [and] all the talks that were going on, and I think that was a massive sort of breakthrough for trying to get information as to where everybody was.[140]

One human rights activist interviewed suggested that the significance of this inclusion was two-fold:

> I think it's significant on two levels … first of all that the families are sufficiently well-organised and connected in order to get that mention. The political process by which you get anything inserted into a presidential speech is very complex. You have to go through many layers of bureaucracy … and you have to have political clout … The second element of significance is the political consequences of it. And if you think back to 1995, and this is at a time when the Republican Movement is working hard … part of the moving out of armed struggle strategy was to build relationships and alliances with key players elsewhere: European Union, SDLP, Irish Government and the Americans … It means that the Republican Movement has to respond at the senior level … if it's something that the President has raised. So it very much gets their attention … That then has a ripple effect beyond the Republican Movement with all of the other political actors, if Clinton is saying that it's important.[141]

These efforts by the families resonate with Lutz and Sikkink's notion of the 'boomerang pattern,' in which domestic activists bypass their states and directly search out international allies to bring outside pressure on their states.[142] US support continued, and in 2005 relatives visited Washington DC to meet with New Jersey Congressman Chris Smith. They were told there would be a special Congressional hearing on the 'disappeared' and were offered assistance with the acquisition of specialist search equipment.[143]

Finally, opportunities for a group to further their goals exist when a state's ability or will to repress dissent diminishes.[144] The main source of repression for the families was in this case a non-state armed group. Opportunity for the families came when that group began its shift away from violence. Margaret McKinney has remarked that "It was not until the ceasefire … that I was able to get my story out."[145] As Monica McWilliams described in interview:

140 Interview, Kieran Megraw, October 2015.
141 Interview, human rights activist with experience of 'dealing with the past' in Northern Ireland, October 2015.
142 Ellen Lutz and Kathryn Sikkink, 'The Justice Cascade: The Evolution and Impact of Foreign Human Rights Trials in Latin America,' *Chicago Journal of International Law*, 2:1, (2001), 1–34, (p. 4).
143 Chris Thornton, 'Washington Pressure over Disappeared,' *Belfast Telegraph*, 14 June 2005.
144 Tarrow, n 114.
145 Bradley, n 91.

> Before the ceasefires and before the Agreement and what happened afterwards … victims' families would have told me they'd be very nervous about speaking out publicly … But once there was permission to do so … there was now a space in which to raise it. And so they were able to take on a much more public profile.[146]

This period of 1994–1999 provided both the opportunity for, and backdrop to, the emergence of the families' campaign. The opportunity existed for families to speak to audiences who would not seek to silence them. Much of the threat of violence had been removed, they had international support in the form of the USA, political manoeuvring not only provided a space for their voices, but also reinforced the Unionist/Republican divide in a way that the families could exploit. As will be explored in Chapter 3, the 'disappeared' became one of several issues that Sinn Féin was being pressured to move on as part of the peace process. At a time when the feasibility of power-sharing was being tested between Unionists and Republicans, the dark shadow cast upon Sinn Féin by this issue gave the families leverage, and the power to embarrass the 'Movement' into action. One interviewee said that he thought, "the impact that the families have had has embarrassed the IRA into cooperating with the Commission."[147]

It should be noted that perhaps there were limited alternative strategies available to the families, as reflected on by one human rights activist:

> If you think back to that time … the alternative kind of campaigning style which was to some extent successful, was the style adopted by groups like Families Against Intimidation and Terror (FAIT) … a group focused exclusively on … the human rights abuse which is and was punishment violence. Their strategy was embarrassment, embarrassment, embarrassment … they followed Gerry Adams around everywhere and they would have pictures of people with broken legs and things like that. So it was a very 'in your face,' confrontational strategy, hugely irritating for the Republican Movement I think, but it got their attention … obviously legal struggle is another way … but it's hard to see what they [the families] could have done … You could take a civil action perhaps, against senior Republicans, very hard to make that stick … As an effective strategy, I don't really see how law would have been that useful to them in the end.[148]

Considering why the families chose the strategy that they did brings us back to the complex victimhood of the 'disappeared':

> It's hard to generalise but the fact that they went – rightly in my view … focusing on the humanitarian issues, may in part be that they thought that

146 Interview, Monica McWilliams, September 2014.
147 Interview, Jeffrey Donaldson, DUP MP, March 2015.
148 Interview, human rights activist with experience of 'dealing with the past' in Northern Ireland, October 2015.

strategically that was the best way to influence the Republican Movement … the fact that some of the individual members within the families are Republicans and therefore would not have been comfortable – even though the Republican Movement had 'disappeared' their loved ones – but would still not have been comfortable with the FAIT-like 'in your face' approach. Plus they may have concluded, probably rightly in my view, that it would have been counterproductive.[149]

4.2. Framing: 'simplifying' complex victims

A frame is defined as 'a schema of interpretation.'[150] To frame is to 'assign meaning to and interpret, relevant events and conditions in ways that are intended to mobilize potential adherents and constituents, to garner bystander support, and to demobilize antagonists.'[151] Influenced by Goffman's work on frame analysis,[152] the concept is used to illustrate how particular issues are given meaning in such a way as to garner support.[153]

As Della Porta and Diani explain, 'social problems … only exist to the extent that certain phenomena are interpreted as such by people.'[154] These phenomena are then simplified and condensed via collective action frames.[155] Snow and Benford[156] distinguished three framing tasks: diagnostic – whereby a problem is identified and blame attributed, prognostic – where a proposed solution is articulated, and motivational – in essence a 'call to arms' or 'rationale for action.'

149 Ibid.
150 Della Porta and Diani, n 51 at 74.
151 David A. Snow and Robert D. Benford, 'Ideology, Frame Resonance, and Participant Mobilization,' *International Social Movement Research*, 1, (1988), 197–217 (p. 198).
152 Erving Goffman, *Frame Analysis: An Analysis on the Organization of Experience* (Harmondsworth: Penguin, 1975).
153 It must be noted that 'framing' has been criticised by some scholars. For some, framing lacks a consistent conceptualisation. Others have argued that certain aspects of framing are under-researched – such as how frames are produced, or the process by which they influence what people think (see e.g. Benford and Snow, n 114; Porismita Borah, 'Conceptual Issues in Framing Theory: A Systematic Examination of a Decade's Literature,' *Journal of Communication*, 61:2, (2011), 246–263; Robert M. Entman, 'Framing: Toward Clarification of a Fractured Paradigm,' *Journal of Communication*, 43:4, (1993), 51–58; James K. Hertog and Douglas M. McLeod, 'A Multiperspectival Approach to Framing Analysis: A Field Guide,' in Stephen D. Reese, Oscar H. Gandy and August E. Grant (eds) *Framing Public Life: Perspectives on Media and our Understanding of the Social World* (Mahwah, NJ: Earlbaum, 2001), pp. 139–161; Thomas J. Scheff, 'The Structure of Context: Deciphering *Frame Analysis*,' *Sociological Theory*, 23:4, (2005), 368–385). Detailed analysis of the limitations of 'framing' is beyond the scope of this book. However, as Entman (convincingly, in my view) contends, framing is useful as a concept for 'directing our attention' to the details of how a communication 'exerts its power' (Entman 1993, 55–56), and that is how it is used here.
154 Della Porta and Diani, n 51 at 74.
155 Benford and Snow, n 114.
156 Snow and Benford, n 151; see also Benford and Snow, n 114.

The diagnostic framing of the 'disappeared' issue is summarised in the first *Belfast Telegraph* headline: 'Give Us Back Our Dead, Mr Adams.'[157] The problem is identified: the missing remains of family members, and blame attributed through the call to Adams and inherent link to the Republican Movement. The families' diagnostic framing is clear throughout their campaign: their loved ones have been 'disappeared,' they want their bodies to be returned, and they consider this the responsibility of the Republican Movement.

The prognostic task is equally clear on the part of families. Although specific strategies are not outlined in their early statements to media, the overall solution of provision of either the bodies or information relating to them by the Republican Movement is clarified. As Snow and Benford posit,[158] there is a direct correlation between the diagnostic and prognostic frames. Blame is directed at the Republican Movement, and in the opinion of families, therein lies the solution: they believe the 'Movement' is in possession of the information needed to facilitate the return of their loved ones' bodies.

Although diagnostic and prognostic frames can overlap, motivational frames are somewhat different, in that they must function as 'prods to action.'[159] With regards the 'disappeared,' although the families can articulate their issue in a straightforward and relatively simple way, what they need to demonstrate is why anyone else should be concerned with it – particularly in a post-ceasefire context where thousands have been affected by the conflict and there are many issues to be addressed.

Framing involves elevating the salience of certain pieces of information.[160] Della Porta and Diani argue that 'Collective action becomes possible at the point at which mobilizing messages are integrated with some cultural component from the population to which they are addressed.'[161] This is 'frame alignment,' i.e. how a movement's message resonates with the population it is hoping to mobilise.[162] This is where the strength of the campaign of the families lies: their framing draws on cultural values intrinsic to wider society and effective motivational framing is reliant on the use of frames that are accessible to many.[163] The families made more 'noticeable, meaningful or memorable'[164] the significance of family relationships, the importance of Christian burial, and the humanitarian or non-political nature of their demands. In so doing the families communicated their grief with a relatable simplicity that was difficult to respond to with anything other than support. As summarised by Viscount Brookeborough, the families' request was one that "no reasonable person could deny."[165]

157 Acheson, n 133.
158 Snow and Benford, n 151.
159 Ibid. at 202.
160 Entman, n 153.
161 Della Porta and Diani, n 51 at 82.
162 Della Porta and Diani, ibid.; Snow and Benford, n 151; David A. Snow, E. Burke Rochford, Jr., Steven K. Worden and Robert D. Benford, 'Frame Alignment Processes, Micromobilization, and Movement Participation,' *American Sociological Review*, 51:4, (1986), 464–481.
163 Snow and Benford, n 151.
164 Entman, n 153 at 53.
165 House of Lords Debates (HL Deb) 18 May 1999, vol 601, cc. 153–190.

4.2.1. The significance of family

In Latin America, Tully describes how groups of mothers 'use their traditional roles as mothers and protectors of families to call attention to the unresolved issue of the disappeared.'[166] Similarly, Schirmer argues that the women searching for their sons 'are not protesting as women (i.e., feminists), but as "mothers looking for our children."'[167] Although the focus on the mother is perhaps not as obvious in the families' campaign in Northern Ireland as it once was (due in part to the passing of time and children 'taking over' from their parents in campaigning), the importance of family relationships is a key theme in accounts of the 'disappeared.' Such a focus speaks to the importance of family in Irish political, social, and communal life. As Byrne describes:

> In Ireland, the story of the family is one of the 'great stories' inextricably bound up with the construction of national identity. Familism is an ideology in which the marital family is treated as a social, cultural, political, economic and affective unit.[168]

'Familism' has been a dominant narrative in shaping Irish society,[169] and the family is 'an important symbol of collective identity, unity and security.'[170] Both historically and in the present, family maintains a significant and central place both socially and politically.[171] Family is viewed as important across Irish society, with Fahey et al. reporting that 93% of Catholics considered family 'very important' in their life.[172] In Northern Ireland specifically, Sir Harold Black's influential 1979 *Report of the Children and Young Persons Review Group* stated that the family and extended family 'has always been a strong force within society.'[173]

As in Latin America,[174] the Catholic Church influenced the ideals of family,[175] and specifically motherhood.[176] 'Womanhood' in Ireland 'has been historically attained and recognised through heterosexual attachment, marriage

166 Tully, n 79 at 1602.
167 Schirmer, n 75 at 26.
168 Anne Byrne, 'Developing a Sociological Model for Researching Women's Self and Social Identities,' *The European Journal of Women's Studies*, 10:4, (2003), 443–464, (p. 443).
169 Anne Byrne and Deirdre O'Mahony, 'Family and Community: (Re) Telling Our Own Story,' *Journal of Family Issues*, 33:1, (2012), 52–75 (p. 56).
170 Pat O'Connor, *Emerging Voices: Women in Contemporary Irish Society* (Dublin: Institute of Public Administration, 1998), p. 89.
171 John Canavan, 'Family and Family Change in Ireland: An Overview,' *Journal of Family Issues*, 33:1, (2012), 10–28.
172 Cited in ibid. at 22.
173 Cited in Liz McShane and John Pinkerton, '"The Family" in Northern Ireland,' *Studies: An Irish Quarterly Review*, 75:298, (1986), 167–176 (p. 167).
174 Schirmer, n 75.
175 Canavan, n 171; Michelle Millar, Liam Coen, Ciara Bradley and Henrike Rau, '"Doing the Job as a Parent": Parenting Alone, Work, and Family Policy in Ireland,' *Journal of Family Issues*, 33:1, (2012), 29–51.
176 Ivana Bacik, 'From Virgins and Mothers to Popstars and Presidents: Changing Roles of Women in Ireland,' *The Irish Review*, 35, (2007), 100–107.

and reproduction.'[177] Motherhood specifically 'was socially and legally sanctioned as the 'natural' role for Irish women'[178] with the Irish state morally, legally, culturally, and ethically 'maternalizing' women.[179] Despite recent changes in this regard,[180] there is some continuity in traditional patterns of the division of labour, with women spending more time involved in housework and caring for others.[181] During fieldwork in Dublin in the 1990s, Throop found that many she encountered still considered childbearing and rearing in the home as a 'natural' role for women. This was in part due to the influence of the Church's perspective of a mother as 'the heart of the family.'[182] 'Ideologically,' O'Connor argues, 'women's 'destiny' lies in subsuming their identity in, and committing their time and energy to, 'the family.'[183] In this regard, in searching for the remains of their children, the mothers of the 'disappeared' are – like those in Latin America – fulfilling this expected role.

The relationship between parent and child features frequently in the accounts of the families. Margaret McKinney has commented that, "any mother who loses a child will know you have to keep on searching."[184] This sense of 'any mother' runs through family accounts, and serves to frame the 'disappeared' in such a way as to allow a much broader section of society to relate to the family's grief than a specific consideration of the circumstances of the victims' 'disappearances' would perhaps allow.

The 'disappearances' have had a lasting impact on the relationships of the families left behind. As a result of their separation between different care facilities, Jean McConville's children, her son Michael has said, "became strangers to each other"[185] and her daughter Helen has described them as "family in name only."[186] Kevin McKee's sister has described the impact on their family of her mother's recurring mental health problems since his 'disappearance.'[187] The impact of the 'disappearance' of Gerry Evans is suggested to have been a motivating factor in his father's death in 1995.[188] The *Belfast Telegraph* reported: 'those who knew him say he died of a broken heart.'[189]

177 Byrne, n 168 at 443.
178 Elizabeth Kiely and Máire Leane, '"What Would I be Doing at Home All Day?": Oral Narratives of Irish Married Women's Working Lives 1936–1960,' *Women's History Review*, 13:3, (2004), 427–446 (p. 428).
179 Bacik, n 176.
180 Ibid.
181 Canavan, n 171.
182 Elizabeth A. Throop, *Net Curtains and Closed Doors* (Westport: Bergin and Garvey, 1999), p. 95.
183 O'Connor, n 170 at 89.
184 Bradley, n 91.
185 Suzanne Breen, 'We All Sympathise with the McConville Children Now, But Back in 1972 Nobody Cared,' *Daily Mail*, 3 May 2014.
186 Tanya Acheson, 'End Silence Over Dead and Let Us Mourn in Peace,' *Belfast Telegraph*, 28 April 1995.
187 *BBC News* [online], 'Still Waiting to Find Her Brother After 38 Years,' 27 October 2010, www.bbc.co.uk/news/uk-northern-ireland-11633757 [accessed 10 August 2018]; WAVE, n 38.
188 Suzanne Breen, 'Put That Family Out of its Misery,' *Sunday Tribune*, 18 January 2009; Harnden, n 39.
189 Acheson, n 133.

Another aspect of this frame is the need for parents to have their children's bodies returned for burial before they themselves pass away. The deaths of a number of parents of the 'disappeared' received media attention.[190] These reports demonstrate both the importance of the parent–child relationship and the hope that the rupture will be repaired, even if only in death. Related to this is the fact that in a number of cases families have put the names of their 'disappeared' loved ones on the family gravestone.[191] For Philomena McKee, the recovery of Kevin's body was "about bringing him back to his family," so that he could be "reunited" with his mother in death by being buried in the family grave with her.[192]

The focus on family relationships, and reuniting parents with lost children, is a cause that many can relate to or at least empathise with. During the House of Commons debate in 1999, in his statement against the passing of the Bill, one UUP MP argued that 'We are told about family grief, we have all had that … Bereavement is … always a painful experience … Such horrors have been visited on literally thousands of families in Northern Ireland.'[193]

However, rather than lessening the significance of the families' loss, that many can relate to the grief of familial loss strengthens the campaign of the families, as greater frame 'resonance' is likely to result in a more successful framing effort.[194] As Healing Through Remembering's Kate Turner described in interview: 'You have brothers or mothers or sons … which I think lets a lot more people put themselves in that situation … it means people can empathise much more with the people they see as the campaigners.'[195]

The DUP's Jeffrey Donaldson shared this view:

> If you're sitting at home and you're watching the television and you hear … Columba McVeigh's mother come on and talk about losing her son, for example, you know if you're a parent, or you're a son or a daughter, and you're thinking about that … you're thinking, what must that woman be going through?[196]

190 See e.g. Claire Regan, 'Tragic Mother Passes Away,' *Belfast Telegraph*, 26 June 2001; Dominic Cunningham, 'Mother of "Disappeared" Man Has Died,' *Irish Independent*, 10 May 2007; 'Funeral for Disappeared Campaigner Margaret McKinney,' *The Irish News*, 6 February 2017; Susan McKay, 'Death of Mother of "Disappeared" Man,' *The Irish Times*, 10 May 2007.

191 See e.g. Claire McNeilly, 'I Just Want to Give Him Proper Burial, Says IRA Murder Victim's Niece,' *Belfast Telegraph*, 14 May 2015; 'Hoping Turned to Haunting,' *The Irish Times*, 12 May 2007; Susan McKay, 'Lost Boys,' *Field Day Review*, 9, (2013), 128–147; WAVE, n 38.

192 Una Bradley, 'Kevin, and the Pain that has Never Disappeared,' *Belfast Telegraph*, 30 August 2013.

193 House of Commons Debates (HC Deb) 12 May 1999, vol 331, col 382.

194 William A. Gamson, *Talking Politics* (Cambridge: Cambridge University Press, 1992); Snow et al., n 162.

195 Interview, Kate Turner, September 2014.

196 Interview, Jeffrey Donaldson, March 2015.

4.2.2. Importance of Christian burial

When asked why the families' campaign garnered such widespread support, journalist and writer, Susan McKay, proposed that one reason was:

> In Ireland, burial of the dead is regarded as being a hugely significant rite … the idea of … not allowing [the families] to recover the bodies so that they can give [them] a proper Christian burial … there's not allowed to be any closure because there isn't any ceremony of death … it's the inhumanity of it, and also the absolute disrespect in a culture – i.e. the Republican culture – which highly regards the … rites of passage of death.[197]

Funeral rites are hugely significant both internationally (see Chapter 1) and within Irish Catholicism and Republicanism. Witoszek claims that 'the most evident hallmark of the Irishness of Irish culture' is a 'persistent, centuries-old preoccupation with death.'[198] While not all scholars might go so far, death and the rituals surrounding it retain a significant place in Irish culture. As Power writes, although the extent of ritual surrounding death and burial in Ireland has diminished, it remains 'a major event,' involving a level of ritual that exceeds the Western European 'norm.' The cultural centrality of burial is linked to the relatively widespread practice of Catholicism (about 90% in the Republic of Ireland and 40% in Northern Ireland at the time Power was writing).[199] There is a 'deep sense of respect' for the body within Catholicism and Catholic cemeteries are considered to be 'sacred places.'[200]

Within the Catholic tradition, burial comprises three stages: a wake, the carrying out of funeral rites during Mass, and the deposition of the body in a place set aside for that specific purpose.[201] 'The physical location of the body in relation to the liturgical observance of the community,' is a key element of the religious process. The Church regulates the placement of the body during the Mass, the procession to the place of burial, and the final placement of the body in consecrated ground.[202] The ability to observe these rites is of course removed when that body is absent. Furthermore, commemorating a dead body is an important component in a process of 'closure.'[203] The stages of funerary ritual provide opportunities for remembering and eulogising a lost loved one.[204] During the wake, those who

197 Interview, Susan McKay, July 2014.
198 Nina Witoszek, 'Ireland: A Funerary Culture?' *Studies: An Irish Quarterly Review*, 76:302, (1987), 206–215 (p. 207).
199 Rosemary Power, 'Death in Ireland: Deaths, Wakes and Funerals in Contemporary Irish Society,' in Donna Dickenson and Malcolm Johnson (eds) *Death, Dying and Bereavement* (London: Sage Publications, 1993), pp. 21–25 (p. 21).
200 James H. Provost, 'Canonical Aspects of the Treatment of the Dead,' *The Jurist*, 59, (1999), 203–213, (pp. 206; 208).
201 Ibid.
202 William J. Wagner, 'Death, Dying, and Burial: Approaches in Religious Law and Practice,' *The Jurist*, 59, (1999), 135–146 (p. 141).
203 Kieran McEvoy and Heather Conway, 'The Dead, The Law, and the Politics of the Past,' *Journal of Law and Society*, 31:4, (2004), 539–562.
204 Wagner, n 202.

knew the deceased can come to view the body, pray, leave mass cards, and give their condolences to the family.[205] Viewing the body, Power states, 'is still regarded an essential part of the grieving process … the close family are deemed … to suffer in the grieving process' if for some reason they are unable to view the body.[206] The celebration of Mass is an opportunity for the community to mark the death and serves as 'a kind of final farewell.'[207] Again, these traditions are denied to families of the 'disappeared.' The emphasis on the importance of Christian burial is another example of frame 'elaboration' or 'amplification' in which the frame is made more significant by reference to particular beliefs or cultural institutions.[208]

From the earliest reports,[209] families emphasise that what they want is to give their relatives Christian burials, with, for example, Helen McKendry stating of her mother, Jean McConville: "all we want is to bury her with dignity."[210] For families whose relatives' remains have been returned to them for burial, there is a sense (for some) of 'closure.' John McClory's sister remarked that she felt "relief, just contentment now that we can take him home and bury him and have somewhere to go to visit."[211] For those families whose loved ones' remains are yet to be found, this continues to be a priority, with Columba McVeigh's brother, Oliver, saying in 2018: "one day I want to walk behind Columba in Donaghmore. And that will be a glorious day. It is maybe strange to say that but I made that promise to my mother. And that's all we want."[212]

The need for formal burial is given further impetus by the significance of burial rites within the Republican Movement itself. For Witoszek, 'the impresario of politically informed funerary rites is undoubtedly the Provisional IRA.'[213] Toolis has written of the significance of death rituals within Catholicism, and in turn, the significance of Catholic culture within Irish Republicanism; the forced abstention on families from such rituals as imposed by 'disappearing' is consequently significant.[214] As will be examined in Chapter 3, the campaign by the Republican Movement to have the remains of executed IRA member Tom Williams exhumed from his burial place at Crumlin Road Gaol and reinterred at Milltown Cemetery exemplifies the significance of burial rites for the Movement. When the decision was taken to exhume Williams' remains, Seamus McKendry voiced his support. In remarking: "everyone deserves a Christian burial," he aligned the Republican Movement's campaign with his own, and that of the other families.[215]

205 Power, n 199; Wagner, ibid.
206 Power, ibid. at 23.
207 Wagner, n 202 at 141.
208 Benford and Snow, n 114; Della Porta and Diani, n 51; Snow et al., n 162.
209 E.g. Breen, n 37; Carmel McQuaid, 'A Wife's Fruitless Hunt for Missing Husband,' *The Glasgow Herald*, 23 November 1994; David Sharrock, 'Families Hope Ceasefire May Solve Mystery of Ulster's "Disappeared",' *The Guardian*, 3 October 1994.
210 Acheson, n 133.
211 McKittrick et al., n 98 at 756.
212 Duggan, n 101.
213 Witoszek, n 198 at 211.
214 Kevin Toolis, *Rebel Hearts: Journeys within the IRA's Soul* (London: Picador, 1995).
215 Martin Breen, 'Digs Resume for Disappeared: Provos "Have Re-Visited Sites",' *Belfast Telegraph*, 2 September 1999.

4.2.3. The cause as humanitarian, not political

During the debate on the LVR legislation in May 1999, DUP MP Peter Robinson remarked: "it is the IRA's responsibility to undo the evil that it has done – it is not the responsibility of the House or of society."[216] Others also suggested that the resolution to the issue should be sought in Republican and Nationalist communities, with the MP William Ross claiming 'their own' community, church, and politicians should have the power to motivate a response from the IRA.[217] Despite these attempts to situate responsibility within Republicanism and the Nationalist community more generally, the 'disappeared' were framed, at least by the families, in a way that excluded the political, and emphasised the humanitarian issue at hand. A petition linked to the campaign of the Families gathered names and addresses to 'pledge my support to the campaign for the Christian and humanitarian burial of the "disappeared."'[218] Lefranc argues that 'the avoidance of the political … is a general characteristic of humanitarian action.'[219] In this case, we are working at a smaller scale than 'humanitarianism' as 'a belief that promotes immediate action to end suffering across the globe.'[220] However, like humanitarian work, the families' framing appeals to our emotions, and calls on us to empathise with their suffering as fellow humans, rather than as – in some cases – the political 'other.' There are two facets to this frame. The first is through what Wilson and Brown describe as 'the mobilization of empathy,'[221] and the second is the relative avoidance of the political – what Tully describes in the context of Nicaragua as 'political nonalignment.'[222]

Suffering, Humphrey and Valverde suggest, provides the 'emotional bedrock' for those seeking to uphold human rights.[223] Indeed, the historical roots of humanitarian aid lie in 'the expression of empathy with common humanity.'[224] In

216 HC Deb 10 May 1999, vol 331, col 62.
217 HC Deb 12 May 1999, vol 331, cols 381–384.
218 Petition (unsigned and undated) stored in Linenhall Library's collection of ephemera on victim support organisations.
219 Sandrine Lefranc, 'A Critique of "Bottom-Up" Peacebuilding: Do Peaceful Individuals Make Peaceful Societies?' in Bruno Charbonneau and Genevieve Parent (eds) *Peacebuilding, Memory and Reconciliation: Bridging Top-Down and Bottom-Up Approaches* (New York: Routledge, 2012), pp. 34–52, (p. 41).
220 Richard Ashby Wilson and Richard D. Brown, 'Introduction,' in Richard Ashby Wilson and Richard D. Brown (eds) *Humanitarianism and Suffering: The Mobilization of Empathy* (Cambridge: Cambridge University Press, 2009), pp. 1–30, (p. 3).
221 Ibid. at 18.
222 Tully, n 79 at 1602.
223 Michael Humphrey and Estela Valverde, 'Human Rights Politics and Injustice: Transitional Justice in Argentina and South Africa,' *International Journal of Transitional Justice*, 2:1, (2008), 83–105 (p. 89).
224 David Chandler, 'The Road to Military Humanitarianism: How the Human Rights NGOs Shaped a New Humanitarian Agenda,' *Human Rights Quarterly*, 23:3, (2001), 678–700, (p. 700). See also Pierluigi Musarò, 'The Banality of Goodness: Humanitarianism Between the Ethics of Showing and the Ethics of Seeing,' *Humanity: An International Journal of Human Rights, Humanitarianism, and Development*, 6:2, (2015), 317–335.

considering what draws humanitarians to address a particular 'narrative of suffering,' Wilson and Brown examine 'the mobilization of empathy' – a necessary component of which, they suggest, are the individual narratives of victims. For example, they point to 'the dearth of well-publicized narratives of suffering by Congolese victims' as a reason why the massive loss of life in the Democratic Republic of Congo between 1998 and 2006 received relatively limited attention when compared to other contemporary conflicts.[225] Core to the families' campaign has been their sharing of their own 'narratives of suffering,' and in so doing they have – as Wilson and Brown suggest – generated compassion.[226] Danny Morrison, former director of publicity for Sinn Féin, said of the families' accounts: they "would turn a stone … the suffering is just so deep, and lasting."[227] Similarly, for Sinn Féin's Declan Kearney: "It was a story of absolute human heartbreak. How could you not be influenced by those stories, and by the huge hurt and suffering that families were still left to carry?"[228]

The suffering of families was referred to by all Republicans interviewed, with one senior Republican suggesting this is what motivated Republicans to act: "Republicans were eager to help bring closure to those families that were still suffering. That would be my belief."[229] In articulating their suffering, the families have helped to avoid any criticism that may have been directed their way. The journalist and writer Malachi O'Doherty commented in interview: "I couldn't bring myself to criticise people who've suffered as much as they have done, and who have articulated that suffering so well."[230]

To draw on Humphrey and Valverde's terminology, the families became a small 'community of suffering' connected through their pursuit of information regarding the fate of their loved ones.[231] This collective identity was grounded in their shared experience of individual trauma, rather than in any notion of political identity. In one of their few public statements, the family of IRA volunteer Seamus Wright said they had "grieved as any other family. Our loss is no greater or no less than anyone else's."[232] This sense of common suffering is what is key to the effectiveness of such a humanitarian approach to what can be a very political crime. As Wilson and Brown posit: 'When individuals experience the same abject conditions, they suffer in more or less the same way, regardless of their gender, cultural or religious identity, or political persuasion.'[233]

Victims' Commissioner, Kenneth Bloomfield, drew on this humanitarian frame in his Report of 1998: 'Common humanity cries out for this modest act of

225 Wilson and Brown, n 220.
226 Ibid. at 19.
227 Interview, Danny Morrison, January 2015.
228 Interview, Declan Kearney, April 2015.
229 Interview, senior Republican ex-combatant, April 2015.
230 Interview, Malachi O'Doherty, August 2015.
231 Humphrey and Valverde, n 223 at 89.
232 Statement by Briege Wright, 'My Brother, Seamus Wright,' *An Phoblacht*, 15 November 2013.
233 Wilson and Brown, n 220 at 5.

mercy … it is one of the most fundamental of human instincts to seek certain knowledge of the fate of a husband or wife, son or daughter, brother or sister.'[234]

Kovras contends that 'framing the problem [of the missing] in humanitarian terms is critical.'[235] Attempting to avoid specific political allegiances is a strategy exemplified in campaigns by relatives of the 'disappeared' internationally. For The Nicaraguan Association of Mothers and Relatives of the Kidnapped and Disappeared, 'official political nonalignment' was significant 'in the fractious climate of Nicaragua.'[236] In Cyprus, depoliticisation of the issue was key to the success of the Committee on Missing Persons (CMP).[237] Although the families in Northern Ireland made the link between their cause and Adams, Sinn Féin, and the IRA from the beginning of their campaign, they have generally avoided aligning themselves with or against any political party. For example, in 1996, the mothers of Brian McKinney and John McClory wrote to all Northern Ireland political parties to highlight their plight and ask for help.[238] A 1996 Press Statement reads: 'The Families of the Disappeared are not engaged in political point-scoring, we simply wish to see the return of our loved ones remains.'[239] Following accusations of hypocrisy from the DUP over Adams' calls for information on the 'disappeared,' Kathleen Armstrong said: "I never knew who was behind it and I still don't know. We are looking to everybody for help."[240] Eugene McVeigh discussed how his family had received support from politicians "right across the board," and pointed to the DUP's former leader, Ian Paisley, meeting with his mother as an example of the non-partisan nature of political support for the families.[241] In interview, the DUP's Jeffrey Donaldson described how this issue "transcended the political divide … that was due in no small part to the very strong advocacy of the families themselves … they, their lobbying, the representations they have made were very powerful."[242]

The non-political nature of the families' campaign arguably transcended party politics into a wider societal empathy. However, it should be noted that no Unionist politician supported the bill in the House of Commons.[243] During the debate on the LVR legislation in the Commons, the non-political nature of the families' campaign was alluded to when mention was made of their drawing support from cross-community groups.[244] Similarly, when debate moved to the Lords, Lord Blease pointed out that the Bill was 'welcomed in many areas of

234 Bloomfield, n 63 at 38.
235 Kovras, n 1 at 51.
236 Tully, n 79, 1602.
237 Kovras, n 1.
238 Carton, n 134.
239 Families of the Disappeared, 'Press Statement for Linenhall Library,' 26 June 1998, located in Linenhall Library's collection of ephemera on victim support organisations.
240 Margaret Canning, 'Adams Call for Information on "Disappeared" Angers DUP,' *The Irish Times*, 12 August 2006.
241 Interview, Eugene McVeigh, August 2015.
242 Interview, Jeffrey Donaldson, March 2015.
243 HC Deb 10 May 1999 vol 331 cc. 38–83.
244 HC Deb 10 May 1999, vol 331, col 44.

Northern Ireland'[245] with Lord Hylton remarking that "the only communication I have received … came from an organisation whose office is on the Shankill Road. That is perhaps a little surprising … where the nationalist point of view is almost totally unrepresented."[246] The way in which the families have conducted their campaign has enabled this widespread support. As Brian Gormally of the Committee for the Administration of Justice said in interview: "it is perfectly possible to be a completely devoted and loyal supporter of Republicanism and still support the families' campaign."[247] In interview, Kieran Megraw described how the families made a conscious effort to not take sides politically:

> We've tried to make sure that it doesn't get used for that, very much so. And if it had cropped up at times we would maybe get a message [across] and say, that's not what we're about. Because we did meet all the parties, we met all the different governments and we always said, it's not to be used. And there might have been one or two tried to do that but I think generally most of them did follow our request as such not to politicise it … everybody can relate to the fact that you haven't got the grave or you haven't got the body. So, it's tended to transcend party politics. Most of the parties at times provided different help.[248]

The families' general avoidance of involving themselves in political partisanship has not deterred them from criticising those involved in the process when they viewed it as necessary. These critiques have been targeted at both Republicans specifically, and the two governments. For instance, when the IRA's March 1999 statement was followed by a refusal to give up information relating to burial sites without some amnesty legislation in place, the families' reactions were of frustration and anger, with Helen McKendry, Margaret McKinney, and Mary McClory accusing the IRA of falsely raising their hopes.[249] As years passed and the pace of progress did not meet expectations, or succeed in the way the headlines of 1999 had suggested, the scope of the families' criticism broadened. By 2005, the families were 'increasingly disappointed and frustrated by the lack of progress and attention given by Republicans and the British and Irish governments'; they voiced criticism of the lack of 'meaningful results' despite the readiness of 'many' to use 'the issue of the Disappeared for political gain.'[250] Just as the families had once embarrassed Republicans into action, this strategy was now used against the British and Irish governments. Following a visit to America, where she met with Congressman Chris Smith, Charlie Armstong's daughter, Anna McShane, commented, "the

245 HL Deb 24 May 1999, vol 601, cc. 639–664.
246 HL Deb 18 May 1999, vol 601, cc. 153–190.
247 Interview, Brian Gormally, November 2014.
248 Interview, Kieran Megraw, October 2015.
249 Suzanne Breen, 'Relatives Accuse IRA on Missing Bodies,' *The Irish Times*, 9 April 1999.
250 Chris Thornton, 'Families of Missing in Appeal for End to Wait,' *Belfast Telegraph*, 26 April 2005.

amount of support we got was unbelievable, especially compared to our own governments."[251]

5. The families, cohesion, and risks to the process

Della Porta and Diani posit that 'collective action cannot occur in the absence of a "we" characterised by common traits and a specific solidarity,' emphasising the importance of the existence of 'relationships of trust' between actors in a movement.[252] Following this line of argument, the maintenance of cohesion between the families of the 'disappeared' is key to the success of their campaign. Indeed, as examined earlier, efforts to recover the 'disappeared' in Lebanon have been complicated by relatives groups being fragmented, with different groups established in response to 'disappearances' by particular perpetrator organisations.[253]

Peter Wilson's sister, Patricia, described the bond between the families: 'We and the other Families of the Disappeared are all in this together, we rejoice when a body is found and we share in the sadness and frustration of those families that are still waiting.'[254]

Yet, just as the 'disappeared' are not a homogenous group, nor are their families. Differences in approach to the campaign exist between and within families. The fraught relationships of Jean McConville's children were brought into public view during the search for Jean's remains on Templetown beach, and have been reported on elsewhere.[255] The relationships between the families are, as Kate Turner of Healing Through Remembering described in interview, "more complicated than I think we stop and realise."[256] The families' opinions and identities are of course not fixed in time, as exemplified by this story shared by Turner, regarding a family member whom she preferred not to name:

> She suddenly said to me, 'you know I'm finding it really hard, because, what am I now? I'm not a mother of a "disappeared," because I've got [my loved one]. And when I look at the other families, I feel really guilty that I've got [my loved one] and they haven't got their family members. And yet, I don't belong with anybody else, so now, I've got [my loved one], but I feel like I've

251 Thornton, n 143.
252 Della Porta and Diani, n 51 at 93–94.
253 Jaquemet, n 1; Kovras, n 1. See n 76.
254 WAVE, n 38, at 30.
255 *BBC News* [online] 'McConville Remains Return Home,' 30 October 2003, http://news.bbc.co.uk/go/pr/f/-/1/hi/northern_ireland/3225755.stm [accessed 10 August 2018]; *BBC News* [online] 'Daughter Will Attend Funeral,' 30 October 2003 http://news.bbc.co.uk/go/pr/f/-/1/hi/northern_ireland/3229131.stm [accessed 10 August 2018]; Jacqueline McIntyre, 'Disappeared Family Split by Search,' *The Irish News*, 5 April 2000; 'Family in Bitter Row Over Book on Victim,' *News Letter*, 5 May 2000; John Cassidy, 'Hunt for Disappeared is Over,' *Sunday Mirror*, 21 May 2000; Mary Fitzgerald, 'Our Mum was Tortured says Victim's Daughter,' *Belfast Telegraph*, 2 October 2003; McKendry, n 45.
256 Interview, Kate Turner, September 2014

lost everything else.' And you know … It was quite obvious the other families weren't looking at her like that. Instead they looked … and saw hope.[257]

The core of the families' campaign was and is of course the recovery of the bodies of the 'disappeared,' and their cohesion is at its most evident in their support for each other in this task. As Eugene McVeigh described, "The thing is . . . people whose loved ones have returned, want to remain supportive to the people whose loved ones haven't returned."[258] This has been made evident in a number of comments to the media.[259] Even those families who are less publicly vocal, such as that of Danny McIlhone, have voiced their support for the other families, stating that their "thoughts and prayers remain with and will always be with the families whose anguish and loss continue."[260]

From the earliest days of their campaign the McKendrys stated that they did not want prosecution, only the return of Jean McConville's remains.[261] However, over the years since McConville's remains have been returned, the demands of at least some family members appear to have changed and by 2012, family members were asking for both truth and justice. Helen McKendry has said that since the body was located, "every day is a struggle because we don't know the real truth … I want to clear my mother's name and I want to see them [the IRA] brought to justice for what they did."[262] In this same article, Michael McConville said he is "not really worried about prosecution but the people that murdered my mother, I would like them to be named and shamed."[263] But in a book published by WAVE in that same year he states that he wants prosecutions in the case, arguing, "those that took my mother away and senior Sinn Féin figures that supported them should be rounded up and made to stand trial in the War Crimes Tribunal in the Hague."[264] The reasons for the

257 Ibid.

258 Interview, Eugene McVeigh, August 2015.

259 See e.g. Dan Keenan, 'Funeral of Young "Disappeared" Man Takes Place, 37 Years After Killing,' *The Irish Times*, 18 December 2010.

260 Dan Keenan, 'Human Remains Identified as Missing Man Killed by IRA,' *The Irish Times*, 20 December 2008.

261 Liam Clarke and Andrew Alderson, 'Revealed,' *The Sunday Times*, 18 June 1995.

262 Anna Maguire, 'McConville Family Hails Ruling by US Court that Terror Tapes Must be Given to Police Here,' *Belfast Telegraph*, 17 June 2012.

263 Ibid.

264 WAVE, n 38 at 22. It should be noted here that the 'disappearance' of Jean McConville should not be described in this way. A 'war crime' is one that takes place 'in the context of' an international or non-international armed conflict. There are difficulties in defining these categories (Boot 2009) and following Cassesse et al.'s (2008, 71) definition of 'large-scale armed hostilities,' it is questionable the extent to which the violence in Northern Ireland can be made to fit such a description. Second, the ICC has jurisdiction 'in respect of war crimes in particular when committed as part of a plan or policy or as part of a large-scale commission of such crimes.' While this does not preclude acts committed on a lesser scale (Byron 2009), Askin (1999) contends that this 'effectively prevents random acts, isolated crimes, or less serious offenses' from coming within the Court's jurisdiction. Although 'serious,' Jean McConville's 'disappearance' is a relatively isolated incident. As one interviewee argued: "one of the features of the Northern Ireland conflict is a lack of precision with regard to language, and one gets this quite often on victim-related issues. There are specific legal meanings to the notion of a war crime … It

changing demands by McConville's family are at this stage unclear and, as has been mentioned, there are differences of opinion between the siblings in this family. It is possible that they believed the return of the body would bring them the required 'closure' but subsequently, for some at least, this has not been the case. Several interviewees have described how what victims want may change over time.[265] It could be the case that revelations regarding the Boston College interviews[266] have led the family to believe that more is possible in terms of truth recovery and prosecution than they had once thought. A further point of note is that, as McConville's remains were found accidentally by a passer-by, rather than located by the ICLVR, forensic evidence found during the examination of her remains can be used in prosecution.[267]

The strength of the families' campaign lies in their message being a simple request for the return of bodies; Sandra Peake of WAVE has described this as "the powerful simplicity of the message."[268] As Kate Turner touched on in interview:

> What they [the families] are looking for … because the campaign is about getting the bodies, it's not about pulling at threads of what happened here, that worries people from all sorts of backgrounds … what that involves … what that exposes … or destabilises.[269]

This 'simplicity' is arguably diminished if individual families begin making separate demands for prosecution, and the hopes of those families still waiting are potentially thrown into further doubt. For example, at the 2013 launch of WAVE's book on the 'disappeared' – in which Michael McConville made his call for a war crimes tribunal – Columba McVeigh's brother, Oliver, reiterated the Families' original message: "We don't even want answers about what happened. We just want a grave to visit."[270] He had previously stated that he believed there are

does not meet the criteria. There are very few of the more extreme … stronger legal terms e.g. genocide, war crimes – they don't match what happened here, it wasn't the nature of our conflict and it doesn't do any of us any good" (Interview, community activist with over 20 years' experience working with ex-combatants, October 2015) (Kelly D. Askin, 'Crimes Within Jurisdiction of the International Criminal Court,' *Criminal Law Forum*, 10:1, (1999), 33–59; Machteld Boot, *Genocide, Crimes Against Humanity, War Crimes* (Intersentia, 2002); Christine Byron, *War Crimes and Crimes Against Humanity* (New York: Palgrave MacMillan, 2009); Antonio Cassesse, Paola Gaeta, Laurel Baig, Mary Fan, Christopher Gosnell and Alex Whiting, *Cassesse's International Criminal Law* (Oxford: Oxford University Press, 2008); Rome Statute of the International Criminal Court, A/CONF.183/9 (17 July 1998), www.icc-cpi.int/nr/rdonlyres/ea9aeff7-5752-4f84-be94-0a655eb30e16/0/rome_statute_english.pdf [accessed 2 August 2018]).

265 Interviews with Susan McKay, July 2014; Adrian McNamee of the Commission for Victims and Survivors, November 2014; Monica McWilliams, September 2014.

266 See Chapter 3, footnote 229.

267 'McConville Son Says Family Endured 31 Years of "Hell",' n 105.

268 'Tour for Troubles' "Missing" Exhibition,' *Belfast Telegraph*, 27 January 2014.

269 Interview, Kate Turner, September 2014.

270 Una Bradley, 'Hope in the Air as Disappeared Families Tell Harrowing Stories of Loss and Pain,' *The Irish Times*, 22 June 2013.

people out there with information who are not coming forward.[271] The implications of the pursuit of justice over the McConville case for the families still waiting are potentially significant. In the days following Gerry Adams' arrest (see Chapter 3), the ICLVR released a statement reaffirming that those bringing information to them could do so with confidence, that this information was 'the lifeblood of the ICLVR's work,' and would be used solely for recovering victims' remains.[272] This suggests that the ICLVR was nervous that the arrests and subsequent media coverage might have a deterrent effect on those coming forward with information. In a BBC interview following the arrest of Adams, Dympna Kerr (sister of Columba McVeigh) was asked her views on the McConvilles' pursuit of prosecution, and allegations that Adams' arrest was politically motivated. In response she said: 'I have no political motivation in this at all … The only thing I would ask him [Gerry Adams] … [is] to get us the help to find out where Columba is … That is the only thing I would want of him.'[273]

This issue brings us to a problematic nexus where the needs of individual families and the collective collide, as touched on by Geoff Knupfer in interview:

> I suppose I'm a bit sort of schizophrenic about this, because I can understand absolutely where family members … wish to see the people who were responsible prosecuted, but I also have to look at it from the Commission's point of view and the other families' point of view, that going down that route would perhaps not be helpful to our cause.[274]

Those individuals who belong to a particular collective identity may consider this only one of multiple identities that they feel they belong to. These different identities can complement each other, or there can be tension between them.[275] This could be what is at play here, as Jean McConville's family have their collective identity as one of the Families of the Disappeared, however they also identify as Jean McConville's family (an identity which is in itself fractured – as touched on previously), and their decision to pursue a course of action that could be detrimental to the hopes of the other families may reflect a tension between these different identities. Hamber and Wilson examine how processes for arriving at 'closure' can differ at the individual and collective level, suggesting that 'calls for punishment of perpetrators … need to be understood as rituals of closure in

271 John Mulgrew, 'Help Us Find the Lost Seven,' *Belfast Telegraph*, 31 August 2012.

272 Independent Commission for the Location of Victims' Remains, 'Reassurance on Information Regarding the Disappeared,' [Press Release], May 2014, www.iclvr.ie/en/ICLVR/ICLVR%20Press%20Release%20May%202014.pdf/Files/ICLVR%20Press%20Release%20May%202014.pdf [accessed 22 August 2018]. See also Steven McCaffery, 'PSNI Bid "may harm the search for bodies",' *Belfast Telegraph*, 4 July 2011.

273 *BBC News* [online], 'The Disappeared: Sister of Columba McVeigh Talks to BBC,' 2 May 2014, www.bbc.co.uk/news/uk-northern-ireland-27251094 [accessed 10 August 2018].

274 Interview, Geoff Knupfer, Senior Investigating Officer of the ICLVR, July 2014.

275 Della Porta and Diani, n 51.

themselves.'[276] At an individual level, McConville's children are pursuing their own path towards 'closure.' This potential clashing of goals between the families of the 'disappeared' is in a way a microcosm of the debate outlined by Hamber and Wilson, of how effective national processes of truth recovery and reconciliation that are addressed to a collective can be in terms of responding to individual suffering.[277]

6. Is the recovery of remains enough?

The 'intractable problem' of any reparations process, Hamber suggests, is that nothing can bring back the dead.[278] Ultimately, no response can be truly 'enough' as these 'disappearances' cannot be undone. The families campaigned for the right to bury their loved ones and a compromise was made to enable the fulfilment of this request. In terms of how satisfied the families feel with this compromise, a consideration of their responses so far reveals a broad – and at times changing – spectrum from the family of Joe Lynskey, at one end, who have said they are satisfied that his existence has been acknowledged to Michael McConville, at the other, who believes justice should be sought via a war crimes tribunal.[279] Elsewhere on this spectrum are those who want more information regarding the 'disappearance' of their loved ones,[280] those whose loved ones have been recovered but appeal on behalf of those families still waiting,[281] and of course, those who continue to seek information regarding the burial locations of their own relatives. This latter group continues to echo the families' call of April 1995. As Geoff Knupfer of the ICLVR said in interview, "there are no generalisation here. Some families are comfortable with what's happened … others less so. But it's an individual issue, not a general one."[282] For Kieran Megraw, interviewed a year after the recovery of his brother's remains:

> You're still probably dealing with the fact that he has been found. I know it is over a year but … you know you found out eventually where he was and you got his body back, and you're getting the grave sorted and then you're probably, some formal inquest or whatever so you're still very much dealing with those type of things. But for us, the target was always to get him back … It was really: let's get him back home.[283]

For others, the LVR legislation was a compromise that has not yet met expectations. In interview, Eugene McVeigh reflected on the families' campaign:

276 Hamber and Wilson, n 80.
277 Ibid.
278 Brandon Hamber, *Transforming Societies After Political Violence: Truth, Reconciliation and Mental Health* (New York: Springer, 2009), p. 101.
279 WAVE, n 38.
280 See e.g. *The Forgiveness Project*, n 91; WAVE, n 38.
281 WAVE, ibid.
282 Interview, Geoff Knupfer, July 2014.
283 Interview, Kieran Megraw, October 2015.

> I think what motivated most people in the first instance was to get their loved ones returned. Now … in the intervening years quite a lot of people have been returned. Remarkably perhaps, greater than I ever thought could happen. But … if we're waiting on 100% success rate here – do you get 100% in anything? So you know, somebody might be left out, could be us. Who knows? … you've got to go back and say: 'are we in a better place now than we would have been without the Agreement, without WAVE, without the Commission' … you'd have to say, 'are we in a better place or a worse place?' Now in our case we haven't had a resolution. But I think we're in a better place.[284]

7. Conclusion

The strength of the families and their campaign has been central to progress in recovering remains. Geoff Knupfer said in interview:

> we have to admire the families for their fortitude, for their perseverance, and for the desire to get to the truth … Astonishing work they've done to get their cause in the headlines and to get somebody to do something about it.[285]

The families mobilising as a group was an important stage in the progression of this issue. Monica McWilliams said in interview: "often the best resolution to issues and indeed support comes from others who've been through what you have been through."[286]

Bouris proposes that there exists a 'need to simplify the actors in a conflict.'[287] Part of the effectiveness of the families' campaign lies in their ability to simplify a complex problem in a way that appeals to a wide audience. As examined, many of the 'disappeared' do not fit with the 'typical' image of a victim. Those families that have spoken publicly have not tried to disguise the reality of their loved one's involvement in activities that could be seen as diverging from those expected from a truly 'innocent' victim. However, they have succeeded in simplifying their overall message by framing it within cultural values to which wider society can relate.

Taussig proposes that the 'space of death is pre-eminently a space of transformation.'[288] It can be argued that through the act of 'disappearance,' if not their deaths, the 'disappeared' were transformed by being given a value as victims that some may have otherwise contested. The 'greyness' of the 'disappeared' as victims has to an extent been negated through their having been 'disappeared.' The gulf of time that has passed since their 'disappearance' has created a space in which we have been able to focus on the wickedness of the act inflicted upon them and the

284 Interview, Eugene McVeigh, August 2015.
285 Interview, Geoff Knupfer, July 2014.
286 Interview, Monica McWilliams, September 2014.
287 Bouris, n 64 at 49.
288 Michael Taussig, 'Culture of Terror – Space of Death. Roger Casement's Putumayo Report and the Explanation of Torture,' *Comparative Studies in Society and History*, 26:3, (1984), 467–497 (p. 468).

suffering that caused their families. This space has enabled us to see that, although some of the 'disappeared' do not fit the image of a typical innocent victim, nor do they fit the image of a 'terrorist' or a 'criminal' or an 'informer.' Smyth and Fay are proponents of the need to overcome the polarising dynamic of accounting for the conflict in terms of right and wrong.[289] The suspension of the families of the 'disappeared' in a sort of limbo has enabled the wider community to focus on their loss and grief, rather than the details of the victims themselves. In this sense the reaction to the 'disappeared' as victims blurs the traditional boundaries of 'victimhood' in Northern Ireland. The 'disappeared' thus hold quite a unique place outside the debate on who constitutes a victim. As one interviewee suggested:

> Perhaps cynically you would say that Unionist politicians that did support the families and who did use it [the issue of the 'disappeared'] as a stick to beat the Republican Movement were airbrushing the fact that some of these people who were killed were IRA members ... Otherwise you could say that it's an example ... [of] the capacity of these families to frame their issue as a humanitarian issue, and Christian burial and all of that – [that] in some ways you could say if you were less cynical, superseded the victim hierarchy ... But it's a very nice example of the capacity of families to frame an issue in such a way that can overcome quite rigid hierarchies ... So in the normal run of events, they [the 'disappeared'] would have been at the bottom of the victim hierarchy but the fact that they were 'disappeared' meant that the victim hierarchy was able to be brushed aside in some ways politically.[290]

The MP Harry Barnes once described the 'disappeared' issue as 'a complex matter of right and wrong,'[291] and this is as applicable now as it was then. On the one hand, the response to the 'disappeared' as a group demonstrates that it is possible to have a more complex and nuanced understanding of victimhood in the Northern Ireland context, to accept that many are, to use Bouris' term 'grey,' and that, because a victim comes from the 'other side' does not make their families' pain and suffering any less. However, the converse of this is also demonstrated by the 'disappeared.' McEvoy and McConnachie argue that in some transitional contexts, 'the "innocent" victim is placed at the apex of a hierarchy of victimhood and becomes a symbol around which contested notions of past violence and suffering are constructed and reproduced.'[292] A 'hierarchy' has emerged of the 'disappeared,' with Jean McConville at the apex. Weinstein argues that any attempt to solve a problem or reach a definite conclusion in a transitional context can result in

289 Marie Smyth and Marie Therese Fay (eds), *Personal Accounts from Northern Ireland's Troubles: Public Conflict, Private Loss* (London: Pluto Press, 2000).

290 Interview, community activist with over 20 years' experience working with ex-combatants, October 2015.

291 HC Deb 10 May 1999, vol 331, col 68.

292 McEvoy and McConnachie, n 10 at 532.

'painful debate about whose views have priority,'[293] The arrest of Adams in 2014 provided a snapshot of this very issue, raising the question of whether the pursuit of justice over one 'disappearance' was to be prioritised over the possibility of recovering the remains of those individuals yet to be found. As explored earlier, debate exists as to the extent to which victims' voices are listened to during the development of transitional policies. The 'disappeared' internationally and in Northern Ireland provide examples of policies that are often victim-driven, and yet it is evident in the Northern Irish context that within the victims' 'voice' there are multiple voices and identities at play, not all of which can be satisfied.

Despite the many complexities outlined in this chapter, the families' campaign has witnessed significant success in terms of the recovery of remains. At the time of writing, the remains of 13 of the 16 'disappeared' have been recovered. The simplicity of how the families framed their needs not only disguised the logistical and political realities of what they needed, it also made it difficult for anyone to challenge. In the debate on the LVR Bill (see Chapter 5), those who did not support what the families wanted appeared at best unsympathetic and at worst self-serving. Although the families have stressed the humanitarian nature of their cause, their methods and opportunities are grounded in the messy political reality of Northern Ireland. This process remains "an enormous compromise,"[294] however by taking advantage of the new atmosphere of peace, and drawing local, national, and international support the families ensured that, in a context where the legacy of the conflict was not (and at the time of writing is not) being 'dealt with' in any comprehensive way, some of their needs have been met, at least in part. When asked what we can learn from all of this, Eugene McVeigh reflected: "When people who had no hope, have some hope, and have some conclusion, then you have to say that was a good thing. Will that be the case for everybody? Maybe not."[295]

293 Harvey M. Weinstein, 'Editorial Note: The Myth of Closure, the Illusion of Reconciliation: Final Thoughts on Five Years as Co-Editor-in-Chief,' *International Journal of Transitional Justice*, 5:1, (2011), 1–10 (p. 5).

294 Interview, Geoff Knupfer, July 2014.

295 Interview, Eugene McVeigh, August 2015.

3 The Republican Movement

Rationalising, leadership, and resolving the 'disappeared'

1. Introduction

The killing of John Joseph Kavanagh on 27 January 1971 is believed to be the first 'execution' of an alleged informer by the IRA during the 'Troubles.' His body was found on the banks of Belfast's Blackstaff River.[1] Although the border of south Armagh and Louth would become the 'traditional dumping ground' for the bodies of alleged informers killed by the IRA,[2] the public nature of the disposal of Kavanagh's body was to become a feature of many IRA 'executions.'[3] The disposal of the bodies of those executed for informing in such a public fashion arguably served a number of purposes. First, it operated as a visible warning to others to deter them from informing.[4] Second, such public declaration that an execution had taken place 'underlined' the IRA's belief in the legitimacy of the killing.[5] Third, in a number of instances, the bodies of those who had been executed or areas surrounding the body were booby-trapped to attempt to kill members of the security forces.[6]

As will be examined in this chapter, the majority of the 'disappeared' were, according to IRA statements, 'guilty' of either informing, stealing IRA weapons, or some other internal disciplinary violation.[7] This raises the question of why the

1 Martin Dillon and Denis Lehane, *Political Murder in Northern Ireland* (Penguin Books, 1973); David McKittrick, Seamus Kelters, Brian Feeney, Chris Thornton and David McVea, *Lost Lives: The Stories of the Men, Women and Children who Died as a Result of the Northern Ireland Troubles* (Edinburgh; London: Mainstream Publishing, 2007).

2 Toby Harnden, *'Bandit Country': The IRA and South Armagh* (London: Hodder and Stoughton, 1999), p. 15.

3 Ron Dudai, *The IRA and the Shadow of the Informer: Punishment, Governance, and Dealing with the Past* (Unpublished PhD Thesis, Queen's University Belfast, 2012) pp. 84–85.

4 Tim Pat Coogan, *Michael Collins: A Biography* (London: Hutchinson, 1990); Ed Moloney, *Voices from the Grave: Two Men's War in Ireland* (London: Faber and Faber, 2011).

5 Tim Wilson, *Frontiers of Violence: Conflict and Identity in Ulster and Upper Silesia 1918–1922* (Oxford: Oxford University Press, 2010), p. 151.

6 Dudai, n 3.

7 'IRA Investigation Locates Grave Sites,' *An Phoblacht*, 1 April 1999; 'Investigation Confirms 1972 Disappearance,' *An Phoblacht*, 11 February 2010.

decision was made to 'disappear' these individuals rather than execute them and leave their bodies where they would be discovered and, ultimately, returned to their families. In those cases of 'disappearance' where the IRA has acknowledged involvement, they have given an explanation for the killing, without offering much of an additional rationale for the 'disappearing' of the body.

This chapter will explore three aspects of the 'Movement's' response to the 'disappeared' issue.[8] First, its rationalising of the issue will be examined, in terms of how the Republican narrative has been constructed and presented, both to Republicans themselves and to the broader public. Second, the timing of Republican involvement will be considered, in terms of how their response to the issue has changed over time, and why. Finally, the practical engagement of the Republican Movement in locating the 'disappeared' will be considered, with specific reference to the role of leadership. While it is perhaps easy for those critical of the

8 Although the 'Republican Movement' and the 'Movement' are referred to throughout this book for purposes of brevity, I am conscious that the 'Movement' is not a monolith, and when using these terms I understand that they cover a complex movement with shifting alliances and power balances. Part of what I do later in this chapter is explore Republican attempts to manage these disparities within their own constituency in their response to the 'disappeared' issue. For analysis of the challenges for armed groups in transition see e.g. Michael E. Allison and Alberto Martín Alvarez, 'Unity and Disunity in the FMLN,' *Latin American Politics and Society*, 54:4, (2012), 89–118; Marc W. Chernick, 'Negotiated Settlement to Armed Conflict: Lessons from the Colombian Peace Process,' *Journal of Interamerican Studies and World Affairs*, 30:4, (1988), 53–88; Véronique Dudouet, 'Dynamics and Factors of Transition From Armed Struggle to Nonviolent Resistance,' *Journal of Peace Research*, 50:3, (2013), 401–413; Cynthia L. Irvin, *Militant Nationalism: Between Movement and Party in Ireland and the Basque Country* (Minneapolis: University of Minnesota Press, 1999); Paul D. Kenny, 'Structural Integrity and Cohesion in Insurgent Organisations: Evidence From Protracted Conflicts in Ireland and Burma,' *International Studies Review*, 12:4, (2010), 533–555; Kieran Mitton, 'Engaging with Disengagement: The Political Reintegration of Sierra Leone's Revolutionary United Front,' in Mats Berdal and David H. Ucko (eds) *Reintegrating Armed Groups After Conflict: Politics, Violence and Transition* (Oxon: Routledge, 2009), pp. 172–198; Jeffrey J. Ryan, 'The Impact of Democratization on Revolutionary Movements,' *Comparative Politics*, 27:1, (1994), 27–44; Matthew Soberg Shugart, 'Guerrillas and Elections: An Institutionalist Perspective on the Costs of Conflict and Competition,' *International Studies Quarterly*, 36, (1992), 121–152; Stephen John Stedman, 'Spoiler Problems in Peace Processes,' *International Security*, 22:2, (1997), 5–53. With specific regard to the Irish Republican Movement see e.g. Gerry Adams, *Hope and History: Making Peace in Ireland* (London: Brandon, 2003); Rogelio Alonso, *The IRA and Armed Struggle* (Oxon: Routledge, 2007); Tony Blair, *A Journey* (London: Hutchinson, 2010); Deaglán de Bréadún, *The Far Side of Revenge: Making Peace in Northern Ireland* (Cork: The Collins Press, 2008); Richard English, *Armed Struggle: The History of the IRA* (London: Pan Books, 2012); John A. Hannigan, 'The Armalite and the Ballot Box: Dilemmas of Strategy and Ideology in the Provisional IRA,' *Social Problems*, 33:1, (1985), 31–40; Eamonn Mallie and David McKittrick, *The Fight for Peace: The Secret Story Behind the Irish Peace Process* (London: Heinemann, 1996); Tommy McKearney, *The Provisional IRA* (London: Pluto Press, 2011); Andrew Sanders, *Inside the IRA: Dissident Republicans and the War for Legitimacy* (Edinburgh: Edinburgh University Press, 2011).

Republican Movement to make accusations of evasion, the on-the-ground reality belies such categorical condemnation. At the time of writing, Republican engagement in the search process has resulted in the location of the remains of 13 of the 'disappeared.'[9] This progress prompted one journalist, who has in the past written scathingly about Republican involvement in 'disappearing,' to suggest that Republicans have gone "a long way toward trying to resolve this."[10] There are attempts at circumvention with regards some aspects of the issue, and, as will be examined, Republican motives for engaging may to an extent be self-serving, but engage they have, and the significance of this move should not be disregarded. While it may be difficult for many to see past the brutality of 'disappearing,' it is important to recognise that progress has been made on an issue that is both politically and logistically challenging.

2. Rationalising the 'disappeared'

Based on the notion that an Ireland united is legitimate, where divided it is not, and that the British state's denial of Irish self-determination legitimates the use of violence in response,[11] the legitimacy of the IRA's goal, and use of violence to achieve this goal, is central to its ideology. Legitimacy demands a level of transparency; it requires explaining what you are doing and why.[12] When one considers that the 'essence' of a 'disappearance' is argued to be the provision of 'maximum deniability at the time and afterward,'[13] that the hiding of a body is a key aspect of so-called 'ordinary crime' murders,[14] that the killing of informers was legitimated through the public disposal of their bodies[15] and that the IRA gave no account of their actions at the time,[16] a dissonance exists between the perpetration of 'disappearances' and the Republican perspective on the legitimacy of violence. As one interviewee contended, the act of 'disappearing' "doesn't fit with their notion of themselves as having reacted to brutality and only killed British soldiers, and only killed people who, in their view, were legitimate targets."[17]

9 See Introduction.
10 Interview, Malachi O'Doherty, August 2015.
11 English, n 8.
12 Mark C. Suchman, 'Managing Legitimacy: Strategic and Institutional Approaches,' *Academy of Management Review*, 20:3, (1995), 571–610.
13 Stanley Cohen, 'State Crimes of Previous Regimes: Knowledge, Accountability, and the Policing of the Past,' *Law & Social Inquiry,* 20:1, (1995), 7–50 (p. 14).
14 Samantha Lundrigan and David Canter, 'A Multivariate Analysis of Serial Murderers' Disposal Site Location Choice,' *Journal of Environmental Psychology,* 21:4, (2001), 423–432.
15 Wilson, n 5.
16 One exception is the case of Robert Nairac. His 'execution' was admitted but his body hidden (see e.g. 'Hunt for Missing Officer is Switched,' *Belfast Telegraph*, 19 May 1977; 'Missing Soldier "Executed" Say Provos,' *Belfast Telegraph*, 16 May 1977; 'No Real Lead to Missing Officer,' *Belfast Telegraph*, 20 May 1977; 'Search Goes on for Missing Officer,' *The Irish Times*, 20 May 1977; 'SAS Captain Executed,' *Republican News*, 21 May 1977).
17 Interview, journalist and writer Susan McKay, July 2014.

As detailed in Chapter 1, one rationale applied for 'disappearing' internationally is to remove 'unwanted categories.'[18] Given the IRA's self-presentation as 'the legal and lawful government of the Irish Republic,'[19] effectively a government or state in waiting,[20] that promotes a strategy of killing only 'legitimate' targets,[21] one should expect to find a similar attempt at legitimation in its 'disappeared' narrative. Indeed, that the 'disappeared' were legitimate targets is the most immediately apparent, and most consistent, rationale given by the IRA.

The punishment of 'criminals, collaborators, and informers' to defend 'the war of liberation' is outlined in the IRA's constitution (*The Green Book*) as one element of the IRA's five-fold strategy of guerrilla warfare.[22] Given the close-knit nature of Republican communities, informers had to be recruited from within as outsiders attempting to infiltrate from without faced very significant difficulties in not 'standing out.'[23] Described as 'expendable as far as both sides [were] concerned'[24] and 'the epitome of all we (Republicans) abhor,'[25] informers posed such a risk that the IRA leadership restructured the entire organisation during the 1970s, from the more traditional format of commands – brigades, battalions, and companies – to a cellular structure.[26] The IRA's response to informers was 'multi-faceted.'[27] While this included 'court martial' and execution in some cases, at various times during the conflict amnesties would be offered to those informers who gave details of their activities, or suspected informers would be ordered to leave the country.[28] During the 'Troubles,' the use of information collected from these informers became critical to state efforts against the IRA,[29] and there is a fiercely contested debate as to the extent to which infiltration by informers contributed to ending the IRA's campaign of violence.[30] Both expendable and hated, informers are an

18 Ralph Rozema, 'Forced Disappearance in an Era of Globalization: Biopolitics, Shadow Networks, and Imagined Worlds,' *American Anthropologist*, 113:4, (2011), 582–593 (p. 583).
19 Tim Pat Coogan, *The IRA* (London: Harper Collins, 2000), p. 544.
20 J. Bowyer Bell, *The Secret Army: The IRA* (New Jersey: Transaction Publishers, 1997) p. 254, fn. 12; James Dingley, *The IRA: The Irish Republican Army* (California: Praeger, 2012), p. 111.
21 Dudai, n 3.
22 Coogan, n 19 at 555.
23 Kevin Toolis, *Rebel Hearts: Journeys within the IRA's Soul* (London: Picador, 1995).
24 Martin Dillon, *The Dirty War* (London: Arrow Books, 1991), p. 34.
25 'Loose Talk Can be Fatal,' *Republican News*, 25 January 1974.
26 Coogan, n 19.
27 Ron Dudai, 'Informers and the Transition in Northern Ireland,' *British Journal of Criminology*, 52, (2012), 32–54.
28 Dudai, n 3 and ibid.
29 Steve Hewitt, *Snitch! A History of the Modern Intelligence Informer* (New York: Continuum, 2010), p. 64.
30 Rory Finegan, *Targeted Killings in Northern Ireland: An Analysis of their Effectiveness and Implications for Counter-Terrorism Policies* (Unpublished PhD Thesis, Dublin City University, 2014).

example of a category of victims who have less 'moral relevance' than others,[31] and certainly constitute an 'unwanted category.'[32]

It is within this narrative of informing, threat, and the need to protect the organisation that the IRA's own 'rationale' for 'disappearing' is framed. Following Captain Robert Nairac's killing,[33] the IRA boasted that he was one of the SAS's 'most high-ranking officers,' interrogated for information on SAS activities and executed as an undercover member of that organisation.[34] In a March 1999 statement, the IRA claimed of those who they had 'disappeared,' "some ... were members of *Oglaigh na hEireann* who were executed for activities which put *Oglaigh na hEireann* personnel at risk or jeopardised the struggle."[35] Included was a list of nine of the 'disappeared' and their 'offences.' Kevin McKee, Seamus Wright, Columba McVeigh, Brendan Megraw, Eamonn Molloy, and Jean McConville were accused of informing for, or working as agents or *agents provocateurs* for, the British Army or the police. McKee, Wright, and Megraw were also accused of 'membership' of the Military Reaction Force (MRF). John McClory, Brian McKinney, and Danny McIlhone[36] were accused of stealing IRA weapons and using them in armed robberies.[37] The admittance of Joe Lynskey's 'disappearance' in 2010 was accompanied by a statement that he was "court-martialled for breaches of IRA standing orders," specifically for having ordered the shooting of another IRA volunteer with whose wife he had been having an affair.[38] These statements suggest that in IRA terms, 'disappearances' were a method of enforcing internal discipline. *The Green Book* makes clear that 'treason' (informing) and 'treachery' (this includes seizing IRA weapons) are both punishable by death.[39] In interview, a senior Republican ex-combatant contended: "There was always a reason as to why these people were killed in the first place." He went on to explain: "The IRA were always going to kill people for stealing their weapons. They were always going to kill people for informing, and for working with the British. Because it's the Achilles heel of any popular resistance."[40]

31 Garrett O'Boyle, 'Theories of Justification and Political Violence: Examples from Four Groups,' *Terrorism and Political Violence*, 14:2, (2002), 23–46 (p. 27).
32 Following Rozema, n 18 at 583.
33 This was the only 'disappeared' case in which the killing was admitted to at the time – Nairac was a British Army officer involved in 'intelligence gathering' (Parker 1999, xiv) who was allegedly trying to infiltrate Republican communities in south Armagh when he was abducted (Anthony Bradley, *Requiem for a Spy* (Cork; Dublin: Mercier Press, 1993); John Parker, *Death of a Hero: Captain Robert Nairac, GC and the Undercover War in Northern Ireland* (London: Metro, 1999)).
34 'SAS Captain Executed,' n 16.
35 'IRA Investigation Locates Grave Sites,' n 7.
36 The accusation against McIlhone was later retracted. An IRA statement ('IRA Statement,' *An Phoblacht*, 15 August 2002) stated that although involved in robberies, McIlhone was not using IRA weapons. This report claimed that McIlhone was killed in a struggle with a volunteer who was guarding him.
37 'IRA Investigation Locates Grave Sites,' n 7.
38 'Investigation Confirms 1972 Disappearance,' n 7.
39 Dillon, n 24.
40 Interview, senior Republican ex-combatant, April 2015.

From this perspective, the Republican Movement's beliefs regarding informing resulted in the 'execution' of the 'disappeared.' As examined in Chapter 2, in several cases, families have indicated that there may have been some foundation to these claims whereas in others, families have refuted the IRA's accusations.

While it is possible that 'disappearing' can be seen as one of a range of possible responses to informing (examined above),[41] why this particular response was selected in certain circumstances and not in others suggests something more complex was at work rather than simply random choice. As I argue elsewhere, while these individuals may have been 'executed' as a result of informing or some other internal disciplinary violation, the decision to 'disappear' their bodies speaks to a desire to avoid the embarrassment of the killing being made known.[42]

Embarrassment is described as an emotion closely linked with social interaction,[43] involving some form of self-evaluation or self-reflection.[44] The origins of feelings of embarrassment lie in situations where there is a dissonance between expected or appropriate behaviour, and that which actually occurs, or in negative evaluations by others.[45] One of the two main threads of embarrassment is this contravention of social expectation – i.e. the role of identity, social conventions, and the importance of how one is evaluated by others.[46] The second thread is what separates embarrassment from other 'self-conscious emotions'[47] such as shame and guilt. This is the need for an audience to be present to witness the departure from social norms.[48] With embarrassment linked to the role of public perception of behaviour,[49] in a 'disappearance,' the hiding of the body results in the removal of any potential audience. As argued by Cohen, the 'essence' of a 'disappearance' is to provide 'maximum deniability at the time and afterward.'[50]

41 See Dudai, n 3 and Dudai, n 27 for an in-depth exploration of Republican responses to informing.

42 Lauren Dempster, 'The Republican Movement, "Disappearing" and Framing the Past in Northern Ireland,' *International Journal of Transitional Justice*, 10:2, (2016), 250–271.

43 Erving Goffman, 'Embarrassment and Social Organisation,' *American Journal of Sociology*, 62:3, (1956), 264–271; June Price Tangney, 'The Self-Conscious Emotions: Shame, Guilt, Embarrassment and Pride,' in Tim Dalgleish and Mick J. Power (eds) *Handbook of Cognition and Emotion* (Chicester: Wiley & Sons Ltd., 1999), pp. 541–568.

44 Tangney, ibid.

45 Ibid.

46 Goffman, n 43; Dacher Keltner and Brenda N. Buswell, 'Embarrassment: Its Distinct Form and Appeasement Functions,' *Psychological Bulletin*, 122:3, (1997), 250–270; Tangney, n 43; June Price Tangney, Rowland S. Miller, Laura Flicker and Deborah Hill Barlow, 'Are Shame, Guilt and Embarrassment Distinct Emotions?' *Journal of Personality and Social Psychology*, 70:6, (1996), 1256–1269.

47 Tangney, n 43.; Tangney et al., ibid.

48 Anja Eller, Miriam Koschate and Kim-Michelle Gilson, 'Embarrassment: The Ingroup-Outgroup Audience Effect in Faux-Pas Situations,' *European Journal of Social Psychology*, 41, (2011), 489–500; Goffman, n 43; Tangney, n 43.

49 Keltner and Buswell, n 46.

50 Cohen, n 13 at 14.

The removal of a body via 'disappearing' hides knowledge of the crime itself, removes much of the potential for establishing culpability, and consequently quashes any potential embarrassment this may have entailed. Such reasoning has been evidenced in the international arena; for example, in Argentina, one of the theories offered is that killings were kept secret to avoid the opprobrium of the Pope, and subsequent damage to the country's international reputation.[51]

Embarrassment is related to a sense of deficiency in the presented self and situation-specific failures.[52] In the context being examined here this would relate to failures, or perceived failures, in the Republican Movement's self-presentation, particularly in relation to particular actions. The term 'Paddy Factor' was allegedly used by the British to refer to mistakes made by the IRA,[53] and examples of operational decisions or errors that have resulted in embarrassment pepper the history of the Troubles. These include the kidnapping of Thomas Niedermayer in 1973,[54] the Shankill bomb of 1993,[55] the Remembrance Day bombing in Enniskillen in 1987, the killings of 3-year-old Jonathan Ball and 12-year-old Tim Parry in the Warrington bomb of March 1993, and myriad other operations in which civilians were killed.[56]

With regards embarrassment in relation to the 'disappeared,' one interviewee suggested that "when you start examining it you start going, these people? When you look at the detail of the people that are 'disappeared,' they don't fit your [Republican] narrative."[57] In interview, Danny Morrison proposed:

> Why was it done in secrecy? Clearly, they wanted to avoid publicity or, in some cases, the circumstances of betrayal by an IRA Volunteer were embarrassing or scandalous. I think, particularly in the case of Jean McConville there had to have been a feeling that they couldn't stand over it, couldn't take the condemnation or criticism, particularly given that she was a widowed mother of ten, and couldn't justify it in the way they would with informers whose killings were claimed. Therefore silence, everything – you don't talk about it, no statements are issued about it, the families aren't told the truth.[58]

Martin McGuinness aired a similar rationale in a 2014 radio interview:

> The arguments that they made to me that the person in this particular case [Patrick Duffy] was from the local area and … they thought that at a time when they were in conflict with the British that it wasn't … something they

51 Horacio Verbitsky, *Confessions of an Argentine Dirty Warrior* (New York; London: The New Press, 2005), p. 100.
52 Keltner and Buswell, n 46; Tangney, n 43; Tangney et al., n 46.
53 Coogan, n 19; Hannigan, n 8.
54 Coogan, ibid.
55 Mallie and McKittrick, n 8.
56 English, n 8.
57 Interview, Kate Turner of Healing Through Remembering, September 2014.
58 Interview, Danny Morrison, former Director of Publicity for Sinn Féin, January 2015.

> wanted to be publicly associated with … the public execution of people who were from their own community who had been in the employ of, or agents for, British state forces … They wanted the focus to be on the conflict between the IRA and the British state forces as opposed to civilians.[59]

McGuinness' comment suggests a deliberate avoidance on the part of the IRA of disposing of the bodies of local informers publicly in their own area in order to avoid public censure and to keep the Republican constituency on side. A similar argument is used by an IRA source, interviewed by Suzanne Breen about the case of Gerry Evans. He claimed when the bodies of informers from the local area were left by the roadside in south Armagh:

> These deaths didn't go down well with some in our community … there was a bit of a backlash. South Armagh is clannish. Gerry Evans had a large extended family. There are dozens of Evanses around Crossmaglen. It wasn't in our interests to kill Gerry openly just in case we alienated any of them. It was easier to do it secretly.[60]

These comments highlight two possible, if overlapping, audiences whose condemnation the IRA may have wished to avoid through 'disappearing': localised Republican communities and a broader audience, including Republicans and perhaps the wider Northern Ireland community. Within these audiences, the possibilities for embarrassment are three-fold. First, the bodies may have been hidden to save the Republican Movement from the embarrassment of others finding out about the killing (as alluded to in the earlier statements). Second, it is possible that victims were 'disappeared' to prevent the wider community finding out about the full extent of informing that was taking place. And third, the 'disappearance' was carried out to protect the victim's family from the embarrassment of the wider Republican community finding out about their relative's role as an informer.

With regards those cases that received some publicity at the time, two in particular have aspects that could potentially have caused embarrassment for the IRA had the killings been made public. In these cases, the headlines are telling: such as,

59 Martin McGuinness in interview with Marian Finucane, RTE 1 Radio Interview 31 May 2014, www.rte.ie/radio1/marian-finucane/programmes/2014/0531/620815-marian-finucane-saturday-31-may-2014/ [accessed 7 August 2018]. Patrick Duffy was abducted, murdered, and buried in a bog by the IRA in August 1973. Duffy's body was exhumed two weeks later and left in a coffin in a car on a border road following public appeals from his wife and priests and, allegedly, pressure from within the Republican community (Suzanne Breen, 'McGuinness Unit "Told to Stop Having Informers Disappeared",' *Irish Mail on Sunday*, 2 October 2011; 'Give Me My Husband's Body – Plea,' *Belfast Telegraph*, 17 August 1973; 'Priest Joins in Plea About Man's Body,' *The Irish Times*, 21 August 1973; 'Executed Man's Body in Car – Army Told,' *The Irish Times*, 25 August 1973; 'Body Found in Coffin at Border,' *The Irish Times*, 27 August 1973).

60 Suzanne Breen, 'Put That Family Out of its Misery,' *Sunday Tribune*, 18 January 2009.

'Retarded Man Still Missing' (in relation to Peter Wilson)[61] and 'Widow with 10 Children Reported Kidnapped' (in relation to Jean McConville).[62] Peter Wilson was not the only young person with learning difficulties killed by the IRA. In 2004, the IRA apologised to the family of Bernard Teggart, a 15-year-old who they shot and killed in 1973, accused of being a 'tout.' Following the killing, Teggart's family described that he had the mental age of 8 or 9 and would not have understood the implications of what he had been accused of.[63] Jean McConville was not the only woman to be killed by the IRA. Other women were killed, allegedly as informers, albeit this was rare, occurred much later in the conflict, and generated negative publicity.[64] Catherine Mahon was shot as an alleged informer in west Belfast in 1985, and Caroline Moreland was taken from west Belfast and shot as an alleged informer in 1994; her body was found near the border the following day.[65] The killings of Wilson and McConville were therefore not unique in their circumstances, but it remains possible that the decision was taken at the time of their killings to secretly bury their remains to avoid censure. Some echoing of the potential reaction to Wilson and McConville's killings can be seen in more recent media reports. Stories covering the search for Peter Wilson refer to his youth, his vulnerability, and his innocence.[66] Jean McConville's case remains the focus of much attention and media reports tell of not only her struggles as a widowed mother, but the impact of her 'disappearance' on her children.[67]

The second form of embarrassment relates to the 'disappearing' of Seamus Wright and Kevin McKee, and is suggested by Ed Moloney. He argues that the two men were 'disappeared' in order to hide the extent of British intelligence infiltration in the IRA and to prevent the tarnishing of the 'success' of the Four Square Laundry operation,[68] in which Wright and McKee were

61 *The Irish Times*, 29 September 1973. In the case of Peter Wilson, it should be pointed out that a senior Republican source claimed that Peter Wilson was not killed by the IRA (see Introduction, footnote 52).
62 *The Irish Times*, 17 January 1973.
63 McKittrick et al., n 1 at 400.
64 E.g. '"Outrage and Abhorrence" at Young Mother's Murder,' *Andersonstown News*, 23 July 1994; 'Woman's Body Lies for 13 Hours on the Border,' *Belfast Telegraph*, 18 July 1994.
65 McKittrick et al., n 1.
66 Dan Keenan, 'Search Begins in Beauty Spot for Body of Man "Disappeared" During Troubles,' *The Irish Times*, 27 October 2010; Dan Keenan, 'Funeral of Young "Disappeared" Man Takes Place, 37 Years After Killing,' *The Irish Times*, 18 December 2010.
67 Tanya Acheson, 'IRA Women Took Mum and Left Me in Living Nightmare,' *Belfast Telegraph*, 28 April 1995; Suzanne Breen, 'We All Sympathise with the McConville Children Now, But Back in 1972 Nobody Cared,' *The Daily Mail*, 3 May 2014.
68 This was an operation by the MRF involving a mobile cleaning service – the Four Square Laundry. Clothes were collected from Catholic areas of Belfast by a van operated by undercover members of the Royal Military Police. Before the clothes were cleaned and returned to their owners, they were tested at a forensic laboratory. According to Martin Dillon, it was Kevin McKee who exposed to the IRA the real nature of this operation – information he had learned through his own involvement

implicated.[69] The latter part of Moloney's argument could be accurate, however his first suggestion is difficult to support. It has been argued that the level of infiltration of the IRA by informers is impossible to determine as various claims have been made, and these are of varying levels of reliability.[70] As previously discussed, informer activity is believed to have been so significant as to have played a role in bringing the conflict to an end. Sutton's 1994 assessment counted 59 alleged informers killed by the IRA[71] and McKeown has counted 68 killings of alleged informers between 1969 and 2001.[72] When one considers these figures, to 'disappear' two individuals to hide the extent of informing seems somewhat futile.

That said, reputational damage to the organisation by the fact that informers have been successful at operating under the radar (especially if this is close to the leadership) is a strong motivation for the IRA responding in different ways to such rumours.[73] Given that the Four Square Laundry attack was considered a failure 'converted to a triumph' in the 'forensic war,'[74] it may be the case that the organisation wanted to keep the memory of that event untarnished by association with informers. It is possible that, when combined with the fact that Wright and McKee were local men connected with prominent Republican families,[75] such factors may have combined to result in their being 'disappeared' rather than just being executed. In interview, Danny Morrison said of these two cases:

> you can see the circumstances … the embarrassment of your own members, being involved in setting up your own members, and being involved in working with British undercover, British intelligence services, dark forces, and they are turned and of course, again they are 'disappeared.'[76]

As noted, the third potential manifestation of 'embarrassment' is a desire to protect families from the embarrassment of it being known that their relative was killed as an informer. There is a 'social stigma' attached to informing and

with the MRF. On 2 October 1972, the Laundry van was ambushed and the driver killed. Two business premises also linked to the activities of the MRF were targeted on the same day and following the attacks the IRA boasted that they had killed 'five British spies,' though the British Army claimed the only death was that of the van driver. See Dillon, n 24 at 31; Tony Geraghty, *The Irish War* (London: Harper Collins, 1998).

69 Ed Moloney, *A Secret History of the IRA* (London: Penguin Books, 2007), p. 121.

70 Dudai, n 3.

71 Malcolm Sutton, *Bear in Mind These Dead* (1994), cited at http://cain.ulst.ac.uk/sutton/book/#append [accessed 7 August 2018].

72 Michael McKeown, 'Post-Mortem,' at http://cain.ulst.ac.uk/victims/mckeown/mckeown01.pdf [accessed 7 August 2018].

73 Dudai, n 27.

74 Geraghty, n 68 at 89–90.

75 Dillon, n 24. See also Moloney, n 4.

76 Interview, Danny Morrison, January 2015.

informers' families can be ostracised in their communities or become a target for retribution.[77] Martin Dillon has similarly suggested this as an alternative reason for the 'disappearing' of Kevin McKee and Seamus Wright, as both were connected to prominent Republican families.[78]

I argue elsewhere that the embarrassment surrounding 'disappearances' has continued into the post-conflict period, resulting in a dissonance between Republican rhetoric on this issue, and the reality of their engagement in the search process. Republican framing of the 'disappeared,' on the one hand, speaks to a distancing from responsibility for 'disappearing.' On the other hand, we see attempts to legitimate the choice of target – effectively to bring 'disappearing' within the bounds of the IRA's 'moral compass.'[79] Such efforts have been criticised.

The inclusion of the alleged 'crimes' of the 'disappeared' in the IRA's March 1999 statement led to criticism from media commentators, political opponents, and some families. Malachi O'Doherty remarked that, 'no Republican is saying it was wrong to shoot Jean McConville. Nothing that Gerry Adams or anyone else in the Movement has said suggests any difficulty with the decision taken to kill her, or any of the other Disappeared.'[80] The Social Democratic and Labour Party's (SDLP's) Denis Haughey commented, "It is very regrettable that the IRA statement contains no apology for the murder, only the length of time it has taken to admit to it,"[81] and Eileen Bell of the Alliance Party described it as "'regrettable' that the IRA could not simply inform families of their loved ones' graves without besmirching their reputation."[82] Seamus McKendry, son-in-law of Jean McConville, called the allegations "lies and propaganda."[83]

In relation to the case of Stephen Hayes,[84] English quotes one Republican of that period as saying: "for the IRA the Stephen Hayes case was a Catch 22 situation. If he was guilty it did them harm in a public relations sense, if not it was even worse."[85] When faced with the need to speak out on the 'disappeared,' the IRA was in a similar 'Catch 22' position. To 'disappear' the bodies of victims was bad enough, without the justifiability of the original killing itself being called into question. From a Republican

77 Dudai, n 3 at 60–61; Toolis, n 23 at 231. See e.g. account of Margaret Valente in Marie Smyth and Marie-Therese Fay (eds) *Personal Accounts from Northern Ireland's Troubles: Public Conflict, Private Loss* (London: Pluto Press, 2000).

78 Dillon, n 24.

79 Dempster, n 42.

80 Malachi O'Doherty, 'The Indelible Stain of Barbarity,' *Belfast Telegraph*, 1 June 1999.

81 Monika Unsworth, 'Mowlam Welcomes IRA Disclosure on Graves of Victims,' *The Irish Times*, 31 March 1999.

82 Ibid.

83 Martin Breen, '"Disappeared" Families Allowed to Bury Dead,' *Belfast Telegraph*, 30 March 1999.

84 Stephen Hayes was an IRA Chief of Staff in the 1940s in Dublin. He was court-martialled for treachery, found guilty and sentenced to death. He managed to escape and lived until 1974, maintaining his innocence throughout his life. The two possible 'truths' for the organisation at the time were that their Chief of Staff was a traitor, or that he was loyal but had been imprisoned, beaten, and sentenced to death by senior IRA officers (English, n 8).

85 Ibid. at 58.

perspective the 'guilt' of those who were 'disappeared' is almost essential. To maintain their own legitimacy in relation to the killings, they have to be able to provide justification for the initial act of abduction and killing, even if they are berated for it. Historian Richard English suggested that, "The IRA have to say, 'we got the right people,' because if they look like they're war criminals and they're also incompetent war criminals, that looks even worse."[86]

The decision to maintain the narrative that the 'disappeared' were legitimate targets may have been a prudent tactical decision for the Republican Movement.[87] In order to satisfy the Movement's internal audience, the decisions made to execute these individuals in the first place cannot be disowned.[88] As one interviewee pointed out: "These are authorised IRA actions. So it would be a bit rich if the leadership came in and said: 'well, why did you do that?' 'Because you fucking ordered me to' would be the obvious response."[89]

Statements that legitimise the choice of target within a Republican framework speak to the internal audience: the Republican Movement and its community. The 'disappeared,' according to the IRA, defied the boundaries set by the Republican Movement and as a result, they were executed in a '*Green Book*-compliant' manner. Reassuring volunteers of the importance of the role they played in past struggles was one way by which the leadership managed the IRA through the transition from conflict.[90] One facet of this, English suggested, is the need to ensure that those who killed in the past continue to feel that they did so for a legitimate reason:

> Organisations, whether the IRA or an orthodox army, have to have some sense of what the community of those who did it feel in their post-war life … if you've got people who went to jail for sixteen years … if you say, 'well not only did you go to jail for 16 years, "Seamus," but also 25% of the people you shot were the wrong people' … That would have been more of a problem …[91]

As another interviewee argued:

> … the management of the constituency is: these were different times, what you did was legitimate in IRA terms, in terms of the killing, obviously the

86 Interview, Richard English, August 2014.
87 Dempster, n 42.
88 As examined in footnote 8, this 'internal audience' is not a homogenous group. However, this terminology is used here to differentiate between Sinn Féin's outward political 'face' at the time of the transition and their attempts to manage the Republican Movement internally.
89 Interview, community activist with over 20 years' experience working with ex-combatants, October 2015.
90 Kevin Bean, *The New Politics of Sinn Féin* (Liverpool: Liverpool University Press, 2007).
91 Interview, Richard English, August 2014.

> burials themselves – we all wish that hadn't happened, but let's do what we can to try to help those families … that's the way they would have framed it. But it would not have worked … if the IRA leadership were trying to disavow what had been done previously, because these were authorised IRA actions, in a lot of the cases … And … they have to manage that reality.[92]

One argument that can be made with relative certainty is that 'disappearing' comes across as an *ad hoc* response in particular cases, rather than standard practice. In interview, Danny Morrison suggested: "I can imagine it not being a thought-out policy, that it was quite you know [an] *ad hoc* or a panic response." He pointed out the lack of consistency: "there's huge periods when there are no 'disappeared,' but the IRA still shoots informers."[93] The *ad hoc* nature of the practice, however, does not render these acts any less organised, or – what is of particular significance from a transitional justice perspective – any less significant in impact.

Although it has been suggested that, generally, victims of 'disappearance' are 'as a rule misrepresented by those responsible,'[94] the Republican Movement remains, on the whole, consistent in their construction of the 'disappeared' as legitimate targets – albeit less vociferously in recent years.[95] This is evident in the 'Movement's' responses to the refutation by Jean McConville's family of the accusations made against her.[96] Cognisance of the political sensitivities aside, there is still a durable Republican mantra which suggests that the original murders at least were justified – but that the 'disappearing' itself was a 'wrong.' For example, in 2006, following a request from her family, the IRA carried out an investigation into the death of Jean McConville, concluding that their investigation "confirmed that Jean McConville was working as an informer for the British Army."[97] Billy McKee (former IRA OC in Belfast) remarked in an interview that, "All I know is that Mrs McConville was found out … working for the Brits."[98] In 2012, Sinn Féin's Mitchel McLaughlin was

92 Interview, community activist with over 20 years' experience working with ex-combatants, October 2015.

93 Interview, Danny Morrison, January 2015.

94 Jeffrey A. Sluka, 'Introduction: State Terror and Anthropology,' in Jeffrey A. Sluka (ed.) *Death Squad: The Anthropology of State Terror* (Philadelphia: University of Pennsylvania Press, 2000), pp. 1–45, (p. 5).

95 See footnote 36 on case of Danny McIlhone.

96 In 2006, the Police Ombudsman's investigation into the abduction and murder of McConville concluded that they found no evidence that she had been working as an agent at any time (Office of the Police Ombudsman for Northern Ireland, *Report into the Complaint by James and Michael McConville Regarding the Police Investigation Into the Abduction and Murder of Their Mother Mrs Jean McConville* (Belfast: Office of the Police Ombudsman for Northern Ireland, 2006)). See also Chapter 2.

97 'IRA Carried Out "Thorough Investigation" Into McConville Death,' *An Phoblacht*, 13 July 2006.

98 'Adams' IRA Denial is a Joke, Says Ex-Provo,' *Belfast Telegraph*, 16 May 2011.

criticised in the Northern Ireland Assembly (NIA) for refusing to retract a comment made in 2005, in which he suggested that the killing of Jean McConville was not a criminal act.[99] It should be noted here that this refrain changed following the beginning of a spate of arrests in relation to the abduction and murder of Jean McConville.[100] At the time he was arrested, Adams said: "I believe the killing of Jean McConville and the secret burial of her body was wrong and a grievous injustice to her and her family."[101] The following month, in an RTÉ interview, McGuinness described 'disappearing' as a practice that was "very, very wrong," and for him had "no rationale."[102]

The campaign of the families of the 'disappeared' could be responded to without disowning decisions made in the past by the IRA. This has resulted in an apparent dissonance between rhetoric and action.[103] Republican framing of the issue left them open to criticism, however their commitment to the recovery of the remains of the 'disappeared' has resulted in significant progress, with the remains of 13 of the 16 'disappeared' having been located. The next section will explore the timing of, and motivation for, Republican engagement in the search process.

3. Denial, timing, and shifting silences

In this section, the shifting 'boundaries of silence'[104] on the part of the Republican Movement will be examined. In the continuing silence following the 'disappearances,' as the need and desire of families to know increased over the years, the information held by those who perpetrated these acts became more valuable. Those who hold secrets can have power.[105] Consequently one must consider why the Republican Movement decided to give this information up, and why they agreed to do so when they did. Although, as explained previously, little academic research has been carried out into the 'disappeared' issue in Ireland, several scholars have suggested motivating factors. Dudai has proposed three reasons for the IRA's engagement in the 'disappeared' issue: compelling

99 'IRA's Secret Burials of Disappeared "Wrong and Unjust," says McLaughlin,' *Belfast Telegraph*, 17 April 2012.

100 'McConville Case – Gerry Adams Comments,' *An Phoblacht*, 23 March 2014.

101 Christine Bohan, 'Gerry Adams Arrested by Police Over Jean McConville's Murder,' *The Journal*, 30 April 2014, http://jrnl.ie/1442163 [accessed 7 August 2018].

102 Martin McGuinness in interview with Marian Finucane, n 59.

103 Dempster, n 42.

104 Jay Winter, 'Thinking About Silence,' in Efrat Ben-Ze'ev, Ruth Ginio and Jay Winter (eds) *Shadows of War: A Social History of Silence in the Twentieth Century* (Cambridge: Cambridge University Press, 2010), pp. 3–31 (p. 24).

105 Of their experience of researching in South Africa, Foster et al. write: 'there is no place in which silence and secrets have greater currency than the arena of violence. Around violence, people in general and perpetrators in particular most frequently prefer to maintain silence. Secrets acquire value … the more one party wants to acquire the information, the greater its value. Because of its value, secret-holders have some power' (Don Foster, Paul Haupt and Marésa De Beer, *The Theatre of Violence: Narratives of Protagonists in the South African Conflict* (Cape Town: Institution of Justice and Reconciliation, 2005), p. 93).

pressure from the outside, a willingness to admit this form of response to informing was wrong, and the ability to do something concrete about it.[106] With regards the latter, Campbell and Connolly have argued for three key messages in the IRA's approach to the issue: (i) aimed at the families, a demonstration of their dedication to locating remains, (ii) a broader attempt at self-cleansing and atonement, and (iii) showing that the IRA can be effective in delivering on transitional justice processes.[107] These suggestions will be considered in light of the arguments presented in this section.

3.1. Timeline of Republican Engagement

In the aftermath of the 'disappearances,' although (as will be explored in Chapter 4) rumours and whispers circulated, the 'Movement' remained officially silent, and attempts by families to approach Republicans for information proved futile. One mother spoke of how "the IRA denied involvement for years and continually lied."[108] In most cases, this silence continued for at least 20 years. As Chapter 6 will explore, as no form of truth recovery process yet exists, any sort of full disclosure of the circumstances surrounding the 'disappearances' themselves is absent. The 'boundaries of silence'[109] have therefore been shifted, but not removed entirely.

During the earliest years of the families' campaign, a number of Republicans continued to deny knowledge of the practice of 'disappearing.' In 1995, a Sinn Féin spokeswoman said, "Sinn Féin knows nothing about these people"[110] and Sinn Féin councillor Joe Austin stated: "I don't know where the bodies are and in many of the cases, it doesn't appear that anyone knows who is responsible for these disappearances."[111] Alex Maskey, a Sinn Féin councillor and cousin of John McClory, refused to comment on the case in 1995 and acted "like a stranger" to his aunt (John's mother), Mary McClory.[112] Maskey's response at this time changed rapidly. On July 8, he refused to comment, telling the *Belfast Telegraph* he "wouldn't be interested in talking about it."[113] On July 14, he spoke out on the families' "right to know what has happened," and described how he had, "over the years ... privately sought information about my cousin John McClory." Mrs McClory – mother of John – remarked in response: "It is great to hear he is now working for us – maybe his conscience has pricked him ... he says he has been seeking information ... but he has never come forward or called at the house."[114] In June 1998, prior to the IRA

106 Dudai, n 3.
107 Colm Campbell and Ita Connolly, 'The Sharp End: Armed Opposition Movements, Transitional Truth Processes and the *Rechtsstaat*,' *International Journal of Transitional Justice*, 6:1, (2012), 11–39.
108 Suzanne Breen, 'For Victims, Deeds Speak Louder than Words,' *The Irish Times*, 18 July 2002.
109 Winter, n 104 at 24.
110 Tanya Acheson, 'End Families' Torment,' *Belfast Telegraph*, 9 August 1995.
111 Tanya Acheson, 'Family Asks Clinton to Help Find Bodies,' *Belfast Telegraph*, 12 May 1995.
112 Denis Campbell 'Let Them Rest in Peace,' *Scotland on Sunday*, 9 July 1995.
113 Tanya Acheson, 'Maskey's Cousin Murdered by IRA,' *Belfast Telegraph*, 8 July 1995.
114 Tanya Acheson, 'Maskey Speaks Out on Disappeared,' *Belfast Telegraph*, 14 July 1995.

revealing that it was carrying out an internal investigation, Adams' responses remained ambiguous (emphasis author's own): "*if* people are missing, *if* they have been killed, that information should go to the families."[115] Winter proposes that 'catalysts' are required to change the 'boundaries of silence.'[116] The latter parts of this section will explore what these catalysts may have been for the Republican Movement. It should of course be noted that Sinn Féin's denial of knowledge might have been rooted in the truth – at least for some. Danny Morrison has argued that "most Republicans" were not aware that these 'disappearances' had taken place:

> I was interned in November 1972, and Jean McConville went missing in December '72. And people from the Falls area ... people would have been coming in, being interned from that area, and yet I never heard of this woman until 20, maybe 25 years later, when it became public knowledge ... And yet there is a tendency among some people to loose talk, and yet I was never aware of that case, and I think that that was probably the same for most Republicans in the Movement unless they had been intimately involved in those incidents.[117]

On the part of the IRA, as noted earlier, one of the first public comments came in an *An Phoblacht* interview published in September 1998, in which an IRA spokesperson admitted that the IRA was 'responsible for the execution and burial of a small number of people.'[118] This acknowledgment came decades after the 'disappearances' themselves, and almost four years after Jean McConville's daughter, Helen McKendry, went public about her family's campaign to find her mother's remains in a Radio Ulster *Talkback* interview in December 1994.[119] In the same *An Phoblacht* interview the IRA spokesperson explained that an internal investigation was under way into the location of the burial sites.[120] An official statement to a similar effect was issued in December 1998.[121] Following the 1998 admission by the IRA, and specifically the acknowledgement, apology, and list of 'disappeared' released in March 1999, events unfolded quickly, with the passing of legislation on the Location of Victims' Remains (see Chapter 5) and formation of the ICLVR leading to heightened expectations of the rapid recovery of the remains of the victims, with newspapers claiming that the remains were 'expected to be recovered within weeks'[122] or even days.[123]

115 Jim Cusack, 'Gardai Are "Hopeful" of IRA Moves on "Disappeared" as Adams Urges End to Tragedy,' *The Irish Times*, 27 June 1998.
116 Winter, n 104 at 24.
117 Interview, Danny Morrison, January 2015.
118 'Omagh Bomb Group Must Disband – IRA. Push Now to Fulfil Potential of Good Friday Document,' *An Phoblacht*, 3 September 1998.
119 Seamus McKendry, *Disappeared: The Search for Jean McConville* (Dublin: Blackwater Press, 2000).
120 'Omagh Bomb Group Must Disband,' n 118.
121 'IRA Continues Search for Missing Bodies,' *An Phoblacht*, 10 December 1998.
122 Chris Thornton, 'Missing Bodies Located "Soon",' *Belfast Telegraph*, 31 August 1998.
123 Darwin Templeton, Martin Breen, and Michael Devine, 'Peace at Last,' *Belfast Telegraph*, 28 May 1999; Jim Cusack, 'Eight More Bodies Expected to be Found Over Weekend,' *The Irish Times*, 29 May 1999.

On the day the LVR legislation came into force, the remains of Eamonn Molloy were left in a coffin in a cemetery at Faughart, Co. Louth. But, the assertion in the 1999 statement, that the 'whereabouts' of the burial sites of nine individuals had been 'established,'[124] did not fully capture the realities of what would be a complex and time consuming search process. After the retrieval of Molloy's remains, it was another month before the remains of John McClory and Brian McKinney were recovered. Although the IRA statement of March 1999 stated that their inquiry had concluded,[125] in June 1999, despite insistence by the IRA that it had given over all information,[126] and reinforcement of this statement by Gerry Adams[127] and Martin McGuinness,[128] this claim was criticised by victims' families,[129] and journalists started to question the sincerity of the IRA's engagement in the process.[130]

Months and years passed, and expectations of prompt recovery proved to be overly ambitious. In 2003 the remains of Jean McConville were accidentally found by a passer-by, although this came after an IRA 'review' of the information they had previously provided to the ICLVR.[131] Similarly, with regards the body of Gerry Evans, recovered in 2010, 'no new information had been provided … but there may have been a clarification of the original information.'[132] Furthermore, despite the insistence that those individuals named in the March 1999 statement were the only cases for which the IRA was responsible[133] (a statement that was repeated in 2003),[134] by 2013, Adams referred to 13 cases for which the IRA had acknowledged responsibility.[135] The cases of Joe Lynskey,[136] Peter Wilson,[137] and Eugene Simons[138] were added to the ICLVR's list.

124 'IRA Investigation Locates Grave Sites,' n 7.
125 Ibid.
126 'Hope Remains for Return of Missing Bodies,' *An Phoblacht*, 3 June 1999.
127 Michael O'Toole and Liz Trainor, 'Search Yields Only Despair,' *The Irish News*, 1 June 1999.
128 Sharon O'Neil, 'Adams is Accused of Justifying Deaths,' *The Irish News*, 1 June 1999.
129 Deaglan de Bréadún and Clare Murphy, 'IRA Claim That it Has no Further Information Criticised,' *The Irish Times*, 2 June 1999.
130 Mary Holland, 'IRA Gesture on Missing Persons Has Gone Badly Wrong,' *The Irish Times*, 3 June 1999.
131 'Remains Located After IRA Review,' *An Phoblacht*, 4 September 2003.
132 'Family Waits After Remains Found in "Disappeared" Dig,' *Belfast Telegraph*, 16 October 2010.
133 'IRA Investigation Locates Grave Sites,' n 7.
134 'Remains Located After IRA Review,' n 131.
135 'Gerry Adams Appeals for Information on Victims Secretly Buried by the IRA,' *An Phoblacht*, 21 June 2013.
136 'Investigation Confirms 1972 Disappearance,' n 7.
137 Allison Morris, 'Exclusive – "Secret" IRA Victim on Disappeared List,' *The Irish News*, 30 October 2009. It should be noted that a senior Republican source has said that Peter Wilson was not killed by the IRA (Introduction, footnote 52)
138 See Introduction, footnote 52.

Once responsibility for the 'disappearances' was acknowledged, the need became one of displaying the continued commitment of the IRA to finding the remains (rather than a one-off effort), through proving that accurate information had been given. The need to find remains is of course vital to the families of victims, but simultaneously, recovery of the bodies also became important to prove the ***bona fides*** of the IRA and Republican Movement more broadly. Without remains being recovered, the veracity of the IRA's information would remain in doubt. As Adams remarked with regards the recovery of Danny McIlhone's remains, this was "evidence that republicans consider this issue a priority and continue to work diligently."[139] Each body recovered not only brings some comfort to the family, but is also tangible evidence of the IRA's commitment to the search. The gradual emergence of information, combined with media coverage of unsuccessful searches, resulted in expressions of doubt from some families, and Sinn Fein's political opponents, accusing the IRA of withholding, or providing inaccurate, information[140]

3.2. Internal factors and the timing of Republican engagement

Arguments for internal factors motivating Republicans to engage in the search process broadly fall into two categories: political and ethical.

Politically, there is a sense that the Republican leadership had to address demands coming from its own constituency. That the 'disappeared' were in many cases from Republican communities may have been a motivating factor for the 'Movement.' English proposed that "because it's intra-communal, because it's about Catholics, it's a way of saying to your own community, actually we realised this was a human rights violation."[141] When the pressure to return remains is coming from within the Republican constituency, Dudai suggests, it's difficult to ignore or dismiss as propaganda on the part of the state.[142]

Republicans also needed something with which to bargain. As English argued:

> If Republicans are going to say, 'we want to be treated this way and this way and this way in the reform of the North,' people say 'well come on, you've got to give us something, and this is something you can give.'[143]

The 'disappeared' were something the IRA could 'give' that strengthened the negotiating hand of Sinn Féin, while simultaneously doing something positive for

139 'Gerry Adams Welcomes Discovery of Remains in Wicklow,' *An Phoblacht*, 13 November 2008.

140 See e.g. Noel McAdam, 'Durkan in Renewed Call to IRA for Bodies,' *Belfast Telegraph*, 29 December 2004; Northern Ireland Assembly Debates (NIA Deb)16 April 2012, vol 74A, pp. 17–25; Sharon O'Neill and Maeve Connolly, 'Victims' Families Pour Scorn on IRA Apology,' *The Irish News*, 25 October 2003.

141 Interview, Richard English, August 2014.

142 Dudai, n 3.

143 Interview, Richard English, August 2014.

families from the Republican community. Of course, these political motivations did not go unnoticed by families, and Columba McVeigh's brother, Eugene, described how this issue "became … one of the boxes to be ticked."[144]

One ex-combatant interviewed denies that the motivations were political: "Republicans weren't doing it for … any reason other than to help the families concerned to get closure."[145] Indeed, Dudai has proposed that the return of the 'disappeared' was a demonstration of the IRA's willingness to admit this form of response to informing was wrong.[146] In a similar vein, as noted earlier, Campbell and Connolly suggest it is an attempt at self-cleansing and atonement.[147]

The debacle over the body of Patrick Duffy[148] demonstrated that even contemporaneously, Republicans questioned the legitimacy of 'disappearing.' For Derry Republican, Mickey Donnelly, it was "anathema to our principles."[149] Billy McKee has said with relation to Jean McConville: "I wouldn't have buried her. I would have executed her alright, no problem, but I would not have buried her."[150] Of this same case, Danny Morrison remarked: "it was wrong, it was a disaster, and it was the wrong response."[151]

One aspect on which several interviewees (both Republican and non-Republican) agree is that, internally, there was an ethical or moral sense that something had to be done. Veteran human rights activist, Mike Ritchie, in considering the potential political motivations, suggested that, "the decision was taken in good faith … to try and resolve this, and resolve it for families."[152] Brendan Megraw's brother, Kieran, although recognising the potential political motivations behind Republican engagement in the search, shared this view:

> I'd say probably the vast majority [of Republicans] for this process of the 'disappeared' feel like it was a wrong thing to be done. And the vast majority would say that, whether it was publicly or privately … I think the vast majority of them were … hoping that the bodies would be recovered and brought back again because … a Christian burial is so important in our culture and our country … And again we might never find that bit out but I think the vast

144 Interview, Eugene McVeigh, brother of Columba McVeigh, August 2015.
145 Interview, senior Republican ex-combatant, April 2015.
146 Dudai, n 3.
147 Campbell and Connolly, n 107.
148 See n 59.
149 Breen, n 59.
150 Jim Cusack, 'The IRA's "Disappeared" Return to Haunt Adams,' *Irish Independent*, 3 November 2013. It should be pointed out that McKee is an outspoken critic of Adams, especially his denial of IRA membership. In fact, in an interview two years previously he commented of McConville, 'If there was some reason to hand her body over … then all right but if there was some reason to bury her somewhere then I'd have done that too' ('Adams' IRA Denial is a Joke, Says Ex-Provo,' n 98).
151 Interview, Danny Morrison, January 2015.
152 Interview, Mike Ritchie, October 2014.

majority of Republicans, whether they were still involved or not, were keen to see that the bodies were recovered.[153]

This sense that 'disappearing' was wrong speaks to something beyond morality, reinforcing the notion that a level of organisational embarrassment existed about the perpetration of these acts (see above). Geoff Knupfer, Senior Investigating Officer (SIO) of the ICLVR has said, "I think there's huge embarrassment … within the Republican Movement. I think everybody accepts that it was a grievous wrong to do what they did."[154] The language used by Republican leaders, notoriously careful about terminology, is also quite instructive. Gerry Adams has described it as a "wrong" that must be put "right,"[155] and Martin McGuinness has said 'disappearing' was "one of the worst things that ever happened" during the conflict.[156] As one interviewee suggested, it was the leadership's decision to act that ultimately motivated movement on this issue:

> I think genuinely there is an embarrassment in the Republican Movement … I've never heard anyone justify the practice … Even in pretty hard bitten ex-combatant work … [about] the gritty end of violence – I've never heard anyone try to justify this … they were embarrassed as an organisation and it's a shameful period in Irish Republican history. So their line will be [regarding cooperation with the ICLVR]: we didn't get much credit for it, but then we didn't do it for the credit. We did it because it was the right thing to do. And they were embarrassed. So it wasn't just that they were being moral – they ignored the pleas of the families for years and lied to them and all of that. But I think once – it's like any other big institution – once the leadership directed: we are going to engage and we are going to do this properly, broadly, that happened.[157]

There is of course a point where these motivations intertwine. One interviewee contended:

> The nature of making peace means also trying to undo wrongs where it is within your competence or your ability to do that … if we can do anything about undoing that pain and suffering … then there's a moral and a political responsibility on political leaders to do so.[158]

153 Interview, Kieran Megraw, October 2015.
154 Interview, Geoff Knupfer, July 2014.
155 Noel McAdam, 'Pressure Steps Up On Disappeared,' *Belfast Telegraph*, 4 August 2006.
156 Martin McGuinness in interview with Marian Finucane, n 59.
157 Interview, community activist with over 20 years' experience working with ex-combatants, October 2015.
158 Interview, Sinn Féin's Declan Kearney, April 2015.

3.3. External pressures and the timing of Republican engagement

As mentioned, one of the suggestions given by Dudai as to why the Republican Movement involved themselves in the search for victims was compelling pressure from the outside.[159] This pressure came from victims' families and the wider political process. Of the Republican motivation for engaging in this issue, one DUP (Democratic Unionist Party) MP remarked:

> They are not immune to public opinion … I think that they recognised that the families were heavily influencing public opinion … and in Sinn Féin's desire to rehabilitate itself, in Sinn Féin's desire to move from being associated with a violent, armed, terrorist organisation to being recognised as a proper political party, they understood that this was one of the things that they needed to do, this was one of the things they needed to address.[160]

The campaign by victims' families was analysed in Chapter 2. As argued, the significance of their campaign cannot be underestimated; however, as has been highlighted, families speaking out about their experiences did not immediately motivate a response of acknowledgement from the Republican Movement. This would suggest that other factors had a part to play.

The continuation of some violence after a formal peace process has been established is not unusual. Northern Ireland was no different in this respect and paramilitary violence and low-level disorder at sectarian interfaces has continued.[161] In the aftermath of the Good Friday Agreement, three specific issues regularly and repeatedly came into contention with regards the 'end' of violence: 'punishment' attacks, the decommissioning of weapons, and the 'disappeared.' In reviewing the various local and national newspapers during these years, huge space is given over to coverage of these three issues, all of which speak to some extent about the seriousness or not of Republicanism in ending the armed struggle.

With regard to 'punishment' attacks, individuals would be beaten or shot as 'punishment' for involvement in drug-dealing, criminal activity, or 'anti-social behaviour,' or for other behaviour deemed an infraction by the different paramilitary groupings (including breaches of organisational discipline). Such attacks actually increased in both frequency and ferocity after the ceasefires.[162] Although in more recent years, these attacks have been associated more with Loyalist paramilitaries, in the years immediately following the ceasefires, around 60% of punishment beatings were attributed to Republican

159 Dudai, n 3.

160 Interview, Jeffrey Donaldson, March 2015.

161 Neil Jarman, 'From War to Peace? Changing Patterns of Violence in Northern Ireland, 1990–2003,' *Terrorism and Political Violence*, 16:3, (2004), 420–438.

162 Rachel Monaghan, '"An Imperfect Peace": Paramilitary "Punishments" in Northern Ireland,' *Terrorism and Political Violence*, 16:3, (2004), 439–461; Andrew Silke, 'Rebel's Dilemma: The Changing Relationship Between the IRA, Sinn Féin and Paramilitary Vigiliantism in Northern Ireland,' *Terrorism and Political Violence*, 11:1, (1999), 55–93; Jarman, ibid.

groups.[163] While punishment beatings have been described, inwardly, as unpopular with many members of the IRA and of Sinn Féin,[164] and, outwardly, as "an embarrassment and a political obstacle" to Republicans,[165] the appropriate leadership response to the issue was not clear-cut. From the perspectives of the perpetrators, punishment attacks were a form of 'policing' rather than military action that might contravene the ceasefires.[166] Consideration had to be given also to the existence of some support for such punishment at a local level, within the wider constituency.[167] In those communities where the Royal Ulster Constabulary's (RUC's) legitimacy was in doubt (examined further in Chapter 4), an alternative response to criminal or anti-social behaviour was considered by some to be necessary.[168] Continued involvement of Republicans in 'punishment' violence threatened wider ambitions of Sinn Féin development in the post-ceasefire period,[169] and the issue of 'punishment' beatings was included in both Kenneth Bloomfield's 1998 *Report of the Northern Ireland Victims Commissioner* [170] and the 1996 *Report of the International Body on Arms Decommissioning* (also known as the Mitchell Report)[171] as an area that required attention. That they continued, alongside other forms of paramilitary violence, cast doubt on the commitment of paramilitary organisations to the ceasefires. This in turn raised questions on the ability, and desire, of political parties to put a stop to this behaviour within paramilitary groups with which they were associated.[172]

The decommissioning of weapons has been described as following a similar pattern to the process for locating victims' remains. Both arrangements involved an Ireland–UK agreement, and domestic legislation in each state created dedicated institutions and provided partial amnesty (or limited immunity, in the case of the ICLVR).[173] Decommissioning became one of the 'hurdles' of the peace process, with the lack of decommissioning of IRA weapons proving a point of contention. The Ulster Unionist Party (UUP) was reluctant to enter into government with Sinn Féin without movement on the issue, while at the same time the SDLP was refusing to enter government without Sinn Féin.[174] As with punishment attacks,

163 Jarman, n 161.
164 Silke, n 162.
165 Alban Maginness (SDLP), quoted in 'Republican Shootings Halted "by September 11th",' *The Irish News*, 16 November 2001.
166 Kieran McEvoy and Harry Mika, 'Restorative Justice and the Critique of Informalism in Northern Ireland,' *The British Journal of Criminology*, 42:3, (2002), 534–462.
167 Jarman, n 161; Silke, n 162.
168 McEvoy and Mika, n 166.
169 Silke, n 162.
170 Kenneth Bloomfield, *"We Will Remember Them": Report of the Northern Ireland Victims Commissioner* (Belfast: HMSO, 1998).
171 International Body on the Decommissioning of Arms, *Report of the International Body on Arms Decommissioning*, 22 January 1996.
172 Monaghan, n 162.
173 Campbell and Connolly, n 107.
174 Eamonn O'Kane, 'The Perpetual Peace Process? Examining Northern Ireland's Neverending but Fundamentally Altering Peace Process,' *Irish Political Studies*, 4, (2013), 515–535.

this was seen as an issue that required movement in order to demonstrate the IRA's commitment to the peace process and democratic politics.[175]

To complete this triumvirate of issues, local, national, and international pressure increased on the Republican Movement to make progress on the 'disappeared' issue. The 'disappeared' were also referred to in the Bloomfield[176] and Mitchell[177] Reports and the issue was raised in the House of Commons.[178] Perhaps more significantly for Sinn Féin, the issue was presented on an international stage in May 1995 when President Clinton, during his address to the Washington Economic Conference, remarked, "many innocents disappeared during the troubles ... Today their families have still not had the chance to grieve in peace, to visit the graves of their loved ones."[179] As examined in Chapter 2, the families' success in having this included in the President's speech was quite a coup, especially because of the potential influence on the Republican Movement, due to the importance of the relationship between Irish Republicans and the USA.[180]

An additional motivation may have been the publicity surrounding the National Graves Association (NGA) in 1995,[181] and in particular on two news items that highlighted how contradictory Republican attitudes towards burial practice could be. Featured in *The Irish News* on consecutive days, the first is a story about the body of Tom Williams, an IRA member buried at Crumlin Road jail following his execution in 1942. The NGA was campaigning to have his remains exhumed and reinterred in the Republican plot at Milltown cemetery.[182] The story on the second day concerned the NGA's backing of the Families of the Disappeared's campaign.[183] Media attention on both these cases indicated the contrast between Republican campaigning for the moving of a body of one of their own to the burial location of their choice, and a number of other families, some of whom are also of a Republican background, not knowing where their loved ones are buried at all. Mary McClory drew attention to this contradiction in an early newspaper interview. With regards to the lack of help she had received from the Republican Movement, she said: "they're always going on to the Brits about the sanctity

175 Roger MacGinty, 'American Influences on the Northern Ireland Peace Process,' *Journal of Conflict Studies*, 17:2, (1997).
176 Bloomfield, n 170.
177 International Body on the Decommissioning of Arms, n 171.
178 'Questions on IRA Victims,' *The Irish News*, 24 May 1995.
179 'Clinton Address to Washington Economic Conference,' *The Irish News*, 26 May 1995.
180 MacGinty, n 175.
181 Originating in Dublin as a Memorial Committee for the 1867 Fenian Rising, the NGA is usually viewed as a very traditional element of the broader Republican Movement. Thus, their support for the families of those who were 'disappeared' is significant (see National Graves Association, 'A Brief History of the National Graves Association,' www.nga.ie/history.php [accessed 7 August 2018]).
182 Brendan Anderson, 'Fresh Hope for IRA Re-burial,' *The Irish News*, 22 June 1995.
183 Gerard Millar, 'Graves Group Backs Families Search,' *The Irish News*, 23 June 1995.

of the bodies of their people who've died and how they shouldn't be left in prison graves."[184]

3.4. The 'disappeared' as a symbol of transitioning Republicanism

As has been described, these tangible remnants of IRA violence – 'punishment' attacks, weapons, and the (at that time) unfound bodies of the 'disappeared' – became obstacles during the peace process, particularly in relation to the formation and operation of a power-sharing assembly, as they cast doubt on the commitment of the Republican Movement to the peace process. As was remarked at the time, it would have been "hypocritical [for Sinn Féin] to expect the status of a full democratic party while the issue of the missing bodies of IRA victims remains unresolved."[185] A willingness to co-operate was needed on these issues to enable political progress, and with regards the 'disappeared,' local and international pressure combined with the need to compromise on key issues and the internal factors examined previously provided the motivation necessary for Republican involvement.

There were both push and pull factors for Republicans. As English has summarised, "at its best it's part of maybe showing that they're wanting to engage in a different way. At its worst it's that they couldn't have gone on saying nothing about it."[186] When IRA decommissioning did begin, one observer suggested to Fionnuala O'Connor that it was 'a kind of formal confirmation that a phase has been left behind.'[187] The same can be said of locating the 'disappeared.' In a way, returning the bodies of those it 'disappeared' was part of the process of the IRA dismantling its apparatus of conflict. In 1995, IRA sources had allegedly linked the return of the bodies to the end of conflict and development of the peace process. Father Denis Faul reported that when he made inquiries of the IRA following the abduction of Thomas Niedermayer,[188] he was told "the body would be returned at the end of the war."[189] With regards those who became known as the 'disappeared,' Republican sources told *Scotland on Sunday* in

184 Suzanne Breen, 'Missing Presumed Dead,' *The Irish Times*, 13 August 1994.

185 Fabian Boyle, '"Disappeared" Families Lash Sinn Féin,' *The Irish News*, 26 June 1995.

186 Interview, Richard English, August 2014.

187 Fionnuala O'Connor, *Breaking the Bonds: Making Peace in Northern Ireland* (Edinburgh: Mainstream Publishing, 2002), p. 49.

188 Thomas Niedermayer managed the Grundig plant in Dunmurry, on the outskirts of Belfast. He was abducted from his home in Belfast on 27 December 1973. His remains were found buried in a shallow grave at Colinglen, Belfast, in March 1980. Three men were charged with involvement in Neidermayer's killing and with IRA membership, one of whom – John Christopher Bradley – was sentenced to 20 years for his manslaughter ('Abducted German Declared Dead,' *The Irish Times*, 11 August 1976; 'Appeal to Kidnappers of German,' *The Irish Times*, 5 January 1974; 'Body may be Niedermayer's,' *The Irish Times*, 12 March 1980; 'Grundig Chief: Wife's Appeal,' *Belfast Telegraph*, 4 January 1974; David McKittrick, 'Britain Admits Threat to Kill Niedermayer Received,' *The Irish Times*, 29 January 1974; McKittrick et al., n 1; 'Niedermayer Kidnapper Sentenced to 20 Years,' *The Irish News*, 17 February 1981; 'Niedermayer: The Last Hours,' *Belfast Telegraph*, 16 February 1981).

189 Tanya Acheson, 'End Silence Over Dead and Let Us Mourn in Peace,' *Belfast Telegraph*, 28 April 1995.

September 1995 that graves would be located but not "in the current political climate – where the British seem to be hell-bent on pursuing an IRA surrender."[190] Republican Sinn Féin president, Ruari O'Bradaigh said in August 1998, "the impression I get [from veteran Republicans] is that when the conflict is finally over and the British Government leave Ireland for good the bodies will be handed back to the families."[191] One Republican ex-combatant told me that Republicans became involved in the search process because: "Republicans always realised that … whenever the war is over, whenever the conflict ends, you have to begin the process of healing the wounds … there was always going to be a willingness to help bring closure, where closure was needed."[192]

Locating the 'disappeared' demonstrated the leaving behind of violent conflict, and served as a symbol of Republican commitment to the peace process. Unlike punishment beatings, or perhaps even unlike putting weapons beyond use, returning the body of a 'disappeared' victim to their family has, in a sense, a permanence attached to it. Of course, as examined in Chapter 1, to focus on one thing silences something else.[193] For journalist Malachi O'Doherty:

> It enables them now to say, 'look we do make an effort,' but … there's … various other things that they don't admit they did. But they can get away with all that in a sense, by bringing the thing to focus on one emblematic issue, like the 'disappeared.' And show some good faith in that, you know.[194]

The return of the remains suggested that the Republican Movement was now playing by different rules, and operating under an amended value system by suggesting that something that was once, in their view, right, is no longer appropriate. Barker has written of the need for 'public displays of legitimation.'[195] Participating in the search for the remains of those it 'disappeared' can be read as an attempt by Republicans to demonstrate publicly their legitimacy as a movement now dedicated to peaceful political means. Many of those 'executed' as informers were left in public, their bodies a symbol of the legitimacy of the killing.[196] 'Disappearing' was, for some, another legitimate response

190 Denis Campbell, 'IRA Makes Pledge to Give Up Bodies of the "Disappeared",' *Scotland on Sunday*, 3 September 1995; Marie Foy, 'New Appeal on "Disappeared",' *Belfast Telegraph*, 4 September 1995.

191 'IRA Murder Victims "Buried in Donegal": Gardai Pass New Lead to Families of Disappeared,' *Belfast Telegraph*, 11 August 1998. This comment from O'Bradaigh could, it should be noted, reflect a lack of desire to engage with the issue in any significant way.

192 Interview, senior Republican ex-combatant, April 2015.

193 Michel-Rolph Trouillot, *Silencing the Past: Power and the Production of History* (Boston: Beacon Press, 1995).

194 Interview, Malachi O'Doherty, August 2015.

195 Rodney S. Barker, *Legitimating Identities: The Self-Presentation of Rulers and Subjects* (Cambridge: Cambridge University Press, 2001), p. 107; James H. Liu and Denis J. Hilton, 'How the Past Weighs on the Present: Social Representations of History and Their Role in Identity Politics,' *British Journal of Social Psychology*, 44, (2005), 537–556.

196 Wilson, n 5.

during a time of conflict. Attempting to locate the bodies signified that keeping the burial locations secret was not a legitimate action in a time of peace.

4. Resolving the 'disappeared': the role of leadership

The exercise of leadership is a key element in the process of recovering remains. In broad terms, the importance of leadership both in the context of conflict and transition cannot be over-stated.[197] Leadership expresses, shapes, and curbs conflict; it can be both an inciting force and one of mediation.[198] One of the more frequently cited leadership scholars, Burns, proposes that 'leadership over human beings is exercised when persons with certain motives and purposes mobilise, in competition or conflict with others, institutional, political, psychological, and other resources so as to arouse, engage, and satisfy the motives of followers.'[199]

For Burns,[200] and others,[201] leadership is multi-dimensional and dynamic. It can be influenced and constrained by followers, opponents, and the wider political context. Leadership has played a dominant role in the transition from conflict in Northern Ireland. Indeed, O'Connor argues that the personalities of leaders have 'mattered more, perhaps, than they ought.'[202] The leadership of a movement that was involved both directly in violence and in politics can be expected to be one that must be multifaceted in nature. Given the shift from being at the forefront of conflict to being at the forefront of the drive for peace, these facets may at times seem paradoxical.

In movements that pursue a dual strategy of military and political activity, the leadership risks becoming a 'prisoner of the political strategy it has adopted' and thus losing credibility, support, and members.[203] In Northern Ireland, the Republican Movement during the transitional period has, on the whole, avoided

197 See e.g. Michael Colaresi, 'When Doves Cry: International Rivalry, Unreciprocated Cooperation, and Leadership Turnover,' *American Journal of Political Science*, 48:3, (2004), 555–570; Betty Glad, 'Passing the Baton: Transformational Political Leadership from Gorbachev to Yeltsin; from de Klerk to Mandela,' *Political Psychology*, 17:1, (1996), 1–28; Cathy Gormley-Heenan, 'Chameleonic Leadership: Towards a New Understanding of Political Leadership During the Northern Ireland Peace Process,' *Leadership*, 2:1, (2006), 53–75; Louis Kriesberg, 'Transforming Conflicts in the Middle East and Europe,' in Louis Kriesberg, Terrell A. Northrup and Stuart J. Thorson (eds) *Intractable Conflicts and Their Transformation* (New York: Syracuse University Press, 1989), 109–131; Stephen John Stedman, *Peacemaking in Civil War: International Mediation in Zimbabwe, 1974–1980* (London: Lynne Rienner Publishers, Inc., 1991).

198 James MacGregor Burns, *Leadership* (New York: Harper & Row, 1978), pp. 37–38.

199 Ibid. at 18.

200 Ibid.

201 Jean Blondel, Jean-Louis Thiébault with Katarzyna Czernica, Takashi Inoguchi, Ukrist Pathmanand and Fulvio Venturino, *Political Leadership, Parties and Citizens: The Personalisation of Leadership* (Abingdon: Routledge, 2010); Robert Elgie, *Political Leadership in Liberal Democracies* (Basingstoke; London: Macmillan Press Ltd., 1995).

202 O'Connor, n 187 at 11.

203 Irvin, n 8 at 23.

such risks. The challenge for the Sinn Féin leadership was 'to sell a new strategy to the wider movement without appearing to sell out traditional republicanism.'[204] Splits were expected, as Sinn Féin had to make an agreement that many within their constituency were not happy with (as with the leaders of other parties during the peace process),[205] and from the perspective of Adams and McGuinness, had to be avoided.[206] Adams has recounted: 'One of our goals in the peace process was to keep republicans united ... the first thing on any republican agenda is the split.'[207] It was essential that the Republican Movement 'move away from violence ... as a unified coherent entity. At all costs ... splits ... had to be averted.'[208] Splits had damaged the 'Movement' in the past,[209] and were a risk during transition; however, they did not happen to the extent predicted.[210] That the majority of Republicans did stay on side as the 'Movement' charted a new path, Ruane contends, is a result of the demonstration of 'formidable political skills' on the part of the leadership.[211] Tony Blair describes how 'throughout, Gerry and Martin feared a split, as had happened before to Republicanism, with disastrous consequences. This meant taking their people step-by-step, leading them, cajoling them ... it was a tough task and they performed it with immense skill.'[212]

As has been set out previously, the challenge with regards the 'disappeared' involved not only holding on to Republican support, but persuading political opponents and the wider public that their involvement in the search process was genuine, and would produce results. The satisfaction of one audience was then dependent on the other. If those Republicans with information that may assist the search came forward, the likelihood of recovering remains would increase, and therefore, at least on paper, this should satisfy (insofar as locating the body of a 'disappeared' person can 'satisfy') a wider audience. The success of the return of the 'disappeared' as a political 'move' depended on the co-operation of those former combatants with knowledge of 'disappearing.'

4.1. Political leadership and the 'disappeared'

A central aspect of political leadership is how individuals in positions of authority can influence the outcome of a decision-making process.[213] In a transitional context, a leader's role is two-fold. On the one hand, a leader is concerned with his or

204 Paul Dixon, 'Political Skills or Lying and Manipulation? The Choreography of the Northern Ireland Peace Process,' *Political Studies*, 50:4, (2002), 725–741 (p. 728).
205 Gormley-Heenan, n 197.
206 Adams, n 8.
207 Adams, ibid. at 317.
208 Mallie and McKittrick, n 8 at 201–202.
209 Deaglán de Bréadún, n 8; Mallie and McKittrick, ibid.; Sanders, n 8.
210 Gormley-Heenan, n 197.
211 Joseph Ruane, 'Contemporary Republicanism and the Strategy of Armed Struggle,' in John Coakley (ed.) *From Political Violence to Negotiated Settlement: The Winding Path to Peace in Twentieth Century Ireland* (Dublin: UCD Press, 2004), p. 9.
212 Blair, n 8 at 197.
213 Elgie, n 201.

her external audience. They must consider the expectations of others,[214] and, for the leader of a revolutionary movement such as the Republican Movement, an additional concern is 'the role of public opinion in legitimating the revolutionary cause.'[215] On the other hand, a leader must consider his or her own position, in terms of their own interests, support base, and how these are to be managed, particularly if the movement departs in a new direction.[216] For Republican leaders like Gerry Adams, one might expect to see him attempting to generate external support, while ensuring that his position and that of other Republican leaders remained secure – in effect taking the 'Movement' with him. Needless to say, other actors such as the British and Irish governments also had a significant investment in ensuring that such efforts to maintain Republican cohesion were successful.

Adams, as the president of Sinn Féin, became a figurehead for the Republican Movement's position on the issue of the disappeared. His status as spokesperson was and is made additionally complicated because of, as will be discussed, the accusations made regarding Adams' alleged involvement in the 'disappearances' (specifically that of Jean McConville) which connect him to the issue in a more direct way. Considering this connection, one might have expected Adams to delegate the responsibility of spokesperson on this issue to someone else. In some ways Martin McGuinness was a more obvious spokesperson on this issue. Where Adams has been accused of involvement in the 'disappearance' of Jean McConville (see later), there is evidence, in the case of Patrick Duffy,[217] to suggest that Derry IRA actively disassociated itself from 'disappearing.' With the exception of an inaccuracy in a 2014 radio interview,[218] McGuinness' remarks regarding the 'disappeared' were arguably more consistently empathetic, and therefore might have carried more weight beyond

214 Gormley-Heenan, n 197.
215 Hannigan, n 8 at 31.
216 Burns, n 198; Gormley-Heenan, n 197.
217 See footnote 59.
218 In Interview with Marian Finucane in May 2014, McGuinness alleged that he was in Portlaoise prison at the time of Duffy's 'disappearance,' but on his release voiced his opposition to the secret burial of Duffy's remains. Following this, McGuinness claimed, Duffy's body was returned to his family. However, it emerged that the dates McGuinness provided were inaccurate, and at the time of Duffy's 'disappearance,' he was instead 'on the run' in the Republic. On the blogs of Anthony McIntyre (*The Pensive Quill*) and Ed Moloney (*The Broken Elbow*), an article was posted suggesting that McGuinness deliberately misled Finucane. McGuinness released a statement saying that his error in the date was genuine, and that he did voice opposition to Duffy's 'disappearance' ('Did Martin McGuinness Pull the Wool Over Marian Finucane's Eyes?' *The Broken Elbow*, 10 June 2014, http://thebrokenelbow.com/2014/06/10/did-martin-mcguinness-pull-the-wool-over-marian-finucanes-eyes/ [accessed 7 August 2018]; Martin McGuinness in interview with Marian Finucane, n 59; 'Martin McGuinness Misled Marian Finucane,' *The Pensive Quill*, 11 June 2014, http://thepensivequill.am/2014/06/martin-mcguinness-misled-marian-finucane.html [accessed 7 August 2018]; 'McGuinness Acknowledges Memory Lapse on Murder Date,' *The Newsletter*, 15 June 2014).

Republicanism given the broader respect that he has engendered in Northern Ireland over the transition. In a 2009 *Belfast Telegraph* poll McGuinness was voted the top-performing minister in the Northern Ireland executive, with 45% of Catholics and 11% of Protestants voting for him as the minister who had 'impressed them the most.'[219] However, Adams remained the main spokesperson. In his analysis of Adams as a leader, Bean outlines how, although Adams 'embodies the movement's essential characteristics,'[220] he largely remains above or outside of events. In the case of the 'disappeared,' and specifically with regards Jean McConville, any such distinction is blurred. In making himself spokesperson, Adams placed himself even more firmly in the firing line for criticism. In the next few paragraphs I outline several – at times overlapping and contradictory – reasons why Adams may have taken on this role of spokesperson.

One possibility is that Adams had little choice but to come to the fore. From the earliest headlines in 1995: 'Give Us Back Our Dead, Mr Adams,'[221] Adams became the Republican figure synonymous with the fate of the 'disappeared.' The counter argument to this of course is that, arguably, many more headlines exist linking Adams to the 'disappeared' because he took on this spokesperson role himself. It may also be the case that Adams is protecting his own constituency. A number of these people were from, and in some cases abducted from, west Belfast, some at a time when Adams is alleged to have been Belfast OC (Officer Commanding) of the IRA.[222] When the armalite had been abandoned in favour of the ballot box, this same area became Adams' 'fiefdom,'[223] where in 2001 he won 27,096 votes, 66% of the total. But again, one could argue, this might equally have motivated Adams to put distance between himself and these cases.

It is possible that Adams is trying to emphasise the importance of the issue for Republicanism. His rhetoric alludes to his taking personal responsibility for overseeing the Republican involvement in the search process. On the release of the Bloomfield Report in 1998, Adams commented that, "These people have a very, very genuine and just case … I don't make commitments lightly. I don't intend to let the issue go until it is resolved."[224] As time passed and bodies were not recovered as rapidly as had been expected, Adams gave more details on Republican engagement in the search process, in order to try and quell the criticism being directed at the Republican Movement. This included promoting the proactive behaviours of Sinn Féin, such as the introduction of the services of the forensic

219 'McGuinness: First Among Stormont's 14 Ministers,' *Belfast Telegraph*, 30 November 2009.
220 Bean, n 90 at 116.
221 Tanya Acheson, 'Give Us Back Our Dead, Mr Adams,' *Belfast Telegraph*, 28 April 1995.
222 Bowyer Bell, n 20; Moloney, n 4 and n 69.
223 O'Connor, n 187 at 18.
224 Kathryn Torney, 'Adams Pledge on "the Disappeared",' *Belfast Telegraph*, 13 May 1998.

expert,[225] and also giving more detail on the search process. Where early reports emphasised the work of 'intermediaries' between the Republican Movement and Commission, in later years Adams described how 'individuals with primary knowledge' were meeting directly with the Commission staff at the search sites.[226] Adams described this one-to-one engagement as "evidence of its [the IRA's] determination to right this wrong."[227]

It could be the case that as it's a highly sensitive issue, particularly for Adams himself, that he wants to manage and communicate the Republican response himself. Repeated accusations have been made regarding Adams' involvement in 'disappearances' specifically in relation to his alleged involvement in Jean McConville's death and subsequent secret burial. For example, Helen McKendry has called him a 'hypocrite,' remarking: 'Gerry Adams … hasn't come out and publicly apologised to our family … he refuses to admit his knowledge about my mother's disappearance. My mother will haunt him for the rest of his life.'[228]

The suspicions of Adams' guilt were fuelled further following allegations contained in the Boston College recordings,[229] in which Brendan Hughes speaks of Adams' direct involvement in giving the order for McConville to be 'disappeared.'[230] Following this, and allegations that Dolours Price also discussed the details of McConville's disappearance during her interviews for the project, the PSNI began a legal bid to access the tapes. In May 2014, Adams was arrested in connection to the 'disappearance' of Jean McConville.[231]

Despite repeated denials of involvement from Adams,[232] the political spectre of the McConville case continues to 'haunt' him, linking him to the conflict in a way that has

225 Gerry Adams, 'The Truth About the Disappeared,' *The Irish Times*, 9 November 2013; 'Republican Efforts Continue to Retrieve Missing Bodies,' *An Phoblacht*, 13 July 2006.
226 'Gerry Adams Welcomes Discovery of Remains in Wicklow,' n 139.
227 McAdam, n 155.
228 Catherine McCurry, 'Jean's Family Slam "Hypocrite" Adams Over Thatcher Apology,' *Belfast Telegraph*, 12 April 2013.
229 Boston College's 'Belfast Project' was an oral history project, directed by Ed Moloney, which involved interviews with former Republican and Loyalist combatants. The publication of Moloney's book (n 4) in 2011 which included extracts from an interview with Brendan Hughes (who died in 2008) naming Adams as having been connected to McConville's 'disappearance,' and the release of a documentary, combined with the publication of a *Sunday Life* article referring to Dolours Price's 'taped confessions' relating to the 'disappearance' of Jean McConville drew attention to the project and the 'potentially incriminating information' the Boston archive contained (Palys and Lowman 2012, 283). Subsequently, the interview recordings and transcripts became the subject of legal wrangling as two sets of subpoenas – initiated by the Police Service of Northern Ireland (PSNI) – were issued to Boston College (Ruan O'Donnell, 'Oral History and the Politics of the Troubles: The Boston College Tapes,' *History Ireland*, 20:2, (2012), 10–13; Ted Palys and John Lowman, 'Defending Research Confidentiality "To the Extent the Law Allows:" Lessons From the Boston College Subpoenas,' *Journal of Academic Ethics*, 10:4, (2012), 271–297).
230 Moloney, n 4.
231 'Gerry Adams Arrested by McConville Murder Police,' *Belfast Telegraph*, 1 May 2014.
232 See e.g. Noel McAdam, 'Minister Accuses Adams over IRA "missing",' *Belfast Telegraph*, 21 June 2005; Gerry Moriarty, 'Gerry Adams Questioned over McConville

thus far proven impossible to shake off. Allegations of Adams' involvement have been raised on multiple occasions in both the Dáil and Stormont, particularly in the aftermath of a 2013 documentary on the 'Disappeared.'[233] Although released without charge, his arrest again pushed his alleged association with the McConville case into the spotlight. Yet, the press conference he gave following his release provided an opportunity for him to refute, once again – and, given the level of international attention this story had received – to a global audience, the allegations made against him and to assert the efforts he has made to bring some sort of resolution to the affected families:

> Let me be very clear: I am innocent of any involvement in any conspiracy to abduct, kill, or bury Mrs McConville. I have worked hard with others to have this injustice redressed and for return of the bodies of others killed during the conflict and secretly buried by the IRA, and I will continue to do so.[234]

For one interviewee, Adams' performance at this press conference was "very interesting":

> It had the potential to be destabilising on the Republican Movement … It was a worldwide event … Gerry Adams being arrested was a very big deal … I thought his performance in the press conference afterwards was excellent: much tighter, much more robust and articulate and persuasive than he often is … I think Adams will have realised: they have nothing on me. This is a case that's been hanging over him for years … And … he was providing leadership, he was recommitting the Republican Movement to unarmed struggle and all of that, so it was a good moment for him.[235]

As spokesperson, Adams has had control over the Republican response. His role is pivotal, connecting both Sinn Féin's political response and the on-the-ground search process. As Sinn Féin's Declan Kearney suggested in interview:

> At the point in time where the Commission came into being, the IRA still existed. The IRA has now left the stage. So the Commission is entirely reliant now on the efforts of the Sinn Féin leadership to continue to say publicly and

Murder,' *Irish Times*, 1 May 2014; Adrian Rutherford and Steven McCaffery, 'Sinn Féin Chief Denies Involvement in Murder of McConville,' *Belfast Telegraph*, 30 March 2010.

233 See e.g. Dáil Éireann Debates (DE Deb) 27 November 2013, vol 822, no 4; NIA Deb 19 November 2013, vol 89, pp. 22–25 and 62–80. See also Chapter 6.

234 Gerry Adams speaking at a press conference following his release, accessed at 'The Release of Gerry Adams – Press Conference,' www.youtube.com/watch?v=qxcgDT8A4lQ [accessed 7 August 2018].

235 Interview, community activist with over 20 years' experience working with ex-combatants, October 2015.

> privately that it is an imperative that, if possible, the remains which have not been discovered, are recovered and returned to families.[236]

A further possibility, which links back to the importance of managing the Republican constituency, is that in making himself spokesperson Adams is maintaining a connection to these acts, and while not admitting any involvement, is also not turning his back on Republicanism's violent past. As explored earlier, demonstrating continuing loyalty to former combatants and their actions was a vital part of the Republican narrative surrounding the 'disappeared.' Irvin suggests that at a time of transition to increased political involvement, the leadership will strive to make public declarations of their commitment to revolutionary ideals, as this is a time when the identity of the organisation can be under threat.[237] Adams has emphasised his continued loyalty to those Republicans involved in the armed struggle. At the Easter Rising commemoration in 2010, speaking of the campaign of the 1960s and 1970s, Adams stated:

> We relied totally on the support of the people to protect us. And we, in turn, protected the people as best we could. We did not divulge their names, their roles, their actions. That is still my position ... let no one think that I will bend.[238]

With regards the 'disappeared,' remarks such as that describing Eamonn Molloy as "an informer and that is something which is reviled in all aspects of society on this island"[239] demonstrate this same loyalty. This remark brought criticism,[240] yet reflects a duality in Adams' self-presentation that was not new, as exemplified by Mallie and McKittrick's assessment of Adams' lifting of the coffin at the funeral of Thomas Begley (one of the Shankill bombers) in 1993, an action which resulted in a public outcry:

> Adams used unusually strong language, saying the attack was wrong and could not be excused. None the less, he shouldered Begley's coffin. He knew very well that this action would associate him with the worst excesses of the IRA, but in republican terms he simply had no choice ... whatever the damage to his political moves, Adams had to shoulder the coffin: for he and Thomas Begley were part of the same Republican Movement.[241]

236 Interview, Declan Kearney, April 2015.
237 Irvin, n 8.
238 '"I'm Glad the War is Over," Says Adams: Easter Rising Commemoration Told Relatives Deserve Truth about Victims of Republican Violence,' *Belfast Telegraph*, 5 April 2010.
239 'Cheap Shots,' *Fortnight*, No. 379, (June 1999), p. 5.
240 One commentator accused Adams of 'suggesting that ... the Irish people are complicit in these murders ... we are being asked to write off murder. To pretend that because it was murder for the cause, it was of a different moral value' (T. P. O'Mahoney, 'No Cause Can Justify This Horror,' *The Examiner*, 3 June 1999).
241 Mallie and McKittrick, n 8 at 201–202.

For Adams not to shoulder the coffin would have been a disownment of the volunteer, and in turn, the IRA. This example demonstrates the necessity, from Adams' perspective, of satisfying two competing audiences, by performing as both peacemaker and loyal Republican. In taking the lead in Sinn Féin's response to the 'disappeared,' he put himself in a position where he could manage this duality.

4.2. Military leadership and the 'disappeared'

It has been suggested that 'the principal benchmark for judging military leadership in … transition is … the capacity to maintain organisational integrity and the related diminution or removal of political violence.'[242] The maintenance of organisational integrity has been demonstrated in the search for the 'disappeared.' As touched on previously, the headlines of 1999 declared the recovery of remains within days or weeks. Even if it had been a case of 'X' marks the spot with regards the locations provided by the IRA at that time, these timeframes would have been hugely optimistic. The challenges of searching for the remains of the 'disappeared' have proved to be a result of both human and environmental factors, with the passage of time exacerbating both sets of challenges.

In terms of human factors, the first stage of the process requires that those people with information come forward. Those involved may have since passed away, either of natural causes or having been killed in the conflict. Indeed, two of the men linked to the murder of Seamus Ruddy were killed.[243] There are also issues with individuals not wanting to bring information forward, either for personal or political reasons. As Knupfer has outlined, those involved in the 'disappearances':

> could have moved on … they might have been involved in paramilitary activity as young men, left the 'Movement' … and are [now] seen within their community as peace-loving and responsible members of society … the last thing they want to do is be seen standing next to the likes of us, helping us to recover victims … we are aware that there are people out there who would fall into that category.[244]

It is also possible that people "assume, naively, that information has been passed on to the Commission by somebody else."[245] This is problematic, as everyone involved may have had a slightly different perspective, and may remember different things.[246] A further factor, as one ex-combatant pointed out in interview, is that

242 Kieran McEvoy and Peter Shirlow, 'Re-Imagining DDR: Ex-Combatants, Leadership and Moral Agency in Conflict Transformation,' *Theoretical Criminology*, 13, (2009), 31–59 (p. 43).

243 Ian Geldard and Keith Craig, *IRA, INLA: Foreign Support and International Connections* (London: Institute for the Study of Terrorism, 1988).

244 Interview, Geoff Knupfer, July 2014.

245 Ibid.

246 Ibid.

to give up information about your activities during the conflict goes against the grain for Republicans:

> When someone would approach them [former combatants] and say, 'look folks, you were about whenever this particular incident happened,' the immediate response, or the immediate inclination is to say, 'I don't know what you're talking about it.' Simply because that is the way Republicans have always acted. Whatever you're involved in it's between you and the people who were with you whenever that happened. And that's where it stays … there's that whole secretive nature.[247]

If these problems are overcome and contact has been made with those who have information or were involved, the next challenge involves remembering the exact burial location. Geoff Knupfer points out that the choice of location was not random, and sites were selected specifically because they would be difficult to find again: "these areas were chosen for their … anonymity, they're just barren wastelands … when the burials occurred … there was never any intention of anybody going back."[248]

A consideration of the environmental factors indicates that, ultimately, the successful recovery of the remains of all of the 'disappeared' is beyond human control. Search areas can be vast, for example the area being searched in 2015 for the remains of Joe Lynskey measured approximately six hectares.[249] Many of the sites are in bogland or other difficult terrain.[250] The landscape may have changed in the intervening years. For example, in the area of Bragan bog where Columba McVeigh's remains are believed to be buried, a dense forest has grown in the 40 years since his 'disappearance.'[251] To consider taphonomy, as outlined by one of the forensic archaeologists working for the ICLVR, if a body is buried in acidic soil, the chances of preservation are significantly less than if the remains are buried in alkaline soils.[252]

As argued in this section so far, the conditions for recovering the remains of the 'disappeared' were challenging. In the IRA's March 1999 statement, the organisation showcases the actions being taken to help locate these remains. This included the establishment of a 'special unit under the command of one of our most senior officers.'[253] It has been claimed that Bobby Storey, allegedly former

247 Interview, senior Republican ex-combatant, April 2015
248 Interview, Geoff Knupfer, July 2014. See also '"Disappeared" Expert Hopeful on New Finds,' *Belfast Telegraph*, 2 August 2010; 'Search for Northern Ireland's Disappeared,' *Belfast Telegraph*, 7 August 2010.
249 'Dig to find "Disappeared" Lynskey,' *Belfast Telegraph*, 12 March 2015.
250 '"Disappeared" Expert Hopeful on New Finds,' n 248.
251 Susan McKay, 'Team of Many Skills on Trail of Disappeared,' *The Irish Times*, 23 April 2012
252 'Digging for the IRA Disappeared. Moors Murders Police Officer Searching for Peat Bog Victims,' *Mirror Online*, 8 June 2013.
253 'IRA Investigation Locates Grave Sites,' n 7.

Director of IRA Intelligence, later Belfast Sinn Féin Chairperson, was this 'senior officer.'[254] Following his November 2014 arrest (and release on the same day) in relation to the 'disappearance' of McConville, a 'Republican source' told the *Belfast Telegraph* that Storey was named in the Boston College interviews as having made inquiries as to the burial locations of the 'disappeared.'[255] If Storey was the figure selected to lead the internal investigation into the 'disappeared,' this choice is likely to have been a strategic one – and one that demonstrates the importance of this task for Republicans. Described by Bowyer Bell as 'confident, audacious, and convincing,'[256] Storey is suggested to be a close ally of Adams, and described as having played a pivotal role in securing Republican support within the IRA for Adams' peace process strategy.[257] The journalist Liam Clarke alleged that Storey was a key figure in 'troubleshooting' the IRA ceasefire. He quoted a 'security force source' as describing Storey as having been brought in to "police the peace within the IRA ... He has the sort of respect, the track record ... He ... has considerable leadership ability and ... commands widespread respect within the IRA."[258] If these claims are to be believed, Storey is an important lynchpin between the 'Movement's' military past and political present, with the leadership skills and extensive support needed to drive the investigation into the 'disappeared.' The ability to uncover information about burial locations, several decades later, suggests the continued existence and maintenance of organisational structures within the IRA that facilitated this process of finding out the required information. Tonge has described the relative cohesion within Republicanism throughout the peace process, and the ability of the IRA to assist in locating remains is a further demonstration of this cohesion.[259]

With regards to why those individuals who had information chose to bring it forward, the continuance of military-style organisation and discipline from the years of conflict has seemingly played an important part. A Republican ex-combatant interviewed outlined differing levels of co-operation:

> People responded to the leadership's call. You also had people who would have been understanding of the plight of the families, and sympathetic of that ... people fall within different levels of motivation, and other people, information had to be dragged out of them. And that's just the way people are, especially when you are delving back into history.[260]

254 Moloney, n 4.
255 'Jean McConville Murder: Police Forced to Free Ex-IRA Boss Bobby Storey After Learning of Immunity,' *Belfast Telegraph*, 1 December 2014.
256 Bowyer Bell, n 20 at 473.
257 Deborah McAleese, 'Jean McConville: Sinn Féin's Gerry Kelly Slams Arrest of Bobby Storey,' *Belfast Telegraph*, 28 November 2014; Moloney, n 69.
258 Liam Clarke, 'IRA Calls in Peace "Fixer",' *The Sunday Times*, 8 January 1995.
259 Jonathan Tonge, '"They Haven't Gone Away, You Know," Irish Republican "Dissidents" and "Armed Struggle",' *Terrorism and Political Violence*, 16:3, (2004), 671–693.
260 Interview, senior Republican ex-combatant, April 2015.

Mike Ritchie suggested that the "chain of command" and a sense of "comradeship" were motivating factors in encouraging people to come forward:

> there's not technically a chain of command now. But perhaps a previous chain of command. A kind of political commitment to Republicanism more generally. So if there's a decision by Republicanism, either secret or open, to get the bodies back, then you'll participate in that vicariously or directly.[261]

In their work with former political prisoners, Shirlow et al. found that former IRA prisoners, through community work, continued to have a sense of having a place within the Republican Movement, and for some this created a sense of pragmatism with regards the steps the 'Movement' was taking.[262] Bean has written of the entwined relationship of the Republican leadership and the grassroots, a relationship forged in part by the loyalty established between long-standing activists during years of shared struggle.[263] This relationship between the leadership and those further down the rungs of the organisation is an important one. That former combatants either wanted to or were encouraged to participate in the Republican Movement's mechanisms of peace-building has proved vital. Richard English drew attention to the irony of the changing attitudes towards Republican cohesion:

> Part of the thing that the British state used to lament was the IRA's kind of hard control over its own people and its attention to its own audience, but during the peace process the British state were quite glad about that because it meant more people moved with them.[264]

It has been argued that the support of former combatants has been essential in securing the compromises that have been necessary for conflict transformation.[265] The location of the bodies of the 'disappeared' is tangible evidence of this cohesion, and of the necessity of it in the transition from conflict. For Danny Morrison, the relative success of the search, "probably reflects that the majority of Republicans went along with the peace process ... there are a number of people, if they have the information ... will cooperate."[266]

The relative success of the internal investigation has been demonstrated in, not only the recovery of remains, but also in terms of the reliability of information given. Geoff Knupfer has said that "information ... passed to the Commission in the late 1990s by intermediaries ... really and truly the information available hasn't

261 Interview, Mike Ritchie, October 2014.

262 Peter Shirlow, Jonathan Tonge, James McAuley and Catherine McGlynn, *Abandoning Historical Conflict? Former Political Prisoners and Reconciliation in Northern Ireland* (Manchester: Manchester University Press, 2010).

263 Bean, n 90.

264 Interview, Richard English, August 2014.

265 Shirlow et al., n 262.

266 Interview, Danny Morrison, January 2015.

changed dramatically since ... the information has remained pretty constant throughout.'"[267]

This is evidence not only of the genuine nature of the IRA's involvement, but indicates that the gradual recovery of remains is the result of a long process of reviewing and revisiting information in order to make it more accurate. As Healing Through Remembering's Kate Turner discussed:

> information has been passed on. And then it's been revised ... it's not just 'right, here I've done it'. It's 'OK right did that not work? Well, maybe that stream wasn't there, or ...' You know I ... find ... that persons had to go back and kind of rethink that, and see 'well if that wasn't there maybe I've confused that with something ...' I think that showed a real commitment.[268]

As touched on previously, IRA statements that remains were found after a 'review' of existing information may have come across as disingenuous. Indeed, as Turner highlighted:

> I do know from talking to some people in the families that ... they find quite interesting that I see that as positive. They go, 'they keep misleading us,' or 'do they not know?' Because to them ... they remember the minute details of the last day they saw that person, every little thing. So how can this person that was involved in that part of it not?[269]

In fact these references to 'reviews'[270] and 'clarifications'[271] reflected the reality of the process of collating all information as to the burial location, then narrowing it down over time to a more precise site. This process on the part of the INLA in relation to the location of Seamus Ruddy's remains has been described by Willie Gallagher, spokesperson for the Irish Republican Socialist Party:

> I was over a number of times with the disappeared body ... along with other people – we went through the whole forest and down that particular path and we were always in the right area but we didn't have the exact precision. This time we had more precision ... I don't know how close the actual body was found to where we marked 'X marks the spot' but it was pretty close – we're talking about yards and I think, if my information is right, that the last dig in 2008 maybe fell short of approximately forty yards from where the body was – that's how close.[272]

267 Interview, Geoff Knupfer, July 2014.
268 Interview, Kate Turner, September 2014.
269 Ibid.
270 'Remains Located After IRA Review,' n 131.
271 'Family Waits After Remains Found in "Disappeared" Dig,' n 132.
272 BBC Radio Foyle, Willie Gallagher in Interview, BBC Radio Foyle, 8 May 1999. Available at http://rfe123.org/willie-gallagher-bbc-radio-foyle-interview-transcript-8-may-2017 [accessed 30 June 2018].

5. Conclusion

Bean suggests that the 'militarisation of politics gave the IRA vital symbolic and practical functions that were essential to the success of the transition from armed struggle to constitutional politics.'[273] The search for the 'disappeared' demonstrates this. Acknowledgement of its involvement in 'disappearing' and helping to locate remains symbolises the end of armed struggle and its replacement with full commitment to politics by democratic means. It is 'an implicit confirmation of the IRA's shift from political violence to peaceful engagement,'[274] 'a declaration that a chapter has closed … an affirmation, in the IRA's symbolism, that the war is finally over.'[275]

The ability to locate burial sites, however, required much practical engagement. During the period of transition, the Republican leadership stressed the continued strength of the 'Movement,' and that the IRA had not been defeated.[276] The search for the 'disappeared' exemplifies this. For the IRA to successfully find places where individuals were buried several decades previously required continued internal cohesion and organisation within the 'Movement,' and also a remaining air of militarism. In essence, the IRA needed to have not "gone away, you know."[277] As examined earlier, although officially no chain of command still existed, the remnants of military control and a sort of ghost military structure were needed to push forward the process of recovering information. The importance of this was demonstrated by the reported installation of Bobby Storey to oversee the internal investigation.

The response to the 'disappeared' has also – as has been explored in this chapter – highlighted some of the challenges, both internal and external, for the 'Movement.' Internally, while the relative success in locating some remains demonstrates that individuals have come forward with information, the lack of progress on other cases indicates that some have not. Geoff Knupfer has said: "We know in some cases there are people alive who have not managed to speak to us yet; for whatever reason they won't engage with the Commission."[278] Some of the reasons for this were explored earlier, however reluctance to bring information forward is evidence of a more fundamental fracture in the 'Movement's' structure.

As already examined, the Republican Movement did not fracture as much as some may have expected during the transition. However, opponents to the Sinn Féin strategy did emerge. These included some former prisoners and intellectuals

273 Bean, n 90 at 189.
274 Dudai, n 3 at 240.
275 'Hope Grows From Tragedy,' *The Irish Times*, 31 May 1999.
276 Ruane, n 211.
277 At a 1995 Republican rally, Adams remarked of the IRA that 'They haven't gone away, you know' (David McKittrick, 'The IRA Has Not Gone Away, Adams Warns Ministers,' *The Independent*, 14 August 1995).
278 Gerry Moriarty, 'Investigator Makes Appeal Over Cases of Columba McVeigh, Robert Nairac, Joe Lynskey and Four Other IRA Victims,' *The Irish Times*, 30 September 2013.

who opposed violence, and those who opposed the ending of violence.[279] There are a number of indications, from Republicans, from the ICLVR, and from victims' families, that some of these dissenters may hold information about the 'disappeared' that they are not bringing forward. In interview, Danny Morrison suggested "many of those that claimed to have been involved in it ['disappearing'], will not take direction from the Republican Movement."[280] In the IRA's 2010 statement in which the 'disappearance' of Joe Lynskey was admitted,[281] the source, in referring to problems hindering the search for information, referred to "open hostility towards current republican politics from others approached for information." In February 2012, the ICLVR specifically appealed to those who had "moved away politically' or had become 'members of a different organisation" to come forward.[282] Families have also spoken out. Oliver McVeigh, brother of Columba, suggested that there remain "people out there who are not coming forward."[283] In 2010, the family of Seamus Wright was critical of reports that Dolours Price, a former IRA member described by Adams as having 'set herself against the Sinn Féin leadership on many occasions,'[284] had information about Wright's 'disappearance.' Wright's family released a statement questioning Price's motives, and criticising those who might use the 'disappeared' 'for their own narrow political ends.'[285] Following on from this, in 2013, Wright's sister, Breige, wrote an open letter to *An Phoblacht*, outlining that Price had not brought forward any information, and that with regards the search for Seamus' remains, one of the difficulties was "the hostility of some, who might have information."[286] With regards to Jean McConville, Danny Morrison described:

> How they became suspicious of her, how they discovered it, what she said under questioning – I have no idea, and I'm not even sure if that information is extant, whether or not it died with the people who were involved in it and who, through gossip, I understand weren't helpful to the Republican Movement when they tried to resolve this injustice. And when it tried to bring some sort of end to the family, closure to the family. The people who were involved were uncooperative.[287]

279 Tonge, n 259. See also Kevin Hearty, 'From "Former Comrades" to "Near Enemy": The Narrative Template of "Armed Struggle" and Conflicting Discourses on Violent Dissident Irish Republican Activity (VDR),' *Critical Studies on Terrorism*, 9:2, (2016), 269–291.
280 Interview, Danny Morrison, January 2015.
281 'Investigation Confirms 1972 Disappearance,' n 7.
282 Allison Morris, 'Investigators Urge Dissidents to Help Locate Disappeared,' *The Irish News*, 17 February 2012.
283 John Mulgrew, 'Help Us Find the Lost Seven,' *Belfast Telegraph*, 31 August 2012.
284 'Wright Family Responds to Price's Claims in Irish News: Gerry Adams Comments,' *An Phoblacht*, 25 February 2010.
285 Ibid.
286 'Family of Seamus Wright Respond to BBC/RTÉ Programme "The Disappeared",' *An Phoblacht*, 15 November 2013.
287 Interview, Danny Morrison, January 2015.

These comments indicate that it is highly possible that despite the will of the Republican Movement as a whole, there are dissenters who are unwilling to provide information.

Campbell and Connolly argue that transitional justice processes provide armed groups with new political opportunities to be exploited.[288] The issue of the 'disappeared' has cast a long shadow in terms of the legacy of IRA violence. And, as outlined, there are many factors that make the recovery of their remains a hugely difficult task. Yet, the issue remains a political opportunity for Republicans. Although circumstances are difficult, dealing with the issue is a chance for the 'Movement' to involve itself directly in 'dealing with the past' and its engagement has revealed both strengths and weaknesses, and successes and challenges in this regard. O'Connor proposed that 'the biggest riddle' during the transition from conflict was, 'were the Provos for real …?'[289] Locating the bodies of the 'disappeared' was an opportunity to prove that they were.

288 Campbell and Connolly, n 107.
289 O'Connor, n 187 at 48.

4 The community

Rumour, whispers, and 'bystander complicity'

1. Introduction

> I do remember in '94, when Helen McKendry gave her interview to *Talkback* and I remember just being astonished. I mean, I had by then written a book on the 'Troubles' … I'd done an enormous amount of journalism, I knew nothing about the 'disappeared' … I was on the *Talkback* programme when Helen McKendry gave her interview … I was with … a senior journalist … and … others … probably six of us who would all have been journalists, well acquainted with the Northern Ireland stories and the notion of 'disappearance' of victims was completely new to all of us. So if that's an indicator, that shows that we just did not know this. And we were appalled, you know, we were appalled.[1]

This quote, from writer and journalist Malachi O'Doherty, is representative of a widespread view regarding Northern Ireland's 'disappeared': that nothing was known about them until their families began to speak out publicly. Yet, 1994 – when Helen McKendry gave this interview on *Talkback* – was not the beginning of this story. Jean McConville's abduction from her home was reported in the news,[2] as was that of Brendan Megraw – with a front-page story on his abduction published in the *Belfast Telegraph* three days after it took place.[3] West Belfast's local paper – *Andersonstown News* – ran 'Missing Persons' pieces on Brian McKinney and John McClory.[4] The cases of Robert Nairac,[5] Patrick

1 Interview, Malachi O'Doherty, August 2015.

2 'Help Trace Kidnapped Mother – MP's Appeal to Falls,' *Belfast Telegraph*, 17 January 1973; 'Inquiry into Widow's Disappearance,' *The Irish Times*, 18 January 1973; 'Missing Mother Reported to be Back in Belfast,' *The Irish News*, 19 January 1973; 'Snatched Mother Missing a Month,' *Belfast Telegraph*, 16 January 1973; 'Widow with 10 Children Reported Kidnapped,' *The Irish Times*, 17 January 1973.

3 'Hunt on for Kidnap Gang,' *Belfast Telegraph*, 11 April 1978; 'Kidnap Hunt Goes On – But Few Clues,' *Belfast Telegraph*, 12 April 1978; 'Still Waiting,' *Andersonstown News*, 27 May 1978; 'Where is Brendan Megraw?' *Andersonstown News*, 20 May 1978.

4 'Missing Persons,' *Andersonstown News*, 17 June 1978.

5 E.g. 'Five Charged with Officer's Murder,' *The Irish Times*, 28 May 1977; 'Five Men Jailed for Link with Nairac Kidnap-Murder,' *The Irish Times*, 16 December 1978; 'Gardai Say Body Found in Bog May be Nairac's,' *The Irish News*, 17 May 1984; 'Hunt for Missing Officer is Switched,' *Belfast Telegraph*, 19 May 1977; 'Missing Soldier "Executed" Say

Duffy,[6] and Eugene Simons[7] were all reported to some extent in the media. The 'strong speculation' following the murder of Patrick Duffy in 1973 'that he was kidnapped and killed across the border and his body hidden,'[8] was in fact what had happened to Duffy and demonstrates that such behaviour was not unimaginable. That the IRA were involved in abducting, killing, and hiding the remains of some victims was therefore not unknown.[9] In a 1981 appeal for information on the whereabouts of Eugene Simons, Father Denis Faul suggested that 'unexplained disappearances' were 'on the increase.'[10] The term 'disappeared' was first used in the Northern Ireland context in a 1983 newspaper report on a sermon given by Cardinal Tomás Ó Fiaich, in which he spoke of the disappearance of three local men and two Belfast men.[11] The following year, an article reporting an appeal from Charlie Armstrong's family stated that he was 'one of three Crossmaglen men who have disappeared within the past five years,' referring also to Gerry Evans and Sean Murphy.[12]

Provos,' *Belfast Telegraph*, 16 May 1977; 'Nairac Death Trial Goes On,' *The Irish Times*, 12 October 1977; 'No Real Lead to Missing Officer,' *Belfast Telegraph*, 20 May 1977; 'Nairac: Police Quiz Men,' *Belfast Telegraph*, 26 May 1977; 'Provisionals Admit Killing Officer,' *The Irish Times*, 17 May 1977; 'Search Goes on for Missing Officer,' *The Irish Times*, 20 May 1977; 'What was Nairac Doing?' *The Irish Times*, 10 November 1977.

6 'Body Found in Coffin at Border,' *The Irish Times*, 27 August 1973; 'Derry IRA Victim Still Not Traced,' *Belfast Telegraph*, 18 August 1973; 'Derry Funeral of IRA Victim,' *Belfast Telegraph*, 27 August 1973; 'Executed Man's Body in Car – Army Told,' *The Irish Times*, 25 August 1973; 'Give Me My Husband's Body – Plea,' *Belfast Telegraph*, 17 August 1973; 'Killers Put Body of Victim in Coffin,' *Belfast Telegraph*, 25 August 1973. See Chapter 3, footnote 59 for details of Duffy case,

7 'Body Found in Bog Identified,' *The Irish Times*, 23 May 1984; 'Co Down Man Believes Body is His Son's,' *The Irish Times*, 21 May 1984; 'Doubts Remain on Identity of Body,' *The Irish Times*, 18 May 1984; 'Down Family in New Appeal,' *The Irish Times*, 21 December 1981.

8 'Killers Put Body of Victim in Coffin,' n 6.

9 Also reported in the media were cases in which the IRA did not leave the bodies of their victims were they could be easily discovered. For example, in the cases of Wallace Allen and William Turbitt, the killings were admitted, but the bodies were recovered only after a search by security forces ('Provisionals Admit to Border Killings,' *The Irish Times*, 5 September 1980; 'War News,' *Republican News*, 19 June 1978; 'Constable Executed Say Provos,' *Belfast Telegraph*, 19 June 1978).

10 'Down Family in New Appeal,' n 7.

11 Fionnuala O'Connor, 'Suspicion and Fear Over the "Disappeared",' *The Irish Times*, 20 July 1983.

12 'Missing Man's Family Appeals,' *The Irish Times*, 20 August 1984. Sean Murphy was 'disappeared' from Crossmaglen in December 1981. His remains were found in a car recovered from Dundalk Bay during dredging in July 1986. No group acknowledged involvement in his killing; however, McKittrick et al. describe the area from which he was taken as 'largely controlled by the IRA.' Other than a reference in Seamus McKendry's book, Murphy has not featured in any lists of the 'disappeared' nor have I found any evidence to suggest his family has involved itself with the other families whose loved ones were 'disappeared' (Seamus McKendry, *Disappeared: The Search for Jean McConville* (Dublin: Blackwater Press, 2000); David McKittrick, Seamus Kelters, Brian Feeney, Chris Thornton and David McVea, *Lost Lives: The Stories of the Men,*

These snippets in news reports, grouping these occurrences together, hint at some connection or similarity between the cases. At this stage the picture was far from complete, but these murmurings suggest that there were those in society who were beginning to pull some of the threads together.

Chapter 2 introduced some of the literature on framing and its impact on public perception of the families' campaign. Edelman says of framing:

> What we 'know' about the nature of the social world depends upon how we frame and interpret the cues we receive.... Those cues would be very confusing if our minds did not give them particular meanings by focusing on a few and ignoring most and by placing those that receive attention into specific categories.[13]

Broadly speaking, the actors involved in 'disappearing' have also been placed into specific categories by the media, by politicians, and by society more widely – an (albeit significant) 'few' have been focussed on, and many others have been ignored. Cohen's 'atrocity triangle' of victims, perpetrators, and observers or bystanders,[14] is instructive here. We have the victims – the 'disappeared' and their families (as explored in Chapter 2) – and the perpetrators, in the form of the Republican Movement (Chapter 3). By default, in the widely accepted narrative captured by the quotation at the beginning of this chapter, everyone else falls into the category of observer or bystander – once unknowing and since the mid-1990s, shocked and empathetic. Where the first two categories have been the focus of significant media, political, and public attention, this latter category has for the most part been ignored. This chapter seeks to rectify this imbalance by charting the response of, and within, the communities in which 'disappearances' were perpetrated. Three, at times overlapping, behaviours will be explored: rumour, whisper, and complicity.

2. 'Contemptuous silence and insidious rumour'[15]: communities standing by?

Gerry Evans' brother, Noel, has described how his family, following Gerry's 'disappearance,' "lived in an ignorant limbo, a kind of purgatory."[16] One of the most difficult elements of the 'disappeared' issue in Ireland as elsewhere is the need for families to confront 'the forced silence imposed on them.'[17] Victims were 'disappeared' not just

Women and Children Who Died as a Result of the Northern Ireland Troubles (Edinburgh; London: Mainstream Publishing, 2007), p. 890).

13 Murray Edelman, 'Contestable Categories and Public Opinion,' *Political Communication*, 10, (1993), 231–242 (p. 231).

14 Stanley Cohen, *States of Denial: Knowing about Atrocities and Suffering* (Cambridge: Polity Press, 2001), p. 14.

15 'Hope Grows From Tragedy,' *The Irish Times*, 31 May 1999.

16 Paul Francis, 'Families in Fresh Disappeared Plea as Book Launched,' *Belfast Telegraph*, 22 June 2013.

17 Gabriel Ruiz Romero, 'Voices Around Us: Memory and Community Empowerment in Reconstruction Efforts in Colombia,' *International Journal of Transitional Justice*, 6:3, (2012), 1–11 (p. 6).

physically, but also almost entirely from the public consciousness, for years, or even decades. Yet, the years between the perpetration of the 'disappearances' and the first major media coverage were not completely characterised by silence, as touched on previously. Families have spoken of hearing rumours about their loved ones and there are indications in newspaper reports that there were whispers of the reality of what had taken place. This section explores the role played by the community in 'disappearing' through analysing the evidence for, and impact of, silence, whisper, and rumour. Before considering these elements of the community response, some consideration will be given to the characteristics of these communities at the time of the 'disappearances.'

In geographical terms, the conflict in Northern Ireland was experienced most intensely in specific locales, with Belfast (specifically north and west), Derry, and County Armagh experiencing some of the highest numbers of fatalities.[18] A degree of segregation between Catholic and Protestant populations in Belfast has existed since the city was founded in the early seventeenth century[19] and continues today.[20] A rapid escalation in segregation occurred during the violence and intimidation of 1969[21] and by the 1970s and 1980s around 77% of Belfast residents were living in streets described as 'highly segregated' (i.e. having a Catholic or Protestant population of greater than 90%).[22] The border areas had, historically, significant levels of IRA activity, and were sites of intense conflict, experiencing high rates of violence.[23]

It has been suggested that this level of segregation has enhanced solidarity within the different communities.[24] This solidarity, as outlined by Feldman, could be of an intensely political kind. He described the existence, in Belfast, of a 'tradition of specific politicized communities,' particularly in working class areas. These spaces could be transformed by paramilitary groups into 'bases of operations,' where violence became a daily reality.[25] Particularly in the early days of the conflict these 'highly segregated' areas of the city became battlegrounds, with frequent pitched battles between the security forces, Republicans, and rival paramilitary factions.[26] Former

18 Marie Therese Fay, Mike Morrissey, Marie Smyth and The Cost of the Troubles Study, *Mapping Troubles-Related Deaths and Deprivation in Northern Ireland* (Londonderry: INCORE, 1998).

19 Frederick Boal, 'Belfast: Walls Within,' *Political Geography*, 21, (2002), 687–694.

20 Máire Braniff, 'A Tale of Two Cities? Community Relations in Northern Ireland,' ARK Research Update, (2016), www.ark.ac.uk/publications/updates/update110.pdf [accessed 7 August 2018]; Conflict in Cities Project: Belfast, www.conflictincities.org/Belfast.html [accessed 19 June 2018]; Peter Shirlow, 'Fear and Ethnic Division,' *Peace Review*, 13:1, (2001), 67–74.

21 Boal, n 19; Alan Feldman, *Formations of Violence: The Narrative of the Body and Political Terror in Northern Ireland* (Chicago; London: University of Chicago Press, 1991); Shirlow, ibid.

22 Boal, n 19.

23 Henry Patterson, 'Sectarianism Revisited: The Provisional IRA Campaign in a Border Region of Northern Ireland,' *Terrorism and Political Violence*, 22:3, (2010), 337–356.

24 Boal, n 19.

25 Feldman, n 21 at 38; 39.

26 Victor Mesev, Peter Shirlow and Joni Downs, 'The Geography of Conflict and Death in Belfast, Northern Ireland,' *Annals of the Association of American Geographers*, 99:5, (2009), 893–903.

director of publicity for Sinn Féin, Danny Morrison, described Belfast at this time as "an apocalyptic Belfast … going down to Divis Flats was frightening … If you were stopped [by the British Army] you were getting a kicking or you were getting trailed into a jeep … right across Belfast you'd army checkpoints, the place was saturated."[27]

In those areas with a Catholic majority, it has been suggested that traditional Republican families had a crucial role to play in politicising certain communities or neighbourhoods.[28] Ruane posits that if the IRA were not actively supported by all, their actions were, in general, tolerated.[29] This support, generated at first by the IRA's apparent role as defenders of the community[30] was maintained, as Ruane argues, by a sense that grievances would not otherwise be addressed, and by the threat of violence from loyalist paramilitaries and state forces.[31] The IRA was in part, Coogan argues, 'based on the fears … of the Catholic population.'[32] The Clonard district of west Belfast, for example, 'considered itself under siege … [inhabitants] regarded the loyalists, and later the British army, as tormentors, and the IRA as legitimate and necessary defenders.'[33]

The majority of the 'disappeared' came from or were abducted from some of those working class, highly segregated areas that had become places of frequent violent confrontation and where a high level of tolerance, if not outright support, for the activities of the IRA existed. Joe Lynskey, Kevin McKee, Seamus Wright, Jean McConville, Peter Wilson, Brendan Megraw, John McClory, Brian McKinney, and Danny McIlhone were all from west Belfast. Eamonn Molloy was from the Ardoyne area of north Belfast. Over a third of those who died during the conflict lived in five postal districts, which were all in north or west Belfast.[34] As one interviewee highlighted: "certainly the biggest cluster [of 'disappearances'] is in Belfast, but there again the biggest concentration of Republican activity was in Belfast. So, in some sense, it's proportionate to the level of IRA activity."[35] Gerry Evans and Charlie Armstrong were both from Crossmaglen and Robert Nairac was abducted from Drumintee, both in south Armagh. Infamously referred to by former Northern Ireland Secretary, Merlyn Rees, as "bandit country,"[36] south Armagh gained a level of notoriety during

27 Interview, Danny Morrison, former Director of Publicity for Sinn Féin, January 2015.
28 Feldman, n 21.
29 Joseph Ruane, 'Contemporary Republicanism and the Strategy of Armed Struggle,' in John Coakley (ed.) *From Political Violence to Negotiated Settlement: The Winding Path to Peace in Twentieth Century Ireland* (Dublin: UCD Press, 2004).
30 Richard English, *Armed Struggle: The History of the IRA* (London: Pan Books, 2012); Ruane, ibid.; Peter Taylor, *Provos: The IRA and Sinn Féin* (Bloomsbury Publishing, 1998).
31 Ruane, n 29.
32 Tim Pat Coogan, *The IRA* (London: Harper Collins, 2000), p. 367.
33 Eamonn Mallie and David McKittrick, *The Fight for Peace: The Secret Story Behind the Irish Peace Process* (London: Heinemann, 1996), p. 67.
34 Fay et al., n 18.
35 Interview, Danny Morrison, January 2015.
36 Conor O'Clery, 'Big Army Inquiry After Ambush Deaths,' *The Irish Times*, 24 November 1975.

the conflict years.[37] With a history of Republican activism dating back at least 200 years, a broadly sympathetic community in which to operate, and proximity to the border with the Republic, south Armagh was undoubtedly one of the most militarily challenging areas for the security forces and one of the most 'effective' for the IRA.[38] Columba McVeigh was from Donaghmore in Tyrone, another county that was a key area of operations for the IRA.[39]

2.1. The role of rumour in 'disappearing'

In his influential work, Knapp defines rumour as 'a proposition for belief of topical reference disseminated without official verification.'[40] Rumours, spread frequently by word-of-mouth, disseminate 'information' relating to a person, occurrence, or circumstance, and, to a greater or lesser extent, satisfy the 'emotional needs of the community.'[41] They can ultimately be true or false, but at the time of their telling, the facts are not there to verify the account.[42] The emotional needs they satisfy can be positive: 'pipe-dream' or 'wish' rumours, designed to express wishes or hopes, or negative: 'bogie' rumours that derive from fear or anxiety, and 'wedge-driving' rumours motivated by hatred or aggression that result in breaking down loyalties and dividing groups.[43] Das emphasises the existence of a 'darker side' of rumour[44] and indeed, although rumours can exist at any time,[45] Knapp also argues, persuasively, that such features are exacerbated at times of conflict and social struggle when public feeling is characterised by uncertainty and suspicion.[46] It is the role of rumours as negative expression and in violent contexts that is of most interest here.

During conflict, rumours are propagated for at least two main reasons; first is the need for secrecy and a scarcity of facts, and second is the existence of suspicion, fear, hostility, and uncertainty among the public.[47] Rumours thrive in such contexts as people attempt to express their fears, suspicions, and hostilities and try to make sense of the uncertainties with which they are faced.[48] As rumours thrive,

37 Toby Harnden, *'Bandit Country': The IRA and South Armagh* (London: Hodder and Stoughton, 1999).

38 English, n 30.

39 Patterson, n 23.

40 Robert H. Knapp, 'A Psychology of Rumour,' *Public Opinion Quarterly*, 8:1, (1944), 22–37 (p. 22).

41 Ibid. at 22.

42 Erich Goode and Nachman Ben-Yehuda, *Moral Panics: The Social Construction of Deviance* (Chichester: Wiley-Blackwell, 2009).

43 Knapp, n 40.

44 Veena Das, 'Specificities: Official Narratives, Rumour, and the Social Production of Hate,' *Social Identities*, 4:1, (1998), 109–130 (p. 126).

45 Gordon W. Allport and Leo Postman, 'An Analysis of Rumour,' *Public Opinion Quarterly*, 10:4, (1946), 501–517; Nicholas DiFonzo and Prashant Bordia, 'Rumour, Gossip and Urban Legends,' *Diogenes*, 54:1, (2007), 19–35; Knapp, n 40.

46 Lee Ann Fujii, 'Shades of Truth and Lies: Interpreting Testimonies of War and Violence,' *Journal of Peace Research*, 47:2, (2010), 231–241; Knapp, n 40.

47 Knapp, n 40.

48 Allport and Postman, n 45; DiFonzo and Bordia, n 45; Knapp, n 40.

however, they serve not only to express emotion and to seek to clarify the unclear, but they can perpetuate unrest. Serving as vehicles for encouraging exclusion and spreading stereotypes and violence-provoking beliefs, rumours can play a role in promoting and maintaining violent conflict.[49] By reflecting and reproducing terror and the threat of violence, Kirsch suggests, rumour can make tangible the threat of violence through language. While on the one hand a rumour can serve as a way of expressing concerns or fears about violence, the spreading of such rumours in turn may serve to enhance the sense of threat or terror.[50] Rumours increase in plausibility the more they are told; in this way they become almost self-propagating, as the more they are spread the more successful they become at carrying the public with them.[51] Das explores the ability of rumour to transform words into action and serve as 'an instrument of force' rather than solely as a form of communication. As a rumour spreads, it generates the power to naturalise differences between groups and produce hate.[52] From this perspective even an unfounded narrative can generate power and meaning through being spread as rumour. Consequently, potentially false words can have real impact, as can be demonstrated with regards the 'disappeared.'

Developing some of these themes, Goode and Ben-Yehuda outline four factors that contribute to the production and dissemination of rumour – all of which are relevant to consideration of the 'disappeared' in Ireland.[53] First, the rumour should be about someone or something of importance.[54] Certainly the disappearance and possible murder of a person reaches this threshold. Second, there must be some sort of uncertainty, ambiguity, or doubt. Rumour 'thrives on doubt'[55] and 'lack of news'[56] and thus in a climate where information is lacking the need for rumour will be all the greater.[57] Uncertainty over the fate of a missing loved one is in many ways the defining characteristic of a 'disappearance,' and as explored in Chapter 1, this ambiguity is often a source of additional suffering for relatives. Thus the very nature of a 'disappearance' makes the act a likely subject of rumour. Third, rumour 'flies on fear,' fed by emotionally negative states of fear or anxiety.[58] As outlined earlier in this section, 'disappearances' occurred

49 Ravi Bhavnani, Michael G. Findley and James H. Kulinski, 'Rumour Dynamics in Ethnic Violence,' *The Journal of Politics*, 71:3, (2009), 876–892; Stefan Ionescu, 'Myths, Narratives and Patterns of Rumours: The Construction of "Jewish Subversion" and Retributive Violence in 1940–41 Romania,' *Culture and Psychology*, 15:3, (2009), 327–336.
50 Stuart Kirsch, 'Rumour and Other Narratives of Political Violence in West Papua,' *Critique of Anthropology*, 22:1, (2002), 53–79.
51 Knapp, n 40.
52 Das, n 44.
53 Goode and Ben-Yehuda, n 42.
54 Allport and Postman, n 45; Goode and Ben-Yehuda, n 42.
55 Goode and Ben-Yehuda, n 42 at 132.
56 Allport and Postman, n 45.
57 Knapp, n 40.
58 Daniel Goleman, 'Anatomy of a Rumor: It Flies on Fear,' *The New York Times*, 4 June 1991.

mostly in those areas most deeply affected by violence. In these communities, people lived not only in fear of the 'other'[59] but also, as analysed in Chapter 3, under the strict and at times brutal control of the IRA. Fourth, rumours require credulity, in that some individuals or audiences must be willing to perceive them as true. In the case of the 'disappeared,' there were ready audiences in the families and loved ones looking for an explanation. In some cases, the rumours were highly credible, arguably more so than the reality. At that time, as several interviewees described, for a person to leave, perhaps suddenly, for a long period of time with little or no contact with their family was far from implausible. Indeed, Gerry Evans' family has spoken of how they thought he might return once the ceasefires were in place,[60] and Columba McVeigh's family thought he had perhaps moved to England or America.[61] His brother Eugene recounted to me in interview:

> I actually thought he had just maybe … gone off somewhere … 'disappeared' in a different way you know … like young people do … It was easy I think for young people to go off and … get lost and sometimes the longer they left it the more difficult it was to then contact home.[62]

'Disappearances' happened at a time and in communities where the elements needed for 'rumour-mongering'[63] coincided. As for the contours of the rumours that families have reported hearing, these can mostly be split into two broad categories, both of which I would argue served to silence families in some way. First, rumours of travel provided families with a plausible explanation for their loved one's absence. For example, Joe Lynskey's family assumed he was alive for decades, in part as a result of stories from 'friends' of his that he was in America.[64] Danny Morrison said of Lynskey: "on the Falls Road, there was a rumour that he had ran away, and that was such a strong rumour that nearly everybody believed it, obviously apart from those who were intimately involved in his 'disappearance.'"[65]

The families of John McClory and Brian McKinney were told of false sightings of them in Ballycastle, Dublin, and Dundalk. In both these cases the mothers of the young men have said they were aware of IRA involvement from the time of the 'disappearance,' but thought their sons may have been ordered to leave the country.[66] The family of Eamonn Molloy did not think he was dead, and heard

59 Shirlow, n 20.

60 David Sharrock, 'Families Hope Ceasefire May Solve Mystery of Ulster's "Disappeared",' *The Guardian*, 3 October 1994; Suzanne Breen, 'Put That Family Out of its Misery,' *Sunday Tribune*, 18 January 2009.

61 WAVE, *The Disappeared of Northern Ireland's 'Troubles'* (Belfast: WAVE Trauma Centre Publications, 2012).

62 Interview, Eugene McVeigh, August 2015.

63 Goode and Ben-Yehuda, n 42 at 131.

64 Allison Morris, 'Emigration Rumour Hid Lynskey Murder,' *The Irish News*, 8 December 2009; WAVE, n 61.

65 Interview, Danny Morrison, January 2015.

66 Suzanne Breen, 'Missing Presumed Dead,' *The Irish Times*, 13 August 1994; WAVE, n 61.

rumours that he had gone to Libya to train with Gaddafi's forces. Molloy's brother, Michael, believes these stories were 'put out to stop the family asking questions about what really happened.'[67]

The second type of rumour appeared designed to undermine an individual's reputation, in effect to vilify the victim. In the aftermath of Charlie Armstrong's 'disappearance,' his daughter has described:

> As the waiting began, the rumours started. He was supposedly seen with two women. He had run away to join the circus. Someone claimed to have seen him getting off a bus in Drogheda. This was all rubbish … meant only as a distraction to throw us off the scent. It also served to blacken his character.[68]

As Monica McWilliams described:

> All kinds of stories … were put out … these were good men whose reputations were being taken – that they'd run off with people … or they'd some association with the army or something. And in small communities like that, those kinds of things are very disruptive.[69]

The most damaging rumours of this kind were those that related to informing, or some sort of involvement with the security forces.[70] As discussed previously, the charge of informing is one of the most visceral accusations to lodge against someone in the Irish Republican tradition.[71] In interview, Danny Morrison described how this hatred of informers permeated the community, creating the backdrop to the 'disappearances':

> Informers were just the lowest of the low. Imagine squealing on your own community after what your community had come through. So informers were despicable. And there was that, that was the atmosphere: very tense, very dark, frightening. You know, a lot of the rules had gone.[72]

The families of Kevin McKee and Eamonn Molloy have described hearing such rumours.[73] A former neighbour of Peter Wilson recounted how "People used to say

67 WAVE, n 61 at 36.
68 WAVE, n 61 at 81.
69 Interview, Monica McWilliams, a senior academic who has been involved with WAVE and the families' campaign, September 2014.
70 Although (see Chapters 2 and 3) the IRA alleged that a number of the 'disappeared' were executed as informers, it will ultimately be impossible to know for sure if they were involved in informing.
71 Ron Dudai, *The IRA and the Shadow of the Informer: Punishment, Governance, and Dealing with the Past* (Unpublished PhD Thesis, Queen's University Belfast, 2012); and see Chapter 3.
72 Interview, Danny Morrison, January 2015.
73 WAVE, n 61.

they saw him in the back of a Saracen … the talk was that he was with the Brits."[74] It is reported that rumours circulated in Republican circles in the aftermath of Gerry Evans' 'disappearance' that he was killed by the British, having agreed to work for them but failing to deliver.[75] Jean McConville's daughter, Helen, has described the circulation of rumours in the aftermath of her 'disappearance' that Jean was informing for the British, or had abandoned her family to embark on an affair with a British soldier or Loyalist paramilitary. One reporter, writing in 2014, described seeing graffiti in Belfast on her way to interview Helen, denouncing Jean McConville as a 'tout.'[76] As one interviewee described, "there was a big stigma … if your relative was accused of being an informer."[77] These sorts of rumours would have served to isolate the families of the 'disappeared' from their communities and impede attempts to generate support or assistance. One former ex-combatant and community activist described to Ron Dudai that:

> when somebody was outed as an informer, the families felt themselves distanced from the republican community … they partly withdrew, because of the shame. The civilian population, especially young adults, didn't help because they inflicted a lot of cruelty on them.[78]

This comment suggests a double distancing or isolation for families. Those who would have been close to the Republican community felt distanced from it, and would also have faced abuse from the wider community. Seamus McKendry has written of the 'callousness' of the McConville children's neighbours following their mother's abduction.[79] In interview, Kate Turner of Healing Through Remembering recalled conversations with some families in which they spoke of "the years they had where people crossed the road and didn't talk to them … they had a lot of feelings about that being people thinking 'well your relative disappeared, they must be a tout.'"[80]

As to the rationale for the origins of these rumours, a number of theories have been put forward. For example, Moloney has suggested a sinister and instrumental origin to some rumours – deliberately started by the IRA to mislead,[81] and this is a view endorsed by some families, as considered previously. Those deliberately spreading false accounts sought to forge a barrier between the loved ones of those who were taken and the truth. We see here aspects of Knapp's 'wedge-driving'

74 Alison Morris, 'The Disappeared: Peter Wilson,' *The Irish News*, 31 October 2009.
75 Breen, n 66.
76 Elizabeth Day, 'Jean McConville's Daughter: "If I Give Up Fighting, They've Won",' *The Observer*, 6 July 2014.
77 Interview, Mike Ritchie, veteran human rights activist, October 2014.
78 Ron Dudai, 'Closing the Gap: Symbolic Reparations and Armed Groups,' *International Review of the Red Cross*, 93:883, (2012), 783–808, fn. 103.
79 McKendry, n 12.
80 Interview, Kate Turner, September 2014. See also WAVE, n 61. In her Introduction to the book, Sandra Peake explains that the circulation of rumours 'undermined any support [families] would have received from neighbours and friends' (p. 2).
81 Ed Moloney, 'The "Disappeared" is Most Shameful Episode in IRA's History,' *Sunday Tribune*, 30 May 1999.

rumours.[82] Perhaps less malevolently, rumours concerning the 'disappeared' may also represent people struggling to make sense of situations that are ambiguous or unusual.[83] In these cases we see elements of Knapp's 'bogie' category of rumours deriving from fear or anxiety.[84] Regardless of their motivation, once started these rumours took on something of a life of their own, transmogrifying into a more widely held community belief or opinion which in turn served to reinforce the 'disappearance.'

2.2. *'Disappearing,' silence, and whispers*

The role of silence in 'disappearing' was introduced in Chapter 1 as a recurring feature of the response to 'disappearances,' both internationally and in the context of Northern Ireland. In this context, as will be considered in Chapter 6, much of the detail surrounding the circumstances of the 'disappearances' remains unknown as the process of information-gathering by the ICLVR is focused solely on recovering remains. This silence, although rooted in the actions of the Republican Movement, is not limited to that organisation and families have spoken of being met with a 'wall of silence' from a range of quarters.[85] However in the midst of this silence, as detailed in the introduction to this chapter, there were whispers of what really was taking place seeping through in media reports both at the time and since. In some cases, families have discovered that there were those in the local community who concealed from them knowledge of their 'disappeared' relatives.[86] Although the extent to which the wider community was aware of 'disappearing' is difficult to gauge, there are suggestions that something of what was going on might have been known in the wider community. Interviewees have spoken of their belief that more people knew about 'disappearing' than those directly involved, and in his research on informers, Dudai has proposed that 'in practice the fact that these individuals were killed as suspected informers became public knowledge relatively quickly.'[87] This is arguably a manifestation of truth being, as argued by Foucault, 'a thing of this world ... the object, under diverse forms, of immense diffusion and consumption.'[88] There is a sense that if 'truth' is 'critical knowledge' or 'critical facts' to use Teitel's terms,[89] that information is there, below the surface, 'retained ... in private memory and consciousness,'[90] and may seep out. The existence of some awareness of what had taken place speaks to

82 Knapp, n 40.
83 DiFonzo and Bordia, n 45; Fujii, n 46.
84 Knapp, n 40.
85 Mary McClory speaking to Suzanne Breen in Breen, n 66.
86 See e.g. Susan McKay, 'Lost Boys,' *Field Day Review*, 9, (2013), 128–147.
87 Dudai, n 71 at 87.
88 Michel Foucault, 'Truth and Power,' in James D. Faubion (ed.) *Power: Essential Works of Foucault 1954–1984 (vol. 3)* (London: Penguin Books, 1994), p. 131.
89 Ruti G. Teitel, *Transitional Justice* (Oxford: Oxford University Press, 2000), p. 88.
90 Stanley Cohen, 'State Crimes of Previous Regimes: Knowledge, Accountability, and the Policing of the Past,' *Law & Social Inquiry*, 20:1, (1995), 7–50 (p. 18).

the gap between knowledge and acknowledgement that is encountered in transitional contexts,[91] a theme that will be explored further in Chapter 6.

'Rumours' about the fate of Brian McKinney and John McClory included that they were buried in secret graves in south Armagh, that they had found an IRA arms dump and given the weapons to the INLA, and that they were shot when trying to escape an execution.[92] This latter story was reported in 1995. The source – a former resident of west Belfast – was interviewed for UTV's *Counterpoint* programme and recounted that following the abduction of the two men, John McClory was shot as he tried to escape, and McKinney was then shot as a witness.[93] This story has been repeated elsewhere and McClory's sister has said in an interview that this is what the family heard had happened.[94] The story relating to the arms dump resonated with the rumours associated with the killing of another 'disappeared' person, Seamus Ruddy. Following Ruddy's 'disappearance,' the media reported that he may have been a victim of an INLA feud,[95] but more recent accounts suggest he was being questioned about arms smuggling prior to his killing,[96] and that his burial site was connected to a former INLA arms dump.[97]

Some of the most common whispers were those that related to the locations of burial sites. Claims were made that the bodies of the 'disappeared' were buried under housing estates, and on Black Mountain, just outside Belfast.[98] An unsuccessful search for the remains of Thomas Niedermayer took place at Waterfoot in Co. Antrim,[99] the location where Peter Wilson's body was recovered in 2010.[100]

91 Cohen, n 90; Naomi Roht-Arriaza, 'The New Landscape of Transitional Justice,' in Naomi Roht-Arriaza and Javier Mariezcurrena (eds) *Transitional Justice in the 21st Century* (Cambridge: Cambridge University Press, 2006), 1–16; Lawrence Weschler, *A Miracle, A Universe: Settling Accounts with Torturers* (Chicago: University of Chicago Press, 1998).

92 Tanya Acheson, 'New Revelation in Hunt for Disappeared,' *Belfast Telegraph*, 18 May 1995; Breen, n 66.

93 Acheson, ibid.

94 Jamie Macaskill, 'Give Back Our Sons,' *Scottish Daily Record*, 8 September 1998; Nick Thorpe, 'Mother's Hope She Can Lay Her Son to Rest,' *The Scotsman*, 27 June 1998.

95 'Family Asks IRSP to Help in Search,' *The Irish Times*, 16 August 1985; 'Missing Man May be Victim of Feud,' *The Irish Times*, 8 July 1985; Ian Geldard and Keith Craig, *IRA, INLA: Foreign Support and International Connections* (London: Institute for the Study of Terrorism, 1988).

96 Martin Breen, 'Secret Grave is Found,' *Belfast Telegraph*, 2 February 1999.

97 Martin Breen, 'Legal Bid to Recover Body of Murder Victim,' *Belfast Telegraph*, 2 March 1999.

98 Liam Clarke and Andrew Alderson, 'Revealed,' *The Sunday Times*, 18 June 1995; Gerry Moriarty, 'IRA Victims Campaign Stepped Up,' *The Irish Times*, 27 June 1995; Thorpe, n 94; Una Bradley, '"Disappeared" Man's Mother "Shattered" by End of Search,' *Belfast Telegraph*, 23 December 1998.

99 Fionnuala O'Connor, 'Tip-Off Starts New Hunt for Body,' *The Irish Times*, 8 November 1978.

100 Dan Keenan, 'Search Begins in Beauty Spot for Body of Man "Disappeared" During Troubles,' *The Irish Times*, 27 October 2010; 'The Disappeared – Peter Wilson – Family in Attendance as Remains Taken From Beach,' *The Irish News*, 4 November 2010.

Niedermayer's body was eventually found in Colin Glen forest in 1980, close to where it was at one time rumoured that the bodies of John McClory and Brian McKinney were buried in the nearby Glen Colin housing estate.[101] In 1995, newspapers reported that sources described a 'graveyard' for suspected 'informers and collaborators' on Black Mountain, and there were rumours that McConville's remains were buried at a location in the Divis Flats area.[102] In 1995, former IRA member – and a prominent British agent – Sean O'Callaghan contacted Margaret McKinney from Maghaberry Prison to inform her that, while drinking with Seamus Twomey (former IRA chief of staff) and another senior IRA figure, he heard that Brian had been killed and buried on Black Mountain.[103] Mrs McKinney was later given a map, allegedly of the location of Brian's burial site.[104] Gerry Evans' aunt was also sent a map of a burial location that proved to be incorrect. An IRA intermediary told reporter Suzanne Breen that he believed "the person who gave it was well meaning but it was based on rumours among republicans shortly after Gerard disappeared."[105] These whispers of false locations, regardless the motivations of those involved, were convincing for some relatives and therefore all the more hurtful when they turned out to be ill-founded. The case of Seamus Ruddy is one example in which a rumour contained accurate information. Willie Gallagher, spokesperson for the Irish Republican Socialist Party (the political organisation linked to the INLA), described in a radio interview how:

> We came across what seemingly seemed an insignificant rumour which we pursued and eventually that insignificant piece of information provided the key to unlock a door in regards to more precision where the body was and basically we were successful in the recovery.[106]

When the first reports emerged that bodies were buried in the border counties, Seamus McKendry was sceptical: "We know for a fact that some of the bodies are buried … in Belfast, so why now is there all this talk about the border areas?"[107] Rumours and accounts such as these, whether or not wholly accurate, hid

101 Eamon Phoenix, 'RUC Files Outline Events After Abduction of Niedermayer,' *The Irish Times*, 30 December 2009; Martin Breen, '"Disappeared" Families Allowed to Bury Dead,' *Belfast Telegraph*, 30 March 1999.
102 'Adams Called on to Pressurise IRA Over Graves of "Disappeared",' *The Irish Times*, 16 August 1995; Moriarty, n 98; Ruth O'Reilly, 'Families Launch Fresh Appeal for Bodies,' *The Irish News*, 19 June 1995; Gerard Millar, 'IRA Victims "Buried in Estate",' *The Irish News*, 21 June 1995.
103 'Police to Quiz Ex-IRA Man on Missing Bodies,' *Belfast Telegraph*, 19 June 1995.
104 'I'll Never Find my Son's Remains,' *Belfast Telegraph*, 22 March 2006.
105 Breen, n 66.
106 BBC Radio Foyle, Willie Gallagher in interview, BBC Radio Foyle, 8 May 1999. Available at http://rfe123.org/willie-gallagher-bbc-radio-foyle-interview-transcrip t-8-may-2017 [accessed 30 June 2018].
107 Claire McGahan, '"Let Me Bury My Son" Pleads Mother,' *Belfast Telegraph*, 26 June 1998.

whispers of the truth, suggesting that some level of information relating to 'disappearances' had leaked out from those who had information.

Although these whispers are clear retrospectively, at the time, as described by Sandra Peake of WAVE, 'the issue … was, by and large, hidden, and there were multiple levels of silence at all levels within the community.'[108] As explored in Chapter 1, although silence is a deliberate or chosen response to an occurrence or set of circumstances, the extent to which that choice is a free one can be limited. Those in power can deter those below them from speaking out through exerting that power to instil fear; as Winter suggests, silencing can be a 'strategy of control.'[109] Such a form of control was witnessed during the Troubles. As has been examined already in this book and as outlined in *The Green Book*, the penalties for 'loose talk' were severe and 'speaking out against the IRA was a kind of taboo subject.'[110] When such a threat exists, silence can serve as 'a means to protect the self and others.'[111] Just as rumours can be almost 'self-propelling,'[112] silence also has a cumulative effect and 'becomes more prohibitive the longer it lasts.'[113] A silence, imposed on a community where speaking out was taboo, could build on itself to become more impenetrable as the years went on.

There are other reasons why silence may have enveloped the issue of the 'disappeared.' As considered previously, in those cases where rumours suggested a person had been an informer, many in the community would have turned away. Another possibility is that during the 1970s and early 1980s when the majority of these 'disappearances' occurred there was simply too much violence for one missing person to receive much attention. In her account of the US response to the Rwandan genocide, Samantha Power describes a conversation with one senior US official from that period who has an awareness that, in spite of a number of possible distractions that he has considered, 'he must simply have chosen to look away.'[114] In the case of the 'disappeared,' there may have been too much to look at. In interview, journalist Brian Rowan described how:

108 WAVE, n 61 at 1.

109 Jay Winter, 'Thinking About Silence,' in Efrat Ben-Ze'ev, Ruth Ginio and Jay Winter (eds) *Shadows of War: A Social History of Silence in the Twentieth Century* (Cambridge: Cambridge University Press, 2010), pp. 3–31 (p. 8).

110 Margaret McKinney in WAVE, n 61 at 53.

111 Fiona C. Ross, 'An Acknowledged Failure: Women, Voice, Violence, and the South African Truth and Reconciliation Commission,' in Rosalind Shaw and Lars Waldorf (eds) *Localizing Transitional Justice* (California: Stanford University Press, 2010), pp. 69–91 (p. 89).

112 Knapp, n 40 at 28.

113 Eviatar Zerubavel, 'The Social Sound of Silence: Toward a Sociology of Denial,' in Efrat Ben-Ze'ev, Ruth Ginio and Jay Winter (eds) *Shadows of War: A Social History of Silence in the Twentieth Century* (Cambridge: Cambridge University Press, 2010), pp. 32–46 (p. 38).

114 Samantha Power, 'Bystanders to Genocide,' *Atlantic Monthly*, 1 September 2001, www.theatlantic.com/magazine/archive/2001/09/bystanders-to-genocide/304571/10/ [accessed 9 August 2018].

> Journalistically ... we went from one event to the next ... I've used this term that people were sometimes dead for a couple of hours, and what I meant was they were the news headline at nine, and somebody else was the news headline at 12.[115]

This highlights the difficulty in maintaining media or public attention on any one case. As one resident of west Belfast explained to reporter Allison Morris of the 'disappearance' of Peter Wilson, "maybe you would have talked about it for a day or two and that would have been it ... It's not that people didn't care. It's just that the situation was so chaotic."[116]

Silence has been described as the 'foremost public form of denial.'[117] As analysed previously, the motivations for spreading rumours, and for remaining silent, with regards the 'disappeared' are complex, intermingled with suspicion and hatred of informers, fear of, and loyalty to, the IRA, and the surrounding mayhem of violent conflict concentrated in specific communities. These factors arguably created a gulf between what was known or suspected privately and what was openly part of public discourse. There existed elements of Zerubavel's 'conspiracy of silence' where 'people collectively ignore something of which each one of them is personally aware,'[118] and this was conducive to reinforcing the act of 'disappearance.' As explored in Chapter 1, Trouillot argues that the 'production of traces is always the creation of silences.'[119] In the case of the 'disappeared,' the spreading of false narratives – some rumours based on plausible but inaccurate explanations, and other whispers not far from the truth – served to create silences. Telling families of sightings elsewhere or plans to emigrate silenced them by removing the need to ask questions. Rumours (whether true or not) that the 'disappeared' were working for the state separated families from their communities and thus created a buffer of silence around them. Finally, whispers of the truth – for those who heard them – may have created a fear of speaking out.

With regards fear, while there is no evidence in the Irish context to suggest that 'disappearing' was used as a form of social repression akin to the Argentinian experience, those connected to the 'disappeared' have spoken of the fear they experienced in the aftermath of the abductions. Following Brendan Megraw's abduction, uncertainty over his fate initially deterred his family from seeking help, as they were concerned that his abductors would do him harm if they informed the police – a threat that remained as long as his killing was not admitted.[120] By not admitting to a person's murder the IRA effectively tied the hands of families, as any attempt to find out what happened could have dangerous repercussions for

115 Interview, Brian Rowan, journalist, commentator, and former BBC security correspondent, September 2014.

116 Morris, n 74.

117 Zerubavel, n 113 at 33.

118 Ibid. at 32.

119 Michel-Rolph Trouillot, *Silencing the Past: Power and the Production of History*, (Boston: Beacon Press, 1995), p. 29.

120 In Megraw's case the police were made aware and undertook an investigation (see references in footnote 3).

their abducted relative who, to their knowledge, may still be alive. In some cases where families attempted to make inquiries, they were threatened.[121] Margaret McKinney, for example, has spoken of being warned against asking too many questions.[122]

Taussig describes how 'cultures of terror are nourished by the intermingling of silence and myth.'[123] A 'disappearance' from a close-knit Republican community, often experiencing the complex dialectic of significant levels of support for the IRA while simultaneously being subject to IRA violence, has the ingredients to produce such a culture. Though the 'Movement' may be officially silent, and this was the response encountered by those families making enquiries, enough of the truth seeped out to create myths that contained whispers of the truth. The effects of such a combination were witnessed in south Armagh when, between 1979 and 1981, Sean Murphy,[124] Gerry Evans, and Charlie Armstrong all 'vanished without trace,' creating 'fear and suspicion among the whole people.'[125] Within the Republican community, and Ireland more broadly, the risk of breaking the rules of the IRA or betraying the cause had been known for generations. Yet, the use of the practice of 'disappearing' may have introduced a previously 'unknown threat,'[126] which served to silence both families and the wider community.

3. Why stand by? The causes of silence, whisper, and rumour

It has been suggested that even in hard-line Republican areas, the public were, at least in later years, disgusted by news of 'disappearing' having taken place.[127] Yet, as has been proposed here, it is evident that even if not widespread, knowledge of what happened, or some suspicion relating to the sort of actions that were being carried out, existed beyond the confines of those directly involved. One of the *Madres* of the Plaza de Mayo asserts that 'one has to speak up; otherwise one becomes an accomplice.'[128] In the cases of the 'disappeared' it seems that in some instances in Northern Ireland there were those who did not 'speak up.' Using the notion of 'the bystander' – described by Cohen as 'those who come to know, see or hear, either at the time or later'[129] – I now wish to examine this phenomenon in a little more detail.

121 WAVE, n 61.
122 WAVE, ibid. at 53.
123 Michael T. Taussig, *Shamanism, Colonialism, and the Wild Man: A Study in Terror and Healing* (Chicago; London: Chicago University Press, 1986), p. 8.
124 See footnote 12 for details of Murphy case.
125 O'Connor, n 11.
126 Antonius C. G. M. Robben, *Political Violence and Trauma in Argentina,* (Philadelphia: University of Pennsylvania Press, 2005), p. 274.
127 Allison Morris, 'The Disappeared – Secretly Buried Remains May Have Been Moved Before,' *The Irish News*, 10 December 2010.
128 Rita Arditti, *Searching for Life: The Grandmothers of the Plaza de Mayo and the Disappeared Children of Argentina* (California: University of California Press, 1999), pp. 90–91.
129 Cohen, n 14 at 15.

In post-conflict processes, Fletcher and Weinstein suggest that bystanders – who did not actively participate in violent acts but also did not actively intervene – are an overlooked category.[130] The notion of an 'innocent bystander' to a conflict has been challenged, given the collective nature of mass violence and the influence of social context.[131] Fletcher argues elsewhere that although the behaviour of bystanders should not be criminalised, she echoes the words of Arditti's interviewee, contending that "doing nothing" is "doing something."[132] Hannah Arendt famously examines these ideas in *Eichmann in Jerusalem*, arguing that focusing on Eichmann's individual deeds precluded exploration of broader questions on the conditions that brought about his actions. Arendt directs our attention to those who knew what was taking place, and those who later came to know but who did not act. She quotes one German army doctor who knew of the activities of the S.S. mobile killing units: "We knew this. We did nothing. Anyone who had seriously protested … would have disappeared."[133]

The failure of the international community to act to prevent or limit the Rwandan genocide in 1994 is another example of standing by on a vast scale. In Power's account of the Clinton administration as 'Bystanders to Genocide,' she analyses the potential actions not taken, and isolates a number of 'justifications' given by the US administration for not taking action on the Rwandan crisis. Ultimately, as Power outlines, the reality of what was taking place in Rwanda was denied. Framing the crisis as a civil war or a peacekeeping issue rather than genocide removed the need for urgent action to be taken.[134] Rwanda provides an example of by-standing on an international scale. However, Cohen articulates the more everyday nature of the behaviour of bystanders, which may be more appropriate for considering the response of the community to the 'disappeared.'[135]

Cohen suggests that dramatic images, such as the CCTV footage of onlookers witnessing Jamie Bulger, prior to his murder, being led away from his mother and beaten, generate a discourse that contrasts too starkly the passive bystander from the good Samaritan, whereas in reality, a range of everyday situations can influence how bystanders behave.[136] Several of the situations outlined are potentially pertinent in the context of the 'disappeared.' Ambiguity can influence the reaction of bystanders to a situation.[137] As considered earlier, although there was uncertainty over the fate of these individuals there were credible explanations in circulation as to why they may have gone missing. It is possible that there were those in the

130 Laurel Fletcher and Harvey M. Weinstein, 'Violence and Social Repair: Rethinking the Contribution of Justice to Reconciliation,' *Human Rights Quarterly*, 24:3, (2002), 573–639.
131 Ibid. See also Hannah Arendt, *Eichmann in Jerusalem: A Report on the Banality of Evil* (Harmondsworth: Penguin Books, 1994).
132 Laurel E. Fletcher, 'From Indifference to Engagement: Bystanders and International Criminal Justice,' *Michigan Journal of International Law*, 26:4, (2005), 1013–1095.
133 Arendt, n 131 at 232.
134 Power, n 114.
135 Cohen, n 14.
136 Ibid. at 69–75.
137 Ibid.

community ready to believe these accounts. Those who heard rumours of these people having been informers may have been concerned about the anticipated reaction of others, if they intervened. Even greater than the risk of social sanction, however, would be the risk of violence to themselves for speaking out. The Cost of the Troubles Study found that in those areas of highest intensity conflict, 71% of respondents very often felt the need to conceal things in order to feel safe.[138] One interviewee suggested that one of the reasons others in the community did not speak out may have been: "the sense of fear about what might happen if they say ... often there are dark things which in something like a war ... people want to stay safe from. There was a lot of looking the other way."[139]

A further suggestion of Cohen's with regard to the passivity of bystanders is that of a sense of social justice and equity, in terms of who is deserving of help.[140] Rumours of people still being alive, having run away with a woman, or having been relocated because of their previous role as an informer may suggest some lack of community empathy for those who were missing. Given the accusations made against the individuals concerned, and the intensity of the conflict at the time, this would not perhaps be entirely surprising. This feeling was expressed in Adams' 1999 remark that Eamonn Molloy "was an informer and that is something which is reviled in all aspects of society on this island."[141] In the case of Jean McConville, Malachi O'Doherty described to the author how "there were people close to the McConville family – geographically close to them ... [who] were prepared to believe all kinds of possible rumours about why this woman had gone missing, and were not particularly helpful to the family."[142]

This apparent lack of empathy was felt by some family members themselves, as illustrated by the following account given by Jean McConville's daughter, Helen. As Helen returned to their flat on the night of Jean's abduction 'it struck [her] as odd that so many people should be standing out on the balconies ... people were staring and whispering.'[143] In the period following the abduction, little attention was apparently paid to the children by police, social workers, or priests, and the flurry of media attention in January 1973 waned.[144] This account raises questions about the responsibilities of the wider community and society more broadly. Kate Turner, of Healing Through Remembering, has spoken of a "guilt on wider society," asking:

> Where's the questions about what happened [to] the McConville family and social services, where were the questions about the media, [they] interviewed

138 Marie Therese Fay, Mike Morrissey, Marie Smith and Tracy Wong, *The Cost of the Troubles Study: Report on the Northern Ireland Survey: The Experience and Impact of the Troubles* (Londonderry: INCORE, 2001), p. 39.
139 Interview, Richard English, historian, August 2014.
140 Cohen, n 14.
141 'Cheap Shots,' *Fortnight*, 379, (June 1999), p. 5.
142 Interview, Malachi O'Doherty, journalist and writer, August 2015.
143 McKendry, n 12 at 18.
144 Ibid.; WAVE n 61.

those kids and then forgot about [them]? … there's something missing about saying what did we not do as a society that said what's happening in these situations?[145]

4. Policing 'disappearances': context and challenges

While the British and Irish governments' responses to the 'disappearances' will be examined in the next chapter, the response by police at the time of the 'disappearances' will be considered here as in at least two cases (see below) where abductions were witnessed, the Royal Ulster Constabulary (RUC) was approached to investigate at the time. Furthermore, as will be examined, relations between police and the communities from which these individuals were 'disappeared' potentially impacted upon the police response.

Searching for information on the role of the police in investigating the 'disappearances' produces minimal results. Two abductions were witnessed by family members and reported to police. In the case of Brendan Megraw, the RUC appealed for information, and succeeded in establishing information on at least one of the cars used.[146] In the case of Jean McConville, a 2006 report by the Office of the Police Ombudsman for Northern Ireland (OPONI) found that although the police were made aware in January 1973 that McConville had disappeared, 'no investigation took place until 1995.'[147] In June of that year, a special police team of eight detectives was appointed and 'concentrated resources' on the cases of the 'disappeared,' resulting in five arrests in January 1996.[148] All were released without charge.[149]

Three particular barriers existed to police investigations into the abductions of the 'disappeared.' The first was, as has been detailed, the sense of fear that existed in some communities, and the power exercised over them by the IRA, which may have served to silence those with information that could assist an investigation. Toolis has described how, following one murder in Belfast, the RUC came 'in search of the eyewitnesses they knew they would never find and who everyone knew had seen nothing.'[150] Indeed, even in 2014 fear continued to prevent Jean

145 Interview, Kate Turner, September 2014.

146 'Hunt on for Kidnap Gang,' n 3; 'Kidnap Hunt Goes On – But Few Clues,' n 3; 'Hunt for Kidnappers Goes On,' *Belfast Telegraph*, 13 April 1978; 'Belfast Kidnap: New Appeal,' *Belfast Telegraph*, 14 April 1978; 'Police Theory in Kidnap Mystery,' *Belfast Telegraph*, 19 April 1978.

147 Office of the Police Ombudsman for Northern Ireland, *Report into the Complaint by James and Michael McConville Regarding the Police Investigation Into the Abduction and Murder of Their Mother Mrs Jean McConville* (Belfast: Office of the Policy Ombudsman for Northern Ireland, 2006).

148 Tanya Acheson, 'Five Men Quizzed on "Disappeared",' *Belfast Telegraph*, 22 January 1996; 'Police to Quiz Ex-IRA Man on Missing Bodies,' n 103; 'RUC Holds 5 in Inquiry on "Disappeared",' *The Irish Times*, 26 January 1996.

149 'Five Freed After Questioning by RUC,' *Belfast Telegraph*, 26 January 1996.

150 Kevin Toolis, *Rebel Hearts: Journeys Within the IRA's Soul* (London: Picador, 1996), p. 2.

McConville's son Michael from naming those involved in his mother's abduction.[151]

The second barrier was the sense of alienation which existed between the RUC and many within the Nationalist community.[152] There was a lack of trust in the organisation, especially within Catholic and Nationalist communities.[153] The religious and political composition of the RUC, its focus on combating 'terrorism' rather than responding to so-called 'ordinary' crime, and its history of involvement in human rights abuses undermined its legitimacy in Nationalist communities, and thus its ability to effectively police these areas.[154] For Republicans, the legitimacy of the RUC was of course further undermined by its association with the British state, their toleration of so-called 'ordinary' crime carried out by those who agreed to inform for them, and a perceived 'inability or unwillingness … to "properly" police Republican areas.'[155]

A third barrier is likely to have been the difficulties faced by police in attempting to enter certain areas. It has been reported that security forces came under attack almost daily and struggled to cope with the volume of incidents that were taking place.[156] These dynamics resulted in an absence of 'normal policing' in some of those areas most affected by the Troubles.[157] English has highlighted how these challenges may have impacted on any investigation into the 'disappeared':

> I don't know that it's true but I suspect that it's true that if you were prioritising as a police person, if you had to choose between which things you were investigating or prioritising and which you weren't, the 'disappearance' of possibly a Republican, from a Republican area, probably killed by Republicans … there's a hierarchy of this, there's only so much time in the day, there's only so much evidence … certain of the places where they'd have

151 Michael McHugh and David Young, 'Gerry Adams Latest: Jean McConville's Son Fears for His Life, Sinn Féin Hits Out at Unionist "Old Guard",' *Belfast Telegraph*, 1 May 2014; Fionola Meredith, 'We Live Distorted Normality Where Fear Still Reigns,' *Belfast Telegraph*, 9 May 2014.

152 Andrew Silke, 'Rebel's Dilemma: The Changing Relationship Between the IRA, Sinn Féin and Paramilitary Vigilantism in Northern Ireland,' *Terrorism and Political Violence*, 11:1, (1999), 55–93.

153 Human Rights Watch (Helsinki), *Children in Northern Ireland: Abused by Security Forces and Paramilitaries* (1992); Kathleen A. Cavanaugh, 'Interpretations of Political Violence in Ethnically Divided Societies,' *Terrorism and Political Violence*, 9:3, (1997), 33–54; Bradley W. C. Bamford, 'The Role and Effectiveness of Intelligence in Northern Ireland,' *Intelligence and National Security*, 20:4, (2005), 581–607.

154 Kieran McEvoy and Harry Mika, 'Punishment, Policing and Praxis: Restorative Justice and Non-Violent Alternatives to Paramilitary Punishments in Northern Ireland,' *Policing and Security*, 11:3–4, (2001), 359–382.

155 Ibid. at 361.

156 Historical Enquiries Team, Review Summary Report, cited in Patricia Lundy, 'Exploring Transitional Justice and its Dilemmas: A Case Study of the Historical Enquiries Team, Northern Ireland,' *International Journal of Transitional Justice*, 3:3, (2009), 321–340; Human Rights Watch, n 153.

157 Human Rights Watch, n 153.

> needed to get evidence, when they went in there they had to have … the army with them to protect them from getting attacked by the people who killed the person whose death they were investigating.[158]

This danger, combined with uncertainty over the circumstances of a person's absence, in part enhanced by the spreading of rumours as outlined earlier, arguably rendered police action even less likely. As Brian Rowan asked in interview: "What is a missing person at that stage? Because these families are being told, 'he's run away', 'he might come back', so you don't have any definitive, definite proof."[159] For Danny Morrison:

> It was a military situation and … looking back now, although we were cynical at the time, even the police resources were overstretched and couldn't cope … so there's a report that somebody went missing – there's lots of people left here. Lots of people ran away from home.[160]

With regards this 'military situation,' one element that has not been fully explored and is beyond the scope of this book is the relationship between military intelligence and the fate of the 'disappeared.' Columba McVeigh's brother Oliver has remarked that Columba "had two enemies … the British Army and the IRA."[161] For his brother, Eugene, the state has questions to answer:

> While the IRA pulled the trigger … I don't dismiss the State's involvement in any of this. Because some of these people were compromised and … they … lost their lives by the machinations of the state who believed these people might have been useful to them…[162]

One interviewee suggested that the role of intelligence was excluded from efforts to address the issue of 'disappearance':

> underlying a lot of it was the role of British intelligence but that wasn't central to the thing. That could be put to one side … it's not just that it didn't raise these particular questions – but, I think everyone was happy to treat it in this self-contained way without looking into these bigger questions.[163]

158 Interview, Richard English, August 2014.
159 Interview, Brian Rowan, September 2014.
160 Interview, Danny Morrison, January 2015.
161 Oliver McVeigh's account in WAVE, n 61 at 40.
162 Interview, Eugene McVeigh, August 2015.
163 Interview, former diplomat who has been engaged in efforts to deal with the past in Northern Ireland, June 2015.

5. The impact of 'standing by'

In a context of mass violence, Fletcher argues that what is relied on is a 'social apparatus' that allows or enables these acts of violence to be carried out.[164] Although the Irish 'disappearances' were sporadic acts of violence, this chapter has established that social conditions existed at that time which allowed these abductions to be hidden, ignored, or to go unnoticed. That these acts could be carried out, with minimal attention from those in the wider community, little in the way of investigation from the police or interest from the media tells us much about the chaos of these times, particularly in those communities most intensely impacted by the conflict. It also offers a stark illustration of the effects of suspicion, mistrust, threat, and fear, not just between communities but also within them. The 'disappeared' became so, not just because they were abducted, murdered, and buried in secret by armed groups, but because these acts occurred at a time and in places where acts such as these could happen.

The suspicion and misunderstanding that can result from a 'disappearance' can be damaging for community relations for decades afterwards.[165] It has been suggested elsewhere that the behaviour of bystanders during a conflict is something that should be considered during reconciliation.[166] In a study of ICTY witnesses, Stover found that one of the biggest obstructions to reconciliation was an unwillingness and inability of those neighbours who stood by as crimes were committed to acknowledge that they did so.[167] Although Stover's example relates to those from different national groups, there is some indication with regards the 'disappeared' that, at least in some cases, although the public focus is very much on the IRA and Adams, the effects of the community's reaction to the relatives of those who were 'disappeared' have had a lasting effect. Eugene McVeigh has described their village, Donaghmore, as 'a nest of vipers' due to the involvement of local IRA men in Columba's 'disappearance.'[168] In interview, when asked if his family received any support in the aftermath of the 'disappearance,' Eugene responded:

> No, nothing. Not a thing … I mean honestly I can say that from 1975 … right through to the Good Friday Agreement period, nothing. We knew nothing. We heard nothing. We were told nothing. And there were people in our community who did know and they were members of the Provisional IRA and Sinn Féin.[169]

164 Fletcher, n 132 at 1026.
165 International Committee of the Red Cross, 'Living with Absence: Helping the Families of the Missing' (ICRC, 2014), www.icrc.org/eng/resources/documents/publication/p4152.htm [9 August 2018].
166 Fletcher, n 132.
167 Eric Stover, 'Witnesses and the Promises of Justice in The Hague,' in Eric Stover and Harvey Weinstein (eds) *My Neighbour, My Enemy: Justice and Community in the Aftermath of Mass Atrocity* (Cambridge: Cambridge University Press, 2004), pp. 104–120.
168 Susan McKay, *Bear in Mind These Dead* (London: Faber & Faber, 2008), p. 177.
169 Interview, Eugene McVeigh, August 2015.

When Susan McKay met with Columba McVeigh's mother in 2005, she found her unable to forgive 'those in the village who knew what had been done but who had said nothing as she watched and waited.'[170] In a similar vein, Kate Turner spoke to the author about deeply embedded mistrust amongst the families of the 'disappeared' towards wider society:

> They were ignored for so long that they do have less trust. Wider society ignored them, and forgot about them … it's not just that they don't trust Republicans … They don't trust the media, they don't trust the rest of us, and I understand completely why.[171]

Such isolation was not the case for all families, it should be noted. For the Megraw family, Kieran recounted:

> Where we lived, everybody was supportive to my mum and the family, within school and all that. And wider family were [supportive] … but we always thought he was coming back, like. And … then it sort of drifted on, some people still … would have said, 'what's happening, was there any word' or whatever.[172]

6. Conclusion

In this chapter I have argued that the response of the local community in the aftermath of the 'disappearances' was a mixture of silence, rumour, and whisper. Although the motivations for these different responses are complex, and may not necessarily be sinister or deliberate, they had a real impact, both at the time and since. The reaction of the community is seldom given much attention in reports on the 'disappeared,' with the media focussing on the families themselves or the Republican Movement. However, as has been contended, the community did have a role and this should not be overlooked. Without detracting from the responsibility of the perpetrators in abducting and killing these individuals, at the time the 'disappearances' were carried out, in the communities where these people were from, and in wider society, conditions existed that reinforced the act of 'disappearing.' Families found themselves misled by rumour and isolated by silence. For those who heard whispers of what was taking place, there was nowhere to turn, particularly if those whispers related to informing. For those cases that did receive media attention, that attention quickly passed on to the next news 'event.'

Jaquemet suggests the missing are 'an ideal testing ground' for processes of how to confront the past.[173] This chapter has introduced some of the challenges of approaching these cases via criminal investigation. One factor which would have

170 McKay, n 86.
171 Interview, Kate Turner, September 2014.
172 Interview, Kieran Megraw, brother of Brendan Megraw, October 2015.
173 Iolanda Jaquemet, 'Fighting Amnesia: Ways to Uncover the Truth about Lebanon's Missing,' *International Journal of Transitional Justice*, 3:1, (2008), 69–90 (p. 90).

likely fundamentally undermined any efforts to locate the 'disappeared' via criminal investigation is that the recovery of remains without information from those directly involved would have been highly unlikely, if not impossible. As journalist Brian Rowan has said, "the people who are best placed to investigate … are not the police. It's the IRA. Because they hold, if not all the information, considerably more."[174] To access the information held by the IRA necessitated a compromise, which the next chapter will examine.

174 Interview, Brian Rowan, September 2014.

5 'Quiet' transitional justice and 'disappearing'

1. Introduction

Following a 1995 meeting with Security Minister Sir John Wheeler, Helen McKendry described her continued hope that political pressure on the Republican Movement would yield results.[1] In February 1999, Victims Minister Adam Ingram called for information and urged those who could do so to pressure those with information to come forward.[2] At this time, although the public approach had changed little, it was becoming evident that the combination of political pressure and public shaming was insufficient to encourage action. Within three months of Ingram's statement, the legislation that would facilitate the establishment of the Independent Commission for the Location of Victims' Remains (ICLVR) was being passed through the Houses of Parliament and the Dáil.[3] This chapter will chart the development of this legislation and argue that this can be considered an example of what I have termed 'quiet' transitional justice. First, I will argue that the legislation can be considered a victim-centred approach, and address the claims made by some that it amounts to an amnesty.

2. The Location of Victims' Remains legislation as a victim-centred approach

In responding to the issue of the 'disappeared' in the aftermath of conflict, there are tensions between the humanitarian needs of families, and prosecutorial needs of a trial.[4] This debate to an extent mirrors wider discussion on the roles of truth

1 Marie Foy, 'Wheeler Pledge Over "Disappeared",' *Belfast Telegraph*, 8 September 1995.

2 Northern Ireland Information Service, *Minister Pledges to Keep up Pressure for Information on the "Disappeared"*, [Press Release], 8 February 1999.

3 Northern Ireland (Location of Victims' Remains) Act 1999 and Criminal Justice (Location of Victims' Remains) Act 1999, respectively.

4 Adam Rosenblatt, *Digging for the Disappeared: Forensic Science After Atrocity* (Stanford: Stanford University Press, 2015); Eric Stover and Rachel Shigekane, 'The Missing in the Aftermath of War: When do the Needs of Victims' Families and International War Crimes Tribunals Clash?' *International Review of the Red Cross*, 84:848, (2002), 845–866.

and justice in post-conflict contexts, bearing in mind of course that the return of a body does not equate to the provision of truth (see Chapter 6). Stover and Shigekane suggest that similar tensions in other contexts between families and international war crimes tribunals are a relatively common phenomenon. Families want to know the fate of their missing relatives and, if they have been killed, to have their remains located and returned. International war crimes tribunals require evidence to secure a prosecution, but this may not require identification of all victims.[5] The debate in Parliament over the true beneficiaries of the Location of Victims' Remains (LVR) legislation speaks to this tension.

Those in favour claimed the Bill was victim-centric, with a humanitarian aim of responding to the needs of the families of the 'disappeared.' They argued that the purpose of the legislation was to demonstrate compassion and bring some closure to the families of the 'disappeared' by making possible the Christian burial of their loved ones. Families were argued to be the "prime beneficiaries"[6] and the Bill's humanitarian nature was at the forefront of arguments in support of the legislation in both the British and Irish parliaments.[7]

Opponents of the Bill argued that it was created for the benefit of the IRA, as a concession or act of appeasement. For Lord Tebbit, the Bill demonstrated "the power of the IRA to extract concessions from the government."[8] Others pointed out different circumstances in which families would not have their relatives' remains returned – such as war, or when a person is lost at sea.[9] In a similar vein, several speakers commented on the relatively small number of 'disappeared' in comparison to the total number of people killed during the Troubles, with Baroness Park suggesting the Bill would, for a small number of families, "compromise justice for all."[10] There was a sense, from these speakers, that the rights of the many should not be compromised for the humanitarian needs of the few.

Some of the strongest criticism of the legislation came from Northern Ireland's Unionist politicians. With regards the Unionist narrative, Lawther contends, 'responsibility for the conflict is laid at the door of the Republican Movement,'[11] and this is reflected in their response to this Bill. Several Unionist MPs argued that the Bill should not be necessary, as it was the terrorists' responsibility to return the

5 Stover and Shigekane, n 4.
6 John McDonnell MP, HC Deb, 10 May 1999, vol 331, col 55.
7 HC Deb 10 May 1999, vol 331, cols 38–83; HC Deb 12 May 1999, vol 331, cols 324–384; HL Deb 18 May 1999, vol 601, cc 153–190; HL Deb 24 May 1999, vol 601, cc. 639–664; DE Deb 5 May 1999, vol 504, no. 2; DE Deb 12 May 1999, vol 504, No. 5; Seanad Éireann Debate 13 May 1999, vol 159, No. 9.
8 HL Deb 24 May 1999, vol 601, cc. 639–664.
9 HL Deb 18 May 1999, vol 601, cc. 153–190.
10 Baroness Park, HL Deb 18 May 1999, vol 601, cc. 153–190. See also comments by Lord Molyneaux in same debate and Ken Maginnis in HC Deb 12 May 1999, vol 331, col 327.
11 Cheryl Lawther, *Truth, Denial and Transition: Northern Ireland and the Contested Past* (Abingdon: Routledge, 2014), p. 31.

remains, and not that of the House, or society at large.[12] William Thompson MP criticised the creation of another all-Ireland body (the ICLVR), claiming its formation was a demonstration of the government's lack of commitment to the Union.[13] During the debate, statements made by Northern Ireland MPs suggested an inability or unwillingness to see beyond their own views in order to assist the families.[14] Their response demonstrates the gap between political rhetoric and the reality of 'dealing with' conflict as explored by Dixon.[15] No Northern Ireland politician put forward a viable alternative solution to the problem of the 'disappeared,' and the debate was instead used as a platform from which to criticise the Republican Movement. This weaponisation of memory will be analysed further in Chapter 6.

While the Bill met with criticism on its passage through both Westminster and the Dáil, it passed in both jurisdictions.[16] For a number of interviewees, this was in part due to the Bill's humanitarian aim, and that passing the legislation was in the interests of the families.[17] Indeed, the introduction of the legislation can be argued to be a victim-centred act. As established in Chapter 2, the families' campaign centred on their call for the return of the remains of their loved ones. In an overview of processes for recovering the 'disappeared,' Nesiah advises that in undertaking a non-judicial process (such as this one) that offers some form of incentive to perpetrators for providing information, the views of victims should be considered.[18] Transitional mechanisms can derive legitimacy from victims,[19] and in the case of this legislation, families declared their support. A number of MPs and Lords mentioned that their decision to support the Bill was influenced by a visit by several families to the House of Commons prior to the debate, and a letter written by them to the Lords. For example, the MP Norman Godman remarked,

12 Peter Robinson HC Deb 10 May 1999, vol 331, col 58; Ken Maginnis HC Deb 12 May 1999, vol 331, col 328; William Thompson HC Deb 12 May 1999, vol 331, col 381.

13 William Thompson HC Deb 12 May 1999, vol 331, col 381

14 See e.g. comments by William Ross, HC Deb 10 May 1999, vol 331, cols 65–68 and Brian Mawhinney, HC Deb 12 May 1999, vol 331, col 324.

15 Paul Dixon, 'Political Skills or Lying and Manipulation? The Choreography of the Northern Ireland Peace Process,' *Political Studies*, 50:4, (2002), 725–741.

16 Bill passed by 324 votes to 5 in the House of Commons. Conservative MPs abstained (except Douglas Hogg) and four Northern Ireland Unionist MPs voted against the Bill (for all debates and votes see: DE Deb 5 May 1999, vol 504, no 2; 12 May 1999, vol 504, no 5; HC Deb 12 May 1999, vol 331, col 384; HL Deb 18 May 1999, vol 601, cc. 153–190; 18 May 1999, vol 601, cc. 639–664; Seanad Éireann Debate (SE Deb) 13 May 1999, vol 159, no 9).

17 E.g. interviews with journalist and writer Susan McKay, July 2014; Adrian McNamee of the Commission for Victims and Survivors, November 2014; DUP MP Jeffrey Donaldson, March 2015.

18 Vasuki Nesiah, 'Overcoming Tensions Between Family and Judicial Procedures,' *International Review of the Red Cross*, 84:848, (2002), 823–844.

19 Sari Kouvo and Dallas Mazoori, 'Reconciliation, Justice and Mobilization of War Victims in Afghanistan,' *International Journal of Transitional Justice*, 5:3, (2011), 492–503.

"I met Mrs Margaret McKinney and another lady ... if I had any doubts about the Bill ... they were dispelled when I met those two ladies."[20]

It is a common theme in the transitional justice literature that political will and compromise are required to develop mechanisms that are effective in dealing with the past.[21] The debate over the passing of this legislation demonstrates both requirements. It is clear when reading the text of the debates that the passing of such legislation goes against the grain for some, yet the thread that runs through many of the speeches is that the Bill responds to the needs of the families, and that only an immunity of this nature will enable the recovery of remains. The overwhelming sense is that the Bill is regrettable but essential to achieve the desired goal – a "necessary evil."[22]

3. The Location of Victims' Remains legislation as amnesty

One of the specific criticisms of the LVR Bill which is worth addressing at length is the claim that it would amount to an amnesty. During the debate on the Bill in Westminster, Lord Fitt claimed the Bill granted "an amnesty to people who have committed some of the most depraved acts in Irish history."[23] The Bill is described as "obnoxious," "dangerous," "offensive," and undermining of the rule of law, the independence of the judiciary, and the very values that Parliament is supposed to represent.[24] Introducing the Bill, Ingram claimed that it was not an amnesty, and was in fact similar to the Northern Ireland Arms Decommissioning Act 1997.[25] Some agreed, with Lord Hylton suggesting that the 'amnesty' term was "an exaggeration."[26] Others drew attention to the practical reality of the situation. Lord Redesdale proposed that if bodies were not found, justice would be unlikely to be achieved anyway.[27] This view was summarised by MP Harry Barnes: "the Bill may allow people to get off the hook, but I do not think that that hook will catch anyone anyway."[28]

20 HC Deb 10 May 1999, vol 331, col 47. An undated 'Statement on behalf of relatives of the disappeared,' stored in the Linenhall Library's collection of ephemera on victim support organisations reads: 'We have no interest in gathering incriminating evidence.'

21 See e.g. Ellen Lutz, 'Transitional Justice: Lessons Learned and the Road Ahead,' in Naomi Roht-Arriaza and Javier Mariezcurrena (eds) *Transitional Justice in the 21st Century* (Cambridge: Cambridge University Press, 2006), pp. 325–341; Robert I. Rotberg, 'Truth Commissions and the Provision of Truth, Justice, and Reconciliation,' in Robert I. Rotberg and Dennis Thompson (eds) *Truth V. Justice: The Morality of Truth Commissions* (Princeton: Princeton University Press, 2000), pp. 3–21.

22 Malcolm Moss, HC Deb 10 May 1999, vol 331, col 46.

23 Rosie Uffindell, '"Disappeared" Law Set to Clear Final Hurdle,' *The Irish News*, 24 May 1999.

24 HC Deb 10 May 1999, vol 331, cols 56–66.

25 HC Deb 10 May 1999, vol 331, cols 40–42.

26 HL Deb 18 May 1999, vol 601, cc. 153–190.

27 HL Deb 18 May 1999, vol 601, cc. 153–190.

28 HC Deb 10 May 1999, vol 331, col 70.

Semantically rooted in the Greek *amnēstia*, meaning forgetfulness or oblivion,[29] amnesty is in some accounts associated with facilitating impunity.[30] For Ricoeur, the link between amnesty and amnesia is more than semantics, as amnesty becomes a process of 'commanded' or 'institutionalised' forgetting, in which memory is denied.[31] The connection between amnesty and forgetting has come to be a dominant perspective in literature on the topic.[32] So-called 'blanket amnesties,' of the type introduced by states in the aftermath of conflict to protect their own agents from prosecution, serve to reinforce this equation of amnesty with impunity.[33]

The rather blinkered view of amnesty as impunity is, Mallinder and McEvoy suggest, in part connected to a narrow definition of accountability, expressed in some transitional justice literature, focussed primarily upon prosecution and punishment.[34] The capacity of amnesty to exclude criminal prosecution to some indicates a continuation of impunity throughout transition, as human rights violations committed under the previous regime go unchecked, or at least are not subject to what many would consider 'justice.'[35] This creates a tension between amnesties and international attempts to combat impunity, rendering amnesty 'like a contraband product' that is considered risky to deal with.[36] Freeman suggests that this reputation creates the perception that amnesties are a 'direct impediment to transitional justice.'[37]

Although this linkage of amnesty to amnesia or oblivion has become increasingly out-dated,[38] the effects of this association persist in some of the transitional justice literature. Amnesty is often associated with the side-lining or silencing of victims,[39] for whom amnesty can be associated with impunity, lawlessness, and

29 Diane F. Orentlicher, 'Settling Accounts: The Duty to Prosecute Human Rights Violations of a Prior Regime,' *The Yale Law Journal*, 100:8, (1991), 2537–2615; Ross Poole, 'Enacting Oblivion,' *International Journal of Politics, Culture and Society*, 22:2, (2009), 149–157.

30 W. James Booth, 'The Unforgotten: Memories of Justice,' *American Political Science Review*, 95:4, (2001), 777–791; Louise Mallinder, *Amnesty, Human Rights and Political Transitions: Bridging the Peace and Justice Divide* (Oxford: Hart Publishing, 2008); Orentlicher, ibid.

31 Paul Ricoeur, *Memory, History, Forgetting* (Chicago; London: University of Chicago Press, 2004).

32 Booth, n 30; Kieran McEvoy and Louise Mallinder, 'Amnesties in Transition: Punishment, Restoration, and the Governance of Mercy,' *Journal of Law and Society*, 39:3, (2012), 410–440; Orentlicher, n 29.

33 Mallinder, n 30.

34 Louise Mallinder and Kieran McEvoy, 'Rethinking Amnesties: Atrocity, Accountability and Impunity in Post-Conflict Societies,' *Contemporary Social Science*, 6:1, (2011), 107–128.

35 Ruti G. Teitel, *Transitional Justice* (Oxford: Oxford University Press, 2000).

36 Mark Freeman, *Necessary Evils: Amnesties and the Search for Justice* (Cambridge: Cambridge University Press, 2009), p. 4.

37 Ibid., 19.

38 Ibid.; Mallinder, n 30.

39 Susanne Karstedt, 'From Absence to Presence, From Silence to Voice: Victims in International and Transitional Justice Since the Nuremberg Trials,' *International Review of Victimology*, 17:1, (2010), 9–30.

political expediency.[40] Motivated by the persistence of this narrow view of amnesty, Mallinder sought to explore the diversity of amnesty laws. She argues, persuasively in my view, that amnesty mechanisms can in fact serve as useful tools in the development of transitional justice processes.[41]

For Freeman, this creates 'the paradox of amnesty.'[42] Although perceived as a threat to establishing accountability, amnesties can prove useful in the development of transitional mechanisms.[43] 'Transitional amnesties,' as Teitel describes them, can play a role in advancing change and can serve to re-establish the rule of law and democratic institutions, through demonstrating prosecutorial restraint.[44] In these scenarios amnesty becomes an 'enabler' of transitional justice rather than its 'antithesis.'[45] The South African TRC is argued to have been a turning point in this regard.[46] The amnesty offered to perpetrators in return for the provision of truth to victims and their families[47] is argued to have functioned as an incentive to truth-telling, rather than a barrier.[48] Internationally, 'increasingly innovative forms of amnesty ... may offer alternative means of fulfilling the obligations of states under international law, where widespread prosecutions are not possible.'[49] In embracing a more constructive view of the role of amnesty, methods to 'account for' violations in ways that do not include prosecution can be sought.[50]

With regards the LVR legislation, it is important to state that it is not, technically, an amnesty. The LVR legislation does not 'remove criminal and/or civil sanctions from specified categories of offenders or offences,' as per Mallinder and McEvoy's definition of amnesty.[51] The legislation neither 'forbids the law from discovering who committed these crimes' nor 'from bringing the suspects to trial.'[52] These cases can be investigated and can be prosecuted. The legislation that facilitated the establishment of the ICLVR did not preclude investigation of these cases by the police, nor did it render those who provided information to the Commission immune from prosecution. As these offences and those who carried them out can still be investigated and prosecuted, the legislation is not, by definition, an amnesty. However, it has a similar effect.

Non-judicial processes for gathering information relating to the missing may require that investigative bodies be 'empowered to use a combination of rewards, incentives and threats to encourage cooperation by reluctant witnesses and

40 Mallinder, n 30.
41 Ibid.
42 Freeman, n 36 at 19.
43 Ibid.
44 Teitel, n 35 at 51.
45 Freeman, n 36 at 19.
46 Karstedt, n 39.
47 Ibid.
48 Mallinder, n 30.
49 Ibid. at 3.
50 Mallinder and McEvoy, n 34.
51 Mallinder and McEvoy, n 34 at 109.
52 Poole, n 29 at 152.

perpetrators.'[53] In the case of the LVR legislation, the 'incentive' was the inclusion of clauses 3 and 4.[54] Clause 3 stated that 'any relevant information provided to the Commission' and 'any evidence obtained (directly or indirectly) as a result of such information being so provided,' 'shall not be admissible in evidence in any criminal proceedings.'[55] Clause 4 restricts forensic testing on any remains recovered to that necessary to determine if an item can be safely moved, to establish the identity of the deceased and establishing – for the purposes of an inquest – how, when, and where that person died.[56] Information given to the Commission cannot be used in the course of a prosecution, and forensic tests cannot be carried out on remains found to, for example, establish who may have been in contact with the deceased. While this legislation does not disallow prosecution for these crimes or those believed to be involved with them, these clauses render prosecution unlikely. As highlighted by Dominic Grieve MP during the Commons' debate: the "Bill does not provide an amnesty … but … its practical effect must be to make it most improbable that anyone will ever stand trial."[57]

For some interviewees, the LVR legislation was amnesty by another name: a "decaffeinated"[58] or "de facto amnesty."[59] As one former diplomat who has been engaged in efforts to deal with the past in Northern Ireland highlighted, such ambiguity is typical of the response to the past in Northern Ireland:

> there's a sort of contradiction or a sort of a dance going on between the players where each side vigorously opposes an amnesty, to a greater or lesser extent.… All sides seem to want prosecutions. But actually … they normally mean the prosecution of the 'other' … it seems to me that a lot of people don't want prosecutions although they argue for prosecutions and they don't want to declare amnesty. Now, coming back to the 'disappeared,' the mechanism fits that quite well. It's not inconsistent with that.[60]

53 Nesiah, n 18.

54 The Northern Ireland (Location of Victims' Remains) Act 1999 was passed by the British government, and the Criminal Justice (Location of Victims' Remains) Act 1999 was passed by the Irish government. The British document will be quoted from here, though the pieces of legislation are almost identical.

55 Northern Ireland (Location of Victims' Remains) Act 1999.

56 Ibid.

57 HC Deb 10 May 1999, vol 331, col 72. It should be noted that former senior IRA member Ivor Bell was charged in connection to the abduction and murder of Jean McConville. In December 2018, criminal proceedings were halted when Bell was ruled unfit to stand trial ('Ivor Bell ruled unfit to stand trial over Jean McConville Murder,' *The Irish Times*, 19 December 2018; 'Republican "Not Fit" to Stand Trial Over McConville Killing, Court Hears,' *The Irish Times*, 14 November 2017; 'Veteran Republican in Custody Over Murder Charges,' *Belfast Telegraph*, 24 March 2014).

58 Interview, Richard English, historian, August 2014.

59 Interview, Mike Ritchie, veteran human rights activist, October 2014.

60 Interview, former diplomat who has been engaged in efforts to deal with the past in Northern Ireland, June 2015. In 2017 the House of Commons Defence Committee

A further point to consider – as one interviewee pointed out – is that a blurring of the line between limited immunity and amnesty is possible if an individual's engagement with the ICLVR has a 'spill over' effect into prosecutorial efforts:

> ... the information provided within that mechanism cannot be used to prosecute people. Whether that legislation has a 'spill over' effect to contaminate other prosecutorial mechanisms is a live debate at the moment ... for example ... one of the arguments concerning Bobby Storey, a senior Republican who, it's alleged ... was involved in the IRA investigation [into the 'disappeared'] ... when he was arrested in relation to Jean McConville ... it is alleged that he played the 'I engaged with the "disappeared" Commission' card and was released ... if you're a prosecutor ... you would see such a release as a 'spill over' ... if the practical consequences of engagement with the Commission are spilling beyond the parameters of the structure itself to other criminal justice processes ... that is ... heading towards an amnesty.[61]

Broader consideration should also be given here to the aim of criminal investigation – identification and prosecution of the perpetrator. While it has been found that domestic trials continue to be one of the most common methods used for dealing with wrongdoings of the past,[62] internationally, there is debate over their effectiveness in dealing with wrongdoing following a period of conflict.[63] It should also be noted that in Northern Ireland there is a

recommended a Statute of Limitations be enacted which would cover all Troubles-related incidents involving former members of the British Armed Forces (House of Commons Defence Select Committee 2017). McEvoy has argued that such a statute would (i) amount to a 'self-amnesty,' (ii) impact upon investigations of collusion between state forces and paramilitaries, and (iii) make prosecution of any Troubles-related prosecutions difficult. The proposal has been opposed by victims from many sides (Kieran McEvoy, 'Is the Price of an Amnesty for the Security Forces Just Too High to Contemplate?' *Belfast Telegraph*, 19 June 2017 and see e.g. David Young, 'Victims Forum Opposed to Amnesty for Security Forces,' *Belfast Telegraph*, 30 November 2017).

61 Interview, community activist with over 20 years' experience working with ex-combatants, October 2015. See also 'Jean McConville Murder: Police Forced to Free Ex-IRA Boss Bobby Storey After Learning of Immunity,' *Belfast Telegraph*, 1 December 2014.

62 Helga Malmin Binningsbo, Cyanne E. Loyle, Scott Gates and Jon Elster, 'Armed Conflict and Post-Conflict Justice,' *Journal of Peace Research*, 49:2, (2012), 731–740.

63 See e.g. Eric Brahm, 'Uncovering the Truth: Examining Truth Commission Success and Impact,' *International Studies Perspectives*, 8, (2007), 16–35; Karstedt, n 39; Jennifer J. Llewellyn and Robert Howse, 'Institutions for Restorative Justice: The South African Truth and Reconciliation Commission,' *The University of Toronto Law Journal*, 49:3, (1999), 355–388; McEvoy and Mallinder, n 32; Naomi Roht-Arriaza, 'The New Landscape of Transitional Justice,' in Naomi Roht-Arriaza and Javier Mariezcurrena (eds) *Transitional Justice in the 21st Century* (Cambridge: Cambridge University Press, 2006), pp. 1–16; Teitel, n 35.

general consensus among relevant organisations and commentators that successful prosecution of Troubles-era crimes is unlikely in the majority of cases.[64]

One of the main criticisms of using criminal trials to deal with past violations that is of particular significance to the case at hand, is that they are perpetrator-focused.[65] Aimed at prosecuting an individual, the information gathered relates to establishing innocence or guilt, rather than providing a complete account of what took place.[66] Generally speaking, given that investigations are designed to establish who is legally culpable, they may not meet broader goals that families of 'disappeared' persons have.[67] Taking this into consideration, not only was criminal investigation unlikely to witness success, it was also unlikely to answer the families' call for the return of their loved ones' remains (see Chapter 2). The recovery of these remains without information from those directly involved would have been highly unlikely, if not impossible.

McEvoy and Mallinder propose that in post-conflict contexts, amnesties are 'often framed as being necessary for "the greater good," with victims asked to sacrifice their desire for the punishment of individuals "in the interests of broader collective objectives."'[68] To an extent, the LVR legislation demonstrates the inverse of this frame as it spoke directly to the families' calls for the return of the remains of the 'disappeared.' It was arguably "the best process they [the families] could get."[69] However, the legislation limits the range of possible future actions, in particular the potential for prosecution. As such it remains "an enormous compromise."[70] One interviewee asked:

64 See e.g. Appendix 5, *Report of the Consultative Group on the Past*, 2009, http://cain.ulst.ac.uk/victims/docs/consultative_group/cgp_230109_report.pdf [accessed 11 August 2018]; Denis Boyd and Sean Doran, 'The Viability of Prosecution Based on Historical Enquiry' (Healing Through Remembering, 2006), http://cain.ulst.ac.uk/victims/docs/group/htr/boyd_doran_1006.pdf [accessed 11 August 2018]; Patricia Lundy, 'Can the Past Be Policed? Lessons From the Historical Enquiries Team Northern Ireland,' *Journal of Law and Social Challenges*, 11, (2009), 109–156; Kieran McEvoy and Anna Bryson, 'Justice, Truth and Oral History: Legislating the Past "From Below" in Northern Ireland,' *Northern Ireland Legal Quarterly*, 67:1, (2016), 67–90.

65 Priscilla Hayner, 'Justice in Transition: Challenges and Opportunities,' Centre for Transitional Justice. Presentation to the 55th Annual DPI/NGO Conference, *Rebuilding Societies Emerging From Conflict: A Shared Responsibility* (United Nations, New York, 9 September 2002); Llewellyn and Howse, n 63; Marie Breen Smyth, *Truth Recovery and Justice After Conflict: Managing Violent Pasts* (London: Routledge, 2007).

66 Brahm, n 63; Richard Ashby Wilson, 'Judging History: The Historical Record of the International Criminal Tribunal for the Former Yugoslavia,' *Human Rights Quarterly*, 27:3, (2005), pp. 908–942.

67 Nesiah, n 18.

68 McEvoy and Mallinder, n 32 at 411.

69 Interview, Monica McWilliams, senior academic who has been involved with WAVE and the families' campaign, September 2014.

70 Interview, Geoff Knupfer, Senior Investigating Officer of the ICLVR, July 2014.

> is that a price you pay … if you're a mother, or … a brother, or … a sister and you've been waiting for 40 years, is that a price you're prepared to pay to get what you want, which is the only thing you can have now?[71]

For Peter Wilson's sister, Patricia, it was 'justice was something we had to waiver in return for getting the information that helped us find the body. I personally think that was a price worth paying.'[72]

Alternatively, Oliver McVeigh, whose brother Columba is yet to be found, has said:

> Immunity for us hasn't … paid any dividends … we went with immunity because it was our only option to get the information about the bodies. For some families it's been comfort, but … we are still looking. The only people really benefitting are the ones who are getting away with prosecution.[73]

Given the amnesty-like nature of the mechanism proposed by the LVR Bill, it is perhaps surprising that it was passed into legislation. A comparison can be made with the so-called 'On The Runs' (OTR) controversy, which came to prominence in 2014. The debacle over the OTRs originated when a case against John Downey, a suspect in the Hyde Park bombing of 1982, collapsed. In passing judgment, Mr Justice Sweeney ruled that Downey could not be prosecuted as he had previously received a letter assuring him that he would not face charges, and he had travelled from the Republic of Ireland to Britain on the basis of that letter, where he was then arrested and charged in connection with the bombing.[74] In this case the PSNI had made an administrative error; they had sent the incorrect letter, but upon realising, did nothing to correct their mistake.[75] The publicity surrounding the collapse of the Downey case drew attention to the 'administrative scheme'[76] of which his letter was part, along with some 156 others.[77] Accusations that the scheme amounted to a de facto 'amnesty' were quick to follow.[78]

71 Interview, Brian Rowan, journalist, commentator, and former BBC security correspondent, September 2014.

72 WAVE, *The Disappeared of Northern Ireland's 'Troubles'* (Belfast: WAVE Trauma Centre Publications, 2012), p. 30.

73 Brian Rowan, 'Revealed: How Haass Aims to Seal a Deal in Six Days,' *Belfast Telegraph*, 13 December 2013.

74 *The Queen v John Anthony Downey* [2014]; *BBC News* [online], 'Reaction to John Downey Judgement,' 26 February 2014, www.bbc.co.uk/news/uk-northern-ireland-26345071 [accessed 25 August 2018].

75 Ibid.

76 Ibid.

77 The Right Honourable Dame Heather Hallett DBE, *The Report of the Hallett Review*, 17 July 2014, https://assets.publishing.service.gov.uk/government/uploads/system/uploads/attachment_data/file/335206/41003_Hallett_Web_Accessible.pdf [accessed 11 August 2018].

78 'Reaction to John Downey Judgement,' n 74; Steven Alexander, 'Kelly "has Chickened out" of OTR Testimony,' *Belfast Telegraph*, 9 July 2014.

Northern Ireland's First Minister, Peter Robinson, denounced Downey's letter as a 'get out of jail free card,' and the OTR scheme as a denial of justice.[79]

As discussed previously, if one looks at the Hansard record for the Commons' and Lords' debates on the Bill, there is much criticism, yet the Bill was passed and little of this controversy seeped through into the public domain. For Monica McWilliams, there is "no comparison" between the "uproar" around the OTR letters and that which existed around the 'disappeared' issue.[80] As one interviewee described:

> the model for dealing with the 'disappeared' seemed to creep up on people, and it was just put in place with not much … public debate. Nobody knew it was happening, everyone was rather calm … it effectively offers a de facto amnesty for anybody who participates … concepts that just spark intense public controversy … And yet it would seem to be possible to do it with very little fuss! And I think that's … quite instructive … first of all these things can be arranged. Secondly with good will and a bit of generosity, and a political will, the models can be found.[81]

Speaking to the Westminster committee set up to investigate the OTR scheme, former Prime Minister Tony Blair stated: "It's not that we decided not to tell people, it's just that it wasn't the focus."[82] In the aftermath of the OTR controversy in 2014, journalist Brian Rowan investigated the extent to which knowledge of the process was already in the public domain. He found that, despite the outpouring of criticism and shock, many 'jigsaw pieces,' amounting to 29 pages of Lady Justice Hallett's review into the scheme, were present in the public domain since its inception in 2000.[83] Rowan described 'a huge gap between full disclosure and knowing nothing,'[84] describing the scheme as 'one element of a peace process, another element much like decommissioning and the procedure to recover the bodies of the Disappeared, that happened offstage and out of sight.'[85]

In some ways the issue of the 'disappeared' has been very prominent in the media. As victims, the 'disappeared' and their families are perhaps one of the most well-known groups of the Troubles. Yet, despite the prominence of some aspects of this issue, the development of the search process happened 'offstage and out of sight.'[86] The remainder of this chapter will examine how the process of locating

79 'Reaction to John Downey Judgement,' n 74.
80 Interview, Monica McWilliams, September 2014.
81 Interview, Mike Ritchie, October 2014.
82 *BBC News* [online], 'OTR Letters: Tony Blair Says NI Peace Process Could Have Collapsed Without Scheme,' 13 January 2015, www.bbc.co.uk/news/uk-northern-ireland-30776891 [accessed 11 August 2018].
83 Brian Rowan, 'Hallett Review: Dealing with Past Needs a New Process,' *Belfast Telegraph*, 18 July 2014.
84 Ibid.
85 Ibid.
86 Ibid.

victims' remains can be considered an example of what I have termed 'quiet' transitional justice. I define this as a practical variant of transitional justice involving a number of components. First, given the focus of transitional justice, it involves an attempt to come to terms with past violence and human rights abuses.[87] Second, it is work that is done behind closed doors. It is a private style of transitional justice which involves negotiations and discussions between the different actors and the concurrent exclusion of the media and broader public from those conversations. In some instances, as will be examined later with regards the case at hand, the outworkings of these deliberations do become public, albeit in a choreographed and carefully managed fashion. Fourth, the mechanism is then implemented and at some level *delivers* what it promised particularly to the victims who are at the centre of all transitional justice processes (rhetorically at least, see Chapter 2).[88] In practice, transitional mechanisms can fail, and there is often disagreement regarding the extent to which measures such as the TRC have 'worked.' However, the version of 'quiet' transitional justice which I advance here and develop elsewhere[89] requires that there be some transition from the *status quo ante*. In Marxist terms, for me at least, it requires praxis.[90] In this chapter, the role of quiet diplomacy, the 'quiet' passage of the legislation, and the implications and impact of this 'quietness' on the development of trust will be examined.

4. Quiet diplomacy and the LVR Bill

In seeking to locate the notion of 'quiet' transitional justice in a broader theoretical framework, I have been drawn to the better-known concept of quiet diplomacy, which has been the subject of considerable academic analysis. Reportedly coined by United Nations Secretary-General of 1953–1961, Dag Hammarskjöld,[91] the term 'quiet diplomacy' described a 'private diplomatic method' that provided an alternative to public-facing 'parliamentary diplomacy.'[92] Associated

87 Cheryl Lawther, Luke Moffett and Dov Jacobs (eds), *Research Handbook on Transitional Justice* (Cheltenham: Edward Elgar Publishing, 2017); Kieran McEvoy and Louise Mallinder, *Transitional Justice: Critical Concepts in Law* (Abingdon: Routledge, 2017); Roht-Arriaza and Mariezcurrena, n 63; Teitel, n 35.

88 Kris Brown and Fionnuala Ní Aoláin, 'Through the Looking Glass: Transitional Justice Futures Through the Lens of Nationalism, Feminism and Transformative Change,' *International Journal of Transitional Justice*, 9, (2014), 127–149; Karstedt n 39; Kieran McEvoy and Kirsten McConnachie, 'Victims and Transitional Justice: Voice, Agency and Blame,' *Social and Legal Studies*, (2013), 1–25.

89 Lauren Dempster, '"Quiet" Transitional Justice: "Publicness," Trust and Legitimacy in the Search for the "Disappeared",' *Social and Legal Studies* (2019). doi: https://doi.org/10.1177/0964663919833027.

90 Geoff Boucher, *Understanding Marxism* (Durham: Acumen Publishing, 2012); Karl Marx, *A Contribution to the Critique of Political Economy* (London: Lawrence and Wishart, 1970); Thomas C. Patterson, *Karl Marx, Anthropologist* (Oxford; New York: Berg, 2009).

91 Sven Åhman, 'Mr. Hammarskjöld's Not-So-Quiet Diplomacy,' *The Reporter*, 4 September 1958.

92 Dag Hammarskjöld, 'The Elements of Privacy in Peacemaking': Address at Ohio University, 5 February 1958 (UN Press Release SG/656, 3 February 1958).

with negotiations undertaken out of the public glare, quiet diplomacy often involves efforts to prevent or mitigate the consequences of violent conflict.[93] In the Northern Ireland context, Arthur has described quiet diplomacy as a form of 'Track Two' diplomacy, involving informal or unofficial interaction between representatives of opposing groups, seeking to develop strategies or create an environment more conducive to the ending of hostilities.[94] For current purposes, quiet diplomacy has three important, overlapping features of relevance, the roots of which can be found in Hammerskjöld's 1950s discourse on the topic.[95] These are: (i) 'back-channel' negotiations outside the glare of publicity, (ii) the creation of space for focused work and relationship-building, and (iii) the implementation of quiet diplomacy in providing effective and trusted channels of communication or in establishing mechanisms for interaction, particularly between state and non-state groups.

One feature of quiet diplomacy is 'back-channel' negotiation.[96] Described as the '"black markets" of negotiation,' back-channels provide 'separate negotiation spaces where bargaining takes place in the shadows,'[97] facilitating secret negotiations between adversaries.[98] Argued to be effective in 'getting the job done' outside the public glare,[99] back-channels are spaces in which issues can be worked through, arguments advanced, and workable solutions developed, on a confidential basis.[100] By its exclusion, an audience is prevented from influencing or disrupting communication, or attacking or damaging the parties involved.[101] With an audience present, parties may seek to generate public approval rather than achieve a negotiated settlement,[102] causing each side to 'pander to their most extreme believers.'[103] Described as the "audience effect," the presence of an audience can cause negotiators to behave more aggressively,

93 Michael Johns, 'Quiet Diplomacy, the European Union and Conflict Prevention: Learning From the HCNM on Issues of Social Cohesion,' *International Journal on Minority and Group Rights*, 19, (2012), 243–265; Walter A. Kemp (ed.), *Quiet Diplomacy in Action: The OSCE High Commissioner on National Minorities*, Office of the OSCE High Commissioner on National Minorities (2001).

94 Paul Arthur, '"Quiet Diplomacy and Personal Conversation": Track Two Diplomacy and the Search for a Settlement in Northern Ireland,' in Joseph Ruane and Jennifer Todd (eds) *After the Good Friday Agreement* (Dublin: University College Dublin Press, 1999), pp. 71–95.

95 See Hammarskjöld, n 92, and Hammarskjöld's 1955 press conference following a visit to China to negotiate the status of detained airmen, 'Dag Hammarskjöld About Quiet Diplomacy,' www.youtube.com/watch?v=2T4YrDCe5Yc [accessed 25 August 2018].

96 Anthony Wanis-St. John, 'Back-Channel Negotiation: International Bargaining in the Shadows,' *Negotiation Journal*, 22:2, (2006), 119–144.

97 Ibid. at 120.

98 Ibid.

99 Arthur, n 94.

100 Ibid.; Johns, n 93; Niall Ó Dochartaigh, 'Together in the Middle: Back-Channel Negotiation in the Irish Peace Process,' *Journal of Peace Research*, 48:6, (2011), 767–780; Wanis-St. John, n 96.

101 Ó Dochartaigh, ibid.

102 Ibid.

103 Johns, n 93 at 246.

as making concessions may be perceived as weakness.[104] Public diplomacy can therefore exacerbate an 'already volatile situation.'[105] Hammarskjöld contends that 'public debate' can be 'useless, or even harmful' if it does not contribute to peace-building.[106] By excluding the audience, a space is created that facilitates moderation and compromise.

It is argued that the more public scrutiny given to an issue, the greater the political cost of failure.[107] By not publicly acknowledging that negotiations are taking place, actors can negotiate without either making or demanding concessions, thus reducing the political cost.[108] In his analysis of back-channel discussions in Northern Ireland, Ó Dochartaigh found that concealing such negotiations from fellow politicians can be valuable. Opponents may attempt to gain political advantage by terminating or condemning quiet diplomatic efforts, especially when the 'legitimacy of parties is contested,'[109] as was the case with Sinn Féin in Northern Ireland at the time of the development of the LVR Bill. Within one's own party, one may face opposition from those who oppose compromise. Back-channel negotiations are a way of side-stepping potential opposition.[110]

The facilitation of negotiations by trusted interlocutors or intermediaries is another feature of quiet diplomatic efforts, one which is particularly useful – and perhaps essential – when communication is taking place between groups that either cannot or will not meet one another, such as state bodies and non-state armed groups.[111] This allows negotiations to happen without states appearing to concede legitimacy to terrorist organisations by officially or publicly engaging in negotiations.[112] Non-Governmental Organisations (NGOs) can be effective in facilitating quiet diplomatic contact between state and non-state actors.[113] NGOs can create 'common ground' based on humanitarian aims, rather than becoming entangled in the politics of peace negotiations.[114] There are resonances here with the ICLVR, for which independence and confidentiality have proven essential to its role as a conduit for information on the burial sites of the 'disappeared.'

104 Wanis-St. John, n 96 at 124. See also Dean G. Pruitt, 'Back-Channel Communication in the Settlement of Conflict,' *International Negotiation*, 13:1, (2008), 37–54.
105 Johns, n 93 at 246.
106 Hammarskjöld, n 92.
107 Matthew A. Baum, 'Going Private: Public Opinion, Presidential Rhetoric, and the Domestic Politics of Audience Costs in US Foreign Policy Crises,' *The Journal of Conflict Resolution*, 48:5, (2004), 603–631.
108 Wanis-St. John, n 96.
109 Ó Dochartaigh, n 100 at 768.
110 Ibid.
111 Guy Oliver Faure, 'Negotiating with Terrorists: A Discrete Form of Diplomacy,' *The Hague Journal of Diplomacy*, 3:2, (2008), 179–200; Pruitt n 104.
112 Faure, ibid.
113 Claudia Hofmann, 'Engaging Non-State Armed Groups in Humanitarian Action,' *International Peacekeeping*, 13:3, (2006), 396–409.
114 Daniela Irrera, *NGOs, Crisis Management and Conflict Resolution: Measuring the Impact of NGOs on Intergovernmental Organisations* (Cheltenham: Edward Elgar Publishing Ltd., 2013), p. 61.

Quiet diplomatic efforts have proved effective in the creation of mechanisms for interaction between parties to a conflict, including both state and non-state armed groups. In Afghanistan, the exchange of a series of letters in 1988 between the UN Coordinator for Afghanistan, the Kabul government, and the leaders of the various Mujahideen factions resulted in a "consensus" between the sides to allow the provision of humanitarian aid across the country.[115] The NGO Geneva Call provided a legal document on the banning of land mines that non-state armed groups could sign to express their adherence to international norms. In this example, and others Hofmann examines, neutral mechanisms, facilitated by NGOs, enable the engagement of non-state armed groups in measures to assuage the effects of violence.[116]

Back-channel communication has become an 'ubiquitous feature' of conflict resolution and political negotiations, and Northern Ireland is no exception.[117] A back-channel of communication between the IRA and the British government between 1990 and 1993 is argued to have been a 'key component' of the 1994 ceasefire and subsequent peace process.[118] Ó Dochartaigh contends that an 'intermittent negotiating relationship' of communication between the IRA and the British government stretching back to the early 1970s created an important base for peace negotiations.[119] This sort of 'prenegotiation,' as will be explored in the next section, has an important place in reducing the uncertainty that exists between parties to a conflict.

4.1. Quiet diplomacy and the 'disappeared'

'Prenegotiation'[120] or 'pre-play'[121] is the period of gestation in which an issue is shaped.[122] At this stage problems can be redefined and a shared commitment to negotiate developed, based on agreed-upon principles.[123] Particularly pertinent in

115 Antonio Donini, 'Negotiating with Terrorists,' in Larry Minear and Hazel Smith (eds) *Humanitarian Diplomacy* (Japan: United Nations University Press, 2007), pp. 153–173.

116 Hofmann, n 113.

117 Ó Dochartaigh, n 100 at 767. See also Pruitt, n 104. It should of course be noted that there are drawbacks in both attempting to pursue and in seeking to understand processes of quiet diplomacy. See e.g. Arthur, n 94 for the challenges in measuring the impact of a series of informal workshops attended by Northern Ireland politicians in the 1990s and Graham (2006) with regards President Mbeki's presidency in Zimbabwe, and the difficulties in recognising the benefits or results of quiet diplomacy (Victoria Graham, 'How Firm the Handshake? South Africa's Use of Quiet Diplomacy in Zimbabwe from 1999 to 2006,' *African Security Review*, 15:4, (2006), 113–127).

118 Ó Dochartaigh, n 100 at 770.

119 Ó Dochartaigh, n 100. See also Arthur, n 94.

120 Chester A. Crocker, Fen Osler Hampson, and Pamela Aall, *Taming Intractable Conflict: Mediation in the Hardest Cases* (Washington: United States Institute of Peace, 2004); Pruitt, n 104; Wanis-St. John, n 96.

121 Arthur, n 94 at 80.

122 Arthur, ibid.

123 Crocker et al., n 120.

contexts where parties do not acknowledge or openly associate with one another,[124] such 'secret diplomacy'[125] is relevant in considering communication between the IRA and the British and Irish governments.

On key aspects of the peace process, such as the decommissioning of paramilitary weapons, carefully pre-arranged choreography between the different actors has been an important element of the transition.[126] Jonathan Powell wrote of these behind-the-scenes efforts:

> We tried to break the process into little steps which would then be choreographed so that both sides had confidence they were moving together, rather than feeling as if they were having to trust the other side to reciprocate if they made the first move.[127]

Such choreography is evident in efforts to address the 'disappeared' issue. In introducing the relevant Bill to the Oireachtas, Minister for Justice, Equality and Law Reform, John O'Donoghue explained the background to the Bill:

> On 29 March 1999 the Government approved the draft text of a statement … [that] indicated that the Government was prepared to facilitate a process in relation to locating the remains through introducing legislation to the effect that evidence resulting from that process could not be used in the prosecution of offences. Shortly afterwards the Provisional IRA issued a statement to the effect that it had succeeded in locating the remains of nine victims.[128]

On the same day as the IRA's March 1999 statement (Chapter 3) was issued, the British and Irish governments released statements announcing that evidence obtained during the search process would not be used in prosecution.[129] Secretary of State for Northern Ireland, Mo Mowlam, clarified the British government's position:

> if it would facilitate the process [of locating remains], I would be willing to consider changing the law to ensure any evidence which emerges in locating the remains will not be used in subsequent criminal proceedings. I understand that is the position of the Irish government also.[130]

124 Ibid.

125 Ibid. at 139.

126 Jonathan Powell, *Great Hatred, Little Room: Making Peace in Northern Ireland* (London: Vintage Books, 2009). See also Dixon, n 15.

127 Powell, ibid., 149–150.

128 DE Deb 5 May 1999, vol 504, no 2.

129 Oonagh Gay, *The Northern Ireland (Location of Victims' Remains) Bill*, House of Commons Research Paper 99/49, 7 May 1999; Clare Murphy and Maol Muire Tynan, 'IRA Says it has Located Burial Places of Nine of its Victims,' *The Irish Times*, 30 March 1999.

130 Northern Ireland Office, 'Secretary of State Welcomes Efforts Being Made to Locate Graves of "the Disappeared",' 29 March 1999, accessed at http://webarchive.na

A similar statement was released by O'Donoghue.[131] The significance of this move on the part of the British and Irish governments is outlined by Rowan:

> I can remember taking the statement in 1999 from the IRA, and before it was read to me … the IRA leadership spokesman [was] waiting for a news bulletin which said that Dublin was going to put this process in place. Had Dublin not done that, that statement wouldn't have been read to me in March 1999 …[132]

When the Bill was being debated in the Dáil, Conor Lenihan alluded to the secretive nature of its development. Pointing out the need for "distasteful but courageous actions" in the peace process, Lenihan continued (emphasis author's own):

> The Minister [O'Donoghue] has played a good and strong role in the process in terms of *sensitive issues about which one cannot boast*. They *cannot be highlighted in the press* but they involve an intense engagement with the security dimension … We have to engage in these practical, though distasteful measures.[133]

Adam Ingram outlines this process more explicitly in the Commons debate on the Bill: 'The British Government have had no contact with the IRA on this issue, which has been handled through an intermediary with the Irish Government.'[134]

Quiet diplomacy also took place on the victims' side. Monica McWilliams explained in interview that, "there was different kinds of lobbying and advocacy going on at different levels, mostly in the background."[135] She described in interview how a representative of the victims' organisation WAVE "thought it would be a good idea if we approached Gerry Adams around the issue. And I remember during the peace talks … [we had] an informal discussion about the possibility of getting more information …"[136]

The 'prenegotiation phase' can be a period of widespread uncertainty, however through using back-channels, parties can continue to publicly behave as adversaries, while privately seeking solutions. This reduces uncertainty as actors can examine the reality underlying their adversary's public posturing and explore

tionalarchives.gov.uk/20020704124508/http://www.nio.gov.uk:80/press/1999/mar/990329g-nio.htm [accessed 11 August 2018].

131 Murphy and Tynan, n 129.

132 Interview, Brian Rowan, September 2014.

133 DE Deb 5 May 1999, vol 504, no 2.

134 HC Deb 12 May 1999, vol 331, col 347.

135 Interview, Monica McWilliams, September 2014.

136 Interview, Monica McWilliams, September 2014. Direct discussions between WAVE, the families, and Adams outside of the media glare also took place after the establishment of the ICLVR (see account of Michael McConville in WAVE, n 72).

avenues for agreement without committing publicly.[137] The likelihood of recovering the remains of the 'disappeared' was very much uncertain. The behind-the-scenes development of the LVR Bill facilitated a phase as outlined by Wanis St.-John, in which possible solutions could be explored without the need for public commitment.[138]

Given the potential for public diplomacy to be designed to appeal to the extremes, it can be preferable when dealing with emotionally charged issues to avoid public glare.[139] As outlined previously, the criticism featured in the outburst of media publicity over the OTR scheme was rooted in the emotionally charged issues of amnesty, justice, and underhand deals. The issue of the 'disappeared' posed the risk of a similar reaction. By undertaking negotiations out of the public glare, this risk was lessened.

Another point to consider is legitimacy. One of the main arguments used against negotiating with 'terrorists' is that to do so would confer legitimacy onto them.[140] Back-channel communication is said to facilitate 'negotiation on the question of legitimacy without conceding legitimacy.'[141] As the LVR Bill was being negotiated, the IRA, although on ceasefire, still existed as an armed and functioning paramilitary organisation. Removing the audience permitted a conversation in which a potential solution could be developed, without those involved appearing to legitimate the IRA, or condone its actions in perpetrating 'disappearances.'

In Northern Ireland more generally during the peace process, one interviewee argued for the value of 'minimising the exposure' of deals being done:

> Insofar as deals were done and concessions were made, they had to be sold to the various constituencies and I think, each side felt that, the more that could be done not to highlight the concessions … then the easier it was to manage.[142]

In the case at hand, "it was, in a sense, a concession, but one which … probably all sides had an interest in dealing with … in a sort of pragmatic, low key way."[143] Quiet diplomacy on this issue allowed the development of a potential solution while excluding those voices that may have halted progress. As Rowan argues,

137 Wanis-St. John, n 96.
138 Ibid.
139 Johns, n 93.
140 Peter Neumann, 'Negotiating with Terrorists,' *Foreign Affairs*, 86:1, (2007), 128–138; Jonathan Powell, 'How to Talk to Terrorists,' *The Guardian*, 7 October 2014; Harmonie Toros, '"We Don't Negotiate with Terrorists!": Legitimacy and Complexity in Terrorist Conflicts,' *Security Dialogue*, 39(4), (2008), 407–426.
141 Ó Dochartaigh, n 100 at 768. See also Pruitt, n 104.
142 Interview, a former diplomat who has been engaged in efforts to deal with the past in Northern Ireland, June 2015.
143 Ibid.

"you need the exploratory conversation, offstage, and then ... you propose your Commission and you say, 'this is how it's going to work.'"[144]

5. 'Quietly' legislating: the passage of the LVR Bill

As examined earlier, the contents of the LVR legislation had the potential to be quite controversial, and this is reflected in the Hansard record of the debates.[145] However, as Monica McWilliams recounted (emphasis author's own): "I don't recall it being that controversial ... I recall it being seen as much needed, and again *it was quietly processed*."[146] This section will examine how legislation can be 'quiet' and how the LVR Bill passed with little public controversy. Three aspects of the Bill and its passage will be considered: the timing and role of the media, the need for some form of 'incentive' to encourage Republicans to provide information on burial site locations, and the 'win win' nature of the legislation.

5.1. The LVR legislation, timing, and the media

As previously noted, Tony Blair has described how the OTR letter scheme was not secret but "just ... wasn't the focus."[147] As Blair intimates, the 'focus' at that time lay elsewhere. As the LVR Bill was being debated, the 'focus' again lay elsewhere. In the Dáil, Minister O'Donoghue pointed out: "We are discussing this legislation at ... a difficult time for the wider [peace] process," indicating decommissioning, the impasse on forming the Executive, and thus, the stalling of implementation of the Good Friday Agreement (GFA).[148] A survey of the *Belfast Telegraph* and *The Irish News* [149] indicates that these issues were the 'focus' at that time. Decommissioning was a frequent front page story.[150] The pressure on Adams to encourage movement on this issue, and the implementation of the GFA, were also

144 Interview, Brian Rowan, September 2014.

145 See DE Deb 5 May 1999, vol 504, no 2; DE Deb 12 May 1999, vol 504, no 5; HC Deb 10 May 1999, vol 331, col 38–83; HC Deb 12 May 1999, vol 331, col 324–386; HL Deb 18 May 1999, vol 601, cc 153–190; HL Deb 24 May 1999, vol 601, cc. 639–664; HL Deb 24 May 1999, vol 601, cc. 678–713; SE Deb 13 May 1999, vol 159, no 9.

146 Interview, Monica McWilliams, September 2014.

147 'OTR Letters,' n 82.

148 DE Deb 5 May 1999, vol 504, no 2.

149 These two newspapers have large readerships in Northern Ireland. The *Belfast Telegraph* has a broadly Unionist stance and *The Irish News* has a broadly Nationalist stance (Bill Rolston, 'News Fit to Print,' in Bill Rolston (ed.) *The Media and Northern Ireland: Covering the Troubles* (London: Macmillan Publishing, 1991), pp. 152–186; Gadi Wolfsfeld, *Media and the Path to Peace* (New York: Cambridge University Press, 2004)).

150 E.g., Martina Purdy, 'Bishop's Plea on Weapons,' *Belfast Telegraph*, 1 May 1999; Martina Purdy and Desmond McCartan, 'Trimble's Deal Pressure,' *Belfast Telegraph*, 17 May 1999; 'Ahern Rejects NIO Arms Plan,' *The Irish News*, 4 May 1999; William Graham, 'Weapons Deal May Spell End for Trimble,' *The Irish News*, 18 May 1999.

recurring stories.[151] Other issues making the front pages included the Orange Order march at Drumcree,[152] accusations of collusion surrounding the killings of Pat Finucane and Rosemary Nelson,[153] and the continuation of Loyalist violence.[154] While the 'disappeared' legislation debate received some attention,[155] these articles were brief and rarely featured on the front page. The front page headlines returned with the successful passage of the Bill into legislation,[156] and the recovery of Eamonn Molloy's remains from Faughart graveyard.[157]

While there was some critical commentary of the legislation,[158] the level of media attention was relatively low. The apparent lack of public interest in this piece of legislation may have been a direct result, as the press can be an important

151 E.g., Martina Purdy and Desmond McCartan, 'Accord Hopes Rising,' *Belfast Telegraph*, 15 May 1999; Martina Purdy, 'Unionists Reaffirm: "No Guns, No Deal",' *Belfast Telegraph*, 18 May 1999; Noel McAdam, 'Trimble Row After "Private" Adams Meeting,' *Belfast Telegraph*, 25 May 1999; Liz Trainor, 'Executive to be Appointed on Thursday,' *The Irish News*, 17 May 1999.

152 E.g. Darwin Templeton, 'Loyalist Parade Plans,' *Belfast Telegraph*, 17 May 1999; Darwin Templeton, 'With Just 46 Days to Drumcree, Do These Pictures Represent the Shape of Things to Come?' *Belfast Telegraph*, 19 May 1999; Chris Thornton and Gavin Mairs, 'Troops on Alert,' *Belfast Telegraph*, 22 May 1999; Martin Anderson, 'Crunch Talks Under Way to Resolve Drumcree Crisis,' *The Irish News*, 4 May 1999; 'Orange Order sets Drumcree Deadline,' *The Irish News*, 17 May 1999.

153 E.g. 'Lawyers' Society Facing Turmoil,' *Belfast Telegraph*, 8 May 1999; Steven McCaffery, 'Nelson Probe Team Includes Collusion Unit,' *The Irish News*, 1 May 1999; Seamus McKinney, 'Finucane Family May Sue UUP Man,' *The Irish News*, 5 May 1999; Seamus McKinney, 'Police Rejected Hermon's "IRA Solicitor" Claim,' *The Irish News*, 11 May 1999.

154 E.g. Liz Trainor, 'RUC Set to Crack Down on Dissident Loyalist Groups,' *The Irish News*, 1 May 1999; Alan Erwin and Sharon O'Neill, 'Loyalists in Knife Attack on Nurse,' *The Irish News*, 3 May 1999; Martin Anderson, 'Boys Foil Loyalist Bookies Massacre,' *The Irish News*, 6 May 1999.

155 E.g. 'Bishop's Hopes Over the Missing Victims,' *The Irish News*, 24 May 1999; 'Bodies May be "Located in Days",' *The Irish News*, 27 May 1999; Desmond McCartan, 'Move on Bill for Missing Opposed,' *Belfast Telegraph*, 12 May 1999; Desmond McCartan, 'Safeguards for Locating Graves Soon to be in Place,' *Belfast Telegraph*, 25 May 1999; Liz Trainor, 'Missing Mother's Family Plan Burial,' *The Irish News*, 11 May 1999; 'Disappeared Legislation Passed,' *The Irish News*, 13 May 1999; Uffindell, n 23; Sharon O'Neill and Paul McKillon, 'New Law Gives Hope to Families of Disappeared,' *The Irish News*, 14 May 1999.

156 Martin Breen and Desmond McCartan, 'Secret Graves "Action in Days",' *Belfast Telegraph*, 27 May 1999.

157 Darwin Templeton, Martin Breen and Michael Devine, 'Peace at Last,' *Belfast Telegraph*, 28 May 1999; Chris Thornton and Peter McVerry, 'The Agony Goes On,' *Belfast Telegraph*, 29 May 1999; 'The Mourning Begins,' *The Irish News*, 29 May 1999; Michael O'Toole and Liz Trainor, 'Families Can Finally Grieve as IRA Hands Over Bodies,' *The Irish News*, 29 May 1999; Alan Erwin, 'Anguish of the Families Continues,' *The Irish News*, 31 May 1999.

158 See e.g. Austen Morgan, 'The Northern Ireland (Location of Victims' Remains) Act 1999: Amnesty, Immunity or What?' *The Irish Jurist*, 37, (2002), 306–321; Kevin Toolis, 'War Crimes of the IRA,' *The Guardian*, 2 June 1999.

influence on public debate.[159] In broad terms, scholarship on the role of the media in conflict and post-conflict contexts reveals a lack of attention given to media coverage of peace processes, in contrast to conflict, both generally,[160] and specifically in relation to Northern Ireland.[161] Where violence and conflict have a central place in news and media coverage, peace is often less exciting, more complicated, and more difficult to communicate.[162]

The relative lack of interest by the media may, however, have been beneficial to the successful passage of the legislation. As examined earlier, high levels of publicity can be detrimental to political progress, particularly on sensitive issues, as politicians can behave differently in the presence of an audience. Although antagonists in a process may turn to the media at a time of crisis, they may also limit access to the news media as a strategy to ensure greater secrecy, as too much media attention is generally assumed to reduce a talks process's chances of success.[163] Wolfsfeld posits that the press plays a destructive role in peace-building attempts and outlines four aspects of news criteria that contribute to this negative role.[164] In the subsequent paragraphs these four criteria will be examined in relation to the case at hand.

Interested in covering events, rather than processes, the immediacy of news is argued to be ill-designed to communicate long-term policies or long-lasting negotiations.[165] While the press covered the development of the Northern Ireland peace process extensively, the stories making the front pages were issues of arms, leaders in crisis, and continuing violence. The passage of the LVR Bill lacked what Rolston describes as the 'instant attraction' which violent conflict holds for the media.[166] If 'drama is the quintessential element of any "good" news story,'[167] then the families' stories and the search for remains fit this bill. It is possible that the deliberations over the legislation were simply not interesting enough at that time, especially when one considers the other news stories that were playing out.

In terms of national media interest in the peace process, Rolston describes, for the British media, a continuation into the peace process years of an 'anti-terrorism paradigm.'[168] The passing of the LVR legislation does not quite fit with this paradigm. As will be examined later, the passing of this legislation gave the Republican Movement a legitimacy that clashes with the 'terrorist' narrative that dominated media coverage. What did fit with the 'anti-terrorism paradigm,' according to Rolston, was the decommissioning issue, something with which, he

159 Wolfsfeld, n 149.
160 Ibid.
161 Bill Rolston, 'Facing Reality: The Media, The Past and Conflict Transformation in Northern Ireland,' *Journal of Crime, Media, Culture*, 3:3, (2007), 345–364.
162 David Miller, *Don't Mention the War: Northern Ireland, Propaganda, and the Media* (London: Pluto Press, 1994); Wolfsfeld, n 149.
163 Wolfsfeld, n 149.
164 Ibid.
165 Ibid.
166 Rolston, n 161 at 346.
167 Wolfsfeld, n 149 at 18.
168 Rolston, n 161 at 347.

describes, 'the media became practically fixated.'[169] As highlighted, this was by far the most frequent headline story as the LVR Bill passed through Parliament and the Oireachtas. In effect, the dominance of decommissioning as an issue allowed some effective 'quiet' transitional justice work to get done.

Headlines that focus on discord or confrontation generate anger.[170] Yet, the headlines declaring Unionist criticism of the Bill[171] did not, it seems, have this effect. One interviewee suggested this was because there was no receptive audience among the wider population for such critique. The views of those who opposed the legislation "were not representative of either the recognition within the political process of what was required or indeed where public opinion was at … people recognised that this was a sensible way to proceed."[172] This idea that Unionist criticism was not representative of the views of wider society is indicative of what Miller describes as a 'perception that unionist parties are bound by their constituencies to repeating a message which may not be popular outside the confines of the unionist community.'[173]

As several interviewees suggested, the momentum, or appetite, for change in this period was significant:[174] "it was a very momentous time, when all sorts of things were agreed upon that it would be very, very difficult to get support for now."[175] As a changing political environment can influence changes in media norms,[176] it is possible that as the political atmosphere became more favourable to compromise the traditional media stance shifted also, to enable this particular compromise to pass relatively below the radar. One interviewee suggested that avoidance of dramatising the issue was a deliberate move on the part of the media:

> It wasn't something that was highlighted … maybe the media chose not to use it because of the emotiveness of the issue … and a realisation that if it was to be successful, then this is probably the only way this could be done.[177]

Another factor to consider is the need for simplicity in news, which can limit the scope of public debate.[178] As this author has discovered, there is no succinct or

169 Ibid. at 348; 347.
170 Wolfsfeld, n 149.
171 Rachel Donnelly, 'Unionists Bitter at "Disappeared" Bill,' *The Irish Times*, 11 May 1999; 'Missing Victims Bill "Reluctantly" Passed: "It's a Down Payment on IRA Ransom Demand",' *News Letter*, 11 May 1999; 'Politics: Molyneaux Talks of "Death Wish",' *News Letter*, 19 May 1999; Sarah Schaefer, 'Parliament: Ministers Attacked for Deal on "Disappeared": Northern Ireland,' *The Independent*, 11 May 1999.
172 Interview, Sinn Féin's Declan Kearney, April 2015.
173 Miller, n 162.
174 Interviews with Susan McKay, July 2014; Richard English, August 2014; Mike Ritchie, October 2014.
175 Interview, Susan McKay, July 2014.
176 Wolfsfeld, n 149.
177 Interview, Adrian McNamee, December 2014.
178 Wolfsfeld, n 149.

'snappy' way to explain the LVR legislation. The news media was perhaps ill-equipped to communicate the proposed process with the necessary complexity.

A final factor outlined by Wolfsfeld is ethnocentrism.[179] Each news medium operates from a particular cultural and political base: the stories they produce are about what happens or might happen to 'us.' News about 'others,' Wolfsfeld suggests, focuses on how it may affect 'us.'[180] With regards the debate on the LVR Bill, it really does not affect wider Northern Ireland society. It was, and continues to be, a self-contained process. Not only is it "intra-communal … about Catholics,"[181] but the legislation applies to only a very small number within this constituency. A further facet to this sense of 'them' and 'us' is, as highlighted by Kate Turner in interview, that at the time this legislation was being passed, there was less public interest in victim-related issues and as such, "there was much less looking at these [victims'] issues then."[182]

One point that should be made here with regards the media role is in relation to Brian Rowan's account of the IRA spokesperson waiting for the news bulletin announcing the governments' willingness to introduce a change in the law. This is an example of 'megaphone diplomacy'[183] in which the news media serves 'as a notice board where it is possible to post messages to the other side.'[184] Governments can communicate messages of clarification or negotiation via the media, arguing that they are not talking to 'terrorists' but rather to journalists.[185] There are of course other methods of communication available to the various parties to negotiations,[186] and indeed the earlier part of this chapter detailed the potential for behind-the-scenes communication. However, in the choreography of this particular case, 'megaphone diplomacy' had a role to play in demonstrating the *bona fides* of the different actors. Through both omission and inclusion, the press played a role in this process of 'quiet' transitional justice.

5.2. The LVR legislation and incentivising Republican engagement

For Graham, quiet diplomacy is aimed at pressurising or persuading an actor to change their behaviour. While this excludes direct military action, it does not exclude the use of persuasive mechanisms such as economic sanctions.[187] As examined, amnesty-type measures can also be used to incentivise behavioural change.[188] To recover the 'disappeared,' Harry Barnes MP declared the need "to

179 Wolfsfeld, ibid.
180 Ibid. at 23.
181 Interview, Richard English, August 2014.
182 Interview, Kate Turner, September 2014.
183 David Miller, 'Diplomatic Vacuity,' *Observer (Uncensored)*, (1993).
184 Kirsten Sparre, 'Megaphone Diplomacy in the Northern Irish Peace Process,' *Harvard International Journal of Press/Politics*, 6:1, (2001), 88–104 (p. 90).
185 Miller, n 183; Miller, n 162; Sparre, ibid.
186 Sparre, n 184.
187 Graham, n 117.
188 Mallinder, n 30.

seek a shift in the IRA's position."[189] The LVR Bill was described by one interviewee as a "lubricant" in this process.[190] Introducing the Bill to the House of Commons, Adam Ingram explained: "It is not within the Government's gift to deliver ... the location of the remains ... That can be done only if those who know their whereabouts come forward with the information."[191]

Given that the state alone could not recover the remains of the 'disappeared,' the legislation is introduced as something the state can offer: an incentive for those who know where remains are buried to come forward. For the DUP's Peter Robinson, such an incentive should have been unnecessary, because "if terrorists want to be part of the democratic process, it is up to them to leave violence behind."[192] However, as former Director of publicity for Sinn Féin, Danny Morrison, proposed in interview (emphasis author's own):

> I mean the Republicans required, in order to go to people, including dissident people who may have been involved, Republicans needed to be able to turn around and say, 'look, none of this is going to be used. If you dropped your diary into the grave ... none of this is going to be used against you.' So *there is an incentive to right this wrong.* [193]

Johns suggests that one aspect of the distinctive nature of quiet diplomacy is that the public don't see the carrots and sticks that are part of the process of coming to political agreement.[194] The LVR legislation has elements of both 'carrot' and 'stick.' The legislation itself was a 'carrot,' designed to tempt those with information on burial locations to provide that to the Commission. Yet, in passing the legislation, the British and Irish governments also created something of a 'stick' in that, with a legislative guarantee of non-prosecution, there was no excuse for the Republican Movement not to co-operate with the ICLVR. The legislation laid "the responsibility at the door of the paramilitaries."[195] Dominic Grieve MP claimed that if the IRA were not to come forward with the information, "nothing could be more damaging to them ... than to be seen to be unable and unwilling to honour their commitment."[196]

The legislation created a level of what Keohane and Nye call 'reputational accountability,' where embarrassment and the subsequent damage to one's reputation, or the reputation of one's organisation, is a sanction.[197] In this case, were

189 HC Deb 10 May 1999, vol 331, col 69.
190 Interview, Richard English, August 2014.
191 HC Deb 10 May 1999, vol 331, cols 41–42.
192 HC Deb 10 May 1999, vol 331, col 58.
193 Interview, Danny Morrison, January 2015.
194 Johns, n 93.
195 Lembit Opik, HC Deb 10 May 1999, vol 331, col 62.
196 HC Deb 10 May 1999, vol 331, col 75.
197 Robert O. Keohane and Joseph S. Nye, Jr., 'Redefining Accountability for Global Governance,' in Miles Kahler and David A. Lake (eds) *Governance in a Global Economy: Political Authority in Transition* (New Jersey: Princeton University Press, 2003), pp. 386–411.

the IRA not to take the opportunity the legislation afforded, it would suffer the 'sanction of embarrassment'[198] within the Republican and Nationalist communities – communities in which Sinn Féin was seeking to develop its political aspirations at that time (see Chapter 3). The use of quiet diplomatic efforts, and the relative lack of media attention as explored in the previous section, meant that in this case the public did not see the carrot or the stick. As Adrian McNamee described in interview, "There was no heralding of this as an amnesty."[199] Other interviewees suggested the same.[200]

5.3. The 'win win' of legislating for the location of victims' remains

Ruane and Todd suggest there is a need to seek 'opportunities for safe compromise' in building peace.[201] This legislation provided such an opportunity. Although, as Lembit Opik pointed out, there is nothing to celebrate[202] with regards this legislation, politically it is a 'win win.' For the two governments, it allowed them to respond to the families' campaign, which had widespread political support from across the spectrum in Northern Ireland and the Republic of Ireland. For Republicans, they were aware the issue needed to be resolved and this provided a mechanism for attempting to do so. For Unionists, the search process would bring focus to "Republican wrongdoing."[203] In interview, one DUP MP touched on this, claiming the debate "was obviously an opportunity to highlight the injustice that had occurred in these cases."[204] As will be examined in Chapter 6, this 'opportunity' has been used throughout the years of search. As one interviewee summarised, the legislation did not "threaten anybody's political position."[205]

A further point to consider here is that, as one interviewee suggested, this was a case of "IRA against their own" without any "cross-group implications."[206] In discussing why this issue garnered relatively widespread support, one interviewee suggested that, "it seems, I think, to people … that it's not actually going to cost the rest of us that much."[207] The LVR legislation does not really impact upon wider society, except, as will be examined later, in terms of the example it sets for

198 Ibid. at 390.
199 Interview, Adrian McNamee, November 2014.
200 Interviews with Susan McKay, July 2014; Monica McWilliams, September 2014; Mike Ritchie, October 2014. See also Dempster, n 89.
201 Joseph Ruane and Jennifer Todd, 'Path Dependence in Settlement Processes: Explaining Settlement in Northern Ireland,' *Political Studies*, 55:2, (2007), 442–458 (p. 450).
202 HC Deb 10 May 1999, vol 331, col 64.
203 Interview, Brian Gormally of the Committee on the Administration of Justice, November 2014.
204 Interview, Jeffrey Donaldson, March 2015.
205 Interview, Brian Gormally, November 2014.
206 Interview, a former diplomat who has been engaged in efforts to deal with the past in Northern Ireland, June 2015.
207 Interview, Kate Turner of Healing Through Remembering, September 2014.

dealing with the past. The process is contained, limited in scope, and potentially dismissible by some as "internal housekeeping" for the Republican Movement.[208] If the LVR Bill was passed and Republicans did not comply, those who would stand to 'lose' would be the families of the 'disappeared' and the Republican Movement. The families would not have their loved ones' remains returned, and this would negatively impact upon already poor perceptions of Republican commitment to the peace process.

6. Trust and locating victims' remains

In its report, the International Body on the Decommissioning of Arms proposed that, were the IRA to return remains, it would serve as a "confidence-building measure."[209] If confidence-building is about taking steps to establish political trust in a way that it is long-term and genuine,[210] then to assess this possibility one must consider what trust is, if and how this process has helped to create it, and the potential risks to its development.

Simultaneously a feeling, attitude, and relationship, trust can be difficult to define.[211] For Hosking, trust is about both relationships with others and expectations for the future.[212] Trust is often associated with expectation, probability, or predictability.[213] The expectation involved is of a positive, desirable, or beneficial outcome, or at least one that is not harmful or damaging.[214] Trust is argued to be essential for co-operation.[215] It alleviates fear,

208 Interview, Brian Rowan, September 2014.

209 International Body on the Decommissioning of Arms, *Report of the International Body on Arms Decommissioning*, 2 January 1996; John McDonnell, HC Deb 10 May 1999, vol 331, col 55; NIA Deb 26 October 1998, vol 1, page 168, col 1; 'Post-Ceasefire Confidence: Mitchell Lynchpin to Progress,' *Belfast Telegraph*, 30 July 1997; 'Where is the Trust? Reducing Division: Steps Needed From Republicans,' *Belfast Telegraph*, 27 July 1998.

210 Ralph M. Goldman and William M. Hardman, *Building Trust: An Introduction to Peacekeeping and Arms Control* (Aldershot: Ashgate Publishing Limited, 1997).

211 Geoffrey Hosking, *Trust: A History* (Oxford: Oxford University Press, 2014). See also Barbara A. Misztal, *Trust in Modern Societies* (Cambridge: Polity Press, 1996) on some of the challenges encountered in seeking to make sense of the notion of trust as it is understood in social science scholarship.

212 Ibid.

213 Morton Deutsch, 'Trust and Suspicion,' *Journal of Conflict Resolution*, 2:4, (1958), 265–279; Hosking, n 211; Peter Hwang and Willem P. Burgers, 'Properties of Trust: An Analytical View,' *Organizational Behaviour and Human Decision Processes*, 69:1, (1997), 67–73.

214 Deutsch, ibid.; Hosking, n 211; Herbert W. Kee and Robert E. Knox, 'Conceptual and Methodological Considerations in the Study of Trust and Suspicion,' *Journal of Conflict Resolution*, 14:3, (1970), 357–366.

215 Willem P. Burgers, 'Apprehension and Temptation: The Forces Against Cooperation,' *The Journal of Conflict Resolution*, 43:1, (1999), 117–130; Hwang and Burgers, n 213; Rafael La Porta, Florencio Lopez-de-Silanes, Andrei Shleifer and Robert W. Vishny, 'Trust in Large Organisations,' *The American Economic Review*, 87:2, (1997), 333–338; Misztal, n 211.

and helps to contain greed by rendering long-term, future co-operation more appealing than short-term gains.[216]

The precise meaning of 'trust' can vary depending on the context in which it is intended to apply.[217] In a transitional justice context, trust is often about rebuilding relationships that have been previously shaped and distorted by the deliberate infliction of violence and suffering. Gaining trust can help people to heal after conflict, and trusting the 'other' may be a basis for greater future reconciliation.[218] In divided societies internationally, continuing uncertainty over the fate of missing persons can fuel mistrust between communities.[219] Alternatively, finding a solution to legacy issues, such as 'disappearances,' can help to build trust.[220] In Northern Ireland, where distrust is argued to be a 'legacy' of the conflict and the peace process,[221] the process of locating the remains of the 'disappeared' may therefore contribute to the building of trust. This section will examine the extent to which this can be argued to be the case.

6.1. 'Quiet' transitional justice, locating remains, and building trust

As Lederach explains, reconciliation is about relationships, and interdependence is key in the development of a peaceful future.[222] In addition to those discussed previously, another of the benefits of quiet diplomacy is that, through the process of communicating with one another in working towards these aims, relationships are built between representatives of adversary groups.[223] During the debate on the Bill in the House of Lords, Lord Hylton drew attention to the Bill as an example of the British and Irish governments working together, remarking that such co-operation was essential in the shift from conflict.[224] Communication itself 'entails recognition of the other,' Sofer tells us, and this can develop into dialogue and understanding.[225] Those involved in 'quiet' diplomatic efforts 'may begin seeing each other as fellow human beings rather

216 Hwang and Burgers, n 213.
217 Kee and Knox, n 214.
218 Janine Natalya Clark, 'Missing Persons, Reconciliation and the View From Below: A Case Study of Bosnia-Hercegovina,' *Southeast European and Black Sea Studies*, 10:4, (2010), 425–442; Ervin Staub, 'Reconciliation After Genocide, Mass Killing, or Intractable Conflict: Understanding the Roots of Violence, Psychological Recovery, and Steps Toward a General Theory,' *Political Psychology*, 27:6, (2006), 867–894.
219 Clark, ibid.
220 Iosif Kovras, 'De-Linkage Processes and Grassroots Movements in Transition,' *Cooperation and Conflict*, 47:1, (2012), 88–105.
221 Patricia Lundy and Mark McGovern, 'A Trojan Horse? Unionism, Trust and Truth-Telling in Northern Ireland,' *International Journal of Transitional Justice*, 2:1, (2008), 42–62.
222 John Paul Lederach, *Building Peace: Sustainable Reconciliation in Divided Societies* (Washington: United States Institute of Peace Press, 1998).
223 Arthur, n 94.
224 HL Deb 18 May 1999, vol 601, col 153–190
225 Sasson Sofer, 'The Diplomat as a Stranger,' *Diplomacy and Statecraft*, 8:3, (1997), 179–186.

than … members of an opposing group.'[226] This can reduce stereotyping and increase levels of respect, empathy, and trust.[227] Joint learning, sharing interests and goals, and the need to rely on one another in a shared purpose contribute to the development of trust.[228] This sense of solidarity is further enhanced through sharing that which is secret.[229]

As discussed earlier, 'quiet diplomacy' has been an important feature of attempts at conflict resolution in Northern Ireland. The repeated contact between the British government and the IRA over a period of more than 20 years is suggested to have built a 'limited degree of trust,' in that interaction became more predictable through repeated contact.[230] Former Chief of Staff under Tony Blair, Jonathan Powell, has said of his informal meetings with McGuinness and Adams from 1997 onwards that 'The shared risks we took [in meeting secretly in Belfast, Derry and Dublin] helped establish a relationship of trust, in which ideas could be explored informally and progress made.'[231]

Ó Dochartaigh proposes that, 'in a situation of armed conflict where one side rejects the legitimacy of the other, the conditions for establishing a relationship of even limited trust are very difficult.'[232] Although the LVR Bill was being debated after the GFA, the continuing struggle to develop trust is omnipresent in media reports from that period, and is fervently expressed in the debate on the Bill.[233] Yet, as previously examined, the Bill's 'offstage' development reduced uncertainty regarding IRA compliance and thus increased the expectation that the desired outcome would be met. Furthermore, that the announcement by the British and Irish Ministers of a willingness to change the law was publicly broadcast creates a level of openness. Although later criticised as an "underhand deal" (see below),[234] that such legislation would be introduced was not secret. Public communication can validate a process.[235]

This legislative change is a further point to consider in relation to trust. Amnesties occupy a 'complex space,' McEvoy and Mallinder argue, where decisions surrounding the process 'speak directly to fundamentally contested versions of the past and indeed often the future of transitional societies.'[236] At the time the legislation was being debated, the IRA had yet to lay down its weapons, and Sinn Féin was striving to assert its new position as fully

226 Pruitt, n 104 at 42.
227 Ibid.
228 Arthur, n 94; Ó Dochartaigh, n 100.
229 Ó Dochartaigh, n 100.
230 Ibid. at 771.
231 Powell, n 126.
232 Ó Dochartaigh, n 100 at 773.
233 HC Deb 10 May 1999, vol 331, cols 38–83; HC Deb 12 May 1999, vol 331, cols 324–386; HL Deb 18 May 1999, vol 601, cc. 153–190; HL Deb 24 May 1999, vol 601, cc. 639–664.
234 Lord Fitt, HL Deb 18 May 1999, vol 601, cc. 153–190.
235 Sparre, n 184.
236 McEvoy and Mallinder, n 32 at 439.

committed to peaceful, democratic means. As Mallinder explains, 'the granting of an amnesty arguably denotes that the actions of non-state actors were political rather than criminal acts.'[237] This speaks to Helena Cobban's argument that amnesties contribute to long-term peace-building in part because they do not use the excluding language of criminalisation.[238]

There were attempts by critics of the Bill to compare the cases of the 'disappeared' with so-called 'ordinary,' non-political criminal acts of abduction, murder, and secret burial. For instance, Lord McConnell argued that if a similar Bill were brought forward for "non-terrorist criminals who have buried their victims," it "would not stand up for very long in this House."[239] This legislation arguably proffered a level of political legitimacy on the Republican Movement. Although not legitimating IRA violence, it did (arguably) legitimate the Republican Movement's new identity as a political actor by giving them an opportunity to right this wrong and continue in the overall peace process. Such a process resonates with Mallinder's view that 'amnesties represent part of a broader process of stripping away the fiction of denial that often characterises state propaganda.'[240] The criminalisation of IRA actions was a frequent refrain of British state propaganda[241] and in introducing this limited immunity, the British government demonstrated a (slight) shift away from this stance.

Transitioning from conflict towards peace provides opportunities for parties to see new opportunities and 're-categorise' their opponents.[242] One of the risks to peace processes and coming to settlement is that these 're-categorisations' can prove to have been mistaken.[243] Locating the bodies of the 'disappeared' was one way in which, as outlined in Chapter 3, the Republican Movement could reinforce its new collective identity as peacemaker and enhance its re-categorisation in the eyes of others. The 'legitimacy' that, some claim, is conferred on 'terrorists' through talking to them is, Powell suggests, 'usually temporary' and dependent on a group's continued involvement in a talks process.[244] Similarly, the impact which the search for the 'disappeared' had on the 're-categorisation' of Republicans depended on their continued and genuine involvement in the search process. For one DUP MP, the confidence-building effects of the process are dependent on the IRA's co-operation:

> The fact that the IRA have cooperated, at least in some cases, is an indication that they recognise that there is a need to address the suffering of these families, and that they are moving on from their involvement in violence to try

237 Mallinder, n 30 at 13.
238 Helena Cobban, *Amnesty After Atrocity? Healing Nations After Genocide and War Crimes* (London: Paradigm Publishers, 2007).
239 HL Deb 18 May 1999, vol 601, cc. 153–190.
240 Mallinder, n 30 at 13.
241 Miller, n 162.
242 Ruane and Todd, n 201 at 454.
243 Ibid.
244 Powell, n 126.

> and at least give some form of, it's not restitution – it certainly isn't – but at least in a humane way to recognise that the families have suffered and have lost, and at the very least, should have their loved ones' remains returned to them … I think if the IRA had refused to cooperate with the Independent Commission, it would have had the opposite effect, of undermining confidence and trust.[245]

Giving up the bodies of the 'disappeared' was a symbolically important move (see Chapter 3). Hosking points to the etymological origins of the word 'symbol' in the Greek *symballein*, meaning to join or throw together.[246] A symbol 'acts as a bridge between the known and the unknown – potentially a creator of trust in the encounter with the Other.'[247] Returning the remains of the 'disappeared' created a 'bridge' between the uncertainty over Republican commitment to the peace process, and the certainty of victims' remains being returned to their families for burial. In interview, historian Richard English spoke of the importance of "gestures" from "the other team;"[248] the return of the remains of the 'disappeared' was one such gesture.

While the success of the search process was important in terms of creating trust, this success was also dependent on the existence of trust – between Republicans and the process. As one interviewee asked: "how do you trust the process?"[249] Some trust is needed for parties to willingly support a transaction.[250] In interviews with Republicans, it is clear that their trust in the process has been vital for its success. As previously considered, the LVR legislation contains no clauses to compel Republicans to act. There is no legal sanction for non-compliance. Although, as discussed, there is a sort of 'stick,' the draw of the 'carrot' is strengthened by trust. Danny Morrison said that the legislation "had the desired effect" because it meant that those Republicans nominated to attempt to gather information "had the authority to turn round to people and say, 'listen, here is the legislation … It's public. You're not going to be arrested. But please help us find these remains.'"[251] In his opinion, the legislation "was a very powerful document, one of the best to come out of the conflict."[252]

Although the legislation provided a legal guarantee that Republicans could have confidence in, trust in the process came with time, and the development of a working relationship with the ICLVR. Trust between those Republicans who are giving information, those Republicans acting as intermediaries between the IRA and the Commission, and the staff of the Commission has been, and continues to

245 Interview, Jeffrey Donaldson, March 2015.
246 Hosking, n 211.
247 Ibid. at 40.
248 Interview, Richard English, August 2014.
249 Interview, Kate Turner, September 2014.
250 Hwang and Burgers, n 213.
251 Interview, Danny Morrison, January 2015.
252 Ibid.

be, essential. One senior Republican ex-combatant interviewed explained, this is what "has been able to unlock all those secrets":[253]

> the people concerned have to be able to have trust in the people that are making the approach. They have to have confidence in those people. They have to be convinced that anything that they divulge to the people who request information will not go beyond that. That the information can be disclosed, but names and personalities will not be. That they will remain anonymous … this whole thing about putting in place a number of very, very, trusted, comrades as the go-betweens between the people – the families and the likes of … Geoff Knupfer – the people who can talk to that side of things in regards to the State, and the people who can talk to the Republican activists and volunteers who were involved in it – the sense of trust, the sense of confidence, and the sense of confidentiality is ensured – that is … the most crucial part of the process.[254]

The evolution of this relationship of trust over time arguably can be seen in how the search has played out. Although I cannot be certain of the mechanics of the search process due to its confidential nature, one interviewee with substantial experience in working with ex-combatants proposed a process which in my view fits well with what has been witnessed in terms of the gradual progress of the search, with large areas being narrowed down over time:

> I think there are a number of elements to the process. The first element is they create their own internal investigation unit. And it starts off by doing bilateral interviews with individuals and then bigger focus groups with individuals, trying to spark memories.… Those interlocutors – the next stage is them engaging with the Commission, then there's a back and forward where interlocutors are going back to the individuals and back again, and I think there's a recognition by all of the parties that that becomes overly cumbersome and eventually they get to a stage where there is sufficient confidence for the individuals themselves … I don't know how it worked practically … that's very secret stuff … But I think that it is right that ultimately individuals who were directly involved in these crimes engaged at some level with the institution.[255]

This theory is supported by Adams' assertion, as examined earlier, that Republicans began meeting directly with the ICLVR staff at search sites.[256] Kieran

253 Interview, senior Republican ex-combatant, April 2015.

254 Ibid.

255 Interview, community activist with over 20 years' experience working with ex-combatants, October 2015.

256 'Gerry Adams Welcomes Discovery of Remains in Wicklow,' *An Phoblacht*, 13 November 2008.

Megraw recounted the outcome of this gradual process in relation to the recovery of the remains of his brother:

> And eventually, Brendan was found on the fourth dig. The first dig was probably a bit further away but the second and third were fairly close. He was found in between the two of them. That was again, somebody had given that final bit of information. Really in most of the cases, that's what it's been.[257]

The Commission, and Geoff Knupfer in particular as Senior Investigating Officer, have proved crucial to progress. A Republican ex-combatant suggested that Republicans "were able to rely on Geoff Knupfer to the same extent that they were able to rely on their comrades."[258] As an independent body, the Commission is in a position to provide valued, objective assessment of Republican involvement. During a debate in the Assembly on dealing with the past, Sinn Féin's Pat Sheehan referred to the Commission's praise of Republican co-operation in the search process as evidence of Republicans having "proved their credentials in dealing with the legacy of the past."[259] Sinn Féin's Declan Kearney spoke of the importance of having this objective viewpoint:

> Geoff Knupfer offered an assessment just a few years ago ... that he felt Republicans had committed 100% to the process, indicates from an entirely objective perspective that Republicans came to this priority with good will and a serious intent to be as helpful as possible.[260]

Lessons for dealing with the past can be learned here. Kearney described:

> that the process could be carried out with absolute confidentiality, that for all involved ... there was a growing and a mutual confidence in one another, and a belief that people were serious ... those are three important ingredients, because that establishes a very firm basis

for, not only the ICLVR, but future mechanisms for dealing with the past; because "it's about how we build confidence, how we create mutual trust."[261] Yet, there were threats to this development of trust.

6.2. Threats to trust: back-channel dealing and the shadow of prosecution

In some studies trust is juxtaposed with suspicion.[262] As its counter or antithesis, suspicion also involves expectation, but in this case expectation of an outcome that

257 Interview, Kieran Megraw, October 2015.
258 Interview, senior Republican ex-combatant, April 2015.
259 NIA Deb 10 October 2011, vol 67, page 170, col 1.
260 Interview, Declan Kearney, April 2015.
261 Ibid.
262 Deutsch, n 213; Kee and Knox, n 214.

may be detrimental or damaging to the person concerned.[263] As explained previously, trust is necessary for co-operation as it alleviates fear. Fear, therefore, threatens this co-operation.[264] Two threats to trust will be analysed: the risks posed by quiet diplomacy, and the fear of prosecution.

Although, as has been outlined, those involved in carrying out quiet diplomacy can develop relationships of trust, for those external to the process who later come to be aware of it, the effect can be the opposite. Although the absence of a public audience increases the chance of finding a diplomatic solution, this can create suspicion over what takes place behind closed doors.[265] Secrecy can create mistrust, which can impact negatively on the development of more widespread support for the compromise reached, as those who were excluded may not support what is proposed.[266] This is the 'paradoxical quality' of back-channel negotiations: although needed to reach agreement, their secretive character may exacerbate the problems already being faced.[267] As Tony Blair recounts of his involvement in the Northern Ireland peace process:

> I had a constant problem of trust, mostly with Unionists, but often with the other side too. It derived partly from the necessarily tricky path that had to be woven through the hazardous thickets of Northern Irish politics, and deals of every description – side, secret and surface – abounded.[268]

In relation to the LVR Bill, the potential damage caused is hinted at in Lord Molyneaux's contribution to the House of Lords' debate:

> Emerging information indicates that, as a result of secret, detailed negotiations between the IRA on the one hand and the MI6 successor to the agent formerly known as 'the mountain climber' on the other, agreed arrangements are already in place. They were in place before this Chamber and the other place began deliberations … the bargains have been struck with the terrorists in great detail … the sole function of your Lordships is now to seal the deal.[269]

The accusatory tone of Lord Molyneaux's contribution highlights the damage to trust that can be caused by 'quiet' negotiations. It also demonstrates how those parties not involved in these strategies can react negatively once dealings are made public. William Ross MP claimed the Bill was evidence of "some deal with the

263 Deutsch, ibid.
264 Hwang and Burgers, n 213.
265 Martin Adelmann, 'Quiet Diplomacy: The Reasons Behind Mbeki's Zimbabwe Policy,' *Africa Spectrum*, 39:2, (2004), 249–276.
266 Ó Dochartaigh, n 100; Wanis-St. John, n 96.
267 Wanis-St. John, ibid. at 138.
268 Tony Blair, *A Journey* (London: Hutchinson, 2010), p. 162.
269 HL Deb 24 May 1999, vol 601, cc. 639–664.

IRA,"[270] and Lord Cooke argued: "This is an IRA Bill. This is not a government Bill."[271]

Where back-channels allow for more 'creative' solutions, these may be more 'daring' or 'risky' and thus less likely to achieve widespread support.[272] During the parliamentary debates some expressed doubt that this mechanism would be effective, as they did not trust the IRA to engage. Viscount Cranborne, for instance, spoke of the IRA's "habit to pocket a concession and give nothing in return."[273]

In transitional processes generally, the threat of trials can threaten hope for truth recovery.[274] In the case at hand, from a Republican perspective, the main threat to trust is the risk of prosecution. One senior Republican interviewed highlighted this risk:

> The danger in anything like this, is the whole idea of, for some of the families of the people concerned, that once … they are able to get whatever closure they want, or they believe they can get with the process of having the remains returned to them, we have seen, it's probably in one particular case – that … is simply the start of a process for them … it's not the end … And … they then seek to go for what they consider to be justice, I suppose, and they seek to bring the people who were involved in the 'disappearance' and all of that … they then seek to get those people into court and to have them sentenced. And that would be a particular worry for Republicans.[275]

Asked if he believed prosecutions would impact on the search process, he answered:

> It's absolutely bound to … they tend to seek to pursue further, whether it's information, whether it's prosecution, whatever it is, and that then can have a negative impact upon the whole process for people who haven't had closure … If it's in the public domain, if it's on the news, that people are being pursued, it means that everyone concerned will be a lot more reluctant to attempt to access information.[276]

However, another interviewee suggested that Republican confidence in the search process "remains pretty strong." This is in part because of "a continued confidence in the 'disappeared' commission." And in part because the only arrests in relation to the 'disappeared' resulted from the Boston College interviews, and that there exists "a lack of sympathy" for those who engaged with that project.[277]

270 HC Deb 12 May 1999, vol 331, col 358.
271 HL Deb 24 May 1999, vol 601, cc. 639–664
272 Wanis-St John, n 96 at 128; 138.
273 HL Deb 18 May 1999, vol 601, cc. 153–190.
274 Freeman, n 36.
275 Interview, senior Republican ex-combatant, April 2015.
276 Ibid.
277 Interview, community activist with over 20 years' experience working with ex-combatants, October 2015. See Chapter 3, footnote 229.

6.3. Locating victims' remains as a confidence-building measure

In the Commons debate on passing the Bill, Peter Robinson remarked that the Bill was "being bandied about as another confidence-building measure."[278] The tone of his comment is clear, but was he right to be so cynical? It can be difficult to measure the impact of 'quiet' processes.[279] While the relative success of the Commission is clear in terms of the remains having been recovered, assessing the extent to which the process has built trust is more challenging. When asked whether or not this measure had the effect of 'confidence-building,' one interviewee raised a useful question: "what would it be like without something being done?"[280] Although the existence of trust is rather intangible, and certainly difficult to measure, the process of search, the Republican Movement's involvement, and the actions of the state in introducing this legislation, can all certainly be argued to be moves in the right direction.

Burgers warns that 'the future casts a shadow back upon the present.'[281] With regards this issue, it is reasonable to suggest that this shadow is less dark as a result of this process. It is difficult to argue that the process has actively built trust between Republicans and their opponents. For some, the building of trust is hindered by the cruelty of 'disappearing.' One interviewee said, "it's hard to describe it as a confidence-building measure given the horror of it … but certainly it put another element of reconciliation in place that needed to happen."[282] However, it can be argued that the contribution of this mechanism is one of lessening the distrust. As one interviewee pointed out: "if these things had unravelled or hadn't worked or couldn't be trusted, then people would lose faith in post-conflict mechanisms or legacy mechanisms generally."[283] Goldman and Hardman suggest that confidence is built as political distrust is reduced,[284] and this is the process we see here.

One senior Republican interviewed argued that confidence-building was not a motivating factor for the IRA.[285] While not their intention, it may have been a side effect. DUP MP Jeffrey Donaldson said in interview:

> I don't think the IRA should be praised for that, I think doing the right thing by those families is something they ought to do. And I don't think in and of itself it contributed significantly to building trust and confidence. But it was certainly a factor in the overall picture … So at the very least, it is neutral, but at best you could say that it helped, to a modest degree, in what the IRA's

278 HC Deb 10 May 1999, vol 331, col 60.
279 See e.g. Arthur, n 94 and Graham, n 117.
280 Interview, Brian Gormally, November 2014.
281 Burgers, n 215 at 118.
282 Interview, Monica McWilliams, September 2014.
283 Interview, a former diplomat who has been engaged in efforts to deal with the past in Northern Ireland, June 2015.
284 Goldman and Hardman, n 210.
285 Interview, senior Republican ex-combatant, April 2015.

motivations were in calling their ceasefire and in Sinn Féin then becoming involved in the political process.[286]

We can see in this statement a level of recognition that Republican involvement in the search has been a positive contribution to the overall process. While it may remain difficult to argue that trust has been built between political opponents, perhaps the most important role for trust here is between Republicans and the process itself, in terms of the Commission. This has set a precedent for a type of process that works, and has created a sense of confidence for Republicans in this type of mechanism. Even limited trust can serve as a foundation[287] and we can see that with this process. As one senior Republican described in interview when asked why the ICLVR was used as a precedent for the Independent Commission on Information Retrieval (ICIR – see Chapter 7), and what lessons could be learned from the ICLVR process more generally, he answered:

> Mainly because the various actors involved in the process were able to have confidence in the Commission … there's very few examples that you could point to, to say that the various actors involved – whether you're talking about at a political level, whether you're talking about former IRA, former comrades, if you don't have initial confidence that the process could work, well then you're not going anywhere … Trust, on both sides, is the big one.[288]

7. Conclusion

Susan Hughes' exhibit 'Quiet Peacemakers' comprises portraits of those individuals whose mostly unseen efforts have contributed to the building of a more peaceful society in Northern Ireland. Of the series of portraits she writes: 'beneath the radar of the big events of the Peace Process are networks of ordinary people moving mountains in courageous and imaginative ways.'[289] This chapter has examined the value of quiet, 'beneath the radar' processes in recovering the remains of the 'disappeared,' finding that using quiet diplomatic efforts helped to create a space in which a solution could be sought and developed. Brian Rowan spoke of the need to focus on one "page" excluding the right and wrong, and the politicking, and focussing on one specific task, as exemplified in De Chastelain's approach to decommissioning.[290] In creating a quiet space to develop and pass this legislation, this allowed the focus to be on one "page," in this case, the return of victims' remains.

286 Interview, Jeffrey Donaldson, March 2015.
287 Ó Dochartaigh, n 100.
288 Interview, senior Republican ex-combatant, April 2015.
289 Susan Hughes, Preface in Publication to accompany *Quiet Peacemakers* exhibition (Ballynafeigh Community Development Association, 2014).
290 Interview, Brian Rowan, September 2014.

This chapter included a comparison between the reaction to the OTR controversy of 2014 and the response to the 'disappeared' legislation, pointing to a relative lack of outcry in response to the latter situation in contrast to the former. The two issues were, however, fundamentally different. As one interviewee pointed out:

> [the 'disappeared'] didn't have huge cross-group implications, and to some extent … the OTRs was a similar sort of thing … [but] with much larger implications because that did involve implications for, as it were, the British army, the Unionists and so on, [it] was much more of a cross-group issue … [it] was another example of … something which was done to try and facilitate the process, but where no one wanted to give it particular publicity and it was only when … a particular case arose that, on one side the Unionists felt that [they] had to politically respond to, that the whole thing was sort of blown open.[291]

The relatively limited and intra-communal nature of the 'disappeared' as a victims' collective made possible the creation of a "bespoke mechanism."[292] With regards dealing with the past in Northern Ireland, Richard English proposed that "any door that's benign and that we can push open we should push open."[293] As has been explored this issue was, in many ways, relatively "benign," and this door was pushed open.

In interview, Rowan elaborated on his 'offstage' suggestion in relation to the 'disappeared' issue:

> the only way they were going to get those bodies back was if they created a process, such as they created around decommissioning, that would allow this to be done offstage, that would provide immunity for information … offstage, doing it quietly, doing it without the police being involved was the only way it was ever going to work. The legislation was inevitable. There had to be a Commission. There had to be that interlocutor process.[294]

English echoed this point:

> it's often the case in the long peace process that there's been less creative generosity than there needed to be and I think sometimes there are things where generosity from one side to the other has sort of brought a certain measure of progress from the other side … what you need therefore is some room for movement … I think, quite often things can be done quietly, behind the scenes more easily.[295]

291 Interview, former diplomat who has been engaged in efforts to deal with the past in Northern Ireland, June 2015.
292 Ibid.
293 Interview, Richard English, August 2014.
294 Interview, Brian Rowan, September 2014.
295 Interview, Richard English, August 2014.

As examined earlier in this chapter, removing the public audience to negotiations reduced the likelihood that participants would play to their extremes. Looking at the debate on the LVR legislation, we can see these extreme views were expressed in the debate on the LVR Bill. That they didn't have a significant impact at that time has been hugely beneficial for this process.

McEvoy and Mallinder suggest that the field of transitional justice is:

> marked by the inherent tensions between principle and pragmatism. On the one hand, there was and is a moral and political impetus towards punishing those who have visited 'extraordinary evil' on their victims. On the other, the legal, practical, and political difficulties inherent in following through on such impulses are manifest.[296]

The mechanism put in place to locate the remains of the 'disappeared' spoke to the pragmatic side of this tension. Although, as has already been discussed, the legislation is certainly a compromise, it is a compromise that facilitated the fulfilment of the families' demand to have the remains of their loved ones returned for burial.

Lederach points to the importance of 'space' in reconciliation:

> reconciliation-as-encounter suggests that space for the acknowledging of the past and envisioning of the future is the necessary ingredient for reframing the present. For this to happen, people must find ways to encounter themselves and their enemies, their hopes and their fears.[297]

As examined in this chapter, the Bill was being debated at a time of much political noise surrounding the implementation of the GFA, pressure to decommission and the establishment of a power-sharing executive. This legislation and the establishment of the ICLVR created a politically 'quiet' space in which progress could be made. Through the use of quiet diplomacy in developing the legislation, the relatively quiet passage of the required legislation, and the operationalising of a limited immunity, political noise was excluded from this process. This supported the creation of a humanitarian and pragmatic space within which the process of searching for remains could begin.

The 'quiet' nature of the process is essential to its success, both in the search for the 'disappeared' and as a model for future transitional processes. One senior Republican interviewed described a series of informal discussions between those in the ex-prisoner community regarding options for truth recovery:

> we in the political ex-prisoner community did a series of discussions … about … how they would feel about becoming involved in a process of truth recovery. First of all we made it very clear to people that what we were not

296 McEvoy and Mallinder, n 32 at 412.
297 Lederach, n 222 at 27.

> talking about was the public trial, taped, televised, show – basically – that you had with the TRC in South Africa … what we had in mind was some sort of a process whereby people on a collective basis could be requested to give information to a group of very trusted and confidential comrades. And that these people then could bring that information forward … And the example that we used was the process of the recovery of the remains. And in the main, most guys would have been comfortable with that.[298]

This quote suggests that a 'loud' transitional justice process, such as the TRC, would not, for the Republicans involved in these discussions, be a viable solution. However, a quiet, confidential, trusted process based around confidentiality and immunity from prosecution is certainly a workable starting point. For human rights activist Mike Ritchie, the 'quiet' nature of the development of the mechanism to recover the bodies of the 'disappeared' is a strength that can be learnt from for the wider process. When asked what can we learn from the process put in place to locate remains, he responded:

> Try and do it sub-rosa … acknowledge that there has to be amnesty or non-prosecution or non-use immunity for the provision of information. Try and create a spirit of public generosity … concentrate on the human factors, the closure that people need. Try and ensure that there's an atmosphere that doesn't focus on punishment, but rather the resolution of practical issues.[299]

298 Interview, senior Republican ex-combatant, April 2015.
299 Interview, Mike Ritchie, October 2014.

6 Acknowledgement, truth, and the collective memory of the 'disappeared'

1. Introduction

Engaging with the memory of past violence is argued by some to be a vital aspect of the transition from conflict.[1] For Misztal, such efforts entail a complex linkage between collective memory and processes of apology, acknowledgement, seeking justice, reconciliation, and, in some instances, the establishment or re-establishment of democracy.[2] As examined in Chapter 5, the mechanism put in place to recover the remains of Northern Ireland's 'disappeared' may be considered an example of 'quiet' transitional justice. The relative absence of, or indeed exclusion of, audience, combined with the lack of a process to recover 'truth' or information beyond that relating to burial site locations, raises questions regarding what constitutes the memory of the 'disappeared' for Northern Ireland as a society.

In Chapter 1 it was argued that the silence surrounding a 'disappearance' is a defining aspect of the act, and that breaking this silence is often a fundamental step for those seeking to establish the fate of the 'disappeared.' As argued in Chapter 2, the families speaking out about 'disappearing' was a vital move in countering the decades of silence they had endured. Although, as will be examined in this chapter, the IRA's acknowledgement of 'disappearing' was significant, the ending of the silence over the fate of these individuals has not led to a deluge of information. Silences remain.

In seeking to better understand these residual silences I have examined some of the relevant theoretical literature. For example, Trouillot tells us how silences can enter into the process of historical production; this can be as facts are created as sources, assembled into archives, retrieved through narrative, or rendered significant as

1 See e.g. W. James Booth, 'The Unforgotten: Memories of Justice,' *American Political Science Review*, 95:4, (2001), 777–791; Priscilla B. Hayner, *Unspeakable Truths: Transitional Justice and the Challenge of Truth Commissions* (2nd ed.) (New York; Oxon: Routledge, 2011); Katharine Hodgkin and Susannah Radstone, 'Introduction: Contested Pasts,' in Katherine Hodgkin and Susannah Radstone (eds) *Contested Pasts: The Politics of Memory* (London; New York: Routledge, 2003), pp. 1–22; Martha Minow, *Between Vengeance and Forgiveness: Facing History After Genocide and Mass Violence* (Boston: Beacon Press, 1998).

2 Barbara A. Misztal, 'Memory and Democracy,' *American Behavioural Scientist*, 48:10, (2005), 1320–1338.

'history.'[3] As Trouillot's theory suggests, the mechanisms of transitional justice can also create such 'silences' as they are inherently selective in terms of both process and outcome. Hamber and Wilson warn that truth commissions can, in attempting to create a homogenised account of the past, silence some individuals, creating 'a new regime of forgetting.'[4] Silences can be created as the 'truth' established is dependent on who provides testimony, and what they choose to say.[5] Further selection occurs in choosing which of this information is included in the final report.[6] Trials can also be silencing as a result of their focus on establishing the innocence or guilt of an alleged perpetrator, rather than uncovering truth.[7] Selectivity in deciding who faces prosecution in the first place is another point at which silence can enter the process.[8] If engaging with the memory of past violence can involve silencing aspects of that past, then it is useful to consider the process of memory construction in any particular case, in order to examine what may have been silenced, and what has been selected as 'worthy of recollection.'[9]

The literature on memory is vast and encompasses various disciplines including psychology, sociology, anthropology, and transitional justice. These accounts on memory range from in-depth analyses of the construction, types, and uses of memory to a broader transitional justice scholarship, in which engaging with the memory of the past may be but one element of efforts to address a legacy of violence. What emerges from these various accounts is that the relationship between what happened in the past and how it is remembered is not straightforward. There is a 'boundary between what happened and that which is said to have happened.'[10] There are of course limitations to that which can be 'said' – as Appadurai proposed, the past is not 'a boundless

3 Michel-Rolph Trouillot, *Silencing the Past: Power and the Production of History* (Boston: Beacon Press, 1995).

4 Brandon Hamber and Richard A. Wilson, 'Symbolic Closure Through Memory, Reparation and Revenge in Post-Conflict Societies,' *Journal of Human Rights*, 1:1, (2002), 35–53 (p. 36).

5 Bill Rolston, 'Dealing with the Past: Pro-State Paramilitaries, Truth and Transition in Northern Ireland,' *Human Rights Quarterly*, 28:3, (2006), 652–675.

6 Audrey R. Chapman and Patrick Ball, 'The Truth of Truth Commissions: Comparative Lessons From Haiti, South Africa, and Guatemala,' *Human Rights Quarterly*, 23:1, (2001), 1–43.

7 Susanne Karstedt, 'From Absence to Presence, From Silence to Voice: Victims in International and Transitional Justice Since the Nuremberg Trials,' *International Review of Victimology*, 17:1, (2010), 9–30; Jennifer J. Llewellyn and Robert Howse, 'Institutions for Restorative Justice: The South African Truth and Reconciliation Commission,' *The University of Toronto Law Journal*, 49:3, (1999), 355–388.

8 Laurel E. Fletcher and Harvey M. Weinstein, 'Violence and Social Repair: Rethinking the Contribution of Justice to Reconciliation,' *Human Rights Quarterly*, 24:3, (2002), 573–639; Minow, n 1.

9 Jaime Malamud Goti, 'Editorial Note: A Turbulent Past and the Problem with Memory,' *International Journal of Transitional Justice*, 4:2, (2010), 153–165 (p. 158).

10 Trouillot, n 3 at 13.

canvas for contemporary embroidery.'[11] However, memory is a site of struggle where the past is linked to present day political and social interests.[12] In his influential work on collective memory, Halbwachs asserted that 'the mind reconstructs its memories under the pressure of society.'[13] For him, collective memory does not preserve the past, but rather 'reconstructs an image of the past which is in accord, in each epoch, with the predominant thoughts of the society.'[14]

Lambek and Antze suggest that memory operates most frequently by means of what they term 'threads of narrative.'[15] Hamber and Wilson similarly contend that, 'memory is … the social practice that constitutes narratives on the past.'[16] In an attempt, at this stage, to circumvent the complex and at times contradictory memory literature, this chapter will begin to explore the construction of memory of the 'disappeared' from the perspective of 'narrative threads.' The idea of 'threads' of narrative is particularly apt here as the result of the lack of any overarching truth recovery mechanism in Northern Ireland (see Introduction), is, arguably, the existence of myriad strands or 'threads of narrative' woven by those engaged in efforts to address the legacy of the conflict. This chapter will examine the IRA's use of apology and acknowledgement, the place of 'truth,' and the use of the memory of the 'disappeared' for political purposes as both 'threads of narrative' and as contributions to the transition in their own right. Finally, the idea of 'collective memory' will be scrutinised in more depth, by engaging with the relevant theoretical literature and teasing out some ideas pertinent to improving our understanding of the case at hand.

2. The 'disappeared,' apology, and acknowledgement

Trouillot describes the significance of an apology as a transitional moment; suggesting that apologies 'mark a temporal transition.'[17] The identification and acknowledgement of a past wrong:

> creates or verifies a new temporal plane, a present oriented towards the future … apologies are premised on the assumption that the state of affairs to

11 Arjun Appadurai, 'The Past as a Scarce Resource,' *Man*, 16:2, (1981), 201–219 (p. 201).
12 Patricia Lundy and Mark McGovern, 'The Politics of Memory in Post-Conflict Northern Ireland,' *Peace Review*, 13:1, (2001), 27–33. See also Chapter 1.
13 Maurice Halbwachs, *On Collective Memory* (ed. trans Lews A. Coser) (Chicago: University of Chicago Press, 1992), 51.
14 Ibid. at 40.
15 Michael Lambek and Paul Antze, 'Introduction: Forecasting Memory,' in Paul Antze and Michael Lambek (eds) *Tense Past* (New York: Routledge, 1996), pp. xi-xxxviii (xvii).
16 Hamber and Wilson, n 4 at 36.
17 Michel-Rolph Trouillot, 'Abortive Rituals: Historical Apologies in the Global Era,' *Interventions: International Journal of Postcolonial Studies*, 2:2, (2000), 171–186 (p. 174).

which they refer does not, or should not, obtain in the present of the actors involved. In claiming a past, they create pastness.[18]

In considering the construction of a collective memory of the 'disappeared,' one should consider this point of apology, this 'temporal transition' between past wrong and a present characterised by new relations.[19] As will be examined, while the IRA's March 1999 statement can be read as an attempt to demonstrate the 'pastness' of IRA violence, the extent to which it can be said to 'create or verify' a newly oriented present, or new relations with those who were wronged, is questionable. However, as I will consider further later, the value of this statement for families lay in the acknowledgement it contained. Acknowledgement, as outlined in Chapter 1, is a valuable first step in responding to the needs of the families of those who have been 'disappeared.'

2.1. Apology, the IRA, and the 'disappeared'

A perceived surge in public apologies by political, state, and religious leaders prompted the declaration of the 1990s and 2000s as the 'Age of Apology,' attracting both popular and academic attention.[20] Apology is, in its most basic form, a 'speech act.'[21] Described as 'illocutionary events denoting to an addressee the repentance of a speaking subject,'[22] the power of apology lies in this expression of repentance from one person to another. Lakoff contends that an apology is 'language politics': it 'changes the world for participants in terms of their relative status and their future relationship.'[23] For some, it is a ritual or performance, its component parts and performative nature rendering it symbolic and imbued with meaning.[24] This ritual starts with a transgression from the norm, the transgression is then framed as such by the victim, their representative, or the media.[25] Apologies serve, or are believed to serve, various purposes, both between the parties involved and between the apologiser and their audience. Between parties, apologies manage rapport[26] and reassert shared values, thus reducing uncertainty in

18 Ibid. at 174.
19 Ibid. at 174.
20 Zohar Kampf and Nava Löwenheim, 'Rituals of Apology in the Global Arena,' *Security Dialogue*, 43:1, (2012), 43–60; Walter Shapiro and Kathleen Adams, 'Mama Mia, That's a Mea Culpa,' *Time*, 146:26, (1997), 18; Sandra Harris, Karen Grainger and Louise Mullany, 'The Pragmatics of Political Apologies,' *Discourse and Society*, 17:6, (2006), 715–737; A. J. Meier, 'Conflict and the Power of Apologies,' *Philologie im Netz*, 30, (2004), 1–17.
21 Kampf and Löwenheim, ibid.
22 Trouillot, n 17 at 174.
23 Robin T. Lakoff, *Language War* (California: California University Press, 2001), p. 23.
24 Kampf and Löwenheim, n 20; Lakoff, ibid.; Danielle Celermajer, 'Mere Ritual? Displacing the Myth of Sincerity in Transitional Rituals,' *International Journal of Transitional Justice*, 7, (2013), 286–305.
25 Kampf and Löwenheim, n 20.
26 Meier, n 20.

relationships.[27] In so doing they restore equilibrium or balance to relationships.[28] Between the apologiser and their intended audience, apologies can serve as a method of 'impression management,'[29] or 'image restoration.'[30] Here, an apology is made in an attempt to repair the damaged image of the speaker.[31]

It should of course be noted that accounts in which families call for an apology are rare. In 2013, Helen McKendry was critical that "Gerry Adams … hasn't come out and publicly apologised to our family."[32] In 2013, Michael McConville told RTÉ's Marian Finucane in interview:

> The biggest thing of me fighting for justice for my mother was to get my mother's body back, and to give her a Christian burial. We have achieved that. The next biggest thing in my mind is to get a proper apology from the IRA. I think that's all our family wants. We want a proper apology from the IRA. We want the IRA to … say that the murder of Jean McConville was wrong, and she wasn't an informant.[33]

Such calls for apology are atypical of remarks made by the families generally, and certainly, a call for an apology is not a component of the families' core message.[34] Indeed, as will be examined, some family members have said that an apology is not something they would value. As analysed in Chapter 2, their public calls were for the return of the remains of their loved ones. However, an apology can have value in a transitional context. Apologies may have a potential political power that renders them 'valuable currency in avoiding or resolving conflict.'[35] When they

27 Ibid.
28 Kampf and Löwenheim, n 20.
29 Meier, n 20.
30 William L. Benoit and Susan L Brinson, 'AT&T: "Apologies are not Enough,"' *Communication Quarterly*, 42:1, (1994) 75–88; William L. Benoit and Shirley Drew, 'Appropriateness and Effectiveness of Image Repair Strategies,' *Communication Reports*, 10:2, (1997), 153–163.
31 Ibid.; Meier, n 20.
32 Catherine McCurry, 'Jean's Family Slam "Hypocrite" Adams Over Thatcher Apology,' *Belfast Telegraph*, 12 April 2013.
33 Michael McConville in interview with Marian Finucane, RTÉ Radio 1, 23 November 2013, www.rte.ie/radio1/marian-finucane/programmes/2013/1123/488613-marian-finucane-saturday-23-november-2013/ [accessed 16 August 2018].
34 The issue of apology has arisen on occasion. For example, in 2003, Dungannon and South Tyrone Borough Council voted unanimously in favour of a motion proposed by the SDLP's Vincent Currie which proposed that the IRA should retract the informer allegations made against Columba McVeigh, apologise to his family, and fully co-operate in efforts to locate his remains. Eight Sinn Féin councillors voted in favour of this motion (Maeve Connolly, 'SF Calls for IRA Apology,' *The Irish News*, 10 September 2003). In 2006, then PSNI Chief Constable, Sir Hugh Orde, apologised to the McConville family following the publication of the OPONI report into the death of Jean McConville, saying that the case should have been better investigated (*RTÉ News*, 'Orde Apologises to McConville Family,' 14 August 2006, www.rte.ie/news/2006/0814/mcconville). See also footnote 64.
35 Meier, n 20.

involve the clarification of what took place, apologies can be a 'vehicle for truth recovery.'[36] Although uncertainty exists over the effectiveness of apology in conflict resolution and the value to victims of an apology,[37] that they continue to be made suggests that political actors see a place for them.[38] For example, Celermajer suggests they have become 'part of the standard toolbox of political transition and historical justice.'[39] In this context, Andrieu proposes that apologies fit into the '"restorative" paradigm … they are considered to be a symbolic form of reparation … their aim is to promote reconciliation through words only, by public acts of contrition and repentance.'[40] Although the act is one based on 'words only,' there is general agreement that the aim of the apology is to achieve something greater than the impact of the words it contains.[41] In a similar vein, Lakoff argues that the 'language politics' of making an apology speak to issues of responsibility and power, in examining or establishing who owes what to whom.[42] With the case of the 'disappeared,' words alone are far from enough, however – in detailing the efforts made to locate the remains of the 'disappeared' – the IRA's March 1999 statement arguably establishes what they believe they 'owe' the families.[43]

Part of what makes an apology effective, Meier suggests, is knowing what one's audience will consider to be effective and appropriate.[44] The likelihood of an apology being accepted is affected by both the extent of the offender's responsibility for the event and the severity of the event.[45] The response to an apology is impacted by the offended party's perception of both the offender and of the offence.[46] In the case of the 'disappeared,' the apologiser – the IRA – can be described as 'highly responsible' for the act, and the outcome of their actions is most certainly 'serious,'[47] factors which Bennett and Earwaker outline as impacting upon the anger experienced and displayed by the offended, the likelihood that further justification or explanation would be required, and thus render the apology less likely to be accepted.[48] For Vera McVeigh, accounts suggest that the anger was just too great. Susan McKay, meeting Mrs McVeigh in 2005, described how

36 Kieran McEvoy, 'Apologies, Acknowledgement and Dealing with the Past in and About Northern Ireland: A Discussion Document,' Draft Report for Healing Through Remembering 2015, p. 32.
37 Celermajer, n 24; Kampf and Löwenheim, n 20.
38 Kampf and Löwenheim, n 20.
39 Celermajer, n 24.
40 Kora Andrieu, '"Sorry for the Genocide": How Public Apologies Can Help Promote National Reconciliation,' *Millennium: Journal of International Studies*, 38:1, (2009), 3–23 (p. 5).
41 Celermajer, n 24.
42 Lakoff, n 23.
43 'IRA Investigation Locates Grave Sites,' *An Phoblacht*, 1 April 1999.
44 Meier, n 20.
45 Mark Bennett and Deborah Earwaker, 'Victims' Responses to Apologies: The Effects of Offender Responsibility and Offense Severity,' *The Journal of Social Psychology*, 134:4, (1994), 457–464.
46 Kampf and Löwenheim, n 20.
47 Bennett and Earwaker, n 45 at 462.
48 Ibid.

'her rage against the killers of her son and those who had kept their secret had not diminished.'[49] In response to a further apology statement made by the IRA in 2003,[50] *The Irish News* reported that Vera McVeigh responded: "I don't want an apology. I want my son's remains … This statement is 28 years too late."[51] Margaret McKinney told one journalist "What use are apologies to me? … I want to know why he was murdered. Sorry doesn't mean anything to me. It has caused so much hurt and harm to our family."[52] In this case, it is clear that further explanation is required. Other factors required in an effective apology include sincerity,[53] the communication of regret,[54] an acknowledgement that the addressee has been wronged and has suffered or recognition of the hurt caused,[55] and an acknowledgement of responsibility for wrongdoing.[56] The delivery of the apology should be in a spirit of respect, sensitivity, and dignity for the recipient.[57] A true apology, Lakoff suggests, should be 'painful.'[58]

One telling interpretation of an apology with regards the case at hand is that of Benoit and Brinson, who argue that in making an apology the apologiser should accept responsibility 'without attempting to diminish the undesirable consequences they [the victim] suffered, and directly apologises for the offensive act.'[59] Breaking this statement down into its two separate parts, it is clear that a significant disparity exists between this ideal and what the IRA offered in March 1999, and comments made by Republicans in the intervening period. Techniques of neutralisation and the contextualisation of 'disappearances' can be read as attempts to 'diminish the undesirable consequences' of the IRA's actions.[60] As recently as 2015, Adams described the 'disappearance' of Jean McConville to CBS

49 Susan McKay, 'Lost Boys,' *Field Day Review*, 9, (2013), 128–147.
50 In a similar vein to the March 1999 statement, the 2003 document reads: "We are sorry that the suffering of those families has continued for so long. We wish to apologise for the grief caused." This statement goes on to provide more detail on the various challenges involved in the search process, such as changing topography, the lapse in time, changes in leadership, and the deaths of some of those involved ('IRA Pledges to try to Bring Closure for Families,' *An Phoblacht*, 30 October 2003).
51 Sharon O'Neill and Maeve Connolly, 'Victims' Families Pour Scorn on IRA Apology,' *The Irish News*, 25 October 2003.
52 Mark Hennessy, 'Victims' Families Reject IRA Apology,' *The Irish Times*, 25 October 2003.
53 Benoit and Drew, n 30; Kampf and Löwenheim, n 20.
54 Benoit and Drew, n 30; Kampf and Löwenheim, n 20; Mathias Thaler, 'Just Pretending: Political Apologies for Historical Injustice and Vice's Tribute to Virtue,' *Critical Review of International Social and Political Philosophy*, 15:3, (2012), 259–278; McEvoy, n 36.
55 Benoit and Brinson, n 30; Lakoff, n 23; McEvoy, n 36.
56 Andrieu, n 40; Benoit and Brinson, n 30; Benoit and Drew, n 30; Kampf and Löwenheim, n 20; Lakoff, n 23; McEvoy, n 36.
57 McEvoy, n 36.
58 Lakoff, n 23 at 23.
59 Benoit and Brinson, n 30 at 80.
60 See Chapter 3 and Lauren Dempster, 'The Republican Movement, "Disappearing" and Framing the Past in Northern Ireland,' *International Journal of Transitional Justice*, 10 (2016), 250–271.

News as "what happens in war."[61] Justifying past wrongs is a 'pitfall' that should be avoided when crafting an effective apology.[62] A direct apology for the 'offensive act' is also not provided. The March 1999 statement states: "We are sorry that this has taken so long to resolve and for prolonged anguish caused to families."[63] This apology is not for the 'disappearances' themselves, but rather the IRA's delayed response to the families' calls for information, and the suffering this caused those families.[64] The inclusion in the statement of the alleged 'crimes' the 'disappeared' were found 'guilty' of also served to undermine any sense of sincerity. Upon reading the statement, Seamus McKendry describes how his wife, Helen, 'cried aloud as she read the affront to her mother's memory.'[65]

It is rare, Harris et al. suggest, 'for the response to a political apology to contain any explicit form of absolution.'[66] The seriousness of the act of 'disappearing' someone, and the depth of the family's suffering, may well render any apology insufficient. Mookherjee et al. raise the question: 'what is the speech-act *worth* against the acts for whose responsibility it also claims some kind of expiation? … What kind of authenticity is carried by the murderer's apology, or even the hangman's?'[67] In considering what response can be expected, Bennett and Earwaker suggest that: 'apologies may have a mitigating effect with respect to the victim's judgments about the offender, but not with respect to unalterable facts, such as the seriousness of the outcome of a transgression.'[68]

With the IRA's 1999 statement,[69] and the similar statement released in 2003,[70] there was a sense that for some it was 'too little, too late.' Margaret McKinney remarked in 2003 that "it has been too many years, so much hurt, so much

61 Philip Ryan, 'Gerry Adams Says Making Jean McConville's Children Orphans is "What Happens in War",' *Belfast Telegraph*, 3 April 2015.

62 McEvoy, n 36 at 22.

63 'IRA Investigation Locates Grave Sites,' n 43.

64 It should be noted that in 2013, Michael McConville reported that during a meeting with Adams, he received an apology from him. McConville told RTÉ's Marian Finucane: "The last time I met with Gerry Adams, he made an apology to me for, he [said] … 'for what it's worth Michael, I'll apologise to you … it was wrong for the Republican Movement to treat your family and yourself the way that what they did.' He says, 'I'm sorry for what happened your mother and I'm sorry for what happened your family.'" However, as mentioned earlier in this chapter, McConville says that the family are still waiting for a similar statement from the IRA (Michael McConville in interview with Marian Finucane, n 33; Patrick Radden Keefe, 'Where the Bodies are Buried,' *The New Yorker*, 16 March 2015).

65 Seamus McKendry, *Disappeared: The Search for Jean McConville* (Dublin, Blackwater Press: 2000), p. 99; p.102.

66 Harris et al., n 20 at 723.

67 Nayanika Mookherjee, Nigel Rapport, Lisette Josephides, Ghassan Hage, Lindi Renier Todd and Gillian Cowlishaw, 'The Ethics of Apology: A Set of Commentaries,' *Critique of Anthropology*, 29:3, (2009), 345–366 (p. 350).

68 Bennett and Earwaker, n 45 at 462.

69 'IRA Investigation Locates Grave Sites,' n 43.

70 'IRA Pledges to try to Bring Closure for Families,' n 50.

harm," and for Kathleen Armstrong: "I still blame them anyway … They lied to families … for years and they are lying to us."[71] It is difficult to argue that the IRA's apology improved their image in the eyes of the families (although, as will be examined later, it is perhaps not the families to whom the apology is directed). Lakoff suggests that in making an apology, status is lost, but credit is gained,[72] and as previously discussed, the management or restoration of one's image can be a motivating factor in making an apology. An apology may be the 'price you pay' in attempting to survive a political storm.[73] The sincerity of a politically motivated apology will always be questioned. However, not apologising can be considered as an act of hostility,[74] and can cause pain.[75] Refusing to acknowledge harm and express regret for past wrongs can widen the gap between perpetrators and victims.[76] Journalist and writer Susan McKay touched on this incongruity:

> I think a lot of people are inevitably a bit cynical about apologies because, in many ways, apologies are for the optics, aren't they? Apologies are for the public image of the organisation. Who knows how sincere they are? … I think people are entitled to have complex and quite painful feelings when they hear these apologies … in Ireland … there have been so many apologies which have been quite self-serving. At the same time, I think it is proper that these apologies are made. … even if there is an advantage and gain for the organisation making them, it's still the right thing to do. And the apologies are due, people are owed apologies so even if there is an element of the self-serving about them, I think it's important that they are made.[77]

That the apology offered in this case is a collective one should also be considered. There are issues with applying the scholarship on interpersonal apologies to collective, public, political ones.[78] Thaler suggests that collective apologies are even more complex than those offered by individuals, rendering the political apology both messy and contestable.[79] As Smith describes, in analysing a collective apology, one must 'lay on a few more coats of grey.'[80] The extent to which a collective can express feelings of regret or remorse has been questioned, given that their decisions and statements are part of a structure of collective representation.[81] Trouillot clarifies this perspective, suggesting that while a collective can be held

71 O'Neill and Connolly, n 51.
72 Lakoff, n 23.
73 Zohar Kampf, 'The Pragmatics of Forgiveness: Judgements of Apologies in the Israeli Political Arena,' *Discourse and Society*, 19:5, (2008), 577–598 (p. 593).
74 Lakoff, n 23.
75 Andrieu, n 40.
76 Ibid.
77 Interview, Susan McKay, July 2014.
78 Harris et al., n 20.
79 Thaler, n 54.
80 Nick Smith, *I Was Wrong: The Meanings of Apologies* (Cambridge: Cambridge University Press, 2008).
81 Thaler, n 54.

accountable or provide compensation, expressing remorse is much more challenging. In this regard, 'identity is always questionable' in collective apologies, and such apologies are, in fact, 'abortive rituals' as they cannot meet their purpose. In attempting to attribute aspects of the free-thinking individual to a collective, there is no hope of succeeding.[82] To find the value of a collective apology, Thaler advises us to look to the 'bigger picture.' While political apologies may provide no direct or immediate reparation, it is possible that such an apology could contribute more broadly to social inclusion.[83] Similarly, Andrieu suggests that apologising can contribute to the building of social trust, which in turn feeds into processes of reconciliation.[84]

The apology presented in this IRA statement can be interpreted as an example of Kampf and Löwenheim's 'purification'-type apology ritual.[85] Designed to address the transgressor's 'notorious past'[86] and create a new self-image, this type of apology ritual is of interest because the offended party's participation is neither necessary nor considered. This type of apology can hinder the development of trust or co-operation as, in attempting to purify him or herself while disregarding the perception of the offended party, the apologiser places him or herself in a symbolically superior position, reinforcing an imbalance in relations and accentuating resentment.[87] As Lakoff outlines, although apologising can place the apologiser in a lower position to his or her addressee, explaining places him in a higher position.[88] In explaining why these acts were perpetrated, rather than apologising for them, the IRA (arguably) maintains a position of superiority. In this regard, the impact of the IRA's apology is potentially a negative one. However, in being combined with a statement of acknowledgement, this IRA communication becomes potentially valuable as a reconciliatory move. Apologies can 'recreate the communication that has been lost through mass violence.'[89] With regards the 'disappeared,' communication was not so much lost as made absent through the IRA's silence. The acknowledgement of responsibility for some 'disappearances' can therefore be considered an important turning point.

2.2. The IRA 'apology' and role of acknowledgement

'Above all, an apology realises a claim to connection.'[90] Acknowledgement of a wrong committed is argued by many to be an important element of an effective apology.[91] It is at this point where one begins to see the value of that March 1999

82 Trouillot, n 17 at 184–185.
83 Thaler, n 54.
84 Andrieu, n 40.
85 Kampf and Löwenheim, n 20.
86 Ibid. at 48.
87 Ibid.
88 Lakoff, n 23.
89 Andrieu, n 40.
90 Mookherjee et al., n 67 at 350.
91 Benoit and Brinson, n 30; Benoit and Drew, n 30; Kampf and Löwenheim, n 20; Lakoff, n 23; Thaler, n 54.

statement. Acknowledging a wrong helps to 'affirm a common moral ground.'[92] This idea links to Trouillot's suggestion examined previously, that in providing an acknowledgement one is demonstrating dedication to a 'new era' of relations.[93] As I argued in Chapter 3, in acknowledging involvement in 'disappearing,' the IRA was also acknowledging that it was entering a new phase, and that violence had been left behind. One former IRA member told a journalist, with 'the peace process … secure. There's no political reason to keep lying.'[94] Yet, this remains a limited example of acknowledgement.

A term more often used than defined, acknowledgement is both component and process. As outlined, acknowledgement of responsibility for a past wrong is considered a necessary component of an apology. Acknowledgement as a transitional mechanism is argued by some to constitute a broader process of engaging with a legacy of violence, and can include prosecutions, truth commissions, commemorations, and apologies.[95] Therefore, we have (small 'a') acknowledgement as a component of apology, which in turn can be part of a process of (capital 'A') Acknowledgement. The former can be described by Stamato's definition of acknowledgement as the admission of 'failed performance or behaviour, to affirmatively indicate that a wrong was done … neither minimizing the offence nor rationalizing the behaviour.'[96] Acknowledgement is also defined as a sort of official 'stamp' of recognition, and this fits into the latter notion of Acknowledgement. In this regard, Weschler quotes Thomas Nagel as describing acknowledgement as "what happens and can only happen to knowledge when it becomes officially sanctioned, when it is made part of the public cognitive scene."[97]

For victims' families, Healing Through Remembering's Kate Turner recounts, the IRA acknowledgement that these individuals had been killed and secretly buried, and at their hands, was significant. The exclusion of several expected names was, however, difficult for those families:

> it was amazing for the families … because … it's been silence, to actually have the list. It was an incredible step that quite often gets forgotten. It is then very difficult for those who aren't there. What does that mean? It's almost an added burden … Something like that lessens what they've gone through. So there were difficulties in that.[98]

92 Andrieu, n 40.
93 Trouillot, n 17 at 174.
94 Suzanne Breen, 'Put That Family Out of its Misery,' *Sunday Tribune*, 18 January 2009.
95 Stanley Cohen, *States of Denial: Knowing about Atrocities and Suffering* (Cambridge: Polity Press, 2001); McEvoy, n 36.
96 Linda Stamato, 'Peace and the Culture and Politics of Apology,' *Peace Review*, 20:3, (2008), 389–397 (p. 394).
97 Lawrence Weschler, *A Miracle, A Universe: Settling Accounts with Torturers* (Chicago: University of Chicago Press, 1998), p. 4.
98 Interview, Healing Through Remembering's Kate Turner, September 2014.

This acknowledgement, coming after decades of silence and uncertainty, took centre stage. From Turner's experience, the apology element of the statement was overshadowed by the acknowledgement:

> You know it's funny because I don't remember much … I think the impact of them actually having done it was so much more interesting there was less focus [on the apology] … Talking to them [the families] since, when they talk back they talk about the list but they don't mention that.[99]

In interview, Brendan Megraw's brother, Kieran, expressed a similar view when asked about the inclusion of the IRA's allegations regarding the 'disappeared,' that the acknowledgement was key:

> Well, probably myself and most people just thought: what is an *agent provocateur*? … Didn't really think much about it … And … at the time you were thinking, you were just glad there's the information that we were going to get his body back and that was the most important part. That information was attached to it but we didn't pay any heed to it.[100]

In acknowledging involvement in 'disappearing' and the pain and suffering this caused to families of the victims, the IRA may be viewed as fulfilling their 'historical responsibility.'[101] This is the need to take into account the impact and effects of what Trouillot has termed the 'structures of power or domination' and to 'evaluate the current losses' induced by those structures.[102] As examined in Chapter 4, that 'disappearances' could happen was in part a symptom of the conditions of the conflict, in which the IRA was a major player. In acknowledging their involvement in this issue and the impact of it, they are evaluating the losses caused by their earlier violent authority, and attempting to answer their historical responsibility. In involving themselves in the search for remains they go some way towards taking 'corrective action,' highlighted as a component part of an apology.[103]

This statement of apology and acknowledgement was an important component in a bigger process of Acknowledgment. Internationally, acknowledgement that a 'disappeared' loved one has been killed is more than a specific transitional mechanism, rather it is a form of recognition that is manifest in various aspects of the response to a 'disappearance' and can have practical, financial, legal, emotional, and psychological benefits for those whose loved one has been 'disappeared.' For families, 'official acknowledgement' of a 'disappearance' can allow them to access the support normally provided to those who have been bereaved, and clarify their

99 Interview, Kate Turner, September 2014.
100 Interview, Kieran Megraw, October 2015.
101 Trouillot, n 17 at 183.
102 Ibid. at 183.
103 Benoit and Drew, n 30 at 156.

legal status.[104] Acknowledgement of emotional suffering can help those affected to heal, or if needed access the appropriate care.[105] At a societal level, Kovras suggests that acknowledgement of the truth about those missing after conflict can also provide 'societal closure.'[106] Recovering remains allows a funeral to take place, which is an opportunity for relatives to acknowledge the life of the deceased.[107] That the IRA acknowledged the fate of the 'disappeared' was an important step in the process of recovering their remains. As examined in Chapter 5, this statement was an essential prelude to the passing of the LVR legislation, which in turn has facilitated the recovery of the remains of 13 individuals.

In considering apology and acknowledgement, this case demonstrates the importance of looking to the context. In considering how the media brings issues of conflict and discord increasingly to the eyes of the world, Trouillot suggests that this 'enhanced gaze … feeds new symbolic demands.'[108] This includes demands for apologies for historical wrongs. That the response to the 'disappeared' was playing out in the so-called 'Age of Apology,'[109] and that apology has now become part of the transitional justice toolkit,[110] points to the IRA apology as something that should be examined. However, in considering the case at hand, the apology is not what is perceived as important. As these cases currently stand, the place for apology is certainly in the shadow of acknowledgement.

The IRA's acknowledgement of its involvement in 'disappearing'[111] was acknowledgement with a small 'a,' a component of a larger statement, admitting involvement in acts in which it was already strongly suspected of having played a hand. A Healing Through Remembering report suggests that an effective acknowledgement should include the naming of wrongs and those harmed by them, the explicit taking of responsibility by those responsible, and a broader collective process that encompasses those who were complicit in the perpetration of abuses, even if not directly involved.[112] The first of these three requirements has been met. Responsibility was not established explicitly; it was couched in justification and context. However, that Republicans have continued to support and contribute to the search process is perhaps a demonstration that this responsibility

104 Margriet Blaauw, '"Denial and Silence" or "Acknowledgement and Disclosure",' *Review of the International Red Cross*, 84:848, (2002), 767–783.

105 Ibid.

106 Iosif Kovras, 'Explaining Prolonged Silences in Transitional Justice: The Disappeared in Cyprus and Spain,' *Comparative Political Studies*, 20:10, (2012), 1–27 (p. 6).

107 Blaauw, n 104.

108 Trouillot, n 17 at 183.

109 Kampf and Löwenheim, n 20; Shapiro and Adams, n 20; Harris et al., n 20; Meier, n 20.

110 Iosif Kovras, *Truth Recovery and Transitional Justice: Deferring Human Rights Abuses* (London: Routledge, 2014).

111 'IRA Continues Search for Missing Bodies,' *An Phoblacht*, 10 December 1998; 'IRA Investigation Locates Grave Sites,' n 43; 'Omagh Bomb Group Must Disband – IRA. Push Now to Fulfil Potential of Good Friday Document,' *An Phoblacht*, 3 September 1998.

112 McEvoy, n 36.

is one they take seriously. As Sinn Féin's Declan Kearney said in interview "until such times as all remains have been recovered and returned to their families ... it has to be seen as unfinished business."[113] The idea of complicity is not something that has been dealt with publicly or academically, however, as introduced in Chapter 4 and as the next section will examine, there is a broader truth to the 'disappeared' that should be engaged with. Stamato asserts that acknowledgement 'requires that truth be told.'[114] The next section will examine what 'truth' we have with regards the 'disappeared.'

3. Truth and the 'disappeared'

Although once considered a 'second-best' alternative to prosecution, the establishment of truth has become a key element of the 'transitional justice toolbox.'[115] Truth commissions, set up to establish 'an accurate historical record,'[116] or 'critical knowledge,' to use Teitel's term,[117] have become 'a staple of the transitional justice menu.'[118] In the transitional justice literature, the effectiveness of truth commissions is debated, and contention exists over the perceived sacrifice of 'justice' to access 'truth.'[119] The ICLVR is not a truth commission, nor does it claim to be. However, elements of these debates resonate with the ICLVR process. Proponents of truth commissions suggest that they end silence and denial through uncovering, acknowledging, and establishing the extent of abuses.[120] As this chapter argues, silences remain over the 'disappeared,' however the recovery of remains has provided tangible evidence of these acts of violence. Where the effectiveness of a truth commission can be difficult to measure and consensus as to their benefits is lacking,[121] the effectiveness and outcome of this self-

113 Interview, Declan Kearney, April 2015.
114 Stamato, n 96 at 394.
115 Kovras, n 110 at 6.
116 Brandon Hamber and Steve Kibble, 'From Truth to Transformation: The Truth and Reconciliation Commission in South Africa,' Catholic Institute for International Relations Report, February 1999.
117 Ruti G. Teitel, *Transitional Justice* (Oxford: Oxford University Press, 2000), p. 88.
118 Naomi Roht-Arriaza, 'The New Landscape of Transitional Justice,' in Naomi Roht-Arriaza and Javier Mariezcurrena (eds) *Transitional Justice in the 21st Century* (Cambridge: Cambridge University Press, 2006), pp. 1–16 (p. 4).
119 See e.g. Booth, n 1; Emilios A. Christodoulidis, '"Truth and Reconciliation" as Risks,' *Social and Legal Studies*, 9:2 (2000), 179–204; Fletcher and Weinstein, n 8; Llewellyn and Howse, n 7; David Mendeloff, 'Trauma and Vengeance: Assessing the Psychological and Emotional Effects of Post-Conflict Justice,' *Human Rights Quarterly*, 31:3, (2009), 592–623; Jack Snyder and Leslie Vinjamuri, 'Trials and Errors: Principle and Pragmatism in Strategies of International Justice,' *International Security*, 28:3, (2004), 5–44; Teitel, n 117.
120 Roht-Arriaza, n 118; Priscilla Hayner, 'Justice in Transition: Challenges and Opportunities,' Centre for Transitional Justice. Presentation to the 55th Annual DPI/NGO Conference: Rebuilding Societies Emerging from Conflict: A Shared Responsibility (United Nations, New York, 9 September 2002).
121 Eric Brahm, 'Uncovering the Truth: Examining Truth Commission Success and Impact,' *International Studies Perspectives*, 8, (2007), 16–35.

contained process is relatively clear. In contrast to perpetrator-centric trials, truth commissions are argued to be victim-centred.[122] Although there is no public platform for victims to voice their experiences,[123] or for perpetrators to potentially express remorse or shame,[124] the ICLVR is ultimately victim-centred, and, as this book has argued, both victims' families and perpetrators have publicly expressed their views through the media as the search process has progressed. Beyond the immediate needs of victims, truth commissions are portrayed as having a wider impact, helping countries and citizens come to terms with their past, informing the wider public of the extent of past violations,[125] and providing a basis for structural and judicial reform that can serve as the starting point for a more positive future.[126] As will be argued, the ICLVR process can have a wider impact and provides a useful and much-needed example of a mechanism of one way of dealing with the legacy of the conflict. As Sinn Féin's Declan Kearney suggested, the ICLVR provides an example from which to develop a truth recovery process: "What we need to do is move to a point, drawing upon positive experiences – such as the process that the Commission has undertaken – to give us the best potential for truth recovery in the future."[127]

As Chapter 5 examined, one of the key points of contention with regards truth commissions is reflected in the work of the ICLVR – establishing 'truth' may mean sacrificing 'justice.' Truth commissions have been criticised as a 'denial of justice,'[128] a 'step backwards' from prosecution.[129] The LVR legislation is similarly (see Chapter 5) a 'step backwards' from this goal. Yet, the ICLVR is more than a 'feel-good idea,' as Brody has described truth commissions,[130] because of the real results achieved for families. As this section will examine, the 'truth' established through this process chimes with Chapman and Ball's assertion that 'truth' is 'an elusive concept.'[131] Rolston's argument is reflected, in that silences are created as the 'truth' established is dependent on who provides testimony, and what they choose to say.[132] Some claim that the 'truth' established via a commission can be partial as a result of a number of factors, such as the subjectivity of memory, the suppression or destruction of evidence, or that testimony may not be given first-

122 Karstedt, n 7.
123 Hayner, n 120.
124 Jonathan Doak, 'The Therapeutic Dimension of Transitional Justice: Emotional Repair and Victim Satisfaction in International Trials and Truth Commissions,' *International Criminal Law Review*, 11:2, (2011), 263–298.
125 Hayner, n 120.
126 Llewellyn and Howse, n 7; Marie Breen Smyth, *Truth Recovery and Justice After Conflict: Managing Violent Pasts* (London; New York: Routledge, 2007).
127 Interview, Declan Kearney, April 2015.
128 Robert I. Rotberg, 'Truth Commissions and the Provision of Truth, Justice, and Reconciliation,' in Robert I. Rotberg and Dennis Thompson (eds) *Truth v. Justice: The Morality of Truth Commissions* (Princeton: Princeton University Press, 2000), pp. 3–21 (p. 14).
129 Brahm, n 121 at 22–23.
130 Reed Brody, 'Justice, the First Casualty of Truth?' *The Nation*, 12 April 2001, www.hrw.org/news/2001/04/12/justice-first-casualty-truth [accessed 6 September 2018].
131 Chapman and Ball, n 6 at 4.
132 Rolston, n 5.

hand (for example, where a relative of a deceased person is providing testimony on their behalf).[133] The practical effects of these factors are evident in the challenges the ICLVR has faced in recovering remains, and of course, the 'disappeared' have no voice of their own, their families represent them. Whatever 'truth' is uncovered with regard to the 'disappeared' is certainly, and inevitably, partial.

The establishment of the fate of the 'disappeared' and the recovery of their remains is identified in some accounts as a special case of truth recovery.[134] Here, uncertainty surrounding the fate of the 'disappeared' is, as Cohen suggests, a 'specific drive behind truth-telling' based on the 'special sensitivity of victims.'[135] It has been argued that difficulties in establishing the truth of any complex event are only exacerbated when this task is being undertaken in a context where divergent and politically loaded versions of the past exist.[136] This is most certainly the case in Northern Ireland. It could be argued that the ICLVR, with its specific remit focussed on locating and recovering the remains of victims, sidesteps many of these problematic issues. As argued in Chapter 5, the ICLVR operates in a sort of apolitical space, and this has been a key strength in terms of its effectiveness. However, the boundaries of this space limit opportunities for establishing a fuller 'truth.'

3.1. Forensic and narrative 'truth(s)' and the need for grey

Internationally, where 'wider truth recovery' involves establishing truth commissions or storytelling projects to give voice to those previously excluded, the gathering of forensic evidence in relation to establishing the whereabouts of the 'disappeared' is sometimes referred to as 'narrow truth recovery.'[137] The 'truth' established via the ICLVR, and through IRA statements, may be similarly described as 'narrow.'

For example, the remit of the Commission, as outlined by its Senior Investigating Officer, Geoff Knupfer, does not include establishing "what happened or why" in these cases.[138] The legislation sets out the functions of the ICLVR: 'receiving relevant information and disclosing such information for the purpose of facilitating the location of the remains to which the information relates.'[139] As Knupfer summarises in introducing the Commission's work: it entails recovery and repatriation. The Commission, as outlined earlier in the book, cannot pass on this 'relevant information' to any other person (other than for the purposes of the search).[140] The only information that can be passed to families is that, '(a) relevant

133 Chapman and Ball, n 6.
134 Stanley Cohen, 'State Crimes of Previous Regimes: Knowledge, Accountability, and the Policing of the Past,' *Law & Social Inquiry*, 20:1, (1995), 7–50; Kovras, n 110.
135 Cohen, ibid. at 19.
136 Chapman and Ball, n 6.
137 Kovras, n 106 at 14; Kovras, n 110 at 7–8.
138 Interview, Geoff Knupfer, July 2014.
139 Northern Ireland (Location of Victims' Remains) Act 1999.
140 Ibid.

information has been provided to the Commission,' and '(b) the place where, according to the information, the victim's remains may be found.'[141] As these extracts from the legislation make clear, the 'truth' established by the ICLVR is a geographical one – relating solely to the locations where bodies are thought to be buried. As one interviewee summarised, "the Commission on the 'disappeared' had a very specific task in respect of very specific cases … the 'Location of Victims' Remains' is simply that, it's about the location of victims' remains … it's about one single task."[142]

The Commission's focus on this single, albeit very challenging, task has been vital to its success. As outlined in the previous chapter, Republican trust in the process is dependent upon their trust in the Commission, and that it is, as described by one interviewee, "hermetically sealed."[143] By design and by necessity, the 'truth' established by the ICLVR is limited to that of a specific, factual nature.

There is a further facet to this notion of geographical truth. The sites from where the 'disappeared' have been recovered, or the locations where remains are believed to be buried, arguably become places of memory. They are places with 'violent, hidden histories'[144] where some element of the 'truth' of the violence perpetrated against these individuals is bound up in the landscape. The process of search – captured in a series of photographs by David Farrell published in 2001 – is described as having 'scarred an otherwise picturesque pastoral scene.'[145] This 'geographical truth' speaks to Derrida's notion of 'hauntology' – of making the absent present through landscape.[146]

As examined in Chapter 3, the IRA's statements acknowledge that some of those who were 'disappeared' were executed by their organisation, and provide a brief 'rationale' for doing so based on a narrative of the threat posed by informing and need for internal discipline. Such statements provide a similarly 'narrow' truth – one aimed at acknowledging involvement in 'disappearing' and legitimating that involvement within a Republican framework – with the proviso of course that it is impossible to verify or dispute these claims without a broader truth recovery process. The information provided to the Commission is also a form of forensic truth. The IRA and the ICLVR have both provided what might be termed 'narrow' truths.

141 Ibid.

142 Interview, a former diplomat who has been engaged in efforts to deal with the past in Northern Ireland, June 2015

143 Ibid.

144 Mark Phelan, 'Not So Innocent Landscapes: Remembrance, Representation and the Disappeared,' in Patrick Anderson and Jisha Menon (eds) *Violence Performed: Local Roots and Global Routes of Conflict* (Palgrave, 2009), pp. 285–316 (p. 290)

145 David Farrell, *Innocent Landscapes* (United Kingdom: Dewi Lewis Publishing, 2001); Derek Gregory, *Geographical Imaginations* (Oxford: Blackwell 1994); Phelan, n 144 at 288–289.

146 Jacques Derrida, *Specters of Marx* (trans. Peggy Kamuf) (London: Routledge, 1994); Nick Peim, 'Spectral Bodies: Derrida and the Philosophy of the Photograph as Historical Document,' *Journal of the Philosophy of Education*, 39:1, (2005), 67–84.

Although narrow, this level of truth is valuable to those whose loved ones have been 'disappeared.' For Robins, 'truth for families of the Missing is most immediately the truth about their loved one that ends ambiguity and allows families to retrieve remains and perform ritual.'[147] In the Northern Ireland context, some families have expressed gratitude for the provision of this information. For example, following the recovery of Brendan Megraw's remains, his brother Kieran said: "Brendan was found because more information came in to refine the search area and we are hugely grateful for whoever provided it."[148] In a joint statement following the recovery of the remains of Seamus Wright and Kevin McKee, their families said they wished to thank "whoever provided the information … without that information this would never have happened."[149]

If the 'truth phase' of a transition from conflict or dictatorship is to be an 'onslaught' on 'denial,'[150] then it is to the families' accounts that we must look. As argued in Chapter 2, in capturing their voice the families combatted decades of Republican silence over these killings. Their stories have value. In assessing the South African TRC, Wilson criticised the privileging of the knowledge created by so-called 'forensic truth' over narrative truths, whose value was believed to lie in their contribution to emotional healing and broader reconciliation. He argued that these narrative truths played a critical role in understanding the causes and context of conflict, and the variants of meaning, subjectivity, and identity involved in past events.[151] The families' accounts of their loved ones provide such narrative truths.

As argued in Chapter 1, engaging with the memory of the 'disappeared,' and bringing private memories into the public domain, can be considered a form of activism. For the families, bringing personal memories of their loved ones into the public arena has had a powerful impact: generating empathy with them and their cause. As one journalist interviewed described, "it humanises the people. It makes people realise this is an ordinary person who is a member of a family."[152] Through the families' public telling of their suffering and recounting of their loved one's stories, memory is restored to the 'disappeared.' As Joe Lynskey's niece Maria says in WAVE's book: 'To me everyone's existence deserves to be acknowledged; I suppose that is why I decided to tell his story in this book, to make sure people know who Joe Lynskey was.'[153]

147 Simon Robins, *Families of the Missing: A Test for Contemporary Approaches to Transitional Justice* (London: Routledge, 2013), p. 49.
148 *BBC News* [online], 'The Disappeared: Meath Remains were those of Brendan Megraw,' 3 November 2014, www.bbc.co.uk/news/uk-northern-ireland-29887678 [accessed 10 August 2018].
149 Tim O'Brien, 'Bodies of Seamus Wright and Kevin McKee Believed Found,' *The Irish Times*, 27 June 2015.
150 Cohen, n 134 at 15.
151 Richard A. Wilson, *The Politics of Truth and Reconciliation in South Africa: Legitimizing the Post-Apartheid State* (Cambridge: Cambridge University Press, 2001), p. 37.
152 Interview, Susan McKay, July 2014.
153 WAVE, *The Disappeared of Northern Ireland's 'Troubles'* (Belfast: WAVE Trauma Centre Publications, 2012), p. 8.

Although the families spoke out to raise awareness of their loved ones and encourage action to be taken in locating remains, a secondary effect has been the contribution, in their accounts of the conflict, of a series of personal, narrative truths.

Although the accounts of the families, particularly those included in *The Disappeared*, [154] are valuable as moving accounts of their relationships with their loved ones, they also provide a snapshot of the context of the conflict, and the lived experience of these families. The families' stories relay the fear and uncertainty of life in their communities during the 'Troubles,' and in some cases outline what they believe motivated their family members to become actively involved in the conflict. These accounts show that the 'disappeared' were, as McKay suggests, "ordinary."[155]

The conflict is further humanised in the families' stories as their domestic, everyday lives are contrasted with the conflict taking place around them. These 'truths' contribute to a breaking down of stark dichotomies between the black and white of the 'Troubles,' between victim and perpetrator or innocent and guilty – instead showing the grey of the conflict, the fluidity of such roles, and the chaos of the rapidly changing backdrop to their loss. As analysed in Chapter 4, reading these stories of rumour and isolation raises questions about the role of the community, the complicity of some within it, and the workings of the state. As mentioned previously, Kate Turner of Healing Through Remembering spoke of: "a guilt on wider society."[156] Through the accounts that have emerged, and facts that have been established, other questions have been opened up. As mentioned previously, Turner mentions: "finding the bodies unravels … what was really happening. It unearths that, in unearthing the bodies, but leaves it lying there unanswered."[157] The narrative truths provided by the families offer accounts of the conflict that go beyond what is debated by politicians and presented in the news.

Despite the limited nature of 'truth' established via exhumations, for Kovras, value remains because '… political exhumations … disrupt hegemonic schemes and legitimize previously unacceptable versions of the truth.'[158] The search for Ireland's 'disappeared' has created a platform for previously silenced voices. There is a risk in truth recovery processes that when the ultimate goal is reconciliation, truths which might be perceived as averse to that aim can be supressed in favour of promoting those truths that contribute positively to it.[159] In this regard, Northern Ireland's lack of an overarching truth recovery process, and the *ad hoc* nature of the response to the issue of the 'disappeared,' may be beneficial. Robins suggests that truth commissions 'are a way of mediating memory.'[160] In the accessibility of accounts from many of those close to these cases, particularly victims' relatives,

154 Ibid.
155 Interview, Susan McKay, July 2014.
156 Interview, Kate Turner, September 2014.
157 Ibid.
158 Kovras, n 110 at 8.
159 Colm Campbell and Catherine Turner, 'Utopia and the Doubters: Truth, Transition and the Law,' *Legal Studies*, 28:3, (2008), 374–395; Hamber and Wilson, n 4.
160 Robins, n 147 at 51.

that have not been edited into a succinct report by a truth commission, what becomes visible is the murkiness of conflict and the challenges of trying to piece this together from a post-conflict perspective. As former Director of Publicity for Sinn Féin, Danny Morrison, told the author in interview:

> It's not until when the peace process comes in, that we look back and see the mess the conflict engendered and trying to navigate our way through it is proving, I mean it's 16 years after the signing of the Good Friday Agreement … we're still trying to work out the past, and of course people are still going to fight over the past, because nobody is going to surrender that they were wrong.[161]

Competing truths exist, and as Kate Turner suggests, the 'disappeared' are:

> an interesting, stark example of this … And part of what we need to do about dealing with the past is to hear that other people have very different perspectives on it and … try and examine that most of those are not black and white and it is much more complicated than that … we've got to accept that 'dealing with the past' is going to prove some things, and it's going to make a lot of things much more grey and much more complicated. And in some ways the 'disappeared' have been teaching us all that.[162]

As Turner summarises, there is a need to establish and accept that any 'truth' will be grey: "It's part of how we look at the conflict, we try and see things as black and white and simple whereas everything's grey, everything's a bit of both."[163]

3.2. The 'disappeared' and competing notions of truth

Despite the prevalence of references to 'truth' and mechanisms to recover it, Kovras suggests that much of the transitional justice literature fails to fully engage with defining 'truth' in all its complexity.[164] Questions arise as to whether it is possible to establish an 'objective truth,' or even 'truths.'[165] Daly captures the challenge: 'truth has certain inherent attributes that make it particularly elusive for transitional governments … truth is not monolithic … even events with a narrow scope,' (such as we are dealing with in the cases of the 'disappeared'), 'often defy truth tellers' efforts as social, political, economic, historical and psychological forces converge in a complexity of layers and pressures.'[166] Truths are multiple and subjective, stories told are the result of choices made by the teller. They are

161 Interview, Danny Morrison, January 2015.
162 Interview, Kate Turner, September 2014.
163 Ibid.
164 Kovras, n 110.
165 Campbell and Turner, n 159 at 381; Chapman and Ball, n 6.
166 Erin Daly, 'Truth Skepticism: An Inquiry into the Value of Truth in Times of Transition,' *International Journal of Transitional Justice*, 2:1, (2008), 23–41 (p. 25).

'often mutually incompatible.'[167] In considering what future truth or truths we might expect surrounding the issue of 'disappearing,' the accounts of families and interviewees have highlighted two main areas of dissonance. The first is whether or not more truth will emerge, and the second is the level of truth that should be expected.

With regards this first point, a number of families have spoken of how they have questions about their loved one's death.[168] In some cases this is at quite a general level. The ICLVR's Geoff Knupfer has said of his experience in speaking with the families:

> In some cases there might be a curiosity as to, 'well I wonder what did happen?' so it's not a case of 'I want this to be pursued,' it's a question mark that they would really like to know the answer to. Not necessarily who did it, but why perhaps.[169]

Eugene McVeigh, brother of Columba, recounted to me in interview:

> I think people always want to know more … want to know detail … in the quietness of an evening or at any time when you reflect on these things, it's hard not to think – for me, it's hard not to think of my brother's last hours on this earth, and how he was treated. And, while I might find it hurtful and while it might open up more anger in me, perhaps to know is still important. There's a narrative here. There's a narrative, and there's a story.[170]

The likelihood of families being provided with more information is perhaps rather slim. Journalist and commentator, Brian Rowan, suggested that the IRA may have said as much as it is going to on this issue:

> the IRA is not going to expose its organisation, either at a leadership level or at an active service level, to scrutiny of that time. So the IRA … internally, go and find out what had to be found out … that becomes the most they're going to do …[171]

There is a sense here that, in agreeing to participate in the ICLVR process, on the part of Republicans, and, on the part of the families, in calling for the return of their loved ones' remains as their core demand, and supporting the passage of the LVR legislation, that an unspoken agreement was entered into, that nothing further would be asked. In interview, one senior Republican alluded to this (this is

167 Ibid. at 26.
168 E.g. see accounts of Kevin McKee's sister, Phil; Peter Wilson's sister, Patricia; Eamonn Molloy's brother, Michael; and Brian McKinney's mother, Margaret in WAVE, n 153.
169 Interview, Geoff Knupfer, July 2014.
170 Interview, Eugene McVeigh, August 2015.
171 Interview, Brian Rowan, September 2014.

tied in to the importance of trust, as examined in the previous chapter – emphasis author's own):

> The danger in anything like this, is … that once … [the families] are able to get whatever closure they want, or they believe they can get … that they then seek to go for what they consider to be justice, I suppose, and *they seek to bring the people who were involved in the 'disappearance' and all of that and the initial thing at the start of it, whatever it was actually happened* … And that would be a particular worry for Republicans.[172]

While this concern is focused around prosecution, there is an allusion to the asking of more information about "the initial thing at the start of it." This comment gives an indication – one that supports Rowan's theory – that, from the perspective captured in this quote at least, a deal has been done that negates the contribution of any further information from the Republican Movement, beyond their continuing involvement with the ICLVR. It should of course be noted that the proposed Independent Commission on Information Retrieval (ICIR – see Chapter 7) may provide another route by which families can seek information.

The second, and arguably more problematic, issue is that the various actors involved have different notions of what 'truth' means. Some families have spoken of a desire to know or meet the individuals directly involved in their family member's 'disappearance.' Peter Wilson's sister, Patricia would like to meet 'those that took him … so they can explain to us why he was taken. This is not so much justice but rather finding out the truth.'[173] Margaret McKinney spoke of the need to establish individual responsibility in order for her to forgive. She told *The Forgiveness Project*: 'I often think about his killer coming to the door. I'd like to sit him down and talk to him, ask if he's sorry … Until that happens I can't say I forgive, because I don't know who to forgive.'[174]

The 'truth' envisaged by the Republican Movement, however, is a collective one. One senior Republican, in describing discussions with former IRA members around these issues, explained:

> what we had in mind was some sort of a process whereby people on a collective basis could be requested to give information to a group of very trusted and confidential comrades. And that these people then could bring that information forward to the panel of whoever it would be that was set up to, you know, to investigate and to supply questions and to liaise with families of people who have been bereaved during the conflict, and who may well have questions and be seeking closure.[175]

172 Interview, senior Republican ex-combatant, April 2015.
173 WAVE, n 153 at 30.
174 *The Forgiveness Project*, 'Margaret McKinney,' accessed at http://theforgivenessproject.com/stories/margaret-mckinney-northern-ireland/ [accessed on 7 June 2018].
175 Interview, senior Republican ex-combatant, April 2015.

When asked to specify if this meant a collective truth, he responded:

> At a corporate level. People said that they didn't have the same problems with a process which dealt with it at a corporate level as opposed to a personal, individual level. That if they were going to be in any way identified, that they would have absolutely nothing to do with it.[176]

An example of what this might mean was pondered by Brian Rowan, during an earlier interview:

> So a truth from the IRA [re: Enniskillen] might now be, we placed the bomb, we exploded the bomb, and in placing the bomb where we placed it, we knew we would kill civilians as well. They could say the same about the Shankill. So it removes the lie, it gives you some more information, it gives you some more truth, but it doesn't go beyond that line to who put it there, who knew it was being put there.[177]

In a 2013 interview, Michael McConville recounted the IRA's operationalisation of this type of mechanism in relation to the 'disappearance' of his mother. In a meeting with the IRA:

> They [the IRA] told us to go away and write everything down on a piece of paper what we wanted answers for. We did that. I went and wrote down a load of questions what I wanted answered. They gave me the answers. There was only one of them that they didn't answer.[178]

In this same interview (as mentioned earlier) Michael McConville said that he wanted the IRA to apologise, and to retract the allegation made that his mother was an informer. Thus, while he had some questions answered, he was not yet at a point where he was satisfied. This collective, or 'corporate' truth, may not satisfy those families who want more individualised information relating to the 'disappeared.' It is also unlikely to satisfy Unionists. Across the main Unionist parties there is a 'widespread cynicism' about the feasibility of a truth recovery process, and the likelihood of Republicans coming forward to provide truthful accounts of the past.[179] This cynicism was vocalised by the DUP's Jeffrey Donaldson in interview:

176 Interview, senior Republican ex-combatant, April 2015. This is similar to the process the Independent Commission on Information Retrieval (ICIR), as outlined in the Stormont House Agreement, is designed to establish. The ICIR will be examined further in Chapter 7.

177 Interview, Brian Rowan, September 2014.

178 Michael McConville in interview with Marian Finucane, n 33.

179 Healing Through Remembering, *Dealing with the Past? An Overview of Legal and Political Approaches Relating to the Conflict in and about Northern Ireland* (Belfast: Healing Through Remembering, 2013), p. 15. See also Introduction and Cheryl

> My experience of all of the paramilitary organisations would tend to suggest to me that the prospect of them telling the truth is limited … we will get partial truth … for example if a victim's family go to this Commission [the Independent Commission on Information Retrieval] and say, we want to know who killed our loved one. I don't think the IRA or UVF or UDA are going to say, here is the name of the person who killed your loved one. I think they will provide information that is circumstantial.[180]

What is described here as 'partial' or 'circumstantial' is, for Republicans, a legitimate form of corporate truth.

As Knupfer suggests, "there are always going to be question marks over some of these cases."[181] In part, this is a result of the horrific nature of the act of 'disappearing.' As Brian Rowan suggests, there is something about the act that renders it unanswerable: "because of the horrific nature of this – not just killing someone, but 'disappearing' their remains – there is no way you can answer that question. The IRA have not been able to answer that question."[182] This idea relates to a point made by Daly:

> Often the truth that victims and others most want to hear is not the forensic truth, not the historical or dialogic truth, but the psychological truth. Why did the perpetrator do this? … To these questions, there are no answers. No truth commission report can explain … the mysteries of human nature, the banality of evil. The most important part of the story may very well remain untold.[183]

A senior Republican in interview described this sense of some questions being unanswerable: "There will always be the pain, and the suffering that goes along with that – the tragedy of what actually happened to their loved one. And that can't really be ameliorated by anything that the IRA could say."[184]

For Cohen, 'to come to terms with the past is to know exactly what happened, to tell the truth, to face the facts.'[185] The 'facts' established regarding the 'disappeared' have been vital in terms of locating their remains and thus providing some semblance of 'closure' for families. Those families' stories have contributed to the 'truths' of the Northern Ireland conflict, even if this was not their intention. As Daly points out, 'to speak is not necessarily to know what happened and to read what happened is not necessarily to know the truth.'[186] The 'truth' that the public have of the 'disappeared' is incomplete. While the truth established by the

Lawther, *Truth, Denial and Transition: Northern Ireland and the Contested Past* (Abingdon: Routledge, 2014).

180 Interview, Jeffrey Donaldson, March 2015.
181 Interview, Geoff Knupfer, July 2014.
182 Interview, Brian Rowan, September 2014.
183 Daly, n 166 at 27.
184 Interview, senior Republican ex-combatant, April 2015.
185 Cohen, n 134 at 12.
186 Daly, n 166 at 26.

ICLVR is of a limited and specific nature, it was neither the rationale behind nor the remit of this organisation to be part of some truth recovery project. It is possible, however, that this process is, for Republicans, considered their contribution with regard the 'disappeared.' Their involvement has been vital and sets an important precedent. As argued previously, the process has contributed to the reduction of mistrust. However, as I have argued herein, dissonance over what 'truth' means to the respective parties to the conflict may yet prove problematic. Ultimately, the collective or corporate truth envisaged by Republicans (and indeed Loyalists)[187] may be unsatisfying to those in search of, or for whom truth means, a more individualised accounting for the past.

4. The 'disappeared' and memory for political ends

Although, as argued in Chapter 1, the 'truth' about the past cannot be directly correlated with 'memory,' in terms of how it is remembered, memory remains part of "telling the story" of the past.[188] Memory is inherently political, and the process of constructing the past is one based on inclusion and exclusion, and is thus inherently linked to who has power over these processes (see Chapter 1). For Misztal: "because memory is a field of the articulation of public and private interests, values and aspirations, it is also the site where contradictions of identities are often contested."[189]

Engaging with the memories of past violence is part of the process of acknowledgement and seeking justice, both of which can be beneficial in building a democracy. However, engaging with the memory of the past can be divisive, and if memory becomes politicised, can induce conflict.[190] As argued in Chapter 1, using the memory of the past as a political weapon can be damaging,[191] and the memory of the past in Northern Ireland remains a site of contention. As regards the development of the peace process, Ruane and Todd describe how everyday experiences of conflict in Northern Ireland have historic depth, and it is this long-term thinking that 'subverted all movements towards settlement.'[192] This sense of being immersed in the past, or at least using it as an argument against agreement, creates hurdles to progress. This point of frustration was picked up during the

187 EPIC, *Truth Recovery Revisited: A Contribution from Within Loyalism* (Belfast: EPIC, 2014).
188 Misztal, n 2 at 1335.
189 Barbara A. Misztal, *Theories of Social Remembering* (Maidenhead: Open University Publishing, 2003), p. 120.
190 Misztal, n 2.
191 Victor Igreja, 'Memories as Weapons: The Politics of Peace and Silence in Post-Civil War Mozambique,' *Journal of Southern African Studies*, 34:3, (2008), 539–556; Luisa Passerini, 'Memories Between Silence and Oblivion,' in Katherine Hodgkin and Susannah Radstone (eds) *Contested Pasts: The Politics of Memory* (London; New York: Routledge, 2003), pp. 238–254.
192 Joseph Ruane and Jennifer Todd, 'Path Dependence in Settlement Processes: Explaining Settlement in Northern Ireland,' *Political Studies*, 55:2, (2007), 442–458 (p. 450).

debate over the LVR legislation, when the MP John McDonnell commented, with regards debates on Northern Ireland issues, that he wished "that we were not reliving every day the vendettas of the past."[193] This section will explore two aspects of the politicisation of the memory of the 'disappeared': the weaponisation of memory and bargaining with the past.

4.1. The 'disappeared' and the weaponisation of memory

Sir Kenneth Bloomfield, in his role as Northern Ireland's Victims Commissioner, warned that 'unhappily, "truth" can be used as a weapon as well as a shield.'[194] We can see this to an extent with regards the 'disappeared,' although there is disagreement between interviewees as to the extent to which this issue has been used as a political weapon. Several interviewees suggested that the issue of the 'disappeared' has not really been politicised, or has been politicised less than other issues.[195] However, two of this group highlighted the case of Jean McConville as an exception to this.[196] As Adrian McNamee commented, "all victims' issues are politicised here … a lot of the politics have been taken out of the 'disappeared' …" however, "I suppose … Jean McConville … is used politically, still. So it's removed to some extent but they're still highly politically charged, emotive issues."[197] As will be examined later, for others, there has been a politicisation of the 'disappeared' which is typical of the approach to the past in Northern Ireland.

The issue of the 'disappeared' has been raised in the Northern Ireland Assembly on a number of occasions in response to calls from Sinn Féin to investigate cases of alleged state collusion. One Ulster Unionist MLA referred to the 'disappeared' – along with others killed by the IRA – in a 2001 Stormont debate on a Sinn Féin motion for an independent public inquiry into allegations of collusion, in questioning the focus on victims of alleged security force collusion.[198] In a 2014 debate on the Haass-O'Sullivan proposals, Arlene Foster of the DUP said of Sinn Féin's Catríona Ruane's speech "We have heard Catríona Ruane say that we have not heard about state collusion: I did not hear about the disappeared from you."[199] In 2015, when Ruane introduced a motion that "this Assembly shares … serious concerns about collusion … [and] calls for a thorough and independent investigation of these matters," the DUP's William Humphrey called out: "Jean McConville" while Ruane was speaking.[200] In his response to the proposed motion, the DUP's Robin Newtown said:

193 HC Deb 10 May 1999, vol 331, col 54.
194 Kenneth Bloomfield, *'We Will Remember Them': Report of the Northern Ireland Victims Commissioner* (Belfast: HMSO, 1998), p. 38.
195 Interviews, Adrian McNamee of the Commission for Victims and Survivors, November 2015; Monica McWilliams, a senior academic who has been involved with WAVE and the families' campaign; September 2014; Mike Ritchie of Relatives for Justice, October 2014.
196 Interviews with Adrian McNamee, November 2014 and Mike Ritchie, October 2014.
197 Interview, Adrian McNamee, November 2014.
198 NIA Deb 27 February 2001, vol 9, page 338, col 2.
199 NIA Deb 13 January 2014, vol 90, no 5, p. 72.
200 NIA Deb 15 June 2015, vol 106, no 6, p. 66–67.

> Sinn Féin has a knowledge of everything that happened around the murder of Jean McConville. If they want to use the high and mighty words that they have used in their motion, let them apply them and reveal the information around on the murder of Jean McConville.[201]

While this is on the one hand arguably part of the 'politicisation of key victims' debates' experienced more generally in Northern Ireland and in other post-conflict contexts,[202] the focus on the 'disappeared' and on Jean McConville in debates on legacy issues and in response to Sinn Féin motions suggests that the issue is used to undermine Sinn Féin by referring to this dark episode of the Republican past. References to the 'disappeared' during debates on unrelated topics would further indicate that this group of victims is at times used for political purposes. A useful example here is the 2013 debate on blood donations by gay men. Northern Ireland's then Minister of Health, Social Services and Public Safety, Edwin Poots, had been found by the High Court to have made an 'irrational' decision which breached the Ministerial Code by maintaining a ban on blood donations by gay men in Northern Ireland which was inconsistent with policy in the rest of the UK. In Poots' contribution to the debate he claimed:

> Is it not remarkable today that, when the public are talking about issues other than gay blood, such as the disappeared … we are discussing – what? – an issue about MSM blood … Is this the big issue of today that the House should be talking about? I do not think so.[203]

This is a fairly blatant example of the memory of the 'disappeared' being used to deflect from current political problems, in this case one specifically related to Poots' Ministerial conduct.

Gerry Adams and other members of Sinn Féin have also been challenged on the issue of the 'disappeared,' both North and South of the border. In November 2008, Nelson McCausland MLA was asked by the speaker to withdraw from the Assembly chamber for not withdrawing remarks made the previous day. The speaker regarded these remarks – regarding Adams' alleged links to the 'disappearance' of Jean McConville – to be 'unparliamentary,' involving 'direct and unsubstantiated allegations of criminal behaviour' about Gerry Adams.[204] In January 2015, Jim Allister of the Traditional Unionist Voice, in a debate on the election of the Assembly Speaker in which Sinn Féin's Mitchel McLaughlin was nominated (and elected), described McLaughlin as "unelectable, because … he … with great notoriety, told the general listening public that that most cruel of crimes, the kidnapping, murder and secret burial of Jean McConville, was not a

201 NIA Deb 15 June 2015, vol 106, no 6, p. 76.

202 Cheryl Lawther, 'The Construction and Politicisation of Victimhood,' in Orla Lynch and Javier Argomaniz (eds) *Victims of Terrorism: A Comparative and Interdisciplinary Study* (Abingdon: Routledge, 2016), pp. 10–30 (p. 29).

203 NIA Deb 5 November 2013, vol 89, page 54, col 1.

204 NIA Deb 4 November 2008, vol 34, no 6, page 263.

crime."[205] In the Republic of Ireland in 2005, then Justice Minister Michael McDowell told a peace conference that senior Sinn Féin members could be 'directly linked' to the deaths of some of the 'disappeared.'[206] In 2013, following the airing of an RTE/BBC documentary on the 'disappeared,' TD Ged Nash accused those in Sinn Féin who did not publicly question Adams' denial of involvement in the 'disappearance' of McConville of "moral cowardice."[207]

There is a certain inevitability to this use of the past as a weapon. Former SDLP MLA Conall McDevitt remarked that, in addressing legacy issues, MLAs were "in a game of historical ping-pong," the outcome of which is that the "duty to deal with" the past is ignored.[208] A number of interviewees agreed that the issue of the 'disappeared' is still politicised in Northern Ireland. Eugene McVeigh, when asked if politicians at times use the issue for their own political gain responded: "Absolutely. Absolutely. No doubt about it." Though it should be noted that McVeigh continued: "perhaps it's unfair to completely condemn every politician right across the board ... because ... we've found them helpful."[209] As Kate Turner suggested: "in a society where ... we're still hooked on who we are and where we're going based on the past, obviously politicians are going to grab the people who represent that to promote their cause or their agenda."[210]

For Brian Rowan:

> the victims issue is still on this battlefield now ... It's about winners and losers. It's about 'I was right and you were wrong.' It's about the ugliness of what happened ... of course it's still a weapon, and it will be a weapon for this generation of politicians.[211]

Susan McKay reflected in interview on the manifestation of this politicisation in the Republic of Ireland:

> there is a political aspect to it ... in the Republic, where there is a huge antagonism towards the Republican Movement ... it has suited anti-Sinn Féin, anti-IRA elements to highlight the 'disappeared' because it's a humiliating and embarrassing episode in the history of the Republican Movement.[212]

Another manifestation of this is that in debate some Unionists appear to ignore or downplay Republican involvement in the search process, and that progress has

205 NIA Deb 12 January 2015, vol 100, no 5, p. 10.
206 Noel McAdam, 'Minister Accuses Adams Over IRA "Missing",' *Belfast Telegraph*, 21 June 2005.
207 Gerry Moriarty, 'Labour TD Rails Against SF's Moral Cowardice,' *The Irish Times*, 8 November 2013.
208 NIA Deb 17 September 2012, vol 77, page 72, col 1.
209 Interview, Eugene McVeigh, August 2015.
210 Interview, Kate Turner, September 2014.
211 Interview, Brian Rowan, September 2014.
212 Interview, Susan McKay, July 2014.

been made in recovering bodies as a direct result. In a 2013 debate on the 'disappeared,' the DUP's Peter Weir described Sinn Féin's "attitude towards the disappeared. It is dodging reality and responsibility, and we get honeyed words instead of practical help."[213] In a debate on an area where direct co-operation between Republicans and the Commission has been evidenced, this is a stance that is difficult to support. This apparent refusal to recognise Republican involvement in bringing some level of resolution to this issue can be exemplified by the DUP's former leader, the late Rev Dr Ian Paisley. On three occasions in the Assembly, Paisley repeats a quote from David Trimble, in which he refers to the issues where progress is needed before the UUP would enter into Executive government with Sinn Féin:

> Democracy dictates that before we will sit in an Executive with Sinn Féin, we require a declaration that the 'war' is over, the standing down of 'active service units,' the handing over of the remains of the 'disappeared,' full co-operation with the Decommissioning Commission, and end to … punishment beatings and … disarmament.[214]

Paisley repeats these words in March 2002[215] and April 2002[216] stating that "all that has not happened"[217] and "the IRA has not measured up."[218] Although by April 2002, only three sets of remains had been recovered by the ICLVR, the fact that Republicans had made some progress on this issue did not seem to be taken into account. These statements read as though the memory of the 'disappeared' as a stain on Sinn Féin's reputation is being given precedence over the fact that progress has been made.

When asked if the memory of the 'disappeared' was used in political point scoring, the DUP's Jeffrey Donaldson answered:

> I don't think that it has, and you know I think … it is right for politicians to highlight where an organisation has acted in an inhumane way … if we don't pass judgment on those who act outside the norms of society, in an unlawful way, then the implication is that we don't regard it as important … I don't think that politicians have used the 'disappeared' as a political issue as such.[219]

Donaldson's response highlights a point of interpretation that is instructive for this discussion. What he argues is highlighting inhumanity, and demonstrating that an issue is considered important, is perceived by others, as, to use Susan McKay's words, 'using the dead to fight old battles.'[220] For Dixon the 'demonisation of "enemies",' is

213 NIA Deb 19 November 2013, vol 89, page 67, col 1–2.
214 NIA Deb 2 November 2001, vol 12, page 450, col 2.
215 NIA Deb 6 March 2002, vol 15, page 92, col 2.
216 NIA Deb 29 April 2002, vol 16, page 35, col 2.
217 NIA Deb 2 November 2001, vol 12, page 450, col 2.
218 NIA Deb 29 April 2002, vol 16, page 35, col 2.
219 Interview, Jeffrey Donaldson, March 2015.
220 Susan McKay, 'Northern Ireland's Peace is Haunted by Ghosts Who Will Not be Silenced,' *The Guardian*, 4 May 2014.

part of the propaganda war in Northern Ireland.[221] We see the memory of the 'disappeared,' and the interviews with McNamee and Ritchie highlight, Jean McConville particularly, used by politicians to 'demonise' Sinn Féin for political gain. As Rowan suggests, when looking for a weapon with which to attack Sinn Féin, "because of the absolute ugliness and darkness of the 'disappeared' … that's the easiest stick in the pack to pull out and use."[222]

In considering the effects of this political weaponisation of memory, one is that of cheapening the memory of victims, by operationalising their suffering for political ends. As Susan McKay said in interview:

> There's no doubt, for example, when you see the Taoiseach … trying to silence Gerry Adams by saying, 'oh what do you know about Jean McConville?' … I think that that is cheap … it is quite distressing to see that sort of thing in circumstances where people ought to know better … obviously the Republican Movement was involved in these ugly activities but … I think it's a bit degrading for the whole process that the Commission is involved in to use it in that way[223]

This links to an idea of Misztal's, that 'dwelling on injustices may … lead to a banalization of the memory of the injustice.'[224] In repeatedly drawing on the name of the 'disappeared' for political purposes, politicians in a way devalue the 'disappeared' and their families. There is also a risk that it will negatively impact upon the search process. In interview, Geoff Knupfer of the ICLVR was asked what he thought regarding the politicisation of the 'disappeared':

> It's not helpful, because all it does is put off the people we would love to talk to, or could potentially put off people we would love to talk to about it and seek their help … I can't say, facts and figures, that it has been negative but it always has the potential to be negative … if I get the opportunity … to appear on a public forum with politicians, there's always the danger that you could end up being used unwittingly as a political football … It's political parties, point-scoring, if you want.[225]

4.2. The 'disappeared' and bargaining with the past

It is not only Sinn Féin's enemies who have used the memory of the 'disappeared' for political ends. As explored in Chapter 3, there is a political motivation (as well

221 Paul Dixon, 'Political Skills or Lying and Manipulation? The Choreography of the Northern Ireland Peace Process,' *Political Studies*, 50:4, (2002), 725–741 (p. 725).
222 Interview, Brian Rowan, September 2014.
223 Interview, Susan McKay, July 2014.
224 Misztal, n 2 at 1326.
225 Interview, Geoff Knupfer, July 2014.

as, arguably, a humanitarian one) behind Republican engagement in this process and, at times, this has been stated relatively unequivocally.

The 'disappeared' have been linked with alleged abuses by British state forces, with Adams commenting on his commitment to recovering the 'disappeared' that he 'couldn't rail against British government injustices in my country if I was not prepared also to oppose injustices where these are perpetrated by republicans.'[226] When commenting on the charging of Ivor Bell in relation to the 'disappearance' of Jean McConville, Adams said:

> The injustice suffered by the McConville family is one of many legacy issues relating to the conflict. We must bear in mind in all of this that there has been a virtual amnesty for British armed forces, including state and state-sponsored killings.[227]

The provision of information by the Republican Movement on the locations of burial sites is linked to the thus far unfulfilled responsibility of the British state to be open about their activities during that period. This idea was made more explicit by Danny Morrison in interview:

> People generally feel, well Nationalists and Republicans generally feel better about … 'our side' so to speak, using quotation marks, is doing its best to sort out the murky past. And, the British should do the same, and of course, they won't.[228]

Rowan makes clear that, in dealing with the past, there is a trade-off in giving up 'truth':

> And that's a reality of the peace process, because, Blair and Ahern, the Unionists, and others, will understand – I wonder do they understand but they should understand … that the more they ask, and probe of others, the more is going to be asked, and demanded of them.[229]

It should be pointed out here that one senior Republican interviewed was critical of the suggestion that Republicans were influenced by politics:

> That's not why Republicans would have done it. Republicans were eager to help bring closure to those families that were still suffering. That would be my belief … having spoken to people … that is what I believe would have been their motivations at the time. The idea of being seen as confidence-building measures and all the rest – that would have been almost incidental.[230]

226 Sharon O'Neil, 'Adams is Accused of Justifying Deaths,' *The Irish News*, 1 June 1999.
227 'McConville Case – Gerry Adams Comments,' *An Phoblacht*, 23 March 2014.
228 Interview, Danny Morrison, January 2015
229 Interview, Brian Rowan, September 2014.
230 Interview, senior Republican ex-combatant, April 2015.

Declan Kearney of Sinn Féin also suggested that issues such as this one should transcend the political mire:

> The reality is that in order for us to effectively deal with the legacy of the past – and the recovery of victims' remains is an absolutely indispensable part of that – [it] needs to be above the political process. It needs to be bereft of recrimination and point-scoring. But it's a sad reality that that is an ever-present part of the society we live within. And it's a direct consequence of the hurt and the pain that has been caused as a result of the conflict, by all sides and to all sides. So at that human level I understand it.[231]

While not all interviewees perceive a politicisation of this issue, there is evidence to show that politicians on both 'sides' of Northern Ireland's cultural divide, and both sides of the Irish border, have at times exploited the memory of the 'disappeared' for political gain. As Rowan suggested in interview (see earlier), there is an inevitability to this. Goti's assertion, that in constructing memory we pick out what is 'worthy of recollection,'[232] is noteworthy here as it appears that certain threads of the story of the 'disappeared' are considered 'worthy of remembering' because of their value as political weapons. In 'selecting' the most harrowing stories to 'demonise' the other side,[233] and particularly in the focus on Jean McConville as one of the most 'typical innocent victims' (see Chapter 2), politicians have played a part in contributing to the development of a rather imbalanced social memory of the 'disappeared.'

5. Unearthing the past? Constructing a collective memory of the 'disappeared'

In interview, Susan McKay argued, "we need to know, what is the history of this conflict? What actually happened? … there's no point in putting into history fictions."[234] As examined previously, composing a history of a conflict can be challenging.[235] In part, this is because of the very nature of history, truth, and narratives of the past. Attempts to interpret or write a history in a post-conflict society are likely to be contested and complex.[236] As Daly posits: 'No period of a nation's history can be described by a single, elegant truth narrative.'[237] As the previous section examined, in any context, particularly a post-conflict one, competing truths can exist and relationships of power can influence which 'truths' or 'facts' or whose accounts enter the historical record, and what is silenced.[238]

231 Interview, Declan Kearney, April 2015.
232 Goti, n 9 at 158.
233 After Dixon, n 221.
234 Interview, Susan McKay, July 2014.
235 Chapman and Ball, n 6.
236 Ibid.
237 Daly, n 166, at 25
238 Trouillot, n 3.

Phillips proposes that the increasing difficulty in attempting to uphold the perspective of a single, authoritative history is what encouraged the framing of memory, or memories, as a way of 'understanding the complex interrelationships among past, present, and future.'[239] Memory, as a construct based around truth, fact, myth, and fiction,[240] provides a lens through which the response to the 'disappeared' can be examined, allowing for the various subjectivities this entails. This section will attempt to tease out the various relevant threads in the vast literature on memory to unpick several ideas relevant to the issue of the memory of the 'disappeared.'

For Misztal, and others, collective memory is social memory.[241] This connection is rooted in Halbwachs' seminal work on the concept of 'collective memory.' Based on his belief that 'studying memory was not a matter of reflecting philosophically on inherent properties of the subjective mind; memory is a matter of how minds work together in society,'[242] Halbwachs argues that 'it is in society that people normally acquire their memories. It is also in society that they recall, recognise, and localize their memories.'[243] That collective and social memory are one and the same concept appears to be widely accepted in the literature (on the whole, see the work of Casey, later). However, an overview of scholarly work on collective memory reveals that Misztal's description of 'a concept defined and interpreted in many different ways'[244] is an accurate one.

One of the difficulties in navigating the collective memory literature is the extent of differentiation, or lack thereof, across its various conceptualisations. For some scholars, 'collective memory' is also known as 'cultural memory,'[245] or 'public memory.'[246] While not merging the two, Misztal treats cultural memory as a separate form of social remembering, involving the institutionalisation of memory through cultural means (e.g. through cultural practices, such as ceremonies, rituals, and festivals, and artefacts such as monuments, statues, and films).[247] Public memory is also considered a form of collective memory, for Misztal this involves the shaping of memory by public institutions such as schools, museums, the courts, and the mass

239 Kendall R. Phillips, 'Introduction,' in Kendall R. Phillips (ed.) *Framing Public Memory* (Alabama: University of Alabama Press, 2004), pp. 1–16 (p. 2).
240 Monica Rico, 'The Limits of Memory: Private and Public in the Remembrance of Prince Albert,' *The Communication Review*, 2:1, (1997), 19–41.
241 Misztal, n 189. See also Misztal, n 2; Jeffrey K. Olick and Joyce Robbins, 'Social Memory Studies: From "Collective Memory" to the Historical Sociology of Mnemonic Practices,' *Annual Review of Sociology*, 24:1, (1998), 105–140; Michael Schudson, 'Cultural Memory: A Special Issue,' *The Communication Review*, 2:1, (1997), 1–2; David M. Smith, 'Tales of Matewan: The Construction of a Usable Past,' *The Communication Review*, 2:1, (1997), 59–88.
242 Olick and Robbins, ibid. at 109.
243 Halbwachs, n 13 at 38.
244 Misztal, n 2 at 1320.
245 Rico, n 240; Schudson, n 241; Smith, n 241.
246 Rico, ibid.
247 Misztal, n 189.

media.[248] Elsewhere, public memory is considered from a different perspective, involving collective remembrance.[249] Here, public memory is associated more with forms of public memorialisation such as museums, monuments, and other heritage sites or artefacts.[250] Kendall divides the interpretation of public memory into two broad categories. For some, it is the 'memory of publics,' where a 'public' entity can be argued to exist, and have memories. For others, it is the 'publicness of memory,' in which memories are visible to many.[251] Others seek to differentiate more explicitly between the branches of memory. For Casey, public, collective, and social memory can each be defined separately.[252] This sample of scholarship shows how various branches of what is conceived as 'collective memory' can be interpreted in different ways.

Drawing on Casey's definition of 'collective memory' as the recollection of the same event by different persons who are not necessarily known to one another,[253] if one considers how unrelated individuals – in this case Northern Ireland society – remember the 'disappeared,' it is possible to argue that present, or recent, interests have influenced the collective memory of the past. The political character of collective memory is inherent in its social nature. Of his memories, Halbwachs suggested:

> There is no point in seeking where they are preserved in my brain or in some nook of my mind to which I alone have access: for they are recalled to me externally, and the groups of which I am a part at any time give me the means to reconstruct them.[254]

In this regard, any social memory of the 'disappeared' will inevitably draw on external factors. Olick and Levy are emphatic about the political nature of collective memory, describing it as 'the conceptually and politically mediated past.'[255]

248 Ibid.

249 Phillips, n 239.

250 Barbara Biesecker, 'Renovating the National Imaginary: A Prolegomenon on Contemporary Paregoric Rhetoric,' in Kendall R. Phillips (ed.) *Framing Public Memory* (Alabama: University of Alabama Press, 2004), pp. 212–247; Gretchen Schafft and Gerhard Zeidler, *Commemorating Hell: The Public Memory of Mittelbau-Dora* (Urbana: University of Illinois Press, 2011). As Marschall posits, public monuments can be both '*loci* of private contemplation and mourning, as well as of public rituals of commemoration,' but also have a role in 'reshaping public memory.' Sites of public memorialisation are both shaped by, and shapers of, public memory (Sabine Marschall, *Landscape of Memory: Commemorative Monuments, Memorials and Public Statuary in Post-Apartheid South Africa* (Leiden: Brill, 2010), pp. 2; 3).

251 Phillips, n 239 at 3–7.

252 Edward S. Casey, 'Public Memory in Place and Time,' in Kendall R. Phillips (ed.) *Framing Public Memory* (Alabama: University of Alabama Press, 2004), pp. 17–44.

253 Ibid.

254 Halbwachs, n 13 at 38.

255 Jeffrey K. Olick and Daniel Levy, 'Collective Memory and Cultural Constraint: Holocaust Myth and Rationality in German Politics,' *American Sociological Review*, 62:6, (1997), 921–936 (p. 922).

That memory is social is, for de Brito et al., what renders it political. They argue that the politics of memory constitutes the attempts made to 'make sense of the present ... based on an assessment of the past.'[256] Collective memory is 'an active process of sense-making.'[257] This chapter has so far analysed the accounts that exist in the public domain regarding the 'disappeared,' and each of these accounts contributes in some way to the body of material available to those trying to 'make sense' of the 'disappeared.'

Trouillot warns that:

> Even when the historical continuities are unquestionable, in no way can we assume a simple correlation between the magnitude of events as they happened and their relevance for generations that inherit them through history ... what we call the 'legacy of the past' may not be anything bequeathed by the past itself.[258]

Although history and memory cannot be considered one and the same, the two concepts are not completely unrelated to one another.[259] Our collective memory shapes our perceptions of history.[260] As a 'negotiation between past and present,'[261] memory is influenced by present conditions and political subjectivities. As Trouillot's work hints at, the "legacy of the past" may be 'bequeathed by' present-day interests rather than 'the past itself.' That the memory of the 'disappeared' holds a relatively prominent place in the 'legacy' of Northern Ireland's past is, arguably, evidence of this.[262]

As noted earlier, while more than 3700 men, women, and children died as a result of the conflict in Northern Ireland,[263] the name everybody knows is Jean McConville. One interviewee stated with regards the Republic of Ireland: "you'll find everybody in the Republic knows the name of Jean McConville. Quite a lot of people ... would struggle to name half a dozen other people who were killed in the Troubles."[264]

This is in part due to the efforts exerted by the families, as examined in Chapter 2. If they had not spoken out, the 'disappeared' would be unknown victims of the conflict in Northern Ireland. However, the pervasiveness of this one name is also a

256 Alexandra Barahona de Brito, Paloma Aguilar and Carmen Gonzalez-Enriquez, 'Introduction,' in Alexandra Barahona de Brito, Carmen Gonzaléz-Enríquez and Paloma Aguilar (eds) *The Politics of Memory: Transitional Justice in Democratizing Societies* (Oxford: Oxford University Press, 2001), pp. 1–39 (p. 39).
257 Olick and Levy, n 255 at 922.
258 Trouillot, n 3 at 16–17.
259 Misztal, n 189; Olick and Robbins, n 241; Smith, n 241.
260 Smith, n 241.
261 Olick and Levy, n 255 at 934.
262 Trouillot, n 3 at 17.
263 David McKittrick, Seamus Kelters, Brian Feeney, Chris Thornton and David McVea, *Lost Lives: The Stories of the Men, Women and Children Who Died as a Result of the Northern Ireland Troubles* (Edinburgh; London: Mainstream Publishing, 2007).
264 Interview, Susan McKay, July 2014.

result of the events surrounding McConville's 'disappearance' and, by association, the other victims of this form of violence, being seared on to the collective memory of the 'Troubles.' The linkage of Gerry Adams' name to the killing of Jean McConville creates yet another dichotomy, a binary shorthand for the conflict, with Adams as (alleged) perpetrator in one of the most heinous acts of the conflict and Jean McConville as the ultimate innocent victim. Schudson argues that public memory exists outside of and beyond physical sites of memory or commemoration.[265] We see this with the 'disappeared.' Their memory persists in part as a result of the politics surrounding this issue. Schudson suggests that, rather than a physical site of commemoration, what he calls the 'primary carrier of memory' is, 'in the span of a human lifetime … the person.' Drawing on the example of President Nixon as a 'memory site' of Watergate, Schudson describes how, in all his public acts, he carried the memory of Watergate with him: 'he could not move without Watergate trailing behind him.'[266] The same can be said of Adams and the 'disappeared,' in particular, Jean McConville. A cartoon published in the *Belfast Telegraph* in November 2013 depicted Adams in a hall of mirrors, with the image of Jean McConville reflected in each one.[267] This connection, English suggested in interview, is in part why this particular issue has gained relevant precedence over other victims' causes:

> There was a set of journalists … who felt that Adams has had a good war and that really, if he'd been a Serb, he'd have been in The Hague … and he shouldn't get away with it. And I think that because he was ambitious and remains ambitious politically, they wanted to chip away at that. But for those journalists giving voice, I think it would have … quietened down … I mean there are lots of other things that happened in the 'Troubles' which were egregious and awful which we never, ever talk about … and I think that the 'disappeared' … it's an amazing story that chipped away at Gerry and that made it something that was particularly attractive.[268]

Adams is a 'memory carrier'[269] of the 'disappeared.' The allegations of involvement inextricably connect him to these events, and every remark made about this in Stormont, or in the Dáil, or in the press, reinforces his place as a carrier of these memories.

In considering the scholarship on remembering the past, and the challenges this entails, one of the frequently occurring ideas is that of a 'trace.' In these accounts, a 'trace' is a remnant, a piece of the puzzle, a fragment, perhaps a

265 Michael Schudson, 'Lives, Laws, and Language: Commemorative versus Non-Commemorative Forms of Effective Public Memory,' *The Communication Review*, 2:1, (1997), 3–17.
266 Ibid. at 6; 7.
267 *Belfast Telegraph*, 5 November 2013.
268 Interview, Richard English, historian, August 2014.
269 Following Schudson, n 265.

piece of evidence; it is a contribution to the production of a representation of the past.[270] Each reference to the 'disappeared' to embarrass Sinn Féin, each news item about a search, each image of the removal of coffined remains from a burial site, these are all 'traces.' The stories the families tell, similarly, are traces, which, although highly personal, in being told – and in being heard – become part of the collective memory of the conflict.

To produce a trace is to create a silence, as to focus on one thing silences something else.[271] In the production of these multiple traces of the 'disappeared,' the suffering of other victims has, perhaps, been silenced. In interview, Malachi O'Doherty described to me how he has "spoken to victims or families of victims who feel that they are overlooked in favour of people that they regard almost as 'celebrity victims.'"[272] As English said (above), lots of other "awful things" happened that are not talked about. Susan McKay also touched on this:

> Jean McConville was not the only mother of many children who was killed in the course of the conflict. People who were mothers were killed by the British Army, they were killed by Loyalists, and … they were killed by police … all sides killed people who were by most people's reckoning, innocent. Sometimes it does seem disproportionate the amount of attention that's given to the 'disappeared,' but that doesn't take away from the fact that the families of the 'disappeared' have a right to as much assistance and support as they can get.[273]

The focus on Adams and McConville silences another aspect of this issue. As outlined previously, much of the context of the 'disappearances' has been silenced. A lot of the 'grey' has been silenced. Focusing on Adams and Republicans silences the responsibility that others had – the state, the local community, wider society. Focussing on McConville silences the profile of the other 'disappeared' as, mostly, young men, some of whom were allegedly involved in low-level criminality or political violence. The collective memory of the 'disappeared' is perhaps a rather simple one, based around Adams as perpetrator, the IRA as the guilty and therefore, responsible party, and Jean McConville as the typical, innocent, 'disappeared' victim – when in fact she is very much atypical. Aretxaga, in examining state violence in Spain, argues that in considering stories of state violence, what is more important – for her purposes – than the 'truth-value,' is what she describes as 'the "truth effects" of the stories which themselves constitute an immediate, affective, charged political reality.'[274] The 'truth

270 See e.g. Francesca Cappelletto, 'Long-Term Memory of Extreme Events: From Autobiography to History,' *The Journal of the Royal Anthropological Institute*, 9:2, (2003), 241–260; Igreja, n 191; Elizabeth Jelin, 'Public Memorialization in Perspective: Truth, Justice and Memory of Past Repression in the Southern Cone of South America,' *International Journal of Transitional Justice*, 1:1, (2007), 138–156; Trouillot, n 3.

271 Trouillot, ibid.

272 Interview, journalist and writer Malachi O'Doherty, August 2015.

273 Interview, Susan McKay, July 2014.

274 Begoña Aretxaga, 'Playing Terrorist: Ghastly Plots and the Ghostly State,' *Journal of Spanish Cultural Studies*, 1:1, (2000), 43–58 (p. 52).

effect' of this collective memory has arguably been beneficial in terms of public perception of, and support for, the families and their attempts to have their loved ones' remains returned. Rico poses the question: 'Why do some versions of the truth resonate within a given culture and not others?'[275] The 'truth effect' here is of a version of the 'truth' that resonates more widely than others might.

6. Conclusion

The campaign of the families of the 'disappeared' has, as in other international contexts, fuelled the development of a transitional justice mechanism. In this case in a context where the approach to the past has been described as 'piecemeal.'[276] Kovras suggests that in unearthing the remains of the 'disappeared,' a space is created that allows for multiple truths to emerge into public debate, and the way is paved for the acknowledgement of suffering.[277] Although based on research in Cyprus and Spain, Kovras' words are equally relevant in the Irish context. As this chapter has explored, although not a truth recovery mechanism, the process of campaigning and searching for the 'disappeared' has facilitated the emergence of various 'truths' – both 'narrow' forensic truths relating to burial site locations, and 'wider' narrative truths through the families' accounts. Acknowledgement, in terms of the IRA's statement acknowledging its involvement, was an important step in this process and, as the issue of 'disappearing' became more public, and has been kept in the public eye by the continuing search process, this has generated a wider, societal acknowledgement of the families' suffering.

Introduced in Chapter 1, Trouillot's work[278] has been drawn on frequently in this chapter. In the story of the 'disappeared' we see the role of power in the production of history in action. Silenced for decades by the power of the IRA, the ceasefires and peace process created a context in which previously silenced voices could speak out and be heard. The impact of the families capturing their voice was hugely significant: it set in motion this entire process. Without this, it is highly unlikely that the IRA would have acknowledged their involvement, or that the state would have introduced the LVR legislation, and the remains of many of the 'disappeared' would not have been found. Yet, we can see the effects of other sources of power. Republicans stay silent on the details of these cases, and are likely to remain so. A fixation by politicians, and, arguably, the media, on the allegations surrounding Gerry Adams and the 'disappearance' of Jean McConville, has produced a collective memory that is rather skewed.

275 Rico, n 240 at 39.

276 Christine Bell, 'Dealing with the Past in Northern Ireland,' *Fordham International Law Journal*, 26, (2002), 1095–1147, (p. 1097); Kieran McEvoy and Graham Ellison, 'Criminological Discourses in Northern Ireland: Conflict and Conflict Resolution,' in Kieran McEvoy and Tim Newburn (eds) *Criminology, Conflict Resolution and Restorative Justice* (Basingstoke: Palgrave Macmillan, 2003), pp. 45–82.

277 Kovras, n 106 at 21.

278 Trouillot, n 3.

The collective memory of the 'disappeared' illustrates both the potential and the pitfalls of engaging with the memory of the past. On the one hand, we see the ability of a broad section of society to sympathise with heart-breaking stories of loss, regardless of the background or affiliations of those directly involved. On the other hand, we see the cynical use of the memory of the suffering experienced by victims by politicians to undermine their opponents. The families' stories have great value in illuminating the lived reality of the conflict, yet the social memory of the 'disappeared' is most greatly influenced by one case – that of Jean McConville. While this story is as heart-breaking as others, it is in many ways not representative of the 'disappeared' as a collective. The prevalence of this case is in part a reflection of present-day political interests. What the 'truth' of the 'disappeared' as told by the families reveals is how ordinary people's lives were impacted by extraordinary events. The reality of these 'disappearances' is as worthy an object of our compassion, one that breaks away from a sense of 'them' and 'us' and sheds light on a grey and complex past. When asked what can we learn from the process of recovering the 'disappeared,' Kate Turner suggested that understanding this 'grey' is what might help avoid a return to conflict:

> We've got to look and find a wider way of saying … how do we accept things that are much more complicated and grey and not as black and white as the narratives we've been led to believe are, because that will help us not go back there.[279]

279 Interview, Kate Turner, September 2014.

7 Conclusion

'Disappearing' and transitional justice – lessons from Northern Ireland

As I write this conclusion, a period of public consultation on 'Addressing the Legacy of Northern Ireland's Past' is ongoing. One of the consultation documents central to this process is the Draft Northern Ireland (Stormont House Agreement) Bill which details the implementation of the Stormont House Agreement (SHA). This agreement, the outcome of lengthy all-party talks at Stormont House in the run-up to Christmas 2014 has been argued to be an important step on the path towards implementing a transitional mechanism for responding to the needs of victims:

> It's the last chance we have for an overarching mechanism for dealing with the past. As you know we've had a piecemeal approach to the past. We've had four serious attempts to do this: so you had the HTR [Healing Through Remembering] process in 2006 … 2009 you've got the Eames-Bradley report, 2013 you've got Haass-O'Sullivan, 2014 you've got [the SHA], this is the last time. If it doesn't work this time it's not going to work … the Stormont House Agreement represents our last chance to do this. If we don't do it, then we will be left with the *status quo ante*, in effect where we will have a largely state-centric approach to dealing with the past based on a criminal justice system … a very unsatisfactory process … so this is our last chance.[1]

Briefer than its predecessors, the SHA provided the framework for a group of four institutions designed to respond to 'The Past.'[2] These are a Historical Investigations Unit (HIU) aimed at providing a prosecutorial route that families can pursue if they so choose, an Independent Commission on Information Retrieval (ICIR) – in essence a truth recovery mechanism, and an Oral History Archive (OHA). An Implementation and Reconciliation Group (IRG) will have a dual role of producing a report on themes and promoting reconciliation. For the purposes of this book, the ICIR is of greatest interest as the SHA states that it will build 'on the

1 Interview, community activist with over 20 years' experience working with ex-combatants, October 2015.

2 Stormont House Agreement, www.gov.uk/government/publications/the-stormont-house-agreement [accessed 16 August 2018].

precedent provided by the Independent Commission for the Location of Victims' Remains.'[3]

With regards 'disappearing' in an international context, Kovras contends that: 'Since the 1970s, the phenomenon of enforced disappearances and the ensuing demand by relatives to acknowledge the truth have shaped the development of transitional justice in societies emerging from conflict.'[4] Robins similarly locates the issue of 'disappearances' within the broader transitional justice debate, suggesting that 'disappearances' have 'driven the development of transitional justice as distinct from a simple prosecutorial approach to violent pasts,' because of the need for truth recovery.[5] To conclude this book, the extent to which the response to the 'disappearances' perpetrated during the conflict in Northern Ireland has 'shaped' – or has the potential to shape – the broader development of transitional justice will be examined. To do this, the notion of the ICLVR as a precedent for the ICIR will be explored, in terms of the rationale behind this decision and the lessons we can learn from the process of recovering remains.

In considering why the ICLVR was used as a precedent for the ICIR, it is to the mechanics of the process itself that we can first look. Both the ICLVR and ICIR have similar purposes: the gathering of information in relation to conflict-related events in a confidential manner. Thus, it follows that the mechanisms for extracting that information should be comparable. Like the ICLVR the ICIR is to be established by legislation in both the British and Irish jurisdictions, it will be independent of the justice system, it will not be able to disclose the information provided to it to either law enforcement or intelligence agencies, and this information will be inadmissible in court proceedings. The identities of those who provide information to the ICIR will also not be disclosed. Like the ICLVR, providing information to the ICIR does not render an individual immune from prosecution. Although the information provided to the ICIR is inadmissible in civil or criminal proceedings, individuals may still be prosecuted if evidence comes to light via other means.[6] One DUP MP who was involved in the negotiations that led to the SHA, said of the decision in interview:

> it was necessary to find a mechanism that enabled them [victims] to ask the questions, and the paramilitary organisations to give the answers. And therefore we looked at the Commission for the 'disappeared,' and the precedents that were created there, the concept that was established … we felt that was probably the most appropriate model because it didn't provide an amnesty, it didn't render people immune from prosecution, but it did offer a mechanism

3 Ibid.

4 Iosif Kovras, 'Explaining Prolonged Silences in Transitional Justice: The Disappeared in Cyprus and Spain,' *Comparative Political Studies*, 20:10, (2012), 1–27 (p. 2).

5 Simon Robins, 'Towards Victim-Centred Transitional Justice: Understanding the Needs of Families of the Disappeared in Postconflict Nepal,' *International Journal of Transitional Justice*, 5:1, (2011), 75–98 (p. 80).

6 Stormont House Agreement, n 2.

> whereby victims could have information and truth and, in the case of the 'disappeared,' hopefully the return of their loved one's remains … there is a correlation between the ICIR and the Commission for the 'disappeared' … the concept behind that … the model of that … how it was dealt with in law, provided a basis for dealing with ICIR … the parallels are not exact, the purposes are slightly different, I think the basic concept, the model, has a lot to do with the fact that the Independent Commission for the 'disappeared' worked, in large measure.[7]

In short, the ICLVR provides an example of a mechanism that works in the way required by the ICIR. More broadly, the experience of the ICLVR shows that forms of limited immunity can be a crucial component of transitional justice and, as argued in Chapter 5, can be argued to be victim-centred. As will be examined in the next few paragraphs, the implications of the ICLVR process exceed the mechanics of the process itself. Several fundamental elements of the process – trust, leadership, context, and the quiet passage of the legislation – have been key to its relative success, and this can and should be instructive for the development of the SHA institutions or indeed other potential future mechanisms for responding to the legacy of conflict either in the context of Northern Ireland or elsewhere.

The importance of building trust features at a number of levels, first of which is the need to manage expectations. As mentioned previously (Chapter 3), early headlines suggested rapid recovery of remains. As Brendan McArdle, a former *An Garda Síochána* Detective Inspector who was involved in the early searches explained in interview, the roots of these expectations were genuine:

> I think we all thought, both media and the people presenting the information, everybody thought this was going to be a very quick process … But it's lingered on … maybe we all rushed in headlong thinking, this is easy, but after 24 hours everybody realised it was going to be extremely difficult, but the media still didn't … And nobody envisaged, at least initially, that it was going to be anything – it was simply you go to a location, mark 'X', 10 feet from a tree and the body's there – it wasn't! It wasn't the case.[8]

Yet given that, as argued previously (Chapter 5), trust is linked with expectation of outcome,[9] making claims that could not realistically be met created conditions for further mistrust to develop. The experience of the ICLVR suggests that one of the first steps in building trust should be the management of the expectations of those with a stake in the process, by being realistic about what is achievable.

7 Interview, Jeffrey Donaldson, March 2015.
8 Interview, Brendan McArdle, Dublin, January 2015.
9 Morton Deutsch, 'Trust and Suspicion,' *Journal of Conflict Resolution*, 2:4, (1958), 265–279; Geoffrey Hosking, *Trust: A History* (Oxford: Oxford University Press, 2014); Herbert W. Kee and Robert E. Knox, 'Conceptual and Methodological Considerations in the Study of Trust and Suspicion,' *Journal of Conflict Resolution*, 14:3, (1970), 357–366.

The legislation that established the ICLVR created a legal foundation upon which trust in the process could develop. This highlights the importance of comprehensive and clear legislation, and yet, the time that has passed since the legislation was introduced arguably indicates that the legislation alone was not enough. It is, after all, some 20 years later and bodies continue to be recovered. While the legislation provided the required legal guarantees, as contended in Chapter 5, the development of working relationships based on trust between those involved has been an equally, if not even more, fundamental factor in the progress that has been made. When asked in interview what lessons can be learned from the process of recovering the remains of the 'disappeared,' one interviewee remarked: "good faith is extremely important, and trust. And it would appear to me that that sort of relationship does exist between the head of the [ICLVR] team and their opposite numbers on the Republican side."[10]

In my reckoning, one of the most significant faults with the ICIR, as proposed in the SHA, is the five-year time limit on its period of operation.[11] To consider the ICLVR, within the first five years, the remains of only four of the 'disappeared' were recovered. Indeed, as Geoff Knupfer of the ICLVR described to me in interview, by 2004 (prior to his instalment as SIO), the process "had dried up, it wasn't going anywhere."[12] While the progress made by that point was no less significant for the families of those four individuals, the rate of retrieval did not really pick up momentum until approaching the ten-year mark, with the remains of other victims recovered in 2008, 2010, 2014, 2015, and 2017. This staggered recovery of remains suggests that more information was provided to the Commission as trust in the process increased, and that this took time. With regards the design of other transitional mechanisms for information recovery – either in Northern Ireland or elsewhere – the experience of the ICLVR suggests that both comprehensive and robust guarantees, and time, are required in order to maximise potential information provision.

A further facet to consider is that the ICLVR arguably demonstrates that this type of mechanism can be trusted. As one interviewee suggested: 'the British and the legal structures have proven their *bona fides* with this. So we now have a mechanism, we now have a system that should be relied upon.'[13]

Part of the value of the ICLVR is that it has been seen to work by those intended to engage with the ICIR mechanism:

10 Interview, Danny Morrison, former Director of Publicity for Sinn Féin, January 2015.

11 In terms of the conclusion of the ICIR's work, the Draft Bill (49 (6)) does allow for, in addition to the period of five years operation, 'any other period which is agreed between Her Majesty's Government in the United Kingdom and the Government of Ireland as the period during which the Commission's functions are exercisable' (Draft Northern Ireland (Stormont House Agreement) Bill, https://assets.publishing.service.gov.uk/government/uploads/system/uploads/attachment_data/file/706283/Draft_Northern_Ireland__Stormont_House_Agreement__Bill.pdf [accessed 25 September 2018]).

12 Interview, Geoff Knupfer, July 2014.

13 Interview, journalist and writer Malachi O'Doherty, August 2015.

> It's something practical that you can point to, to the ex-combatant or former security force constituency to say: this thing can work. Because the misgivings for them will be, well why the hell should we if we're liable to be prosecuted etc. So if you're having that conversation within the IRA structures or within the Loyalist structures ... you can say: this worked, look, if there's good faith here, it's going to work ... it shows it can work, it shows you can construct an institution that has cross-border effect which can carry out a very important element of the transition and no one ends up getting prosecuted as a result of it, I think that's very important.[14]

The issue of the missing, Jaquemet warns, can be 'symbolic of the past poisoning the present.'[15] Yet, in the context of Northern Ireland, the response to the issue of the 'disappeared' has created an opportunity for addressing the legacy of the past by demonstrating the potential of a form of transitional mechanism that could be adapted to address other legacy issues – both in Northern Ireland and in other transitional contexts.

As has been highlighted, trust in those individuals linking the ICLVR with the Republican Movement has been core to the relative success of the search. In considering the lessons that we can take from the response to the issue of the 'disappeared' for the broader challenges of dealing with the past in Northern Ireland, the need for effective leadership is notable. Asked how important leadership has been in this process, one interviewee responded:

> Crucial ... once the Republican leadership – both Sinn Féin and the IRA – engaged with this issue properly and created their own structures in order to manage it, that's when the issue begins to be resolved, you know it's only when they take it seriously. And it's a top-down organisation ... so once ... senior Republicans are calling a meeting for IRA personnel to come and have a discussion about what happened on that operation, people show up. That's how it works. It doesn't work until you have that top-down commitment to making it work. So it's absolutely central. It doesn't happen without that kind of sea change in the attitude of the Republican leadership towards this issue.[16]

On the side of the ICLVR, many of my interviewees referred to Geoff Knupfer specifically. Described as "an impressive character,"[17] one Republican ex-combatant interviewed suggested that Republicans "were able to rely on Geoff Knupfer

14 Interview, community activist with over 20 years' experience working with ex-combatants, October 2015.

15 Iolanda Jaquemet, 'Fighting Amnesia: Ways to Uncover the Truth about Lebanon's Missing,' *International Journal of Transitional Justice*, 3:1, (2008), 69–90 (p. 76).

16 Interview, community activist with over 20 years' experience working with ex-combatants, October 2015.

17 Interview, veteran human rights activist Mike Ritchie, October 2014.

to the same extent that they were able to rely on their comrades."[18] This, he said, has been "crucial."[19] One interviewee suggested why Knupfer is so valued:

> He reminds me slightly of former combatants themselves … you'll see sometimes relationships developing between former IRA personnel, former police officers or former army personnel … they are used to a structure, they are used to a certain hierarchy, discipline, focus … They totally understand each other's worlds … Secondly he has a kind of 'no bullshit' approach to this … it's a practical, task-orientated way of approaching this and also the fact that he made public pronouncements about the fact that the Republican Movement were engaging with this in good faith … He's a … straight-talking military/policing person who's kind of not trying to get too politically clever … but getting on with the task and calling it as they see it, and … I think they like that sort of approach. So for all of those reasons I think he's been a very successful appointment.[20]

What this suggests, with regards the ICIR – or indeed any transitional justice institution – is the importance of selecting the right personnel, as this can influence the extent to which individuals engage with the mechanism. This need is indicated by the inclusion in a model bill produced by a group of academics and practitioners of a list of qualities and experience that the ICIR Commissioners should have. This includes being independent, impartial – and being perceived as such – and being able to handle sensitive information.[21]

As argued in Chapter 2, the power of the families of the 'disappeared' as a small social movement has both generated and maintained attention and support for the recovery of the remains of those who were 'disappeared.' However, a central tenet to the relative success of their campaign has been, as emphasised in some of the social movement literature,[22] the context in which they have sought to bring about change. The backdrop to the families' campaign, as mentioned by several interviewees, has been hugely significant. There was a "momentum"[23] for change

18 Interview, senior Republican ex-combatant, April 2015.
19 Ibid.
20 Interview, community activist with over 20 years' experience working with ex-combatants, October 2015.
21 Stormont House Agreement, Model Implementation Bill, available at www.caj.org.uk/contents/1289.
22 Sandra R. Levitsky, 'Law and Social Movements: Old Debates and New Directions,' in Austin Sarat and Patricia Ewick (eds) *The Handbook of Law and Society* (Wiley Online: 2015), pp. 382–398; Holly J. McCammon and Allison R. McGrath, 'Litigating Change? Social Movements and the Court System,' *Sociology Compass*, 9:2, (2015), 128–139; Michael McCann, 'Law and Social Movements: Contemporary Perspectives,' *Annual Review of Law and Social Science*, 2, (2005), 17–38; Douglas NeJaime, 'Constitutional Change, Courts, and Social Movements,' *Michigan Law Review*, 111:6, (2013), 877–902.
23 Interviews with Susan McKay, journalist and writer, July 2014; Richard English, historian, August 2014; Mike Ritchie, October 2014.

in the post-Good Friday Agreement period that perhaps does not exist now. In interview, veteran human rights activist Mike Ritchie suggested in his 2014 interview, "you know it didn't feel a very happy time, but when you look back at it now there was so much more generosity and willingness to accept that it was time to move on, than there is now."[24] As examined in Chapter 1, there is a time for engaging with the past, and the families' campaign gained momentum during a period when it was this time for Northern Ireland. Whether such 'generosity,' or indeed 'willingness,' exists now, is questionable.

Not only was the context one conducive to the setting up of the ICLVR, but within this context, as argued in Chapter 5, the search mechanism was put in place with "very little fuss."[25] As has been contended, the Commission has proven to be an effective way of uncovering the information needed to locate the remains of the 'disappeared.' However, arguably, had discussions surrounding the development of such a mechanism got caught up in the point-scoring of local politicians, or had the word 'amnesty' been splashed across the front pages, the required mechanism may not have been put in place. That the establishment of the ICLVR can be considered an example of what I have termed 'quiet' transitional justice cushioned the development of this mechanism from potential opposition that may have impeded its progress. In this regard, the SHA is a very different matter. Far from 'quiet,' the claims of 'amnesty' that did not feature in the (relatively minimal) media attention surrounding the passing of the Location of Victims' Remains Bill have surfaced with the SHA.[26] As one interviewee pointed out:

> It's quite interesting if you look at the two issues [the ICLVR and the ICIR]. At the time nobody really jumped up and down to say 'this is an amnesty' and nobody got very excited about the amnesty elements of the 'disappeared' Commission but some of the victims' groups ... are jumping up and down on this issue.[27]

The issue of amnesty raised its head again following a recommendation in 2017 by the House of Commons Defence Committee that a Statute of Limitations be enacted to cover all Troubles-related incidents involving former members of the British Armed Forces.[28] Such a statute would, according to McEvoy, amount to a

24 Interview, Mike Ritchie, October 2014.

25 Ibid.

26 E.g. Jilly Beattie, 'Allister Slams Bid to Dress Up Amnesty,' *Daily Mirror*, 24 September 2015; Jilly Beattie, 'Terrorists and Soldiers Accused of Horrific Murders in Northern Ireland's Troubles Can Confess and Walk Free,' *Daily Mirror*, 10 September 2015; Philip Bradfield, 'Troubles Killers Can Confess ... but Victims Will not be Told,' *News Letter*, 24 September 2015.

27 Interview, community activist with over 20 years' experience working with ex-combatants, October 2015.

28 House of Commons Defence Committee, *Investigations into Fatalities in Northern Ireland Involving British Military Personnel: Seventh Report of Session 2016–17*, 24 April 2017.

'self-amnesty,'[29] and indeed, the proposal has been opposed by victims from across Northern Ireland's political spectrum.[30]

The public nature of the development of the SHA renders it more exposed to the negative effects of publicity as examined in Chapter 5, such as the 'audience effect.'[31] While this cannot be undone, it is important that those politicians who supported the development of the SHA within the confines of Stormont House do not begin to step back from that stance when faced with criticism from their electorate. The experience of the ICLVR indicates that there can be value in working 'quietly.' As I argue elsewhere,[32] while such an approach may seem anathema to the broader principles of transitional justice as they are often understood, the response to the 'disappeared' shows that there can be a pragmatic value in working outside the glare of publicity.

At this point I will enter one caveat to the appropriateness of the ICLVR as a precedent for the ICIR. As mentioned previously, Sinn Féin's Declan Kearney remarked of the ICLVR: "there is a model there, that I think commends itself to the discussion around future, wider truth recovery."[33] As I have argued so far, this could be the case. Yet, one interviewee with significant experience of efforts to deal with the past in Northern Ireland entered a note of caution in this regard which warrants attention:

> To meet the relatives' needs, without opening up the possibility of prosecutions … [the ICLVR's] got a very clearly defined mandate, it goes about its work very discretely … [it] limits wider lessons or wider implications coming out of this … And at least from the government's point of view, the ICIR would be hermetically sealed, and, I think, this is one reason why to build it on the 'disappeared' has sort of wider policy implications, whether intended or unintended. I'm sure intended is the idea that to reassure the public that this has been done before, that it has worked, this isn't some sort of new, explosive, truth recovery process … all those things that have been successful in the 'disappeared' model, can therefore be successful in the truth recovery model. The difficulty with that in my view is that that is a very minimal view of information recovery … the 'disappeared' provides some reassurance that a

29 Kieran McEvoy, 'Is the Price of an Amnesty for the Security Forces Just Too High to Contemplate?' *Belfast Telegraph*, 19 June 2017.

30 See e.g. Mark Devenport, 'Arlene Foster "Concerned" Over Security Force Amnesty,' *BBC News* [online] www.bbc.co.uk/news/uk-northern-ireland-42114814 [accessed 26 August 2018]; 'Forum Members from all Sides Oppose Amnesty for Security Forces in Troubles,' *Belfast Telegraph*, 29 November 2017.

31 Anthony Wanis-St. John, 'Back-Channel Negotiation: International Bargaining in the Shadows,' *Negotiation Journal*, 22:2, (2006), 119–144 (p.124). See also Dean G. Pruitt, 'Back-Channel Communication in the Settlement of Conflict,' *International Negotiation*, 13:1, (2008), 37–54.

32 Lauren Dempster, '"Quiet" Transitional Justice: "Publicness," Trust and Legitimacy in the Search for the "Disappeared",' *Social and Legal Studies* (2019). doi: https://doi.org/10.1177/0964663919833027.

33 Interview, Declan Kearney, April 2015.

> confidential mechanism can be established and can be made to work. It shows that you can get information without risking endangering prosecutions. It shows that you can have a sort of information or sort of factual discovery process without declaring an amnesty … the ICIR could work in very much the same way. But my question is whether it will then do very much.[34]

From this perspective, although the ICLVR mechanism provides a valuable example of the sort of process that can work, future processes should not be bound by its example in terms of its narrow scope and limited remit. The ICLVR mechanism is instructive but should not be constraining. This brings us back to the question raised in Chapter 6: what of the 'grey' truths? At the launch of the draft legislation for the SHA, one audience member asked a question that spoke to this potential gap: would the OHA collect archive material not just related to 'victims' or 'perpetrators' but on everybody else too, as all the lives that were being lived amidst the conflict contribute to the development of narratives of the past? As Chapter 4 explored, we must look beyond the victim/perpetrator dichotomy as not only are these categories problematic, but to focus on them detracts attention away from others, such as the local community, and the state.

In 2015, the story of one of the individuals I refer to earlier in this book appeared again in the news; his story told this time from a different perspective. Bernard Teggart, referred to in Chapter 3 as an example of someone with learning difficulties murdered by the IRA whose body – in contrast to that of Peter Wilson – was disposed of publicly, featured in a news story related to the Historical Institutional Abuse Inquiry. What we learned is that at the time Teggart was abducted he was supposedly in the care of St Patrick's Training School. And yet the IRA was allowed to take him from there and staff did not contact police.[35] Reading this story, I could not help but again think of Kate Turner's question in relation to Jean McConville:

> Where's the questions about what happened [to] the McConville family and social services, where were the questions about the media, [they] interviewed those kids and then forgot about [them]? … there's something missing about saying what did we not do as a society that said what's happening in these situations?[36]

Those who stood by during the conflict here, while not pulling the trigger – either literally or figuratively – had their own part to play, the outcome of which for some, like the 'disappeared' and like Bernard Teggart, was truly tragic. In Adams

34 Interview, a former diplomat who has been engaged in efforts to deal with the past in Northern Ireland, June 2015.

35 *BBC News* [online], 'Historical Institutional Abuse Inquiry: IRA Murder of Bernard Teggart "Most Horrific" Case,' 2 September 2015, www.bbc.co.uk/news/uk-northern-ireland-34130277 [accessed 16 August 2018]; 'IRA Murder of Boy (15) "Horrific Child Abuse," Inquiry Hears,' *The Irish News*, 3 September 2015.

36 Interview, Kate Turner of Healing Through Remembering, September 2014.

and McConville we have been presented with the ideal perpetrator/victim dichotomy – a story that plays out with a familiar circularity. In trying to move away from such a dichotomy, or from a hierarchy of victims, not only must we look at the 'grey' of these categories but we should also look to those who may at first appear outside of such categorisation. As argued in this book, and as suggested by Kate Turner in interview, "everything's grey, everything's a bit of both."[37] As a result, as Turner continued, the events of the past cannot be 'siloed':

> The difficulties are thinking that things are siloed, and that we can silo things, and that there aren't threads running from everything. What we realise is that … everything's connected … we can't silo things off … they're going to be interrelated … every little thing you look at is going to pull at all the other bits.[38]

The ICIR potentially shifts the conversation into less 'siloed' territory. However not everyone may welcome this. As one interviewee remarked:

> The ICIR would potentially be more contested because it's at this nub, the interface between the in-depth part and the sort of wider information part. And, whereas the Commission for the 'disappeared' was always a discrete mechanism, the ICIR … is in a more exposed place.[39]

As journalist and commentator Brian Rowan suggested in interview, this is a place that is still feared by some:

> Politically, there are people who are happy enough about the past being explored and excavated, if it's about exposing Gerry Adams or some Loyalist. If it becomes a bit more complicated, and threatens governments or intelligence agencies or police or army or our politicians, then that becomes the scary bit of the past, and the place where they don't want to go.[40]

Of course, as I argue for the value in teasing out the 'grey' of the conflict, I should note that for the families of the 'disappeared' there has been value in framing their cause in a way that simplifies the issues into black and white. Edelman argues:

> The reduction of multiple, competing claims to moral justification and rational action to neat contrasts between evil and virtue … evokes a herd spirit … Although the imaginary worlds we create do not describe the

37 Ibid.
38 Ibid.
39 Interview, a former diplomat who has been engaged in efforts to deal with the past in Northern Ireland, June 2015.
40 Interview, Brian Rowan, September 2014.

> complicated, often confusing and murky world in which we live, they do powerfully rationalise … outcomes in that world, helping people to adjust to their social situations and accept them.[41]

The 'value' in seeing atrocities in black and white is that it forces the audience to a rational choice. If we see the grey of the 'disappeared' as 'innocent victims,' if we bring in the debate over collusion and the effects of British state policy or strategy in Northern Ireland, this is likely to – as Edelman suggests – 'blur moralistic claims and rational strategies.'[42] As the story of the 'disappeared' exists for most in Irish society it has a simple moral claim and a rational strategy for resolution. The 'herd spirit' evoked has been one favourable to the pursuit of the families' claims.

Since I began researching the ICLVR in 2012, the potential of this process, and the pitfalls, have both played out. The remains of four more of the 'disappeared' have been recovered, bringing the total recovered to 13, with the remains of three – Joe Lynskey, Columba McVeigh, and Robert Nairac – still missing. However, we have seen continued political disruption linked to the fall-out from Boston College, *The Disappeared* documentary of 2013 and, of course, Adams' arrest over the 'disappearance' of Jean McConville. These events make even more evident the need for a process – such as that envisaged by the SHA – to 'deal with' the past. The recovery of remains gives us space to hope, and shows that workable mechanisms can be developed that begin to answer the suffering of victims.

Perhaps surprisingly, it was a DUP MP who alighted on one of the most significant 'lessons' to be learned from the ICLVR for the wider process. Rather than the specific workings of the process itself, he points to the importance of the spirit in which these sorts of issues are approached:

> We live in an imperfect world, and I cannot sit here and say that in every case of every murder, or every victim who feels a sense of loss, that you will be able to find a form of closure … however hard we try to deal with the legacy of our troubled past, the outcome will always be imperfect … But I do think that the Commission on the 'disappeared' is a good example of how these issues can be handled sensitively, pragmatically, and in a principled way. And I hope that that can be replicated in the new institutions that we hope will be established under the Stormont House Agreement.[43]

The pragmatism of those I have interviewed – some of whom have been critical of Sinn Féin in the past – has been a privilege to hear. In a note that Brendan Duddy, intermediary between Republicans and the British government, wrote to

41 Murray Edelman, 'Contestable Categories and Public Opinion,' *Political Communication*, 10, (1993), 231–242 (p. 241).

42 Ibid. at 241.

43 Interview, Jeffrey Donaldson, March 2015

the British in 1975 during negotiations over the making of concessions to strengthen the position of pro-ceasefire IRA leaders, he asked that they "be generous … we're all in this together."[44] The feeling I get from those I have interviewed is that there are many who are prepared to be generous – even in the most tragic of circumstances, such as those the family of Columba McVeigh had to deal with:

> what happened to my brother was awful, but there was a lot of people died here on both sides, all sides – police, soldiers, civilians, civilians in England … My brother's just another victim. While it's obviously painful for myself and my family, I see the movement towards peace – albeit fragile and difficult and all of that – as worthwhile and worthy and … a good thing … even though like a lot of people we've made a sacrifice along the way for it, I feel we have a stake in it because we made a sacrifice.[45]

44 Duddy papers, NUI Galway, POL 35 4/62 cited in Niall Ó Dochartaigh, 'Together in the Middle: Back-Channel Negotiation in the Irish Peace Process,' *Journal of Peace Research*, 48:6, (2011), 767–780 (p. 776).

45 Interview, Eugene McVeigh, brother of Columba McVeigh, August 2015.

List of interviewees

Interviewees are listed alphabetically, showing their organisational affiliation or the position they held at the time of the interview. The locations and dates of the interviews are also indicated. Four interviewees wished to remain anonymous and are identified throughout the main text and in footnotes by a brief description. They are not listed here.

Donaldson, Jeffrey	Democratic Unionist Party MP. Lisburn, 13 March 2015.
English, Richard	Wardlaw Professor of Politics and Director of the Handa Centre for the Study of Terrorism and Political Violence, University of St Andrews. Belfast, 28 August 2014.
Gormally, Brian	Director of the Committee on the Administration of Justice. Belfast, 5 November 2014.
Kearney, Declan	Sinn Féin National Chairperson. Belfast, 23 April 2015.
Knupfer, Geoff	Senior Investigating Officer of the Independent Commission for the Location of Victims' Remains. Belfast, 10 July 2014.
McArdle, Brendan	Retired *An Garda Síochána* Detective Inspector. Dublin, 16 January 2015.
McKay, Susan	Journalist and writer. Belfast, 31 July 2014.
McNamee, Adrian	Head of Policy and Research, Commission for Victims and Survivors. Belfast, 19 November 2014.
McWilliams, Monica	Professor of Women's Studies and Research Fellow in the Transitional Justice Institute at the University of Ulster. Jordanstown, 11 September 2014.
McVeigh, Eugene	Brother of Columba McVeigh, who was 'disappeared' in 1975. Belfast, 10 August 2015.
Megraw, Kieran	Brother of Brendan Megraw, who was 'disappeared' in 1978. Belfast, 26 October 2015.
Morrison, Danny	Former Director of Publicity for Sinn Féin. Belfast, 21 January 2015.
O'Doherty, Malachi	Journalist and writer. Belfast, 4 August 2015.

Ritchie, Mike	Veteran human rights activist and casework manager at Relatives for Justice. Belfast, 22 October 2014.
Rowan, Brian	Commentator, journalist and former BBC security correspondent. Belfast, 17 September 2014.
Turner, Kate	Director of Healing Through Remembering. Belfast, 25 September 2014.

Bibliography

'Abducted German Declared Dead,' *The Irish Times*, 11 August 1976

Acheson, Tanya, 'End Silence Over Dead and Let Us Mourn in Peace,' *Belfast Telegraph*, 28 April 1995

Acheson, Tanya, 'Give Us Back Our Dead, Mr Adams,' *Belfast Telegraph*, 28 April 1995

Acheson, Tanya, 'IRA Women Took Mum and Left Me in Living Nightmare,' *Belfast Telegraph*, 28 April 1995

Acheson, Tanya, 'Family Asks Clinton to Help Find Bodies,' *Belfast Telegraph*, 12 May 1995

Acheson, Tanya, 'New Revelation in Hunt for Disappeared,' *Belfast Telegraph*, 18 May 1995

Acheson, Tanya, 'Ribbon to Remember Missing,' *Belfast Telegraph*, 21 June 1995

Acheson, Tanya, 'Maskey's Cousin Murdered by IRA,' *Belfast Telegraph*, 8 July 1995

Acheson, Tanya, 'Maskey Speaks Out on Disappeared,' *Belfast Telegraph*, 14 July 1995

Acheson, Tanya, 'End Families' Torment,' *Belfast Telegraph*, 9 August 1995

Acheson, Tanya, 'Grieving Families Lobby MPs,' *Belfast Telegraph*, 2 October 1995

Acheson, Tanya, 'Five Men Quizzed on "Disappeared",' *Belfast Telegraph*, 22 January 1996

Achino-Loeb, Maria-Luisa, 'Introduction: Silence as the Currency of Power,' in Maria-Luisa Achino-Loeb (ed.) *Silence: The Currency of Power* (Oxford: Berghahn Books, 2006), 1–22

Achino-Loeb, Maria-Luisa (ed.), *Silence: The Currency of Power* (Oxford: Berghahn Books, 2006)

'Adams Called on to Pressurise IRA Over Graves of "Disappeared",' *The Irish Times*, 16 August 1995

Adams, Gerry, *Hope and History: Making Peace in Ireland* (London: Brandon, 2003)

Adams, Gerry, 'The Truth About the Disappeared,' *The Irish Times*, 9 November 2013

'Adams in New Appeal for Help to Find Missing Victims,' *The Irish Times*, 4 January 2007

'Adams' IRA Denial is a Joke, Says Ex-Provo,' *Belfast Telegraph*, 16 May 2011

Adelmann, Martin, 'Quiet Diplomacy: The Reasons Behind Mbeki's Zimbabwe Policy,' *Africa Spectrum*, 39:2, (2004), 249–276

Aggestam, Karin and Annika Bjorkdahl (eds) *Rethinking Peacebuilding: The Quest for Justice Peace in the Middle East and the Western Balkans* (Abingdon: Routledge, 2013)

Aguilar, Paloma and Iosif Kovras, 'Explaining Disappearances as a Tool of Political Terror,' *International Political Science Review*, (2018)

'Ahern Rejects NIO Arms Plan,' *The Irish News*, 4 May 1999

Åhman, Sven, 'Mr. Hammarskjöld's Not-So-Quiet Diplomacy,' *The Reporter*, 4 September 1958

Aiken, Nevin T., 'Learning to Live Together: Transitional Justice and Intergroup Reconciliation in Northern Ireland,' *International Journal of Transitional Justice*, 4:2, (2010), 166–188

Akhavan, Payam, 'Are International Criminal Tribunals a Disincentive to Peace? Reconciling Judicial Romanticism and Political Realism,' *Human Rights Quarterly*, 31:3, (2009), 624–654

Alexander, Steven, 'Kelly "has Chickened out" of OTR Testimony,' *Belfast Telegraph*, 9 July 2014

Allison, Michael E. and Alberto Martín Alvarez, 'Unity and Disunity in the FMLN,' *Latin American Politics and Society*, 54:4, (2012), 89–118

Allport, Gordon W. and Leo Postman, 'An Analysis of Rumour,' *Public Opinion Quarterly*, 10:4, (1946), 501–517

Alonso, Rogelio, *The IRA and Armed Struggle* (Oxon: Routledge, 2007)

Amnesty International, *'Disappearances' and Political Killings: Human Rights Crisis of the 1990s – A Manual for Action* (Amsterdam: Amnesty International, 1994)

Anderson, Benedict, *Imagined Communities: Reflections on the Origin and Spread of Nationalism* (London; New York: Verso, 2006)

Anderson, Brendan, 'Fresh Hope for IRA Re-Burial,' *The Irish News*, 22 June 1995

Anderson, Martin, 'Crunch Talks Under Way to Resolve Drumcree Crisis,' *The Irish News*, 4 May 1999

Anderson, Martin, 'Boys Foil Loyalist Bookies Massacre,' *The Irish News*, 6 May 1999

Anderson, Patrick, and Jisha Menon (eds) *Violence Performed: Local Roots and Global Routes of Conflict* (Palgrave, 2009), 285–316

Andreopolis, George A. and Peter Zehra Juviler, *Non-State Actors in the Human Rights Universe* (USA: Kumarian Press, 2006)

Andrieu, Kora, '"Sorry for the Genocide": How Public Apologies Can Help Promote National Reconciliation,' *Millennium: Journal of International Studies*, 38:1, (2009), 3–23

Antze, Paul and Michael Lambek, *Tense Past* (New York: Routledge, 1996)

Appadurai, Arjun, 'The Past as a Scarce Resource,' *Man*, 16:2, (1981), 201–219

'Appeal to Kidnappers of German,' *The Irish Times*, 5 January 1974

Arditti, Rita, *Searching for Life: The Grandmothers of the Plaza de Mayo and the Disappeared Children of Argentina* (California: University of California Press, 1999)

Arendt, Hannah, *Eichmann in Jerusalem: A Report on the Banality of Evil* (Harmondsworth: Penguin Books, 1994)

Aretxaga, Begoña, 'Playing Terrorist: Ghastly Plots and the Ghostly State,' *Journal of Spanish Cultural Studies*, 1:1, (2000), 43–58

Aronson, Jay D., 'The Strengths and Limitations of South Africa's Search for Apartheid-Era Missing Persons,' *International Journal of Transitional Justice*, 5:2, (2011), 262–281

Arriaza, Laura and Naomi Roht-Arriaza, 'Social Reconstruction as a Local Process,' *International Journal of Transitional Justice*, 2:2, (2008), 152–172

Arthur, Paul, '"Quiet Diplomacy and Personal Conversation": Track Two Diplomacy and the Search for a Settlement in Northern Ireland,' in Joseph Ruane and Jennifer Todd (eds) *After the Good Friday Agreement* (Dublin: University College Dublin Press, 1999), 71–95

Asian Human Rights Commission, 'Sri Lanka: Mayuri Inoka, Wife Campaigning for Disappeared Husband, Abducted' (2014), www.humanrights.asia/news/press-releases/AHRC-PRL-023-2014 [accessed 2 August 2018]

Askin, Kelly D., 'Crimes Within Jurisdiction of the International Criminal Court,' *Criminal Law Forum*, 10:1, (1999), 33–59

Bacik, Ivana, 'From Virgins and Mothers to Popstars and Presidents: Changing Roles of Women in Ireland,' *The Irish Review*, 35, (2007), 100–107

Bakiner, Onur, 'From Denial to Reluctant Dialogue: The Chilean Military's Confrontation with Human Rights (1990–2006),' *International Journal of Transitional Justice*, 4:1, (2010), 47–66

Bamford, Bradley W.C., 'The Role and Effectiveness of Intelligence in Northern Ireland,' *Intelligence and National Security*, 20:4, (2005), 581–607

Barahona de Brito, Alexandra, Paloma Aguilar and Carmen Gonzalez-Enriquez, 'Introduction,' in Alexandra Barahona de Brito, Carmen Gonzaléz-Enríquez and Paloma Aguilar (eds) *The Politics of Memory: Transitional Justice in Democratizing Societies* (Oxford: Oxford University Press, 2001), 1–39

Barahona de Brito, Alexandra, Carmen Gonzaléz-Enríquez and Paloma Aguilar (eds), *The Politics of Memory: Transitional Justice in Democratizing Societies* (Oxford: Oxford University Press, 2001)

Barahona de Brito, Alexandra, 'Truth, Justice, Memory, and Democratization in the Southern Cone,' in Alexandra Barahona de Brito, Carmen Gonzaléz-Enríquez and Paloma Aguilar (eds) *The Politics of Memory: Transitional Justice in Democratizing Societies* (Oxford: Oxford University Press, 2001), 119–160

Barker, Rodney S., *Legitimating Identities: The Self-Presentation of Rulers and Subjects* (Cambridge: Cambridge University Press, 2001)

Baum, Matthew A., 'Going Private: Public Opinion, Presidential Rhetoric, and the Domestic Politics of Audience Costs in US Foreign Policy Crises,' *The Journal of Conflict Resolution*, 48:5, (2004), 603–631

BBC News [online] 'Daughter Will Attend Funeral,' 30 October 2003 <http://news.bbc.co.uk/go/pr/f/-/1/hi/northern_ireland/3229131.stm> [accessed 10/08/2018]

BBC News [online] 'McConville Remains Return Home,' 30 October 2003 <http://news.bbc.co.uk/go/pr/f/-/1/hi/northern_ireland/3225755.stm> [accessed 10/08/2018]

BBC News [online], 'Still Waiting to Find Her Brother After 38 Years,' 27 October 2010, www.bbc.co.uk/news/uk-northern-ireland-11633757 [accessed 10 August 2018]

BBC News [online], 'Reaction to John Downey Judgement,' 26 February 2014, www.bbc.co.uk/news/uk-northern-ireland-26345071 [accessed 25 August 2018]

BBC News [online], 'The Disappeared: Sister of Columba McVeigh Talks to BBC,' 2 May 2014, www.bbc.co.uk/news/uk-northern-ireland-27251094 [accessed 10 August 2018]

BBC News [online], 'The Disappeared: Meath Remains were those of Brendan Megraw,' 3 November 2014, www.bbc.co.uk/news/uk-northern-ireland-29887678 [accessed 10 August 2018]

BBC News [online], 'OTR Letters: Tony Blair Says NI Peace Process Could Have Collapsed Without Scheme,' 13 January 2015, www.bbc.co.uk/news/uk-northern-ireland-30776891 [accessed 11 August 2018].

BBC News [online], 'Historical Institutional Abuse Inquiry: IRA Murder of Bernard Teggart "Most Horrific" Case,' 2 September 2015, www.bbc.co.uk/news/uk-northern-ireland-34130277 [accessed 16 August 2018]

BBC News [online], 'Timeline: The Disappearance of Lisa Dorrian,' 28 February 2017, www.bbc.co.uk/news/uk-northern-ireland-39116502 [accessed 11 September 2018]

BBC Radio Foyle, Willie Gallagher in interview with BBC Radio Foyle, 8 May 1999. Available at http://rfe123.org/willie-gallagher-bbc-radio-foyle-interview-transcript-8-may-2017 [accessed 30 June 2018]

Bean, Kevin, *The New Politics of Sinn Féin* (Liverpool: Liverpool University Press, 2007)

Beattie, Jilly, 'Terrorists and Soldiers Accused of Horrific Murders in Northern Ireland's Troubles Can Confess and Walk Free,' *Daily Mirror*, 10 September 2015

Beattie, Jilly, 'Secret Terror Amnesty Deal to be Dropped,' *Daily Mirror*, 23 September 2015

Beattie, Jilly, 'Allister Slams Bid to Dress Up Amnesty,' *Daily Mirror*, 24 September 2015

Beattie, Jilly, 'Kicking Up a Storm,' *Daily Mirror*, 7 October 2015

Beattie, Jilly and Martin Breen, 'Missing Bodies of IRA Victims Buried Under Family Homes,' *The People*, 29 June 1997

'Belfast Kidnap: New Appeal,' *Belfast Telegraph*, 14 April 1978

Bell, Christine, 'Dealing with the Past in Northern Ireland,' *Fordham International Law Journal*, 26, (2002), 1095–1147

Benford, Robert D. and David A. Snow, 'Framing Processes and Social Movements: An Overview and Assessment,' *Annual Review of Sociology*, 26, (2000), 611–639

Bennett, Mark and Deborah Earwaker, 'Victims' Responses to Apologies: The Effects of Offender Responsibility and Offense Severity,' *The Journal of Social Psychology*, 134:4, (1994), 457–464

Benoit, William L. and Susan L. Brinson, 'AT&T: "Apologies are not Enough",' *Communication Quarterly*, 42:1, (1994), 75–88.

Benoit, William L. and Shirley Drew, 'Appropriateness and Effectiveness of Image Repair Strategies,' *Communication Reports*, 10:2, (1997), 153–163

Ben-Ze'ev, Efrat, Ruth Ginio and Jay Winter (eds) *Shadows of War: A Social History of Silence in the Twentieth Century* (Cambridge: Cambridge University Press, 2010)

Berdal, Mats and David H. Ucko (eds) *Reintegrating Armed Groups After Conflict: Politics, Violence and Transition* (Oxon: Routledge, 2009)

Berman, Maureen R. and Roger S. Clark, 'State Terrorism: Disappearances,' *Rutgers Law Journal*, 13, (1981), 531–558

Bhavnani, Ravi, Michael G. Findley and James H. Kulinski, 'Rumour Dynamics in Ethnic Violence,' *The Journal of Politics*, 71:3, (2009), 876–892

Biesecker, Barbara, 'Renovating the National Imaginary: A Prolegomenon on Contemporary Paregoric Rhetoric,' in Kendall R. Phillips (ed.) *Framing Public Memory* (Alabama: University of Alabama Press, 2004), 212–247

Binningsbo, Helga Malmin, Cyanne E. Loyle, Scott Gates and Jon Elster, 'Armed Conflict and Post-Conflict Justice,' *Journal of Peace Research*, 49:2, (2012), 731–740

'Bishop's Hopes Over the Missing Victims,' *The Irish News*, 24 May 1999

Blaauw, Margriet, '"Denial and Silence" or "Acknowledgement and Disclosure",' *Review of the International Red Cross*, 84:848, (2002), 767–783

Blair, Johnny, Frederick Conrad, Allison Castellano Ackermann and Greg Claxton, 'The Effect of Sample Size on Cognitive Interview Findings,' *Proceedings of the American Statistical Association, Section on Survey Research Methods*, (2006), 4041–4046.

Blair, Tony, *A Journey* (London: Hutchinson, 2010)

Blondel, Jean, Jean-Louis Thiébault, with Katarzyna Czernica, Inoguchi Takashi, Ukrist Pathmanand and Fulvio Venturino, *Political Leadership, Parties and Citizens: The Personalisation of Leadership* (Abingdon: Routledge, 2010)

Bloomfield, Kenneth, *'We Will Remember Them': Report of the Northern Ireland Victims Commissioner* (Belfast: HMSO, 1998)

Boal, Frederick, 'Belfast: Walls Within,' *Political Geography*, 21, (2002), 687–694

'Bodies May be "Located in Days",' *The Irish News*, 27 May 1999

'Body Found in Bog Identified,' *The Irish Times*, 23 May 1984

'Body Found in Coffin at Border,' *The Irish Times*, 27 August 1973

'Body May be Niedermayer's,' *The Irish Times*, 12 March 1980

Bohan, Christine, 'Gerry Adams Arrested by Police Over Jean McConville's Murder,' *The Journal*, 30 April 2014, http://jrnl.ie/1442163 [accessed 7 August 2018]

Boot, Machteld, *Genocide, Crimes Against Humanity, War Crimes* (Intersentia, 2002)

Booth, W. James, 'The Unforgotten: Memories of Justice,' *American Political Science Review*, 95:4, (2001), 777–791

Borah, Porismita, 'Conceptual Issues in Framing Theory: A Systematic Examination of a Decade's Literature,' *Journal of Communication*, 61:2, (2011), 246–263

Borer, Tristan Anne, 'A Taxonomy of Victims and Perpetrators: Human Rights and Reconciliation in South Africa,' *Human Rights Quarterly*, 25:4, (2003), 1088–1116

Boss, Pauline, *Ambiguous Loss: Learning to Live with Unresolved Grief* (Massachusetts: Harvard University Press, 1999)

Boucher, Geoff, *Understanding Marxism* (Durham: Acumen Publishing, 2012)

Bouris, Erica, *Complex Political Victims* (Connecticut: Kumarian, 2007)

Bowyer Bell, J., *The Secret Army: The IRA* (New Jersey: Transaction Publishers, 1997)

Boyd, Denis and Sean Doran, 'The Viability of Prosecution Based on Historical Enquiry' (Healing Through Remembering, 2006), http://cain.ulst.ac.uk/victims/docs/group/htr/boyd_doran_1006.pdf [accessed 11 August 2018]

Boyle, Fabian, '"Disappeared" Families Lash Sinn Féin,' *The Irish News*, 26 June 1995

Bradfield, Philip, 'Troubles Killers Can Confess … but Victims Will not be Told,' *News Letter*, 24 September 2015.

Bradley, Anthony, *Requiem for a Spy* (Cork; Dublin: Mercier Press, 1993)

Bradley, Una, '"Disappeared" Man's Mother "Shattered" by End of Search,' *Belfast Telegraph*, 23 December 1998

Bradley, Una, 'Hope in the Air as Disappeared Families Tell Harrowing Stories of Loss and Pain,' *The Irish Times*, 22 June 2013

Bradley, Una, 'Kevin, and the Pain that has Never Disappeared,' *Belfast Telegraph*, 30 August 2013

Brady, Tom, 'Hunt for Bodies of Northern Ireland's Remaining Disappeared Intensifies,' *Belfast Telegraph*, 25 June 2018.

Brahm, Eric, 'Uncovering the Truth: Examining Truth Commission Success and Impact,' *International Studies Perspectives*, 8, (2007), 16–35

Braniff, Máire, 'A Tale of Two Cities? Community Relations in Northern Ireland,' ARK Research Update, (2016), www.ark.ac.uk/publications/updates/update110.pdf [accessed 7 August 2018]

Breen, Martin, 'Secret Grave is Found,' *Belfast Telegraph*, 27 February 1999

Breen, Martin, 'Legal Bid to Recover Body of Murder Victim,' *Belfast Telegraph*, 2 March 1999

Breen, Martin, '"Disappeared" Families Allowed to Bury Dead,' *Belfast Telegraph*, 30 March 1999

Breen, Martin, 'Digs Resume for Disappeared: Provos "Have Re-Visited Sites",' *Belfast Telegraph*, 2 September 1999

Breen, Martin and Desmond McCartan, 'Secret Graves "Action in Days",' *Belfast Telegraph*, 27 May 1999

Breen, Suzanne, 'Missing Presumed Dead,' *The Irish Times*, 13 August 1994

Breen, Suzanne, 'IRSP "accepts" that Former Member Dead,' *The Irish Times*, 19 December 1995

Breen, Suzanne, 'Relatives Accuse IRA on Missing Bodies,' *The Irish Times*, 9 April 1999

Breen, Suzanne, 'For Victims, Deeds Speak Louder Than Words,' *The Irish Times*, 18 July 2002

Breen, Suzanne, 'Put That Family Out of its Misery,' *Sunday Tribune*, 18 January 2009

Breen, Suzanne, 'McGuinness Unit "Told to Stop Having Informers Disappeared",' *Irish Mail on Sunday*, 2 October 2011

Breen, Suzanne, 'We All Sympathise with the McConville Children Now, But Back in 1972 Nobody Cared,' *Daily Mail*, 3 May 2014

Brewer, John and Bernadette Hayes, 'Victims as Moral Beacons: Victims and Perpetrators in Northern Ireland,' *Contemporary Social Science*, 6:1, (2011), 73–88

Brewer, John and Bernadette Hayes, 'Victimhood Status and Public Attitudes Towards Post-Conflict Agreements: Northern Ireland as a Case Study,' *Political Studies*, 61:2, (2013), 442–461

Brody, Reed, 'Justice, the First Casualty of Truth?' *The Nation*, 12 April 2001, www.hrw.org/news/2001/04/12/justice-first-casualty-truth [accessed 6 September 2018].

Brody, Reed and Felipe González, 'Nunca Más: An Analysis of International Instruments on "Disappearances",' *Human Rights Quarterly*, 19:2, (1997), 365–405

Brown, Kris and Fionnuala Ní Aoláin, 'Through the Looking Glass: Transitional Justice Futures Through the Lens of Nationalism, Feminism and Transformative Change,' *International Journal of Transitional Justice*, 9, (2014), 127–149

Bryson, Anna and Sean McConville, *The Routledge Guide to Interviewing* (Abingdon: Routledge, 2014)

Burchianti, Margaret E., 'Building Bridges of Memory: The Mothers of the Plaza de Mayo and the Cultural Politics of Maternal Memories,' *History and Anthropology*, 15:2, (2004), 133–150

Burgers, Willem P., 'Apprehension and Temptation: The Forces Against Cooperation,' *The Journal of Conflict Resolution*, 43:1, (1999), 117–130

Burns, James MacGregor, *Leadership* (New York: Harper & Row, 1978)

Burt, Jo-Marie, 'Guilty as Charged: The Trial of Former Peruvian President Alberto Fujimori for Human Rights Violations,' *International Journal of Transitional Justice*, 3:3, (2009), 384–405

Byrne, Anne, 'Developing a Sociological Model for Researching Women's Self and Social Identities,' *The European Journal of Women's Studies*, 10:4, (2003), 443–464

Byrne, Anne and Deirdre O'Mahony, 'Family and Community: (Re) Telling Our Own Story,' *Journal of Family Issues*, 33:1, (2012), 52–75

Byron, Christine, *War Crimes and Crimes Against Humanity* (New York: Palgrave MacMillan, 2009)

Campbell, Colm and Ita Connolly, 'The Sharp End: Armed Opposition Movements, Transitional Truth Processes and the Rechtsstaat,' *International Journal of Transitional Justice*, 6:1, (2012), 11–39

Campbell, Colm and Catherine Turner, 'Utopia and the Doubters: Truth, Transition and the Law,' *Legal Studies*, 28:3, (2008), 374–395

Campbell, Denis, 'IRA Makes Pledge to Give Up Bodies of the "Disappeared",' *Scotland on Sunday*, 3 September 1995

Campbell, Denis, 'Let Them Rest in Peace,' *Scotland on Sunday*, 9 July 1995

Canavan, John, 'Family and Family Change in Ireland: An Overview,' *Journal of Family Issues*, 33:1, (2012), 10–28

Canning, Margaret, 'Adams Call for Information on "Disappeared" Angers DUP,' *The Irish Times*, 12 August 2006

Cappelletto, Francesca, 'Long-Term Memory of Extreme Events: From Autobiography to History,' *The Journal of the Royal Anthropological Institute*, 9:2, (2003), 241–260

Carton, Donna, 'Where are the Bodies?' *News Letter*, 19 April 1996.

Casey, Edward S., 'Public Memory in Place and Time,' in Kendall R. Phillips (ed.) *Framing Public Memory* (Alabama: University of Alabama Press, 2004), 17–44

Cassesse, Antonio, Paola Gaeta, Laurel Baig, Mary Fan, Christopher Gosnell and Alex Whiting, *Cassesse's International Criminal Law* (Oxford: Oxford University Press, 2008)

Cassidy, John, 'Hunt for Disappeared is Over,' *Sunday Mirror*, 21 May 2000

Cavanaugh, Kathleen A., 'Interpretations of Political Violence in Ethnically Divided Societies,' *Terrorism and Political Violence*, 9:3, (1997), 33–54

Celermajer, Danielle, 'Mere Ritual? Displacing the Myth of Sincerity in Transitional Rituals,' *International Journal of Transitional Justice*, 7, (2013), 286–305

Chandler, David, 'The Road to Military Humanitarianism: How the Human Rights NGOs Shaped a New Humanitarian Agenda,' *Human Rights Quarterly*, 23:3, (2001), 678–700

Chapman, Audrey R. and Patrick Ball, 'The Truth of Truth Commissions: Comparative Lessons From Haiti, South Africa, and Guatemala,' *Human Rights Quarterly*, 23:1, (2001), 1–43

Charbonneau, Bruno and Genevieve Parent (eds) *Peacebuilding, Memory and Reconciliation: Bridging Top-Down and Bottom-Up Approaches* (New York: Routledge, 2012)

'Cheap Shots,' *Fortnight*, No. 379, (June 1999)

Chernick, Marc W., 'Negotiated Settlement to Armed Conflict: Lessons from the Colombian Peace Process,' *Journal of Interamerican Studies and World Affairs*, 30:4, (1988), 53–88

Christie, Nils, 'The Ideal Victim' in Ezzata A. Fattah (ed.) *From Crime Policy to Victim Policy* (London: Macmillan, 1986), 17–30

Christodoulidis, Emilios A., '"Truth and Reconciliation" as Risks,' *Social and Legal Studies*, 9:2, (2000), 179–204

Clark, Janine Natalya, 'Missing Persons, Reconciliation and the View From Below: A Case Study of Bosnia-Hercegovina,' *Southeast European and Black Sea Studies*, 10:4 (2010), 425–442

Clarke, Liam, 'IRA Calls in Peace "Fixer",' *The Sunday Times*, 8 January 1995

Clarke, Liam and Andrew Alderson, 'Revealed,' *The Sunday Times*, 18 June 1995

'Clinton Address to Washington Economic Conference,' *The Irish News*, 26 May 1995

Coakley, John (ed.) *From Political Violence to Negotiated Settlement: The Winding Path to Peace in Twentieth Century Ireland* (Dublin: UCD Press, 2004)

Cobban, Helena, *Amnesty After Atrocity? Healing Nations After Genocide and War Crimes* (London: Paradigm Publishers, 2007)

'Co Down Man Believes Body is his Son's,' *The Irish Times*, 21 May 1984

Cohen, Stanley, 'State Crimes of Previous Regimes: Knowledge, Accountability, and the Policing of the Past,' *Law & Social Inquiry*, 20:1, (1995), 7–50

Cohen, Stanley, *States of Denial: Knowing about Atrocities and Suffering* (Cambridge: Polity Press, 2001)

Colaresi, Michael, 'When Doves Cry: International Rivalry, Unreciprocated Cooperation, and Leadership Turnover,' *American Journal of Political Science*, 48:3, (2004), 555–570

Conflict in Cities Project: Belfast, www.conflictincities.org/Belfast.html [accessed 19 June 2018]

Connerton, Paul, 'Seven Types of Forgetting,' *Memory Studies*, 1:1, (2008), 59–71

Connolly, Maeve, 'SF Calls for IRA Apology,' *The Irish News*, 10 September 2003

'Constable Executed Say Provos,' *Belfast Telegraph*, 19 June 1978

Coogan, Tim Pat, *Michael Collins: A Biography* (London: Hutchinson, 1990)

Coogan, Tim Pat, *The IRA* (London: Harper Collins, 2000)

Council on Hemispheric Affairs, 'Forced Disappearance in Colombia' (2011), www.coha.org/forced-disappearances-in-colombia/#_ftn2 [accessed 2 August 2018]

Crenzel, Emilio, 'Argentina's National Commission on the Disappearance of Persons: Contributions to Transitional Justice,' *International Journal of Transitional Justice*, 2:2, (2008), 173–191

Crenzel, Emilio, *Memory of the Argentina Disappearances: The Political History of Nunca Más* (New York: Routledge, 2011)

Criminal Justice (Location of Victims' Remains) Act 1999

Crocker, Chester A., Fen Osler Hampson and Pamela Aall, *Taming Intractable Conflict: Mediation in the Hardest Cases* (Washington: United States Institute of Peace, 2004)

Crossland, Zoe, 'Buried Lives,' *Archaeological Dialogues*, 7:2, (2000), 146–159

Crouch, Mira and Heather McKenzie, 'The Logic of Small Samples in Interview-Based Qualitative Research,' *Social Science Information*, 45:4, (2006), 483–499

Cunningham, Dominic, 'Mother of "Disappeared" Man Has Died,' *Irish Independent*, 10 May 2007

Cusack, Jim, 'Gardai Are "Hopeful" of IRA Moves on "Disappeared" as Adams Urges End to Tragedy,' *The Irish Times*, 27 June 1998

Cusack, Jim, 'Eight More Bodies Expected to be Found Over Weekend,' *The Irish Times*, 29 May 1999

Cusack, Jim, 'McConville Found Herself Isolated as Falls Rejected British Army Role,' *The Irish Times*, 31 May 1999

Cusack, Jim, 'The IRA's "Disappeared" Return to Haunt Adams,' *Irish Independent*, 3 November 2013

Dáil Éireann Debates 5 May 1999, vol 504, no 2; 12 May 1999, vol 504, no 5; 27 November 2013, vol 822, no 4

Dalgleish, Tim and Mick J. Power (eds) *Handbook of Cognition and Emotion* (Chicester: Wiley & Sons Ltd., 1999)

Daly, Erin, 'Truth Skepticism: An Inquiry into the Value of Truth in Times of Transition,' *International Journal of Transitional Justice*, 2:1, (2008), 23–41

Das, Veena, 'Specificities: Official Narratives, Rumour, and the Social Production of Hate,' *Social Identities*, 4:1, (1998), 109–130

Das, Veena, *Life and Words: Exploring Violence and the Descent into the Ordinary* (California: University of California Press, 2006)

'David Never got Over the Passing of his Beloved Wife,' *Belfast Telegraph*, 2 July 2011

David, Roman, 'International Criminal Tribunals and the Perception of Justice: The Effect of the ICTY in Croatia,' *International Journal of Transitional Justice*, 8:3, (2014), 476–495

Day, Elizabeth, 'Jean McConville's Daughter: "If I Give Up Fighting, They've Won",' *The Observer*, 6 July 2014

De Alwis, Malathi, '"Disappearance" and "Displacement" in Sri Lanka,' *Journal of Refugee Studies*, 22:3, (2009), 378–391

de Bréadún, Deaglán, 'IRA Move on Burial Places Expected Soon,' *The Irish Times*, 27 May 1999

de Bréadún, Deaglán, *The Far Side of Revenge: Making Peace in Northern Ireland* (Cork: The Collins Press, 2008)

de Bréadún, Deaglan and Clare Murphy, 'IRA Claim That it Has no Further Information Criticised,' *The Irish Times*, 2 June 1999

De Frouville, Olivier, Chair and Rapporteur of the WGEID in interview, *Oxford University Press Blog*, 'How Can a Human Being "Disappear"?' (2013), http://blog.oup.com/2013/08/enforced-disappearance-international-law-pil [accessed 2 August 2018]

De Greiff, Pablo, *Report of the Special Rapporteur on the Promotion of Truth, Justice, Reparation and Guarantees of Non-Recurrence, on his Mission to the United Kingdom of Great Britain and Northern Ireland*, A/HRC/34/62/Add.1 (17 November 2016), https://digitallibrary.un.org/record/861416/files/A_HRC_34_62_Add-1-EN.pdf [accessed 7 August 2018]

DeJesus, Kevin M., Fernando Bosco and Iman Humaydan, 'Enforced Disappearance: Spaces, Selves, Societies, Suffering,' *ACME*, 13:1, (2014), 73–78

Della Porta, Donnatella and MarioDiani, *Social Movements: An Introduction* (Oxford: Blackwell, 2006)

Dembour, Marie-Bénédicte and Emily Haslam, 'Silencing Hearings? Victim-Witnesses at War Crimes Trials,' *European Journal of International Law*, 15:1, (2004), 151–177

Dempster, Lauren, 'The Republican Movement, "Disappearing" and Framing the Past in Northern Ireland,' *International Journal of Transitional Justice*, 10:2, (2016), 250–271

Dempster, Lauren, '"Quiet" Transitional Justice: "Publicness," Trust and Legitimacy in the Search for the "Disappeared,"' *Social and Legal Studies*, 2019. doi: https://doi.org/10.1177/0964663919833027

Derrida, Jacques, *Specters of Marx* (trans. Peggy Kamuf) (London: Routledge, 1994)

'Derry Funeral of IRA Victim,' *Belfast Telegraph*, 27 August 1973

'Derry IRA Victim Still Not Traced,' *Belfast Telegraph*, 18 August 1973

Deutsch, Morton, 'Trust and Suspicion,' *Journal of Conflict Resolution*, 2:4, (1958), 265–279

Devenport, Mark, 'Richard Haass Talks: Back at a Crossroads,' *BBC News* [online], 31 December 2013, www.bbc.co.uk/news/uk-northern-ireland-25563061 [accessed 14 August 2018]

Devenport, Mark, 'Arlene Foster "Concerned" Over Security Force Amnesty,' *BBC News* [online], www.bbc.co.uk/news/uk-northern-ireland-42114814 [accessed 26 August 2018]

de Waardt, Mijke, 'Are Peruvian Victims Being Mocked? Politicization of Victimhood and Victims' Motivations for Reparations,' *Human Rights Quarterly*, 35:4, (2013), 830–849

de Waardt, Mijke, 'The Politics of Victimhood at the Grassroots Level: Inclusion and Exclusion Among Peruvian Victim Organisations,' in Vincent Druliolle and Roddy Brett (eds) *The Politics of Victimhood in Post-Conflict Societies* (Cham, Switzerland: Palgrave Macmillan, 2018), 133–158

Diaz, Catalina, 'Challenging Impunity from Below: The Contested Ownership of Transitional Justice in Colombia,' in Kieran McEvoy and Lorna McGregor (eds) *Transitional Justice from Below* (Oxford: Hart Publishing, 2008), 189–216

Dickenson, Donna and Johnson, Malcolm (eds) *Death, Dying and Bereavement* (London: Sage Publications, 1993)

'Did Martin McGuinness Pull the Wool Over Marian Finucane's Eyes?' *The Broken Elbow*, 10 June 2014,http://thebrokenelbow.com/2014/06/10/did-martin-mcguinness-pull-the-wool-over-marian-finucanes-eyes/ [accessed 7 August 2018]

DiFonzo, Nicholas and Prashant Bordia, 'Rumour, Gossip and Urban Legends,' *Diogenes*, 54:1, (2007), 19–35

'Digging for the IRA Disappeared. Moors Murders Police Officer Searching for Peat Bog Victims,' *Mirror Online*, 8 June 2013

'Dig to Find "Disappeared" Lynskey,' *Belfast Telegraph*, 12 March 2015

Dillon, Martin , *The Dirty War* (London: Arrow Books, 1991)

Dillon, Martin and Denis Lehane, *Political Murder in Northern Ireland* (Penguin Books, 1973)

Dingley, James, *The IRA: The Irish Republican Army* (California: Praeger, 2012)

'Disappeared,' undated flyer linked to campaign. Linenhall Library collection of ephemera on victim support organisations.

'"Disappeared" Expert Hopeful on New Finds,' *Belfast Telegraph*, 2 August 2010

'Disappeared Legislation Passed,' *The Irish News*, 13 May 1999

Dixon, Paul, 'Political Skills or Lying and Manipulation? The Choreography of the Northern Ireland Peace Process,' *Political Studies*, 50:4, (2002), 725–741

Dixon, Peter and Chris Tenove, 'International Criminal Justice as a Transnational Field: Rules, Authority and Victims,' *International Journal of Transitional Justice*, 7:3, (2013), 393–412

Doak, Jonathan, 'The Therapeutic Dimension of Transitional Justice: Emotional Repair and Victim Satisfaction in International Trials and Truth Commissions,' *International Criminal Law Review*, 11:2, (2011), 263–298

Donini, Antonio, 'Negotiating with Terrorists,' in Larry Minear and Hazel Smith (eds) *Humanitarian Diplomacy* (Japan: United Nations University Press, 2007), 153–173

Donnelly, Rachel, 'Unionists Bitter at "Disappeared" Bill,' *The Irish Times*, 11 May 1999

'Doubts Remain on Identity of Body,' *The Irish Times*, 18 May 1984

'Down Family in New Appeal,' *The Irish Times*, 21 December 1981

Draft Northern Ireland (Stormont House Agreement) Bill, https://assets.publishing.service.gov.uk/government/uploads/system/uploads/attachment_data/file/706283/Draft_Northern_Ireland__Stormont_House_Agreement__Bill.pdf [accessed 25 September 2018]

Druliolle, Vincent, 'Silhouettes of the Disappeared: Memory, Justice and Human Rights in Post-Authoritarian Argentina,' *Human Rights and Human Welfare*, 9, (2009), 77–89

Druliolle, Vincent, 'Recovering Historical Memory: A Struggle against Silence and Forgetting? The Politics of Victimhood in Spain,' *International Journal of Transitional Justice*, 9:2, (2015), 316–335

Druliolle, Vincent and Roddy Brett, 'Introduction,' in Vincent Druliolle and Roddy Brett (eds) *The Politics of Victimhood in Post-Conflict Societies* (Cham, Switzerland: Palgrave Macmillan, 2018), 1–22

Druliolle, Vincent and Roddy Brett (eds) *The Politics of Victimhood in Post-Conflict Societies* (Cham, Switzerland: Palgrave Macmillan, 2018), 25–52

Dudai, Ron, 'Closing the Gap: Symbolic Reparations and Armed Groups,' *International Review of the Red Cross*, 93:883, (2012), 783–808

Dudai, Ron, 'Informers and the Transition in Northern Ireland,' *British Journal of Criminology*, 52, (2012), 32–54

Dudai, Ron, *The IRA and the Shadow of the Informer: Punishment, Governance, and Dealing with the Past* (Unpublished PhD Thesis, Queen's University Belfast, 2012)

Dudai, Ron and Hillel Cohen, 'Dealing with the Past when the Conflict is Still Present,' in Rosalind Shaw and Lars Waldorf (eds) *Localizing Transitional Justice* (California: Stanford University Press, 2010), 228–252

Dudouet, Véronique, 'Dynamics and Factors of Transition From Armed Struggle to Nonviolent Resistance,' *Journal of Peace Research*, 50:3, (2013), 401–413

Duffy, Aoife, 'A Truth Commission for Northern Ireland?' *International Journal of Transitional Justice*, 4:1, (2010), 26–46

Duggan, Keith, 'Columba McVeigh: A Lost Life Brought into Sharper Focus,' *The Irish Times*, 19 May 2018.

Eastmond, Marita and Johanna Mannergren Selimovic, 'Silence as Possibility in Postwar Everyday Life,' *International Journal of Transitional Justice*, 6:3, (2012), 502–524

Edelman, Murray, 'Contestable Categories and Public Opinion,' *Political Communication*, 10, (1993), 231–242

Elgie, Robert, *Political Leadership in Liberal Democracies* (Basingstoke; London: Macmillan Press Ltd., 1995)

Eller, Anja, Miriam Koschate and Kim-Michelle Gilson, 'Embarrassment: The Ingroup-Outgroup Audience Effect in Faux-Pas Situations,' *European Journal of Social Psychology*, 41, (2011), 489–500

Ellis, Walter, 'Army Used Retarded Man – Claim,' *The Irish Times*, 19 September 1973

English, Richard, *Armed Struggle: The History of the IRA* (London: Pan Books, 2012)

Entman, Robert M., 'Framing: Toward Clarification of a Fractured Paradigm,' *Journal of Communication*, 43:4, (1993), 51–58

EPIC, *Truth Recovery Revisited: A Contribution from Within Loyalism* (Belfast: EPIC, 2014)

Erwin, Alan, 'Anguish of the Families Continues,' *The Irish News*, 31 May 1999

Erwin, Alan and Sharon O'Neill, 'Loyalists in Knife Attack on Nurse,' *The Irish News*, 3 May 1999

'Executed Man's Body in Car – Army Told,' *The Irish Times*, 25 August 1973

'Families Get Closure with Verdicts of Unlawful Killing on Disappeared,' *Belfast Telegraph*, 22 September 2011

Families of the Disappeared, 'Press Statement for Linenhall Library,' 26 June 1998. Linenhall Library collection of ephemera on victim support organisations.

'Families "Will Stand Together Until All the Disappeared are Brought Home",' *Belfast Telegraph*, 2 November 2017.

'Family Asks IRSP to Help in Search,' *The Irish Times*, 16 August 1985

'Family in Bitter Row Over Book on Victim,' *News Letter*, 5 May 2000

'Family of Seamus Wright Respond to BBC/RTÉ Programme "The Disappeared",' *An Phoblacht*, 15 November 2013

'Family Waits After Remains Found in "Disappeared" Dig,' *Belfast Telegraph*, 16 October 2010

Farrell, David, *Innocent Landscapes* (United Kingdom: Dewi Lewis Publishing, 2001)

Fattah, Ezzata A. (ed.) *From Crime Policy to Victim Policy* (London: Macmillan, 1986)

Faure, Guy Oliver, 'Negotiating with Terrorists: A Discrete Form of Diplomacy,' *The Hague Journal of Diplomacy*, 3:2, (2008), 179–200

Fay, Marie Therese, Mike Morrissey, Marie Smyth and The Cost of the Troubles Study, *Mapping Troubles-Related Deaths and Deprivation in Northern Ireland* (Londonderry: INCORE, 1998)

Fay, Marie Therese, Mike Morrissey, Marie Smyth and Tracy Wong, *The Cost of the Troubles Study: Report on the Northern Ireland Survey: The Experience and Impact of the Troubles* (Londonderry: INCORE, 2001)

Feldman, Alan , *Formations of Violence: The Narrative of Body and Political Terror in Northern Ireland* (Chicago; London: University of Chicago Press, 1991)

Ferguson, Neil, Mark Burgess and Ian Hollywood, 'Who are the Victims? Victimhood Experiences in Postagreement Northern Ireland,' *Political Psychology*, 31:6, (2010), 857–886

Ferrándiz, Francisco, 'Mass Graves, Landscapes of Terror,' in Francisco Ferrándiz and Antonius C. G. M. Robben (eds) *Necropolitics* (Philadelphia: University of Pennsylvania Press, 2015), 92–118

Ferrándiz, Francisco and Antonius C. G. M. Robben (eds) *Necropolitics: Mass Graves and Exhumations in the Age of Human Rights* (Philadelphia: University of Pennsylvania Press, 2015)

Finegan, Rory, *Targeted Killings in Northern Ireland: An Analysis of their Effectiveness and Implications for Counter-Terrorism Policies* (Unpublished PhD Thesis, Dublin City University, 2014)

Finucane, Marian, interview with Martin McGuinness, RTÉ 1 Radio, 31 May 2014, www.rte.ie/radio1/marian-finucane/programmes/2014/0531/620815-marian-finucane-saturday-31-may-2014/ [accessed 7 August 2018]

Finucane, Marian, interview with Michael McConville, RTÉ Radio 1, 23 November 2013, www.rte.ie/radio1/marian-finucane/programmes/2013/1123/488613-marian-finucane-saturday-23-november-2013/ [accessed 16 August 2018]

Fitzgerald, Mary, 'Our Mum was Tortured says Victim's Daughter,' *Belfast Telegraph*, 2 October 2003

'Five Charged with Officer's Murder,' *The Irish Times*, 28 May 1977

'Five Freed After Questioning by RUC,' *Belfast Telegraph*, 26 January 1996

'Five Men Jailed for Link with Nairac Kidnap-Murder,' *The Irish Times*, 16 December 1978

Fletcher, Laurel E., 'From Indifference to Engagement: Bystanders and International Criminal Justice,' *Michigan Journal of International Law*, 26:4, (2005), 1013–1095

Fletcher, Laurel E. and Harvey M. Weinstein, 'Violence and Social Repair: Rethinking the Contribution of Justice to Reconciliation,' *Human Rights Quarterly*, 24:3, (2002), 573–639

Flick, Uwe, *An Introduction to Qualitative Research* (4th ed.) (London: SAGE Publications Ltd., 2009)

Fontein, Joost, 'Between Tortured Bodies and Resurfacing Bones: The Politics of the Dead in Zimbabwe,' *Journal of Material Culture*, 15:3, (2010), 423–448

'Forum Members From All Sides Oppose Amnesty for Security Forces in Troubles,' *Belfast Telegraph*, 29 November 2017

Foster, Don, Paul Haupt and Marésa De Beer, *The Theatre of Violence: Narratives of Protagonists in the South African Conflict* (Cape Town: Institution of Justice and Reconciliation, 2005)

Foucault, Michel, *Discipline and Punish: The Birth of the Prison* (London: Penguin Books, 1977)

Foucault, Michel, 'Truth and Power,' in James D. Faubion (ed.) *Power: Essential Works of Foucault 1954–1984 (vol. 3)* (London: Penguin Books, 1994)

Foy, Marie, 'New Appeal on "Disappeared",' *Belfast Telegraph*, 4 September 1995

Foy, Marie, 'Wheeler Pledge Over "Disappeared",' *Belfast Telegraph*, 8 September 1995

Foy, Marie, 'Provo Victim Jean's Family Hit Back,' *Belfast Telegraph*, 27 January 2005

Francis, Paul, 'Families in Fresh Disappeared Plea as Book Launched,' *Belfast Telegraph*, 22 June 2013

Freeman, Mark, *Necessary Evils: Amnesties and the Search for Justice* (Cambridge: Cambridge University Press, 2009)

Fujii, Lee Ann, 'Shades of Truth and Lies: Interpreting Testimonies of War and Violence,' *Journal of Peace Research*, 47:2, (2010), 231–241

'Funeral for Disappeared Campaigner Margaret McKinney,' *The Irish News*, 6 February 2017

Galiana, Soledad, 'Searching for the Disappeared,' *An Phoblacht*, 28 January 1999

Gamson, William A., *Talking Politics* (Cambridge: Cambridge University Press, 1992)

García-Godos, Jemima, 'Victims and Victimhood in Reparation Programs: Lessons from Latin America,' in Vincent Druliolle and Roddy Brett (eds) *The Politics of Victimhood in Post-Conflict Societies* (Cham, Switzerland: Palgrave Macmillan, 2018), 25–52

García-Godos, Jemima and Knut Andreas O. Lid, 'Transitional Justice and Victims' Rights Before the End of a Conflict,' *Journal of Latin American Studies*, 42:3, (2010), 487–516

'Gardai Say Body Found in Bog May be Nairac's,' *The Irish News*, 17 May 1984

Garland, David, 'Penal Excess and Surplus Meaning: Public Torture Lynchings in Twentieth-Century America,' *Law and Society Review*, 39:4, (2005), 793–833

Gassiot Ballbé, Ermengol and Dawnie Wolfe Steadman, 'The Political, Social and Scientific Contexts of Archaeological Investigations of Mass Graves in Spain,' *Archaeologies: Journal of the World Archaeological Congress*, 4:3, (2008), 429–444

Gay, Oonagh, The Northern Ireland (Location of Victims' Remains) Bill, House of Commons Research Paper 99/49, 7 May 1999

Geldard, Ian and Keith Craig, *IRA, INLA: Foreign Support and International Connections* (London: Institute for the Study of Terrorism, 1988)

Geraghty, Tony, *The Irish War* (London: Harper Collins, 1998)

'Gerry Adams Appeals for Information on Victims Secretly Buried by the IRA,' *An Phoblacht*, 21 June 2013

'Gerry Adams Arrested by McConville Murder Police,' *Belfast Telegraph*, 1 May 2014

'Gerry Adams Welcomes Discovery of Remains in Wicklow,' *An Phoblacht*, 13 November 2008

Gillespie, Kristen, 'Enforced Disappearance a "Continuous Practice of the Assads",' *Syria Direct*, 16 September 2014, http://syriadirect.org/main/36-interviews/1566-enforced-disappearance-a-continuous-practice-of-the-assads [accessed 2 August 2018]

Giorgou, Irena, 'State Involvement in the Perpetration of Enforced Disappearance and the Rome Statute,' *Journal of International Criminal Justice*, 11, (2013), 1001–1021

'Give Me My Husband's Body – Plea,' *Belfast Telegraph*, 17 August 1973

Glad, Betty, 'Passing the Baton: Transformational Political Leadership from Gorbachev to Yeltsin; from de Klerk to Mandela,' *Political Psychology*, 17:1, (1996), 1–28

Goffman, Erving, 'Embarrassment and Social Organisation,' *American Journal of Sociology*, 62:3, (1956), 264–271

Goffman, Erving, *Frame Analysis: An Analysis on the Organization of Experience* (Harmondsworth: Penguin, 1975)

Goldman, Ralph M. and William M. Hardman, *Building Trust: An Introduction to Peacekeeping and Arms Control* (Aldershot: Ashgate Publishing Limited, 1997)

Goldstone, Jack A., 'More Social Movements or Fewer? Beyond Political Opportunity Structures to Relational Fields,' *Theory and Society*, 33:3–4, (2004), 333–365

Goleman, Daniel, 'Anatomy of a Rumor: It Flies on Fear,' *The New York Times*, 4 June 1991

Goñi, Uki, 'Argentina "Death Flight" Pilots Sentenced for Deaths Including Pope's Friend,' *The Guardian*, 29 November 2017

Goode, Erich and Nachman Ben-Yehuda, *Moral Panics: The Social Construction of Deviance* (Chichester: Wiley-Blackwell, 2009)

Gormley-Heenan, Cathy, 'Chameleonic Leadership: Towards a New Understanding of Political Leadership During the Northern Ireland Peace Process,' *Leadership*, 2:1, (2006), 53–75

Goti, Jaime Malamud, 'Editorial Note: A Turbulent Past and the Problem with Memory,' *International Journal of Transitional Justice*, 4:2, (2010), 153–165

Graham, Victoria, 'How Firm the Handshake? South Africa's Use of Quiet Diplomacy in Zimbabwe from 1999 to 2006,' *African Security Review*, 15:4, (2006), 113–127

Graham, William, 'Weapons Deal May Spell End for Trimble,' *The Irish News*, 18 May 1999

Gregory, Derek, *Geographical Imaginations* (Oxford: Blackwell, 1994)

'Grundig Chief: Wife's Appeal,' *Belfast Telegraph*, 4 January 1974

Haass, Richard, 'An Agreement Among the Parties of the Northern Ireland Executive on Parades, Select Commemorations, and Related Protests; Flags and Emblems; and Contending with the Past,' Proposed Agreement 31 December 2013, http://cain.ulst.ac.uk/events/peace/haass-talks/haass_2013-12-31.pdf [accessed 2 August 2018]

Halbwachs, Maurice, *On Collective Memory* (ed. trans. Lewis A. Coser) (Chicago: University of Chicago Press, 1992)

The Right Honourable Dame Heather Hallett DBE, *The Report of the Hallett Review*, 17 July 2014, https://assets.publishing.service.gov.uk/government/uploads/system/uploads/attachment_data/file/335206/41003_Hallett_Web_Accessible.pdf [accessed 11 August 2018]

Hamber, Brandon, *Transforming Societies After Political Violence: Truth, Reconciliation and Mental Health* (New York: Springer, 2009)

Hamber, Brandon and Richard A. Wilson, 'Symbolic Closure Through Memory, Reparation and Revenge in Post-Conflict Societies,' *Journal of Human Rights*, 1:1, (2002), 35–53

Hamber, Brandon and Steve Kibble, 'From Truth to Transformation: The Truth and Reconciliation Commission in South Africa,' Catholic Institute for International Relations Report, February 1999

Hammarskjöld, Dag, 'The Elements of Privacy in Peacemaking': Address at Ohio University, 5 February 1958 (UN Press Release SG/656, 3 February 1958)

Hammarskjöld, Dag, Press Conference: 'Dag Hammarskjöld About Quiet Diplomacy,' www.youtube.com/watch?v=2T4YrDCe5Yc [accessed 25 August 2018]

Hannigan, J. A., 'The Armalite and the Ballot Box: Dilemmas of Strategy and Ideology in the Provisional IRA,' *Social Problems*, 33:1, (1985), 31–40

Harnden, Toby, *'Bandit Country': The IRA and South Armagh* (London: Hodder and Stoughton, 1999)

Harris, Sandra, Grainger, Karen and Mullany, Louise, 'The Pragmatics of Political Apologies,' *Discourse and Society*, 17:6, (2006), 715–737

Haslam, Emily, 'Subjects and Objects: International Criminal Law and the Institutionalization of Civil Society,' *International Journal Transitional Justice*, 5:2, (2011), 221–240

Hayner, Priscilla, 'Justice in Transition: Challenges and Opportunities,' Centre for Transitional Justice. Presentation to the 55th Annual DPI/NGO Conference: Rebuilding Societies Emerging From Conflict: A Shared Responsibility (United Nations, New York, 9 September 2002).

Hayner, Priscilla B., *Unspeakable Truths: Transitional Justice and the Challenge of Truth Commissions* (2nd ed.) (New York; Oxon: Routledge, 2011)

Healing Through Remembering, *Dealing with the Past? An Overview of Legal and Political Approaches Relating to the Conflict in and about Northern Ireland* (Belfast: Healing Through Remembering, 2013)

Hearty, Kevin, 'From "Former Comrades" to "Near Enemy": The Narrative Template of "Armed Struggle" and Conflicting Discourses on Violent Dissident Irish Republican Activity (VDR),' *Critical Studies on Terrorism*, 9:2, (2016), 269–291

Hearty, Kevin, '"Victims of" Human Rights Abuses in Transitional Justice: Hierarchies, Perpetrators and the Struggle for Peace,' *The International Journal of Human Rights*, 22:7, (2018), 888–909.

Heinz, Wolfgang S., 'Motives for "Disappearances" in Argentina, Chile and Uruguay,' *Netherlands Quarterly Human Rights*, 13, (1995), 50–64

'Help Trace Kidnapped Mother – MP's Appeal to Falls,' *Belfast Telegraph*, 17 January 1973

Hennessy, Mark, 'Victims' Families Reject IRA Apology,' *The Irish Times*, 25 October 2003

Herman, Johanna, Olga Martin-Ortega and Chandra L. Sriram, 'Beyond Justice Versus Peace: Transitional Justice and Peacebuilding Strategies,' in Karin Aggestam and Annika Bjorkdahl (eds) *Rethinking Peacebuilding: The Quest for Justice Peace in the Middle East and the Western Balkans* (Abingdon: Routledge, 2013), 1–46

Hertog, James K. and Douglas M. McLeod, 'A Multiperspectival Approach to Framing Analysis: A Field Guide,' in Stephen D. Reese, Oscar H. Gandy and August E. Grant (eds) *Framing Public Life: Perspectives on Media and our Understanding of the Social World* (Mahwah, NJ: Earlbaum, 2001), 139–161

Hewitt, Steve, *Snitch! A History of the Modern Intelligence Informer* (New York: Continuum, 2010)

Hill, Martin, 'Clinton and Mandela Get Grief Symbol,' *Belfast Telegraph*, 26 June 1995

Hodgkin, Katharine and Susannah Radstone (eds) *Contested Pasts: The Politics of Memory* (London; New York: Routledge, 2003)

Hodgkin, Katharine and Susannah Radstone, 'Introduction: Contested Pasts,' in Katherine Hodgkin and Susannah Radstone (eds) *Contested Pasts: The Politics of Memory* (London; New York: Routledge, 2003), 1–22

Hofmann, Claudia, 'Engaging Non-State Armed Groups in Humanitarian Action,' *International Peacekeeping*, 13:3, (2006), 396–409

Holland, Mary, 'IRA Gesture on Missing Persons Has Gone Badly Wrong,' *The Irish Times*, 3 June 1999

'Hope Grows From Tragedy,' *The Irish Times*, 31 May 1999

'Hope Remains for Return of Missing Bodies,' *An Phoblacht*, 3 June 1999

'Hoping Turned to Haunting,' *The Irish Times*, 12 May 2007

Hosking, Geoffrey, *Trust: A History* (Oxford: Oxford University Press, 2014)

House of Commons Debates 10 May 1999, vol 331, cols 38–83; 12 May 1999, vol 331, cols 324–386

House of Lords Debates 18 May 1999, vol 601, cc. 153–190; 24 May 1999, vol 601, cc. 639–713

House of Commons Defence Committee, *Investigations into Fatalities in Northern Ireland Involving British Military Personnel: Seventh Report of Session 2016–17*, 24 April 2017

House of Commons Defence Select Committee, *Investigations into Fatalities in Northern Ireland Involving British Military Personnel: Government Response to the Committee's Seventh Report of Session 2016–17* (7 November 2017)

Hughes, Susan, Preface in Publication to accompany *Quiet Peacemakers* exhibition (Ballynafeigh Community Development Association, 2014)

Human Rights Watch (Helsinki), *Children in Northern Ireland: Abused by Security Forces and Paramilitaries* (1992)

Human Rights Watch, 'Colombia's Zone of Fear,' 26 August 2001, www.hrw.org/news/2001/08/26/colombias-zone-fear-0 [accessed 2 August 2018]

Human Rights Watch, 'Time for Reckoning: Enforced Disappearances and Abductions in Algeria' (February 2003), www.hrw.org/reports/2003/algeria0203/algeria0203.pdf [accessed 2 August 2018]

Human Rights Watch, 'Mexico's Disappeared,' 20 February 2013, www.hrw.org/reports/2013/02/20/mexicos-disappeared-0 [accessed 2 August 2018]

Human Rights Watch, 'Vanished: The Disappeared of Mexico's Drug War,' 8 January 2014, www.hrw.org/news/2014/01/08/vanished-disappeared-mexicos-drug-war [accessed 2 August 2018]

Human Rights Watch, 'Where are Syria's Disappeared, Detained, and Kidnapped?' 28 October 2017, www.hrw.org/news/2017/10/28/where-are-syrias-disappeared-detained-and-kidnapped [accessed 2 August 2018]

Human Rights Watch, *World Report 2014*, www.hrw.org/sites/default/files/wr2014_web_0.pdf [accessed 2 August 2018]

Humphrey, Michael, 'From Victim to Victimhood: Truth Commissions and Trials as Rituals of Political Transition and Individual Healing,' *The Australian Journal of Anthropology*, 14:2, (2003), 171–187

Humphrey, Michael and Estela Valverde, 'Human Rights Politics and Injustice: Transitional Justice in Argentina and South Africa,' *International Journal of Transitional Justice*, 2:1, (2008), 83–105

'Hunt for Kidnappers Goes On,' *Belfast Telegraph*, 13 April 1978

'Hunt for Missing Officer is Switched,' *Belfast Telegraph*, 19 May 1977

'Hunt on for Kidnap Gang,' *Belfast Telegraph*, 11 April 1978

Hwang, Peter and Willem P. Burgers, 'Properties of Trust: An Analytical View,' *Organizational Behaviour and Human Decision Processes*, 69:1, (1997), 67–73

Igreja, Victor, 'Memories as Weapons: The Politics of Peace and Silence in Post-Civil War Mozambique,' *Journal of Southern African Studies*, 34:3, (2008), 539–556

'I'll Never Find my Son's Remains,' *Belfast Telegraph*, 22 March 2006

'"I'm Glad the War is Over," Says Adams: Easter Rising Commemoration Told Relatives Deserve Truth about Victims of Republican Violence,' *Belfast Telegraph*, 5 April 2010

Independent Commission for the Location of Victims' Remains, 'Reassurance on Information Regarding the Disappeared,' [Press Release], May 2014, www.iclvr.ie/en/ICLVR/ICLVR%20Press%20Release%20May%202014.pdf/Files/ICLVR%20Press%20Release%20May%202014.pdf [accessed 22 August 2018]

Independent International Commission of Inquiry on the Syrian Arab Republic, *Conference Room Paper: Without a Trace: Enforced Disappearances in Syria* (19 December 2013), www.ohchr.org/Documents/HRBodies/HRCouncil/CoISyria/ThematicPaperEDInSyria.pdf [accessed 2 August 2018]

'Inquiry into Widow's Disappearance,' *The Irish Times*, 18 January 1973

International Body on the Decommissioning of Arms, *Report of the International Body on Arms Decommissioning*, 22 January 1996

International Commission of Jurists, *Enforced Disappearance and Extrajudicial Execution: Investigation and Sanction* (Practitioners Guide 9, 2015)

International Committee of the Red Cross, 'Living with Absence: Helping the Families of the Missing' (ICRC, 2014), www.icrc.org/eng/resources/documents/publication/p4152.htm [accessed 9 August 2018]

International Committee of the Red Cross, 'Practice Relating to Rule 98. Enforced Disappearance,' www.icrc.org/customary-ihl/eng/docs/v2_rul_rule98 [accessed 2 August 2018]

International Criminal Tribunal for the Former Yugoslavia, 'Radislav Krstic Becomes the First Person to be Convicted of Genocide at the ICTY and is Sentenced to 46 Years Imprisonment,' [Press Release], OF/P.I.S/609e (2 August 2001), www.icty.org/sid/7964 [accessed 2 August 2018]

'Investigation Confirms 1972 Disappearance,' *An Phoblacht*, 11 February 2010

Ionescu, Stefan, 'Myths, Narratives and Patterns of Rumours: The Construction of "Jewish Subversion" and Retributive Violence in 1940–41 Romania,' *Culture and Psychology*, 15:3, (2009), 327–336

'IRA Carried Out "Thorough Investigation" Into McConville Death,' *An Phoblacht*, 13 July 2006

'IRA Continues Search for Missing Bodies,' *An Phoblacht*, 10 December 1998

'IRA Investigation Locates Grave Sites,' *An Phoblacht*, 1 April 1999

'IRA Murder of Boy (15) "Horrific Child Abuse," Inquiry Hears,' *The Irish News*, 3 September 2015

'IRA Murder Victims "Buried in Donegal": Gardai Pass New Lead to Families of Disappeared,' *Belfast Telegraph*, 11 August 1998

'IRA Pledges to Try to Bring Closure for Families,' *An Phoblacht*, 30 October 2003

'IRA's Secret Burials of Disappeared "Wrong and Unjust," says McLaughlin,' *Belfast Telegraph*, 17 April 2012

'IRA Statement,' *An Phoblacht*, 15 August 2002

Ireton, Kathleen and Iosif Kovras, 'Non-Apologies and Prolonged Silences in Post-Conflict Settings: The Case of Post-Colonial Cyprus,' *Time and Society*, 21:1, (2012), 71–88

Irrera, Daniela, *NGOs, Crisis Management and Conflict Resolution: Measuring the Impact of NGOs on Intergovernmental Organisations* (Cheltenham: Edward Elgar Publishing Ltd., 2013)

Irvin, Cynthia L., *Militant Nationalism: Between Movement and Party in Ireland and the Basque Country* (Minneapolis: University of Minnesota Press, 1999)

'Ivor Bell ruled unfit to stand trial over Jean McConville Murder,' *The Irish Times*, 19 December 2018

Jamieson, Ruth, 'Framing Blame and Punishment: Former Politically-Motivated Prisoners in Post-Conflict Northern Ireland,' *Criminal Justice Matters*, 89:1, (2012), 30–31

Jaquemet, Iolanda, 'Fighting Amnesia: Ways to Uncover the Truth about Lebanon's Missing,' *International Journal of Transitional Justice*, 3:1, (2008), 69–90

Jarman, Neil, 'From War to Peace? Changing Patterns of Violence in Northern Ireland, 1990–2003,' *Terrorism and Political Violence*, 16:3, (2004), 420–438

'Jean McConville Murder: Police Forced to Free Ex-IRA Boss Bobby Storey After Learning of Immunity,' *Belfast Telegraph*, 1 December 2014

Jeffery, Renée, 'Amnesty and Accountability: The Price of Peace in Aceh, Indonesia,' *International Journal of Transitional Justice*, 6:1, (2012), 60–82

Jelin, Elizabeth, 'Public Memorialization in Perspective: Truth, Justice and Memory of Past Repression in the Southern Cone of South America,' *International Journal of Transitional Justice*, 1:1, (2007), 138–156

Johns, Michael, 'Quiet Diplomacy, the European Union and Conflict Prevention: Learning From the HCNM on Issues of Social Cohesion,' *International Journal on Minority and Group Rights*, 19, (2012), 243–265

Kahler, Miles and David A. Lake (eds) *Governance in a Global Economy: Political Authority in Transition* (New Jersey: Princeton University Press, 2003)

Kampf, Zohar, 'The Pragmatics of Forgiveness: Judgements of Apologies in the Israeli Political Arena,' *Discourse and Society*, 19:5, (2008), 577–598

Kampf, Zohar and Nava Löwenheim, 'Rituals of Apology in the Global Arena,' *Security Dialogue*, 43:1, (2012), 43–60

Kansteiner, Wulf, 'Finding Meaning in Memory: A Methodological Critique of Collective Memory Studies,' *History and Theory*, 41, (2002), 179–197

Karl, Sylvia, 'Rehumanizing the Disappeared: Spaces of Memory in Mexico and the Liminality of Transitional Justice,' *American Quarterly*, 66:3, (2014), 727–748

Karstedt, Susanne, 'From Absence to Presence, From Silence to Voice: Victims in International and Transitional Justice Since the Nuremberg Trials,' *International Review of Victimology*, 17:1, (2010), 9–30

Kiely, Elizabeth and Máire Leane, '"What Would I be Doing at Home All Day?": Oral Narratives of Irish Married Women's Working Lives 1936–1960,' *Women's History Review*, 13:3, (2004), 427–446

Kearney, Vincent and Martina Purdy, 'Clinton to Visit in Autumn,' *Belfast Telegraph*, 26 May 1995

Kee, Herbert W. and Robert E. Knox, 'Conceptual and Methodological Considerations in the Study of Trust and Suspicion,' *Journal of Conflict Resolution*, 14:3, (1970), 357–366

Keefe, Patrick Radden, 'Where the Bodies are Buried,' *The New Yorker*, 16 March 2015

Keenan, Dan, 'Funeral of Young "Disappeared" Man Takes Place, 37 Years After Killing,' *The Irish Times*, 18 December 2010

Keenan, Dan, 'Human Remains Identified as Missing Man Killed by IRA,' *The Irish Times*, 20 December 2008

Keenan, Dan, 'Search Begins in Beauty Spot for Body of Man "Disappeared" During Troubles,' *The Irish Times*, 27 October 2010

Keenan, Dan and Liam Reid, 'IRA Derided Over its Defence of McConville Murder,' *The Irish Times*, 10 July 2006

Keltner, Dacher and Brenda N. Buswell, 'Embarrassment: Its Distinct Form and Appeasement Functions,' *Psychological Bulletin*, 122:3, (1997), 250–270

Kemp, Walter A. (ed.), *Quiet Diplomacy in Action: The OSCE High Commissioner on National Minorities* (Office of the OSCE High Commissioner on National Minorities, 2001)

Kenny, Paul D., 'Structural Integrity and Cohesion in Insurgent Organisations: Evidence From Protracted Conflicts in Ireland and Burma,' *International Studies Review*, 12:4, (2010), 533–555

Keohane, Robert O. and Joseph S. Nye, Jr., 'Redefining Accountability for Global Governance,' in Miles Kahler and David A. Lake (eds) *Governance in a Global Economy: Political Authority in Transition* (New Jersey: Princeton University Press, 2003), 386–411

'Kidnap Hunt Goes On – But Few Clues,' *Belfast Telegraph*, 12 April 1978

Kidron, Carol A., 'Toward an Ethnography of Silence,' *Current Anthropology*, 50:1, (2009), 5–27

Killean, Rachel, *Victims, Atrocity and International Criminal Justice: Lessons From Cambodia* (London: Routledge, 2018)

'Killers Put Body of Victim in Coffin,' *Belfast Telegraph*, 25 August 1973

King, Nigel and Christine Horrocks, *Interviews in Qualitative Research* (London: SAGE Publications Ltd., 2010)

Kirsch, Stuart, 'Rumour and Other Narratives of Political Violence in West Papua,' *Critique of Anthropology*, 22:1, (2002), 53–79

Knapp, Robert H., 'A Psychology of Rumour,' *Public Opinion Quarterly*, 8:1, (1944), 22–37

Kössler, Reinhart, 'Facing a Fragmented Past: Memory, Culture and Politics in Namibia,' *Journal of Southern African Studies*, 33:2, (2007), 361–382

Kouvo, Sari and Dallas Mazoori, 'Reconciliation, Justice and Mobilization of War Victims in Afghanistan,' *International Journal of Transitional Justice*, 5:3, (2011), 492–503

Kovras, Iosif, 'De-Linkage Processes and Grassroots Movements in Transition,' *Cooperation and Conflict*, 47:1, (2012), 88–105

Kovras, Iosif, 'Explaining Prolonged Silences in Transitional Justice: The Disappeared in Cyprus and Spain,' *Comparative Political Studies*, 20:10, (2012), 1–27

Kovras, Iosif, *Grassroots Activism and the Evolution of Transitional Justice: The Families of the Disappeared* (Cambridge: Cambridge University Press, 2017)

Kovras, Iosif, *Truth Recovery and Transitional Justice: Deferring Human Rights Abuses* (London: Routledge, 2014)

Kovras, Iosif and Neophytos Loizides, 'Delaying Truth Recovery for Missing Persons,' *Nations and Nationalism*, 17:3, (2011), 520–539

Kriesberg, Louis, 'Transforming Conflicts in the Middle East and Europe,' in Louis Kriesberg, Terrell A. Northrup and Stuart J. Thorson (eds) *Intractable Conflicts and Their Transformation* (New York: Syracuse University Press, 1989), 109–131

Kriesberg, Louis, Terrell A. Northrup and Stuart J. Thorson (eds) *Intractable Conflicts and Their Transformation* (New York: Syracuse University Press, 1989)

Lakoff, Robin T., *Language War* (California: California University Press, 2001)

Lamb, Sharon, *The Trouble with Blame: Victims, Perpetrators and Responsibility* (London: Harvard University Press, 1996)

Lambek, Michael and Paul Antze, 'Introduction: Forecasting Memory,' in Paul Antze and Michael Lambek (eds) *Tense Past* (New York: Routledge, 1996), xi–xxxviii

Lambourne, Wendy, 'Transitional Justice and Peacebuilding after Mass Violence,' *International Journal of Transitional Justice*, 3:1, (2008), 28–48

La Porta, Rafael, Florencio Lopez-de-Silanes, Andrei Shleifer and Robert W. Vishny, 'Trust in Large Organisations,' *The American Economic Review*, 87:2, (1997), 333–338

Lawther, Cheryl, 'Unionism, Truth Recovery and the Fearful Past,' *Irish Political Studies*, 26:3, (2011), 361–382

Lawther, Cheryl, 'The Construction and Politicisation of Victimhood,' in Orla Lynch and Javier Argomaniz (eds) *Victims of Terrorism: A Comparative and Interdisciplinary Study* (Abingdon: Routledge, 2016), 10–30.

Lawther, Cheryl, *Truth, Denial and Transition: Northern Ireland and the Contested Past* (Abingdon: Routledge, 2014)

Lawther, Cheryl, Luke Moffett and Dov Jacobs (eds), *Research Handbook on Transitional Justice* (Cheltenham: Edward Elgar Publishing, 2017)

'Lawyers' Society Facing Turmoil,' *Belfast Telegraph*, 8 May 1999

Lederach, John Paul, *Building Peace: Sustainable Reconciliation in Divided Societies* (Washington: United States Institute of Peace Press, 1997)

Lefranc, Sandrine, 'A Critique of "Bottom-Up" Peacebuilding: Do Peaceful Individuals Make Peaceful Societies?' in Bruno Charbonneau and Genevieve Parent (eds) *Peacebuilding, Memory and Reconciliation: Bridging Top-Down and Bottom-Up Approaches* (New York: Routledge, 2012), 34–52

Levitsky, Sandra R., 'Law and Social Movements: Old Debates and New Directions,' in Austin Sarat and Patricia Ewick (eds) *The Handbook of Law and Society* (Wiley Online: 2015), 382–398

Liebling, Alison, David Price and Charles Elliott, 'Appreciative Inquiry and Relationships in Prison,' *Punishment and Society*, 1:1, (1999), 71–98

Liu, James H. and Denis J. Hilton, 'How the Past Weighs on the Present: Social Representations of History and Their Role in Identity Politics,' *British Journal of Social Psychology*, 44, (2005), 537–556

Llewellyn, Jennifer J. and Robert Howse, 'Institutions for Restorative Justice: The South African Truth and Reconciliation Commission,' *The University of Toronto Law Journal*, 49:3, (1999), 355–388

'Loose Talk Can Be Fatal,' *Republican News*, 25 January 1974

Lundrigan, Samantha and David Canter, 'A Multivariate Analysis of Serial Murderers' Disposal Site Location Choice,' *Journal of Environmental Psychology*, 21:4, (2001), 423–432

Lundy, Patricia, 'Can the Past Be Policed? Lessons From the Historical Enquiries Team Northern Ireland,' *Journal of Law and Social Challenges*, 11, (2009), 109–156

Lundy, Patricia, 'Exploring Transitional Justice and its Dilemmas: A Case Study of the Historical Enquiries Team, Northern Ireland,' *International Journal of Transitional Justice*, 3:3, (2009), 321–340

Lundy, Patricia and Mark McGovern, 'The Politics of Memory in Post-Conflict Northern Ireland,' *Peace Review*, 13:1, (2001), 27–33

Lundy, Patricia and Mark McGovern, 'A Trojan Horse? Unionism, Trust and Truth-Telling in Northern Ireland,' *International Journal of Transitional Justice*, 2:1, (2008), 42–62

Lutz, Ellen, 'Transitional Justice: Lessons Learned and the Road Ahead,' in Naomi Roht-Arriaza and Javier Mariezcurrena (eds) *Transitional Justice in the 21st Century* (Cambridge: Cambridge University Press, 2006), 325–341

Lutz, Ellen and Kathryn Sikkink, 'The Justice Cascade: The Evolution and Impact of Foreign Human Rights Trials in Latin America,' *Chicago Journal of International Law*, 2:1, (2001), 1–34

Lynch, Orla and Javier Argomaniz (eds), *Victims of Terrorism: A Comparative and Interdisciplinary Study* (Abingdon: Routledge, 2016).

Macaskill, Jamie, 'Give Back Our Sons,' *Scottish Daily Record*, 8 September 1998

MacGinty, Roger, 'American Influences on the Northern Ireland Peace Process,' *Journal of Conflict Studies*, 17:2, (1997)

Madlingozi, Tshepo, 'On Transitional Justice Entrepreneurs and the Production of Victims,' *Journal of Human Rights Practice*, 13:2, (2010), 208–228

Maguire, Anna, 'McConville Family Hails Ruling by US Court that Terror Tapes Must be Given to Police Here,' *Belfast Telegraph*, 17 June 2012

Mallie, Eamonn and David McKittrick, *The Fight for Peace: The Secret Story Behind the Irish Peace Process* (London: Heinemann, 1996)

Mallinder, Louise, *Amnesty, Human Rights and Political Transitions: Bridging the Peace and Justice Divide* (Oxford: Hart Publishing, 2008)

Mallinder, Louise, 'Uruguay's Evolving Experience of Amnesty and Civil Society's Response.' Working paper (2009) Transitional Justice Institute Research. Available at SSRN: https://ssrn.com/abstract=1387362

Mallinder, Louise and Kieran McEvoy, 'Rethinking Amnesties: Atrocity, Accountability and Impunity in Post-Conflict Societies,' *Contemporary Social Science*, 6:1, (2011), 107–128

Marschall, Sabine, *Landscape of Memory: Commemorative Monuments, Memorials and Public Statuary in Post-Apartheid South Africa* (Leiden: Brill, 2010)

Marshall, Martin N., 'Sampling for Qualitative Research,' *Family Practice*, 13:6, (1996), 522–525

'Martin McGuinness Misled Marian Finucane,' *The Pensive Quill*, 11 June 2014, http://thepensivequill.am/2014/06/martin-mcguinness-misled-marian-finucane.html [accessed 7 August 2018]

Marx, Karl, *A Contribution to the Critique of Political Economy* (London: Lawrence and Wishart, 1970)

Matza, David, *Becoming Deviant* (New Jersey: Prentice Hall, 1969)

Mbembe, Achille (trans.), 'Necropolitics,' *Public Culture*, 15:1, (2003), 11–40

McAdam, Noel, 'Trimble Row After "Private" Adams Meeting,' *Belfast Telegraph*, 25 May 1999

McAdam, Noel, 'Durkan in Renewed Call to IRA for Bodies,' *Belfast Telegraph*, 29 December 2004

McAdam, Noel, 'Minister Accuses Adams Over IRA "Missing",' *Belfast Telegraph*, 21 June 2005

McAdam, Noel, 'Pressure Steps Up on Disappeared,' *Belfast Telegraph*, 4 August 2006

McAleese, Deborah, 'Jean McConville: Sinn Féin's Gerry Kelly Slams Arrest of Bobby Storey,' *Belfast Telegraph*, 28 November 2014

McCaffery, Steven, 'Nelson Probe Team Includes Collusion Unit,' *The Irish News*, 1 May 1999

McCaffery, Steven, 'PSNI Bid "May Harm the Search for Bodies",' *Belfast Telegraph*, 4 July 2011

McCammon, Holly J. and Allison R. McGrath, 'Litigating Change? Social Movements and the Court System,' *Sociology Compass*, 9:2, (2015), 128–139

McCann, Michael, 'Law and Social Movements: Contemporary Perspectives,' *Annual Review of Law and Social Science*, 2, (2005), 17–38

McCartan, Desmond, 'Move on Bill for Missing Opposed,' *Belfast Telegraph*, 12 May 1999

McCartan, Desmond, 'Safeguards for Locating Graves Soon to be in Place,' *Belfast Telegraph*, 25 May 1999

'McConville Case – Gerry Adams Comments,' *An Phoblacht*, 23 March 2014

'McConville Son Says Family Endured 31 Years of "Hell",' *The Irish Times*, 5 April 2004

McCurry, Catherine, 'Jean's Family Slam "Hypocrite" Adams Over Thatcher Apology,' *Belfast Telegraph*, 12 April 2013

McEvoy, Kieran, 'Is the Price of an Amnesty for the Security Forces Just Too High to Contemplate?' *Belfast Telegraph*, 19 June 2017

McEvoy, Kieran , *Making Peace with the Past: Options for Truth Recovery Regarding the Conflict in and about Northern Ireland* (Belfast: Healing Through Remembering, 2006)

McEvoy, Kieran, 'Apologies, Acknowledgement and Dealing with the Past in and About Northern Ireland: A Discussion Document,' *Report for Healing Through Remembering*, 2015

McEvoy, Kieran and Anna Bryson, 'Justice, Truth and Oral History: Legislating the Past "From Below" in Northern Ireland,' *Northern Ireland Legal Quarterly*, 67:1, (2016), 67–90.

McEvoy, Kieran and Graham Ellison, 'Criminological Discourses in Northern Ireland: Conflict and Conflict Resolution,' in Kieran McEvoy and Tim Newburn (eds) *Criminology, Conflict Resolution and Restorative Justice* (Basingstoke: Palgrave Macmillan, 2003), 45–82

McEvoy, Kieran and Harry Mika, 'Punishment, Policing and Praxis: Restorative Justice and Non-Violent Alternatives to Paramilitary Punishments in Northern Ireland,' *Policing and Society*, 11:3–4, (2001), 359–382

McEvoy, Kieran and Harry Mika, 'Restorative Justice and the Critique of Informalism in Northern Ireland,' *The British Journal of Criminology*, 42:3, (2002), 534–562

McEvoy, Kieran and Heather Conway, 'The Dead, the Law, and the Politics of the Past,' *Journal of Law and Society*, 31:4, (2004), 539–562

McEvoy, Kieran and Kirsten McConnachie, 'Victimology in Transitional Justice: Victimhood, Innocence and Hierarchy,' *European Journal of Criminology*, 9:5, (2012), 527–538

McEvoy, Kieran and Kirsten McConnachie, 'Victims and Transitional Justice: Voice, Agency and Blame,' *Social and Legal Studies*, (2013), 1–25

McEvoy, Kieran and Lorna McGregor (eds) *Transitional Justice from Below* (Oxford: Hart Publishing, 2008)

McEvoy, Kieran and Louise Mallinder, 'Amnesties in Transition: Punishment, Restoration, and the Governance of Mercy,' *Journal of Law and Society*, 39:3, (2012), 410–440

McEvoy, Kieran and Louise Mallinder, *Transitional Justice: Critical Concepts in Law* (Abingdon: Routledge, 2017)

McEvoy, Kieran and Peter Shirlow, 'Re-Imagining DDR: Ex-Combatants, Leadership and Moral Agency in Conflict Transformation,' *Theoretical Criminology*, 13, (2009), 31–59

McEvoy, Kieran and Tim Newburn (eds) *Criminology, Conflict Resolution and Restorative Justice* (Basingstoke: Palgrave Macmillan, 2003)

McGahan, Claire, '"Let Me Bury My Son" Pleads Mother,' *Belfast Telegraph*, 26 June 1998

McGuckin, Oliver, 'Pledge on "Disappeared",' *Belfast Telegraph*, 3 May 1995

'McGuinness Acknowledges Memory Lapse on Murder Date,' *The Newsletter*, 15 June 2014

'McGuinness: First Among Stormont's 14 Ministers,' *Belfast Telegraph*, 30 November 2009

McHugh, Michael and David Young, 'Gerry Adams Latest: Jean McConville's Son Fears for His Life, Sinn Féin Hits Out at Unionist "Old Guard",' *Belfast Telegraph*, 1 May 2014

McIntyre, Jacqueline, 'Disappeared Family Split by Search,' *The Irish News*, 5 April 2000

McKay, Susan, 'Death of Mother of "Disappeared" Man,' *The Irish Times*, 10 May 2007

McKay, Susan, *Bear in Mind These Dead* (London: Faber and Faber, 2008)

McKay, Susan, 'Lost Boys,' *Field Day Review*, 9, (2013), 128–147

McKay, Susan, 'Team of Many Skills on Trail of Disappeared,' *The Irish Times*, 23 April 2012.

McKay, Susan, 'Northern Ireland's Peace is Haunted by Ghosts Who Will Not be Silenced,' *The Guardian*, 4 May 2014

McKearney, Tommy, *The Provisional IRA* (London: Pluto Press, 2011)

McKendry, Seamus, *Disappeared: The Search for Jean McConville* (Dublin: Blackwater Press, 2000)

McKeown, Michael, 'Post-Mortem,' at http://cain.ulst.ac.uk/victims/mckeown/mckeown01.pdf [accessed 7 August 2018]

McKinney, Seamus, 'Finucane Family May Sue UUP Man,' *The Irish News*, 5 May 1999

McKinney, Seamus, 'Police Rejected Hermon's "IRA Solicitor" Claim,' *The Irish News*, 11 May 1999

McKittrick, David, 'Britain Admits Threat to Kill Niedermayer Received,' *The Irish Times*, 29 January 1974

McKittrick, David, 'The IRA Has Not Gone Away, Adams Warns Ministers,' *The Independent*, 14 August 1995

McKittrick, David, Seamus Kelters, Brian Feeney, Chris Thornton and David McVea, *Lost Lives: The Stories of the Men, Women and Children Who Died as a Result of the Northern Ireland Troubles* (Edinburgh; London: Mainstream Publishing, 2007)

McMahon, Donal, 'Family Emotions Run High,' *Newry Reporter*, 10 May 2017

McNeilly, Claire, 'I Just Want to Give Him Proper Burial, Says IRA Murder Victim's Niece,' *Belfast Telegraph*, 14 May 2015

McQuaid, Carmel, 'A Wife's Fruitless Hunt for Missing Husband,' *The Glasgow Herald*, 23 November 1994

McShane, Liz and John Pinkerton, '"The Family" in Northern Ireland,' *Studies: An Irish Quarterly Review*, 75:298, (1986), 167–176

Meier, A. J., 'Conflict and the Power of Apologies,' *Philologie im Netz*, 30, (2004), 1–17

Mendeloff, David, 'Trauma and Vengeance: Assessing the Psychological and Emotional Effects of Post-Conflict Justice,' *Human Rights Quarterly*, 31:3, (2009), 592–623

Meredith, Fionola, 'We Live Distorted Normality Where Fear Still Reigns,' *Belfast Telegraph*, 9 May 2014

Mesev, Victor, Peter Shirlow and Joni Downs, 'The Geography of Conflict and Death in Belfast, Northern Ireland,' *Annals of the Association of American Geographers*, 99:5, (2009), 893–903

Millar, Gerard, 'IRA Victims "Buried in Estate",' *The Irish News*, 21 June 1995

Millar, Gerard, 'Graves Group Backs Families Search,' *The Irish News*, 23 June 1995

Millar, Michelle, Liam Coen, Ciara Bradley and Henrike Rau, '"Doing the Job as a Parent': Parenting Alone, Work, and Family Policy in Ireland,' *Journal of Family Issues*, 33:1, (2012), 29–51

Miller, David, 'Diplomatic Vacuity,' *Observer (Uncensored)*, 1993

Miller, David, *Don't Mention the War: Northern Ireland, Propaganda, and the Media* (London: Pluto Press, 1994)

Milosz, Czeslaw, Nobel Lecture (1980), www.nobelprize.org/nobel_prizes/literature/laureates/1980/milosz-lecture.html [accessed 2 August 2018]

Minear, Larry and Hazel Smith, *Humanitarian Diplomacy* (Japan: United Nations University Press, 2007)

Minow, Martha, *Between Vengeance and Forgiveness: Facing History After Genocide and Mass Violence* (Boston: Beacon Press, 1998)

'Missing Man's Family Appeals,' *The Irish Times*, 20 August 1984

'Missing Man May Be Victim of Feud,' *The Irish Times*, 8 July 1985

'Missing Mother Reported to be Back in Belfast,' *The Irish News*, 19 January 1973

'Missing Persons,' *Andersonstown News*, 17 June 1978

'Missing Soldier "Executed" Say Provos,' *Belfast Telegraph*, 16 May 1977

'Missing Victims Bill "Reluctantly" Passed: "It's a Down Payment on IRA Ransom Demand",' *News Letter*, 11 May 1999

Misztal, Barbara A., *Trust in Modern Societies* (Cambridge: Polity Press, 1996)

Misztal, Barbara A., *Theories of Social Remembering* (Maidenhead: Open University Publishing, 2003)

Misztal, Barbara A., 'Memory and Democracy,' *American Behavioural Scientist*, 48:10, (2005), 1320–1338

Mitton, Kieran, 'Engaging with Disengagement: The Political Reintegration of Sierra Leone's Revolutionary United Front,' in Mats Berdal and David H. Ucko (eds) *Reintegrating Armed Groups After Conflict: Politics, Violence and Transition* (Oxon: Routledge, 2009), 172–198

Moloney, Ed, 'The "Disappeared" is Most Shameful Episode in IRA's History,' *Sunday Tribune*, 30 May 1999

Moloney, Ed, *A Secret History of the IRA* (London: Penguin Books, 2007)

Moloney, Ed, *Voices from the Grave: Two Men's War in Ireland* (London: Faber and Faber, 2011)

Monaghan, Rachel, '"An Imperfect Peace": Paramilitary "Punishments" in Northern Ireland,' *Terrorism and Political Violence*, 16:3, (2004), 439–461

Mookherjee, Nayanika, Nigel Rapport, Lisette Josephides, Ghassan Hage, Lindi Renier Todd and Gillian Cowlishaw, 'The Ethics of Apology: A Set of Commentaries,' *Critique of Anthropology*, 29:3, (2009), 345–366

Morgan, Austen, 'The Northern Ireland (Location of Victims' Remains) Act 1999: Amnesty, Immunity or What?' *The Irish Jurist*, 37, (2002), 306–321

Moriarty, Gerry, 'IRA Victims Campaign Stepped Up,' *The Irish Times*, 27 June 1995

Moriarty, Gerry, 'Armstrongs Mourn 'Disappeared' Father 29 Years After Abduction on Way to Church,' *The Irish Times*, 20 September 2010

Moriarty, Gerry, 'Investigator Makes Appeal Over Cases of Columba McVeigh, Robert Nairac, Joe Lynskey and Four Other IRA Victims,' *The Irish Times*, 30 September 2013

Moriarty, Gerry, 'Labour TD Rails Against SF's Moral Cowardice,' *The Irish Times*, 8 November 2013

Moriarty, Gerry, 'Gerry Adams Questioned over McConville Murder,' *The Irish Times*, 1 May 2014

Moriarty, Gerry, 'Funeral Held for IRA Murder Victim Brendan Megraw,' *The Irish Times*, 14 November 2014

Morris, Aldon, 'Reflections on Social Movement Theory: Criticisms and Proposals,' *Contemporary Sociology*, 29:3, (2000), 445–454

Morris, Allison, 'Exclusive – "Secret" IRA Victim on Disappeared List,' *The Irish News*, 30 October 2009

Morris, Allison, 'The Disappeared: Peter Wilson,' *The Irish News*, 31 October 2009

Morris, Allison, 'Emigration Rumour Hid Lynskey Murder,' *The Irish News*, 8 December 2009

Morris, Allison, 'The Disappeared – Secretly Buried Remains May Have Been Moved Before,' *The Irish News*, 10 December 2010

Morris, Allison, 'Investigators Urge Dissidents to Help Locate Disappeared,' *The Irish News*, 17 February 2012

Mulgrew, John, 'Help Us Find the Lost Seven,' *Belfast Telegraph*, 31 August 2012

Murphy, Clare and Maol Muire Tynan, 'IRA Says it has Located Burial Places of Nine of its Victims,' *The Irish Times*, 30 March 1999

Musarò, Pierluigi, 'The Banality of Goodness: Humanitarianism Between the Ethics of Showing and the Ethics of Seeing,' *Humanity: An International Journal of Human Rights, Humanitarianism, and Development*, 6:2, (2015), 317–335

'Nairac Death Trial Goes On,' *The Irish Times*, 12 October 1977

'Nairac: Police Quiz Men,' *Belfast Telegraph*, 26 May 1977

National Graves Association, 'A Brief History of the National Graves Association,' www.nga.ie/history.php [accessed 7 August 2018]

Nee, Ann and Peter Uvin, 'Silence and Dialogue: Burundians' Alternatives to Transitional Justice,' in Rosalind Shaw and Lars Waldorf (eds) *Localizing Transitional Justice* (California: Stanford University Press, 2010), 157–182

NeJaime, Douglas, 'Constitutional Change, Courts, and Social Movements,' *Michigan Law Review*, 111:6, (2013), 877–902

Nesiah, Vasuki, 'Overcoming Tensions Between Family and Judicial Procedures,' *International Review of the Red Cross*, 84:848, (2002), 823–844

Neumann, Peter, 'Negotiating with Terrorists,' *Foreign Affairs*, 86:1, (2007), 128–138

Ní Aoláin, Fionnuala and Catherine Turner, 'Gender, Truth and Transition,' *UCLA Women's Law Journal*, 16, (2007), 229–279

'Niedermayer Kidnapper Sentenced to 20 Years,' *The Irish News*, 17 February 1981

'Niedermayer: The Last Hours,' *Belfast Telegraph*, 16 February 1981

'No Real Lead to Missing Officer,' *Belfast Telegraph*, 20 May 1977

Northern Ireland Assembly Debates 26 October 1998, vol 1, page 168, col 1; 29 November 1999, vol 3; 27 February 2001, vol 9; 2; 2 November 2001, vol 12; 6 March 2002, vol 15; 29 April 2002, vol 16; 4 November 2008, vol 34, no 6; 10 October 2011, vol 67; 16 April 2012, vol 74A; 17 September 2012, vol 77; 5 November 2013, vol 89;

19 November 2013, vol 89; 13 January 2014, vol 90, no 5; 23 June 2014, vol 96; 12 January 2015, vol 100, no 5; 15 June 2015, vol 106, no 6

Northern Ireland Information Service, *Minister Pledges to Keep up Pressure for Information on the "Disappeared"*, [Press Release], 8 February 1999

Northern Ireland (Location of Victims' Remains) Act 1999

Northern Ireland Office, 'Secretary of State Welcomes Efforts Being Made to Locate Graves of "the Disappeared",' 29 March 1999, accessed at http://webarchive.nationalarchives.gov.uk/20020704124508/http://www.nio.gov.uk:80/press/1999/mar/990329g-nio.htm [accessed 11 August 2018]

Northern Ireland Office and The Rt Hon Karen Bradley MP, 'Press Release,' 11 May 2018, www.gov.uk/government/news/secretary-of-state-launches-public-consultation-on-proposals-to-address-the-legacy-of-northern-irelands-past [accessed 16 June 2018]

Nowgu, Nneoma v., 'When and Why It Started: Deconstructing Victim-Centered Truth Commission in the Context of Ethnicity-Based Conflict,' *International Journal of Transitional Justice*, 4:2, (2010), 275–289

Nuremberg Trial Proceedings Volume 10, 4 April 1946 (Morning Session), http://avalon.law.yale.edu/imt/04-04-46.asp#keitel2 [accessed 20 June 2018]

O'Boyle, Garrett, 'Theories of Justification and Political Violence: Examples from Four Groups,' *Terrorism and Political Violence*, 14:2, (2002), 23–46

Obradovic-Wodnik, Jelena, 'The "Silent Dilemma" of Transitional Justice: Silencing and Coming to Terms with the Past in Serbia,' *International Journal of Transitional Justice*, 7:2, (2013), 328–347

O'Brien, Tim, 'Bodies of Seamus Wright and Kevin McKee Believed Found,' *The Irish Times*, 27 June 2015

O'Clery, Conor, 'Big Army Inquiry After Ambush Deaths,' *The Irish Times*, 24 November 1975

O'Connor, Fionnuala, 'Tip-Off Starts New Hunt for Body,' *The Irish Times*, 8 November 1978

O'Connor, Fionnuala, 'Suspicion and Fear Over the "Disappeared",' *The Irish Times*, 20 July 1983

O'Connor, Fionnuala, *Breaking the Bonds: Making Peace in Northern Ireland* (Edinburgh: Mainstream Publishing, 2002)

O'Connor, Pat, *Emerging Voices: Women in Contemporary Irish Society* (Dublin: Institute of Public Administration, 1998)

Ó Dochartaigh, Niall, 'Together in the Middle: Back-Channel Negotiation in the Irish Peace Process,' *Journal of Peace Research*, 48:6, (2011), 767–780

O'Doherty, Malachi, 'The Indelible Stain of Barbarity,' *Belfast Telegraph*, 1 June 1999

O'Donnell, Ruan, 'Oral History and the Politics of the Troubles: The Boston College Tapes,' *History Ireland*, 20:2, (2012), 10–13

Office of the Police Ombudsman for Northern Ireland, *Report into the Complaint by James and Michael McConville Regarding the Police Investigation Into the Abduction and Murder of Their Mother Mrs Jean McConville* (Belfast: Office of the Police Ombudsman for Northern Ireland, 2006)

O'Kane, Eamonn, 'The Perpetual Peace Process? Examining Northern Ireland's Never-ending but Fundamentally Altering Peace Process,' *Irish Political Studies*, 4, (2013), 515–535

Olick, Jeffrey K. and Daniel Levy, 'Collective Memory and Cultural Constraint: Holocaust Myth and Rationality in German Politics,' *American Sociological Review*, 62:6, (1997), 921–936

Olick, Jeffrey K. and Joyce Robbins, 'Social Memory Studies: From "Collective Memory" to the Historical Sociology of Mnemonic Practices,' *Annual Review of Sociology*, 24:1, (1998), 105–140

'Omagh Bomb Group Must Disband – IRA. Push Now to Fulfil Potential of Good Friday Document,' *An Phoblacht*, 3 September 1998

O'Mahoney, T. P., 'No Cause Can Justify This Horror,' *The Examiner*, 3 June 1999

'One Drugged, One Dead: Incredible Scenes at Basque Dirty Tricks Trial,' *An Phoblacht*, 20 January 2000

O'Neil, Sharon, 'Adams is Accused of Justifying Deaths,' *The Irish News*, 1 June 1999

O'Neill, Sharon and Maeve Connolly, 'Victims' Families Pour Scorn on IRA Apology,' *The Irish News*, 25 October 2003

O'Neill, Sharon and Paul McKillon, 'New Law Gives Hope to Families of Disappeared,' *The Irish News*, 14 May 1999

'Orange Order sets Drumcree Deadline,' *The Irish News*, 17 May 1999

O'Reilly, Ruth, 'Families Launch Fresh Appeal for Bodies,' *The Irish News*, 19 June 1995

Orentlicher, Diane F., 'Settling Accounts: The Duty to Prosecute Human Rights Violations of a Prior Regime,' *The Yale Law Journal*, 100:8, (1991), 2537–2615

O'Toole, Michael and Liz Trainor, 'Families Can Finally Grieve as IRA Hands Over Bodies,' *The Irish News*, 29 May 1999

O'Toole, Michael and Liz Trainor, 'Search Yields Only Despair,' *The Irish News*, 1 June 1999

Ott, Lisa, *Enforced Disappearance in International Law* (Cambridge: Intersentia Ltd., 2011)

'"Outrage and Abhorrence" at Young Mother's Murder,' *Andersonstown News*, 23 July 1994

Palys, Ted and John Lowman, 'Defending Research Confidentiality "To the Extent the Law Allows:" Lessons From the Boston College Subpoenas,' *Journal of Academic Ethics*, 10:4, (2012), 271–297

Parker, John, *Death of a Hero: Captain Robert Nairac, GC and the Undercover War in Northern Ireland* (London: Metro, 1999)

Passerini, Luisa, 'Memories Between Silence and Oblivion,' in Katherine Hodgkin and Susannah Radstone (eds) *Contested Pasts: The Politics of Memory* (London; New York: Routledge, 2003), 238–254

Patterson, Henry, 'Sectarianism Revisited: The Provisional IRA Campaign in a Border Region of Northern Ireland,' *Terrorism and Political Violence*, 22:3, (2010), 337–356

Patterson, Thomas C., *Karl Marx, Anthropologist* (Oxford; New York: Berg, 2009)

Peim, Nick, 'Spectral Bodies: Derrida and the Philosophy of the Photograph as Historical Document,' *Journal of the Philosophy of Education*, 39:1, (2005), 67–84

Pena, Mariana and Gaelle Carayon, 'Is the ICC Making the Most of Victim Participation?' *International Journal of Transitional Justice*, 7:3, (2013), 518–535

Perera, Suvendrini, '"They Give Evidence": Bodies, Borders and the Disappeared,' *Social Identities*, 12:6, (2006), 637–656

Petition (unsigned and undated). Linenhall Library collection of ephemera on victim support organisations.

Phelan, Mark, 'Not So Innocent Landscapes: Remembrance, Representation and the Disappeared,' in Patrick Anderson and Jisha Menon (eds) *Violence Performed: Local Roots and Global Routes of Conflict* (Palgrave, 2009), 285–316

Phillips, Kendall R. (ed.) *Framing Public Memory* (Alabama: University of Alabama Press, 2004)

Phillips, Kendall R., 'Introduction,' in Kendall R. Phillips (ed.) *Framing Public Memory* (Alabama: University of Alabama Press, 2004), 1–16

Phoenix, Eamon, 'RUC Files Outline Events After Abduction of Niedermayer,' *The Irish Times*, 30 December 2009

'Police Theory in Kidnap Mystery,' *Belfast Telegraph*, 19 April 1978

'Police to Quiz Ex-IRA Man on Missing Bodies,' *Belfast Telegraph*, 19 June 1995

'Politics: Molyneaux Talks of "Death Wish",' *News Letter*, 19 May 1999

Polletta, Francesca and James M. Jasper, 'Collective Identity and Social Movements,' *Annual Review of Sociology*, 27, (2001), 283–305

Poole, Ross, 'Enacting Oblivion,' *International Journal of Politics, Culture and Society*, 22:2, (2009), 149–157

'Post-Ceasefire Confidence: Mitchell Lynchpin to Progress,' *Belfast Telegraph*, 30 July 1997

Powell, Jonathan, *Great Hatred, Little Room: Making Peace in Northern Ireland* (London: Vintage Books, 2009)

Powell, Jonathan, 'How to Talk to Terrorists,' *The Guardian*, 7 October 2014

Power, Rosemary, 'Death in Ireland: Deaths, Wakes and Funerals in Contemporary Irish Society,' in Donna Dickenson and Malcolm Johnson (eds) *Death, Dying and Bereavement* (London: Sage Publications, 1993), 21–25

Power, Samantha, 'Bystanders to Genocide,' *Atlantic Monthly*, 1 September 2001, www.theatlantic.com/magazine/archive/2001/09/bystanders-to-genocide/304571/10/ [accessed 9 August 2018]

Press Association News, 26 June 1995

'Priest Joins in Plea About Man's Body,' *The Irish Times*, 21 August 1973

'Provisionals Admit Killing Officer,' *The Irish Times*, 17 May 1977

'Provisionals Admit to Border Killings,' *The Irish Times*, 5 September 1980

Provost, James H., 'Canonical Aspects of the Treatment of the Dead,' *The Jurist*, 59, (1999), 203–213

Pruitt, Dean G., 'Back-Channel Communication in the Settlement of Conflict,' *International Negotiation*, 13:1, (2008), 37–54

Purdy, Martina, 'Bishop's Plea on Weapons,' *Belfast Telegraph*, 1 May 1999

Purdy, Martina, 'Unionists Reaffirm: "No Guns, No Deal",' *Belfast Telegraph*, 18 May 1999

Purdy, Martina and Desmond McCartan, 'Accord Hopes Rising,' *Belfast Telegraph*, 15 May 1999

Purdy, Martina and Desmond McCartan, 'Trimble's Deal Pressure,' *Belfast Telegraph*, 17 May 1999

'Questions on IRA Victims,' *The Irish News*, 24 May 1995

Patton, Michael Quinn, *Qualitative Research and Evaluation Methods* (3rd ed.) (London: SAGE, 2002)

Reese, Stephen D., Oscar H. Gandy and August E. Grant (eds) *Framing Public Life: Perspectives on Media and our Understanding of the Social World* (Mahwah, NJ: Earlbaum, 2001)

Regan, Claire, 'Tragic Mother Passes Away,' *Belfast Telegraph*, 26 June 2001

'Remains Located After IRA Review,' *An Phoblacht*, 4 September 2003

Renshaw, Layla, *Exhuming Loss: Memory, Materiality and Mass Graves of the Spanish Civil War* (California: Left Coast Press, 2011)

Report of the Consultative Group on the Past, 2009, http://cain.ulst.ac.uk/victims/docs/consultative_group/cgp_230109_report.pdf [accessed 11 August 2018]

'Republican Efforts Continue to Retrieve Missing Bodies,' *An Phoblacht*, 13 July 2006

'Republican "Not Fit" to Stand Trial Over McConville Killing, Court Hears,' *The Irish Times*, 14 November 2017

'Republican Shootings Halted "by September 11th",' *The Irish News*, 16 November 2001

'Retarded Man Still Missing,' *The Irish Times*, 29 September 1973

Rico, Monica, 'The Limits of Memory: Private and Public in the Remembrance of Prince Albert,' *The Communication Review*, 2:1, (1997), 19–41

Ricoeur, Paul, *Memory, History, Forgetting* (Chicago; London: University of Chicago Press, 2004)

Ríos, Luis, José Ignacio Casado Ovejero and Jorge Puente Prieto, 'Identification Process in Mass Graves from The Spanish Civil War I,' *Forensic Science International*, 199, (2010), e27-e36

Robben, Antonius C. G. M., 'Disappearance and Reburial in Argentina,' in Jeffrey A. Sluka (ed.) *Death Squad: The Anthropology of State Terror* (Philadelphia: University of Pennsylvania Press, 2000), 93–113

Robben, Antonius C. G. M., *Political Violence and Trauma in Argentina* (Philadelphia: University of Pennsylvania Press, 2005)

Robben, Antonius C. G. M., 'Exhumations, Territoriality, and Necropolitics in Chile and Argentina,' in Francisco Ferrándiz and Antonius C. G. M. Robben (eds) *Necropolitics* (Philadelphia: University of Pennsylvania Press, 2015), 53–75

Robins, Simon, 'Ambiguous Loss in a Non-Western Context: Families of the Disappeared in Postconflict Nepal,' *Family Relations*, 59:3, (2010), 253–268

Robins, Simon, 'Towards Victim-Centred Transitional Justice: Understanding the Needs of Families of the Disappeared in Postconflict Nepal,' *International Journal of Transitional Justice*, 5:1, (2011), 75–98

Robins, Simon, *Families of the Missing: A Test for Contemporary Approaches to Transitional Justice* (London: Routledge, 2013)

Roht-Arriaza, Naomi, 'The New Landscape of Transitional Justice,' in Naomi Roht-Arriaza and Javier Mariezcurrena (eds) *Transitional Justice in the 21st Century* (Cambridge: Cambridge University Press, 2006), 1–16

Roht-Arriaza, Naomi and Javier Mariezcurrena (eds) *Transitional Justice in the 21st Century* (Cambridge: Cambridge University Press, 2006)

Rolston, Bill, 'News Fit to Print,' in Bill Rolston (ed.) *The Media and Northern Ireland: Covering the Troubles* (London: Macmillan Publishing, 1991), 152–186

Rolston, Bill (ed.), *The Media and Northern Ireland: Covering the Troubles* (London: Macmillan Publishing, 1991)

Rolston, Bill, 'Dealing with the Past: Pro-State Paramilitaries, Truth and Transition in Northern Ireland,' *Human Rights Quarterly*, 28:3, (2006), 652–675

Rolston, Bill, 'Facing Reality: The Media, the Past and Conflict Transformation in Northern Ireland,' *Journal of Crime, Media and Culture*, 3:3, (2007), 345–364

Rome Statute of the International Criminal Court (17 July 1998), www.icc-cpi.int/NR/rdonlyres/ADD16852-AEE9-4757-ABE7-9CDC7CF02886/283503/RomeStatutEng1.pdf [accessed 2 August 2018]

Rosenblatt, Adam, *Digging for the Disappeared: Forensic Science After Atrocity* (Stanford: Stanford University Press, 2015)

Ross, Fiona C., 'On Having Voice and Being Heard: Some After-Effects of Testifying Before the South African Truth and Reconciliation Commission,' *Anthropological Theory*, 3:3, (2003), 325–341

Ross, Fiona C., 'An Acknowledged Failure: Women, Voice, Violence, and the South African Truth and Reconciliation Commission,' in Rosalind Shaw and Lars Waldorf (eds) *Localizing Transitional Justice* (California: Stanford University Press, 2010), 69–91

Rotberg, Robert I., 'Truth Commissions and the Provision of Truth, Justice, and Reconciliation,' in Robert I. Rotberg and Dennis Thompson (eds) *Truth v. Justice: The Morality of Truth Commissions* (Princeton: Princeton University Press, 2000), 3–21

Rotberg, Robert I. and Dennis Thompson (eds) *Truth v. Justice: The Morality of Truth Commissions* (Princeton: Princeton University Press, 2000)

Rowan, Brian, 'Move to Distance IRA from Missing West Belfast Man,' *Belfast Telegraph*, 2 November 2009

Rowan, Brian, 'Revealed: How Haass Aims to Seal a Deal in Six Days,' *Belfast Telegraph*, 13 December 2013

Rowan, Brian, 'Hallett Review: Dealing with Past Needs a New Process,' *Belfast Telegraph*, 18 July 2014

Rozema, Ralph, 'Forced Disappearance in an Era of Globalization: Biopolitics, Shadow Networks, and Imagined Worlds,' *American Anthropologist*, 113:4, (2011), 582–593

RTÉ News [online], 'Orde Apologises to McConville Family,' 14 August 2006, www.rte.ie/news/2006/0814/mcconville

Ruane, Joseph, 'Contemporary Republicanism and the Strategy of Armed Struggle,' in John Coakley (ed.) *From Political Violence to Negotiated Settlement: The Winding Path to Peace in Twentieth Century Ireland* (Dublin: UCD Press, 2004)

Ruane, Joseph and Jennifer Todd (eds) *After the Good Friday Agreement* (Dublin: University College Dublin Press, 1999)

Ruane, Joseph and Jennifer Todd, 'Path Dependence in Settlement Processes: Explaining Settlement in Northern Ireland,' *Political Studies*, 55:2, (2007), 442–458

'RUC Holds 5 in Inquiry on "Disappeared",' *The Irish Times*, 26 January 1996

Ruiz Romero, Gabriel, 'Voices Around Us: Memory and Community Empowerment in Reconstruction Efforts in Colombia,' *International Journal of Transitional Justice*, 6:3, (2012), 1–11

Rutherford, Adrian and McCaffery, Steven, 'Sinn Féin Chief Denies Involvement in Murder of McConville,' *Belfast Telegraph*, 30 March 2010

Ryan, Jeffrey J., 'The Impact of Democratization on Revolutionary Movements,' *Comparative Politics*, 27:1, (1994), 27–44

Ryan, Philip, 'Gerry Adams Says Making Jean McConville's Children Orphans is "What Happens in War",' *Belfast Telegraph*, 3 April 2015

Sanders, Andrew, *Inside the IRA: Dissident Republicans and the War for Legitimacy* (Edinburgh: Edinburgh University Press, 2011)

Sarat, Austin and Patricia Ewick, *The Handbook of Law and Society* (Wiley Online: 2015)

'SAS Captain Executed,' *Republican News*, 21 May 1977

Schaefer, Sarah, 'Parliament: Ministers Attacked for Deal on "Disappeared",' *The Independent*, 11 May 1999

Schafft, Gretchen and Gerhard Zeidler, *Commemorating Hell: The Public Memory of Mittelbau-Dora* (Urbana: University of Illinois Press, 2011)

Scheff, Thomas J., 'The Structure of Context: Deciphering Frame Analysis,' *Sociological Theory*, 23:4, (2005), 368–385

Schirmer, Jennifer G., '"Those Who Die for Life Cannot be Called Dead": Women and Human Rights Protest in Latin America,' *Feminist Review*, 32, (1989), 3–29

Schudson, Michael, 'Cultural Memory: A Special Issue,' *The Communication Review*, 2:1, (1997), 1–2

Schudson, Michael, 'Lives, Laws, and Language: Commemorative versus Non-Commemorative Forms of Effective Public Memory,' *The Communication Review*, 2:1, (1997), 3–17

Schwarz-Marin, Ernesto and Arely Cruz-Santiago, 'Forensic Civism: Articulating Science, DNA and Kinship in Contemporary Mexico and Colombia,' *Human Remains and Violence: An Interdisciplinary Journal*, 2:1, (2016), 58–74

Schwarz-Marin, Ernesto and Arely Cruz-Santiago, 'Pure Corpses, Dangerous Citizens,' *Social Research*, 83:2, (2016), 483–510

Scovazzi, Tullio and Gabriella Citroni, *The Struggle Against Enforced Disappearance and the 2007 United Nations Convention* (Leiden; Boston: Martinus Nijhoff Publishers, 2007)

Seanad Éireann Debate 13 May 1999, vol 159, no 9

'Search for Northern Ireland's Disappeared,' *Belfast Telegraph*, 7 August 2010

'Search Goes on for Missing Officer,' *The Irish Times*, 20 May 1977

Shapiro, Walter and Kathleen Adams, 'Mama Mia, That's a Mea Culpa,' *Time*, 146:26, (1997), 18

Sharrock, David, 'Families Hope Ceasefire May Solve Mystery of Ulster's "Disappeared",' *The Guardian*, 3 October 1994

Shaw, Rosalind and Lars Waldorf, 'Introduction: Localizing Transitional Justice,' in Rosalind Shaw and Lars Waldorf (eds) *Localizing Transitional Justice* (California: Stanford University Press, 2010), 3–26

Shaw, Rosalind and Lars Waldorf (eds) *Localizing Transitional Justice* (California: Stanford University Press, 2010)

Shirlow, Peter, 'Fear and Ethnic Division,' *Peace Review*, 13:1, (2001), 67–74

Shirlow, Peter, Jonathan Tonge, James McAuley and Catherine McGlynn, *Abandoning Historical Conflict? Former Political Prisoners and Reconciliation in Northern Ireland*, (Manchester: Manchester University Press, 2010)

Shugart, Matthew Soberg, 'Guerrillas and Elections: An Institutionalist Perspective on the Costs of Conflict and Competition,' *International Studies Quarterly*, 36, (1992), 121–152

Sieber, Joan E. and Barbara Stanley, 'Ethical and Professional Dimensions of Socially Sensitive Research,' *American Psychologist*, 43:1, (1988), 49–55

Silke, Andrew, 'Rebel's Dilemma: The Changing Relationship Between the IRA, Sinn Féin and Paramilitary Vigiliantism in Northern Ireland,' *Terrorism and Political Violence*, 11:1, (1999), 55–93

Simic, Olivera and Kathleen Daly, '"One Pair of Shoes, One Life": Steps Towards Accountability for Genocide in Srebenica,' *International Journal of Transitional Justice*, 5:3, (2011), 477–491

Sluka, Jeffrey A. (ed.) *Death Squad: The Anthropology of State Terror* (Philadelphia: University of Pennsylvania Press, 2000)

Sluka, Jeffrey A., 'Introduction: State Terror and Anthropology,' in Jeffrey A. Sluka (ed.) *Death Squad: The Anthropology of State Terror* (Philadelphia: University of Pennsylvania Press, 2000), 1–45

Smith, David M., 'Tales of Matewan: The Construction of a Usable Past,' *The Communication Review*, 2:1, (1997), 59–88

Smith, Nick, *I Was Wrong: The Meanings of Apologies* (Cambridge: Cambridge University Press, 2008)

Smyth, Marie, *Residual Matters Relating to Victims of the Troubles in Light of the Agreement Document*, Submission to the Northern Ireland Commission on Victims, 22 April 1998 (INCORE)

Smyth, Marie Breen, *Truth Recovery and Justice After Conflict: Managing Violent Pasts* (London: Routledge, 2007)

Smyth, Marie Breen, 'The Uses of Suffering: Victims as Moral Beacons or Icons of Grievance,' in Vincent Druliolle and Roddy Brett (eds) *The Politics of Victimhood in Post-Conflict Societies* (Cham, Switzerland: Palgrave Macmillan, 2018), 211–236.

Smyth, Marie and Marie-Therese Fay (eds) *Personal Accounts from Northern Ireland's Troubles: Public Conflict, Private Loss* (London: Pluto Press, 2000)

'Snatched Mother Missing a Month,' *Belfast Telegraph*, 16 January 1973

Snow, David A. and Robert D. Benford, 'Ideology, Frame Resonance, and Participant Mobilization,' *International Social Movement Research*, 1, (1988), 197–217

Snow, David A., E. Burke Rochford, Jr., Steven K. Worden and Robert D. Benford, 'Frame Alignment Processes, Micromobilization, and Movement Participation,' *American Sociological Review*, 51:4, (1986), 464–481

Snyder, Jack and Leslie Vinjamuri, 'Trials and Errors: Principle and Pragmatism in Strategies of International Justice,' *International Security*, 28:3, (2004), 5–44

Sofer, Sasson, 'The Diplomat as a Stranger,' *Diplomacy and Statecraft*, 8:3, (1997), 179–186

Sparre, Kirsten, 'Megaphone Diplomacy in the Northern Irish Peace Process,' *Harvard International Journal of Press/Politics*, 6:1, (2001), 88–104

Stamato, Linda, 'Peace and the Culture and Politics of Apology,' *Peace Review*, 20:3, (2008), 389–397

Staub, Ervin, 'Reconciliation After Genocide, Mass Killing, or Intractable Conflict: Understanding the Roots of Violence, Psychological Recovery, and Steps Toward a General Theory,' *Political Psychology*, 27:6, (2006), 867–894

Stedman, Stephen John, *Peacemaking in Civil War: International Mediation in Zimbabwe, 1974–1980* (London: Lynne Rienner Publishers, Inc., 1991)

Stedman, Stephen John, 'Spoiler Problems in Peace Processes,' *International Security*, 22:2, (1997), 5–53

Stephen, Lynn, 'Women's Rights are Human Rights,' *American Ethnologist*, 22:4, (1995), 807–827

'Still Waiting,' *Andersonstown News*, 27 May 1978

Stormont House Agreement, www.gov.uk/government/publications/the-stormont-house-agreement [accessed 16 August 2018]

Stormont House Agreement, Model Implementation Bill. Available at www.caj.org.uk/contents/1289

Stover, Eric, 'Witnesses and the Promises of Justice in The Hague,' in Eric Stover and Harvey Weinstein (eds) *My Neighbour, My Enemy: Justice and Community in the Aftermath of Mass Atrocity* (Cambridge: Cambridge University Press, 2004), 104–120

Stover, Eric and Harvey Weinstein (eds) *My Neighbour, My Enemy: Justice and Community in the Aftermath of Mass Atrocity* (Cambridge: Cambridge University Press, 2004)

Stover, Eric and Rachel Shigekane, 'The Missing in the Aftermath of War: When do the Needs of Victims' Families and International War Crimes Tribunals Clash?' *International Review of the Red Cross*, 84:848, (2002), 845–866

Stover, Eric, William D. Haglund and Margaret Samuels, 'Exhumation of Mass Graves in Iraq,' *JAMA: The Journal of the American Medical Association*, 290:5, (2003), 663–666

Suchman, Mark C., 'Managing Legitimacy: Strategic and Institutional Approaches,' *Academy of Management Review*, 20:3, (1995), 571–610

Sutton, Malcolm, *Bear in Mind These Dead* (1994), at http://cain.ulst.ac.uk/sutton/book/#append [accessed 7 August 2018]

Tangney, June Price, 'The Self-Conscious Emotions: Shame, Guilt, Embarrassment and Pride,' in Tim Dalgleish and Mick J. Power (eds) *Handbook of Cognition and Emotion* (Chicester: Wiley & Sons Ltd., 1999), 541–568

Tangney, June Price, Rowland S. Miller, Laura Flicker and Deborah Hill Barlow, 'Are Shame, Guilt and Embarrassment Distinct Emotions?' *Journal of Personality and Social Psychology*, 70:6, (1996), 1256–1269

Tarrow, Sidney, *Power in Movement: Social Movements and Contentious Politics* (Cambridge: Cambridge University Press, 1998)

Taussig, Michael, 'Culture of Terror – Space of Death. Roger Casement's Putumayo Report and the Explanation of Torture,' *Comparative Studies in Society and History*, 26:3, (1984), 467–497

Taussig, Michael T., *Shamanism, Colonialism, and the Wild Man: A Study in Terror and Healing* (Chicago; London: Chicago University Press, 1986)

Taussig, Michael T., *The Nervous System* (New York: Routledge, 1992)

Tayler, Wilder, 'Background to the Elaboration of the Draft International Convention for the Protection of All Persons from Enforced Disappearance,' *The Review/International Commission of Jurists*, 62–63, (2001), 63–72

Taylor, Peter, *States of Terror: Democracy and Political Violence* (Harmondsworth: Penguin, 1994)

Taylor, Peter, *Provos: The IRA and Sinn Féin* (Bloomsbury Publishing, 1998)

Teitel, Ruti G., *Transitional Justice* (Oxford: Oxford University Press, 2000)

Templeton, Darwin, 'Loyalist Parade Plans,' *Belfast Telegraph*, 17 May 1999

Templeton, Darwin, 'With Just 46 Days to Drumcree, Do These Pictures Represent the Shape of Things to Come?' *Belfast Telegraph*, 19 May 1999

Templeton, Darwin, Martin Breen, and Michael Devine, 'Peace at Last,' *Belfast Telegraph*, 28 May 1999

Thaler, Mathias, 'Just Pretending: Political Apologies for Historical Injustice and Vice's Tribute to Virtue,' *Critical Review of International Social and Political Philosophy*, 15:3, (2012), 259–278

'The Disappeared,' at www.iclvr.ie/en/iclvr/pages/thedisappeared [accessed 2 August 2018]

'The Disappeared – Peter Wilson – Family in Attendance as Remains Taken From Beach,' *The Irish News*, 4 November 2010

The Forgiveness Project, 'Margaret McKinney,' http://theforgivenessproject.com/stories/margaret-mckinney-northern-ireland/ [accessed 7 June 2018]

'The Mourning Begins,' *The Irish News*, 29 May 1999

The Queen v John Anthony Downey [2014]

'The Release of Gerry Adams – Press Conference,' www.youtube.com/watch?v=qxcgDT8A4lQ [accessed 7 August 2018]

Thornton, Chris, 'Missing Bodies Located "Soon",' *Belfast Telegraph*, 31 August 1998

Thornton, Chris, 'Families of Missing in Appeal for End to Wait,' *Belfast Telegraph*, 26 April 2005

Thornton, Chris, 'Washington Pressure over Disappeared,' *Belfast Telegraph*, 14 June 2005

Thornton, Chris and Gavin Mairs, 'Troops on Alert,' *Belfast Telegraph*, 22 May 1999

Thornton, Chris and Peter McVerry, 'The Agony Goes On,' *Belfast Telegraph*, 29 May 1999

Thorpe, Nick, 'Mother's Hope She Can Lay Her Son to Rest,' *The Scotsman*, 27 June 1998

Throop, Elizabeth A., *Net Curtains and Closed Doors* (Westport: Bergin and Garvey, 1999)

Tolbert, David, 'Enforced Disappearances: Justice for the Disappeared has a Woman's Face,' *The International Centre for Transitional Justice* (30 August 2013) https://ictj.org/news/justice-disappeared-has-woman's-face [accessed 2 August 2018]

Tonge, Jonathan, '"They Haven't Gone Away, You Know," Irish Republican "Dissidents" and "Armed Struggle",' *Terrorism and Political Violence*, 16:3, (2004), 671–693

Tonkin, Elizabeth, *Narrating Our Pasts: The Social Construction of Oral History* (Cambridge: Cambridge University Press, 1992)

Toolis, Kevin, *Rebel Hearts: Journeys within the IRA's Soul* (London: Picador, 1995)

Toolis, Kevin, 'War Crimes of the IRA,' *The Guardian*, 2 June 1999

Torney, Kathryn, 'Adams Pledge on "the Disappeared",' *Belfast Telegraph*, 13 May 1998

Toros, Harmonie, '"We Don't Negotiate with Terrorists!": Legitimacy and Complexity in Terrorist Conflicts,' *Security Dialogue*, 39:4, (2008), 407–426

'Tour for Troubles' "Missing" Exhibition,' *Belfast Telegraph*, 27 January 2014

Trainor, Liz, 'RUC Set to Crack Down on Dissident Loyalist Groups,' *The Irish News*, 1 May 1999

Trainor, Liz, 'Missing Mother's Family Plan Burial,' *The Irish News*, 11 May 1999

Trainor, Liz, 'Executive to be Appointed on Thursday,' *The Irish News*, 17 May 1999

Trouillot, Michel-Rolph, *Silencing the Past: Power and the Production of History* (Boston: Beacon Press, 1995)

Trouillot, Michel-Rolph, 'Abortive Rituals: Historical Apologies in the Global Era,' *Interventions: International Journal of Postcolonial Studies*, 2:2, (2000), 171–186

Tully, Sheila R., 'A Painful Purgatory: Grief and the Nicaraguan Mothers of the Disappeared,' *Social Science and Medicine*, 40:12, (1995), 1597–1610

Uffindell, Rosie, '"Disappeared" Law Set to Clear Final Hurdle,' *The Irish News*, 24 May 1999

United Nations Commission on Human Rights, *Civil and Political Rights, Including Questions of: Disappearances and Summary Executions, Report Submitted by Mr Manfred Nowak, Independent Expert Charged with Examining the Existing International Criminal and Human Rights Framework for the Protection of Persons from Enforced or Involuntary Disappearances*, E/CN.4/2002/71 (8 January 2002), www.icaed.org/fileadmin/user_upload/G0210026.pdf [accessed 2 August 2018]

United Nations, *Declaration on the Protection of all Persons from Enforced Disappearance*, A/RES/47/133 (18 December 1992), www.un.org/documents/ga/res/47/a47r133.htm [accessed 2 August 2018]

United Nations Economic and Social Council, *Civil and Political Rights, Including the Questions of: Disappearances and Summary Executions – Report of the Working Group on Enforced or Involuntary Disappearances*, E/CN.4/2006/56 (27 December 2005), www.ijdh.org/wp-content/uploads/2005/12/Disappearances-working-group-report_UN2005.pdf [accessed 2 August 2018]

UNGA (United Nations General Assembly), *International Convention for the Protection of All Persons from Enforced Disappearance*, A/RES/61/177 (20 December 2006), www.ohchr.org/en/hrbodies/ced/pages/conventionced.aspx [accessed 2 August 2018]

UNGA (United Nations General Assembly), *Report of the Independent International Commission of Inquiry on the Syrian Arab Republic*, AHRC/27/60 (13 August 2014), www.ohchr.org/Documents/HRBodies/HRCouncil/CoISyria/A.HRC.27.60_Eng.pdf [accessed 2 August 2018]

United Nations Working Group on Enforced or Involuntary Disappearances, *Report of the Working Group on Enforced or Involuntary Disappearances*, A/HRC/36/39 (31 July

2017), https://documents-dds-ny.un.org/doc/UNDOC/GEN/G17/229/15/PDF/G1722915.pdf?OpenElement [accessed 2 August 2018]

Unsworth, Monika, 'Mowlam Welcomes IRA Disclosure on Graves of Victims,' *The Irish Times*, 31 March 1999

Van der Leun, Justine, 'The Odd Couple: Why an Apartheid Activist Joined Forces with a Murderer,' *The Guardian*, 6 June 2015

Verbitsky, Horacio, *Confessions of an Argentine Dirty Warrior* (New York; London: The New Press, 2005)

Verdery, Katherine, *The Political Lives of Dead Bodies: Reburial and Postsocialist Change* (New York: Columbia University Press, 1999)

'Veteran Republican in Custody Over Murder Charges,' *Belfast Telegraph*, 24 March 2014

Vincent, Mary, 'Breaking the Silence? Memory and Oblivion Since the Spanish Civil War,' in Efrat Ben-Ze'ev, Ruth Ginio and Jay Winter (eds) *Shadows of War: A Social History of Silence in the Twentieth Century* (Cambridge: Cambridge University Press, 2010), 47–67

Wagner, William J., 'Death, Dying, and Burial: Approaches in Religious Law and Practice,' *The Jurist*, 59, (1999), 135–146

Wanis-St. John, Anthony, 'Back-Channel Negotiation: International Bargaining in the Shadows,' *Negotiation Journal*, 22:2, (2006), 119–144

'War News,' *Republican News*, 19 June 1978

WAVE, *The Disappeared of Northern Ireland's 'Troubles'* (Belfast: WAVE Trauma Centre Publications, 2012)

WAVE, 'About Us,' www.wavetraumacentre.org.uk/about-us [accessed 7 June 2018]

Weinstein, Harvey M., 'Editorial Note: The Myth of Closure, the Illusion of Reconciliation: Final Thoughts on Five Years as Co-Editor-in-Chief,' *International Journal of Transitional Justice*, 5:1, (2011), 1–10

Weschler, Lawrence, *A Miracle, A Universe: Settling Accounts with Torturers* (Chicago: University of Chicago Press, 1998)

'What was Nairac Doing?' *The Irish Times*, 10 November 1977

'Where is Brendan Megraw?' *Andersonstown News*, 20 May 1978

'Where is the Trust? Reducing Division: Steps Needed From Republicans,' *Belfast Telegraph*, 27 July 1998

'Widow with 10 Children Reported Kidnapped,' *The Irish Times*, 17 January 1973

Wiles, Rose, *What are Qualitative Research Ethics?* (Bloomsbury Publishing, 2012)

Wilson, Richard A., *The Politics of Truth and Reconciliation in South Africa: Legitimizing the Post-Apartheid State* (Cambridge: Cambridge University Press, 2001)

Wilson, Richard Ashby, 'Judging History: The Historical Record of the International Criminal Tribunal for the Former Yugoslavia,' *Human Rights Quarterly*, 27:3, (2005), 908–942

Wilson, Richard Ashby and Richard D. Brown (eds) *Humanitarianism and Suffering: The Mobilization of Empathy* (Cambridge: Cambridge University Press, 2009)

Wilson, Richard Ashby and Richard D. Brown, 'Introduction,' in Richard Ashby Wilson and Richard D. Brown (eds) *Humanitarianism and Suffering: The Mobilization of Empathy* (Cambridge: Cambridge University Press, 2009), 1–30

Wilson, Tim, *Frontiers of Violence: Conflict and Identity in Ulster and Upper Silesia 1918–1922* (Oxford: Oxford University Press, 2010)

Winter, Jay, 'Thinking About Silence,' in Efrat Ben-Ze'ev, Ruth Ginio and JayWinter (eds) *Shadows of War: A Social History of Silence in the Twentieth Century* (Cambridge: Cambridge University Press, 2010), 3–31

Witoszek, Nina, 'Ireland: A Funerary Culture?' *Studies: An Irish Quarterly Review*, 76:302, (1987), 206–215

Wolfsfeld, Gadi, *Media and the Path to Peace* (New York: Cambridge University Press, 2004)

'Woman's Body Lies for 13 Hours on the Border,' *Belfast Telegraph*, 18 July 1994

Wood, Nancy, *Vectors of Memory: Legacies of Trauma in Postwar Europe*, (Oxford: Berg, 1999)

Wright, Briege, 'My Brother, Seamus Wright,' *An Phoblacht*, 15 November 2013

'Wright Family Responds to Price's Claims in Irish News: Gerry Adams Comments,' *An Phoblacht*, 25 February 2010

Young, David, 'Victims Forum Opposed to Amnesty for Security Forces,' *Belfast Telegraph*, 30 November 2017

Young, Michael, 'The Sneer of Memory: Lebanon's Disappeared and Postwar Culture,' *Middle East Report*, 217, (2000), 42–45

Zerubavel, Eviatar, 'The Social Sound of Silence: Toward a Sociology of Denial,' in Efrat Ben-Ze'ev, Ruth Ginio and JayWinter (eds) *Shadows of War: A Social History of Silence in the Twentieth Century* (Cambridge: Cambridge University Press, 2010), 32–46

Index

For Product Safety Concerns and Information please contact our EU representative GPSR@taylorandfrancis.com
Taylor & Francis Verlag GmbH, Kaufingerstraße 24, 80331 München, Germany

www.ingramcontent.com/pod-product-compliance
Ingram Content Group UK Ltd.
Pitfield, Milton Keynes, MK11 3LW, UK
UKHW021301190926
475701UK00009B/385
* 9 7 8 0 3 6 7 7 2 7 9 5 6 *